LIFE OF FRANCIS PAGET

MACMILLAN AND CO., Limited
LONDON · BOMBAY · CALCUTTA
MELBOURNE

THE MACMILLAN COMPANY
NEW YORK · BOSTON · CHICAGO
DALLAS · SAN FRANCISCO

THE MACMILLAN CO. OF CANADA, Ltd.
TORONTO

Always affectionately yours, F. Oxon.

Emery Walker Ph. sc.

FRANCIS PAGET

BISHOP OF OXFORD
CHANCELLOR OF THE ORDER OF THE GARTER
HONORARY STUDENT AND SOMETIME DEAN
OF CHRIST CHURCH

BY

STEPHEN PAGET

AND

J. M. C. CRUM

WITH AN INTRODUCTION BY

HIS GRACE
THE ARCHBISHOP OF CANTERBURY

DOMINUS REGIT ME
ET NIHIL MIHI DEERIT

MACMILLAN AND CO., LIMITED
ST. MARTIN'S STREET, LONDON
1912

TO

MARY CHURCH

PREFACE

AMONG those who have given help toward the writing of this memoir, are Mr. T. Norton Longman, who has let us reprint passages from books published by him ; and Mr. Blackwell, the publisher of the Oxford Diocesan Magazine.

In his letters, Dr. Paget used to follow his father's rule of writing in capitals the Divine Name : he used also to date his letters according to the Church Calendar. We have not thought it necessary, in the printed letters, to mark these observances.

Messrs. Hills and Saunders have lent photographs for some of the illustrations. The frontispiece is from Mr. Sidney Hall's picture, which was presented this year to Cuddesdon ; it is a replica from his large picture, now in Buckingham Palace, of an Investiture of the Order of the Garter.

Miss Church and the Bishop of Stepney have kindly read and corrected the proof-sheets.

S. P.
J. M. C. C.

November 1912.

CONTENTS

PART I

By Stephen Paget

CHAPTER I

CHAPTER II

CHAPTER III

CHAPTER IV

CHAPTER V

ix

PART II

BY J. M. C. CRUM

ILLUSTRATIONS

INTRODUCTION

By the Archbishop of Canterbury

THOUGH I was allowed in the last decade of his life to number Francis Paget among my closest personal friends, I can lay no claim to such knowledge of his earlier years as is possessed by many of the contemporaries whose companionship with him this volume will record.

It is, as I understand, for a different and a specific reason that I have been invited to contribute to its pages some recollections of my own. Probably no living man knows so well as I do the value and weight of his public service, quietly, steadily, conscientiously rendered to Church and Realm during the ten years of his episcopate.

It was my good fortune to be closely associated with his illustrious predecessor Dr. Stubbs,[1] and I recall very vividly the anxieties which, on his death, were felt as to the choice and nomination of a bishop who should worthily sustain the high traditions of the See. That in Paget's hands they were so sustained will not, I think, be questioned by any one. It is of his central work and influence that I can speak with amplest knowledge. From the very first he brought to our councils in matters ecclesiastical a wealth of

---

[1] Apart from other fellowship in public work we were for several years fellow-occupants of the Lollards' Tower at Lambeth.

matured opinion upon the distinctive history, position, and opportunities of the Church of England, which compelled attention. With his power of lucid exposition, his ready and scholarly grace of diction, and his close acquaintance with the masters of Anglican theology, from Richard Hooker to Dean Church, he naturally and almost as a matter of course held from the first a position of quiet and unassuming prominence in council and debate.

When in 1904 a Royal Commission was appointed to consider the difficulties which attend the administration of discipline in matters ecclesiastical, his nomination as a commissioner, though he had not yet been three years a bishop, was approved, I believe, by reasonable men of every school. In the long and trying work of that Commission we used to see him at his best. His historical and liturgical knowledge, his unfailing courtesy, his quiet resourcefulness, and his facility of speech and pen were assets invaluable to the discharge of our task. The same qualities told continuously in our Convocation debates. No one, whatever the trend of his personal opinions, who was a member of the Upper House during Paget's episcopate, would hesitate, I think, to assign to him a front-rank place in those synodical discussions. Whether one agreed with him or not, he possessed the invaluable gift of making one want to agree with him. The somewhat homiletic tone of voice in which his terse, lucid, well-finished sentences fell upon the ear, though not, I think, well suited to a promiscuous public gathering, or specially acceptable in the House of Lords, presented no difficulty in Convocation, where we all knew the value of what he thought and said. And I recall one notable occasion, the great Albert Hall meeting of protest against Congo misrule, when he rose to the level of highest oratory, and his words rang out with incisive force as, after the manner of some prophet of old days, he wielded without loss of dignity the scathing scourge of indignant irony.

In the Lambeth Conference of 1908 he was chairman of the Episcopal Committee which dealt with the anxious question of " the conditions requisite to the due administration of the Holy Communion." No question which came before us required more delicate handling. His speech on presenting the report of his Committee will not be forgotten by those who heard it. But he had a weightier task. When the ecclesiastical historian a few generations hence examines the unpublished papers which have been preserved he will be able, on the evidence of handwriting, to assign unhesitatingly to their respective authors different parts of the great Encyclical Letter in which the 240 bishops spoke to Church and people. Three or four handwritings will be found in the portfolio, and he will see that some of the most important pages of all are Francis Paget's. The time for that higher criticism is not yet.

One more point out of many which I might choose. I should be graceless indeed if I forgot the enthusiastic support, or even leadership, which Paget gave to the special effort, set on foot nearly three years ago by the Archbishops of Canterbury and York, for meeting the exceptional needs of Western Canada. What he did, and what he would fain have done besides, for that high cause, are for a special reason known in their entirety to only a few men on earth. They are known and marked by Him Who seeth in secret.

Great as were his outward gifts, I regard them as

altogether outweighed by his value as a colleague and counsellor in deliberative and administrative work. During the last few years of his life I doubt whether a single week passed in which he and I failed to interchange opinion by letter or talk upon some matter calling for action or argument or elucidation. Needless to say we did not always agree : indeed, on some public matters we found ourselves markedly apart, but I have known no counsellor-friend with whom "differences" were more absolutely free from any vestige of friction or offence.

I learned increasingly to admire the courage with which he faced some of the administrative and disciplinary problems which are sometimes apt to be evaded by a Bishop who realises the difficulty of these questions as sensitively as Paget did. In regard to ritual matters, for example, two parishes at least in his great rural diocese gave him, in successive years, anxiety so deep that I have seen the tears standing in his eyes as he debated with himself and with me in what way he could, with least counterbalancing detriment, take the disciplinary or penal steps from which he was determined not to shrink. Himself, by deliberate conviction, an Anglican High Churchman of the older school, with strong and clear Sacramentarian opinions, it was in proportion to the earnestness of those opinions that he suffered so acutely in the unswerving exercise of his Episcopal authority on behalf of loyalty to the teaching of the Book of Common Prayer. The men whose excesses he felt bound to repress were men who asserted that they based their action upon principles with which he was himself in fullest sympathy.

With each added year's experience of his friendship,

the man as man became greater, and the friendship
more sacred, and one learned to look to him for
fraternal aid and guidance in a score of unintended
ways. The quiet, grave, unquestioning "collected-
ness" of his loyalty to the Church and to the Church's
Lord set a peculiar stamp upon his action and his
advice, and the very fact that he seemed to be comparatively free from the disquieting questionings, social
or theological, which have from time to time troubled
most of us, exercised a sort of steadying power which
it is easier to record than to define. And, if one may
reverently say it, there was a kindred or corresponding
personal force in his mere presence as he quietly and un-
hurriedly took his wonted place, morning and evening,
in our chapel at Lambeth, unconsciously helping his
fellow-worshippers to reach a higher standard, both of
common and of private prayer.

I have always found it hard to analyse the secret of
his spell—for spell he surely wielded in his personal
intercourse. But perhaps it is really simple. I have
worked with him in London for days and nights
together, I have sat at his side on Commissions and
Committees. I have, best of all, travelled with him
abroad, securing in long walks in the Italian Alps great
stretches of his delightful freshness, full of interest,
full of reminiscences, full of stories, full of enthusiasms.
Hardly ever among all the changes and chances of such
days of work and leisure did I see him either seriously
ruffled in temper or lacking in gracious courtesy, or in
resourcefulness and buoyancy of thought. Of course
there was something splendidly infectious in his sometimes exuberant enjoyment of beautiful things in nature
or in music or in art. He would literally shout for
joy (I remember the very occasions) at the sight of a

sunlit glacier on Monte Rosa, or a waterfall among the autumn trees in a steep gorge, or a quiet fresco in a village church. And all the while one felt this to be in no degree inconsistent with the underlying note of gravity and even sadness which from the time of his great sorrow in 1900 had an essential place in the harmony of his methodical and busy life. I remember how, in 1905, when he was during the summer months a weekly guest in our house, I asked him to let me propose him for election to the coterie known distinctively as "The Club,"[1] whereof his father had been a prominent and honoured member. I have unfortunately mislaid the letter which he wrote in reply, but it was to this effect: "A few years ago, I should have welcomed it eagerly. But not now. I can accept quiet pleasures as they come, but I cannot any longer go to seek them. Do not propose me. If elected, I should decline."

The incident, trifling in itself, was significant of a good deal. It illustrates the almost paradoxical contrast between the bright flow of his conversation, eager, graceful, humorous, and the underlying current of sadness to which I have referred. The contrast had a pathetic interest for his friends as we remembered that it was Paget himself who had taught us, years before, through his best-known volume, *The Spirit of Discipline*, to consider carefully the meanings and contrasts of *accidie*, and of *tristitia*, and of " the sorrow of the world." I asked him once—it was on a walk over the Col de Chécouri at Courmayeur, to expand for me afresh his understanding of the phrase he used to quote from Spinoza: *Tristitia est hominis transitio a majore ad minorem perfectionem.* He answered gravely

---

[1] Founded by Dr. Samuel Johnson and Sir Joshua Reynolds in 1764.

and almost in a whisper, "I can never understand Spinoza, but I am quite certain he was right there." One saw at once how the thought had dwelt with him. Did it explain perhaps how we were to reconcile his frequent complaint, that he was constitutionally lazy, with the relentless stress of "busyness" by day and night, which in his later years he imposed upon his own life? Few readers of his famous essay on *accidie* can have forgotten how he returns once and again to the persistent and yet varied picture set before us by such men successively as Cassian and St. Thomas Aquinas and Dante and Chaucer and Botticelli and Ruskin and Keble and Stevenson, of the conflict between what Chaucer calls the "roten sinne" of sluggish gloom, and the *fortitudo* which "maketh folk to undertake hard and grevous thinges by thir owen will, wisely and reasonably." Nor will any one, I think, who knew him well contend that Paget in those later years was unconscious of the corresponding peril, to which such a nature as his was liable, of letting the multiplied activities and the relentless "busyness," however wholesome and effective, become ends in themselves, and thus harm in unsuspected ways the wounded life which they cannot really heal.

I have perhaps dwelt too long upon that particular point, but the matter pressed itself so often upon my thoughts that it may possibly have a similar interest for others who felt for him the same brotherly love and sympathy which he found and responded to in those Lambeth months and years.

I thank God constantly for the privilege of that friendship. I thank God that I was allowed to minister to him at the last in the Sacred Mysteries upon which we had so often thought and talked and worked together. Above all, I thank God for the abiding encouragement which his presence never failed to bring not into my own life only, but into the whole purpose and atmosphere of a busy, sometimes an over-busy home. As he has himself said of another and very different man : "Whatever may be denied to him or criticised in him, this surely may be claimed without misgiving by those who have learnt from him and loved him—that he never failed to make effort seem worth while."

PART I

By Stephen Paget

CHAPTER I

IT is impossible to have full knowledge of a man, or to find exact words for the half-knowledge which is all that we have ; and we go wrong again and again in what we think and say of him. When we write of him, we do it because we loved him, miss him, desire to explain something in him which did not explain itself, and believe that his friends will be glad to read about him. But there should be more than these reasons for a biography. There should be a thesis to be maintained, a point of view to be taken and kept, a design to be brought out ; the later years must gather up the earlier years ; the purpose of his life, the meaning of it, must be seen complete, fulfilled between his birth and his death.

If we have known him, as we call it, all our lives, and are with him at the last, we may see then, as we never saw till then, what he was living for. In the end, everything comes into its right place ; the design is finished, and we see, so far as we can, all of it. By the last few years of his life, and by the manner of his death—" the setting sun, and music at the close "—he lights and interprets the whole of his life.

So it was when Francis Paget died. He was ill for a few days only, but he left his work in good order.

For he was fond of Bishop King's rule—"Make your plans as if you were going to live, and live as if you were going to die"—and he said a few years ago that, if he were to die to-morrow, his successor would be able to take on the work of the diocese within forty-eight hours. It would not have been like him, to let his death add anything to other men's difficulties, or delay and confuse the proper course of affairs. Neither would it have been like him, to die without helping to the utmost of his power those who were with him. They remember how he kept trying to console and please them, praising and thanking them for what he called their wonderful kindness to him ; how he never lost hold for a moment on his love for them, his gratitude, his insight into their thoughts, his wish to be of service to them. He made his death one more occasion for the exercise of courtesy, sympathy, self-restraint, reverence. It was all exactly like him ; it was just what he always was — that is what we say of one who has lately died ; we compare our memories of him, talk them over, and arrange them according to the plan of his life. Point by point we slowly fit them together, till we get a true idea of him. At last, if we knew him well and were often with him, the picture stands out clear, just like him. When we have obtained this good likeness of him, we want to show it to those who did not know him well, nor were often with him. They met him now and again, and they took him as they found him ; but they did not, to our thinking, find him.

The writers of this memoir were closely associated with the late Bishop of Oxford, one of them as his brother, the other for eight years as his chaplain, and afterwards as his son-in-law. They hope that they have given a true account of his work, the conditions under which it was done, the influences which helped to make him what he was, and, above all, the way in which he advanced, through many difficulties, to the attainment of the later years of his life.   They hope, also, that they have not committed the offence of Rosencrantz and Guildenstern—" Why, look you now, how unworthy a thing you make of me ! You would play upon me ; you would seem to know all my stops : you would pluck out the heart of my mystery ; you would sound me from my lowest note to the top of my compass."

Francis Paget was the third child and second son of the famous surgeon Sir James Paget, and was born on March 20, 1851.   His father, in 1851, was Warden of the College of St. Bartholomew's Hospital, and Francis Paget was born in the little house assigned to the Warden, and was baptized in the Hospital church ; the house and the church are both of them inside the walls of the Hospital.   Toward the end of the year, his father resigned the Wardenship, and moved westward to 24 Henrietta Street, Cavendish Square.   Four or five years later, he began to have a great consulting practice ; and in 1858 took a larger house, 1 Harewood Place, Hanover Square.   He was at Harewood Place from 1858 to 1893, thirty-five years ; then he retired to 5 Park Square West, Regent's Park.   There, in 1894, he and Lady Paget kept their golden wedding day.   She died on January 7, 1895, and Sir James on December 30, 1899.

The *Memoirs and Letters of Sir James Paget* (Longmans, 1901) contain many references to the home-life, and many letters from Sir James to Francis Paget. But Sir James did not keep letters, except those which had to do with his work, and those which his wife had

written to him during the seven years of their engagement.   The Bishop of Oxford was able to say, " My
father kept only two letters from any of his children,
and one of them was from me."   Looking back, it is
difficult to see the two lives apart.   At first, of course,
when he was only twelve or thirteen years old, he was
merely vain, as the way of boys is, that he was the
son of a great man ; but, in the later years of life together, he cared only to be serviceable, bringing home his
gifts, for his father's use and enjoyment, as a labourer's
son brings home his wages.   He never came empty-
handed ; he brought them as if they were something
that he had found in a shop window in Bond Street for
his father's birthday.   He was always on the look-out
for a chance of easing the burden of his father's work,
even if it were only to amuse him at dinner with a
new theory, or the latest epigram from Common-room,
or a plan for a holiday, or a little description, exquisitely
light and humorous, of some dull ceremony.   No
duty for him came before filial duty.   The more he
had to give the more he gave, and the more he gave
the more he gained ; thus, his father and he, by
exchange of influences, became, as time went on, more
and more alike.   Seeing them together in the later years,
one hardly thought of them as example and copy ;
rather, the two lives were halves of a stereoscopic
picture, which must be united to get the effect.   But,
in the earlier years, it was example and copy ; and much
of the younger man's happiness, and some of his
difficulties, were in his resolute imitation of his father's
example under the conditions of his own temperament.

The conditions of his childhood and education were
wholly unlike his father's.   Sir James was born and
brought up in the keen air of Yarmouth ; he went to

a small day-school in Yarmouth, and there his school-
ing stopped ; he was apprenticed, at sixteen, to a
Yarmouth surgeon, and did not set foot in London
till he was twenty. Francis Paget was born and
brought up in London ; and would have been the
better for less London and more country. He was
born at a time when his father's life was full of
anxiety. It was kept from the children : unfailing
care and gentleness were given to them, and they
were happy enough ; but the little house in Henrietta
Street would seem very dull and serious now to a
London child. Sixty years ago, it was not the way
of home to provide a long run of amusements for
small children, nor to be always sending them for
change of air ; nor could his father afford it. But
the children had a month or more, every summer,
out of London, though it might be nothing more
countrified than lodgings near Hampstead Heath or
Wimbledon Common ; and there was Cavendish Square
to play in, and Regent's Park for long walks ; and
their lessons were not made wearisome to them. At
first, their mother taught them ; later, a foreign tutor
came daily. They had not such exercise, gymnastics,
and physical culture as now are part of the bringing
up of London children ; they were quietly pleased,
and fairly well, without these advantages ; but London
was too much with them, and here was a child who
greatly needed what the country alone could give him.
For he was more solemn than was good for him, and
had moods of depression which made him, sometimes, difficult ; not aggressive, but very hard to play
with. It is sixty years too late to be wishing that
he had been brought up far from London, and had
run wild in some more inspiring playground than

Cavendish Square, far from the professional atmosphere of that neighbourhood. Even in play he
tended to solemnity : there was a skull in the
children's little museum of curiosities, and he gave
a lecture on it to a nursery audience, the first of all
his many lectures, standing on tiptoes to reach it on
the nursery table—" Gentlemen, the object before us
is a specimen of the human skull." It is good for
children that they should not be afraid of touching
a skull ; but there are livelier playthings for them.[1]
With this sombre temperament, he would have gained
great benefit from a first-rate preparatory school in the
country or at the seaside ; and the present generation
of London children ought to be deeply thankful for
such schools. But, sixty years ago, there were very
few of them, and the value of them was not felt as
it is now ; besides, his father had been paying-off,
for years, certain heavy debts, not his own, and
could not well afford to send the children away for
their education.

For these reasons, Francis Paget and his brothers
went to a day-school in the neighbourhood of
Regent's Park. The house happened to have been
his mother's home when she was a girl. It was not
too far from Harewood Place, and the school may have
been as good as most other London day-schools of that
time. It came to an end long ago ; it was a private
venture, and must not be confused with the present
Marylebone Grammar School. One of the masters,
Mr. Kett, was a careful teacher, and a gentleman ; and

---

[1] When he was about twelve years old, he had a " chemical chest," and used to
give lectures in chemistry, in his bedroom, with many experiments. His bedroom,
at this time, was a strange sight : for he covered the wall, as close as a patchwork
quilt, with little unframed pictures cut out of diverse illustrated papers, and made a
grave little catalogue of them.

some of the boys, among whom were George Romanes
and Clifford Harrison, had a high standard of conduct ;
but the school, on the whole, was hopelessly second-
rate.   There was no gross evil, but there was no spirit,
no tone or go in it.   A boy was made unhappy if his
father were a tradesman.   Prayers were read daily, at
the desk with the cane in it, and those few boys who
were not of the religion of the majority were dismissed
to a little back-room, where they could play marbles till
prayers were over.   The cane was used, now and again,
with horrible severity ; but it seemed to have a way of
avoiding the hands of boys with important fathers.
There was a gravelled playground, which is turfed
now ; here the boys, exposed to the public gaze, played
prisoner's-base, or spun peg-tops, or had a poor sort of
game with chestnuts on strings, or just lounged up and
down and round and round.   It is a pity that they did
not play cricket or football in Regent's Park, just across
the road, nor learn rowing there.   The lessons, mostly,
were done in a slovenly, half-hearted way : one may
put the school a little higher than Dr. Grimstone's, in
Vice Versâ, but a good deal lower than Dr. Blimber's,
in *Dombey and Son*.   The Principal, at his best, was
not unlike Dr. Blimber ; but without his kindliness.
He had a saying, which is still remembered against
him, " Little birds that can sing, and won't sing, must
be made to sing " ; then, down rushed the cane.   It is
hard, after all this time, to forgive that saying, or to
believe that he altogether disliked the giving of pain to
the poor boy.   Once a year, there was a grand prize-
giving, at the old Hanover Square Rooms, with acting
and recitations : the boys presented Shakspere, Plautus,
Molière, Schiller, with more assurance than success.
Paget, at one of these prize-givings, recited a speech

by Pitt. In September, 1864, when he was thirteen, he
went to Shrewsbury. One of his father's brothers had
been mathematical master there ; one of his father's
pupils, Dr. Burd, had the chief practice in Shrewsbury,
and was a good friend to the boy ; and the School
was, and is, renowned over all England for the excellence of its teaching.

Shrewsbury discovered him, and was the making of
him. *Lateritium invenit, marmoreum reliquit*—it found
him of brick, and left him of marble. It found him,
come from a bad preparatory school, a boy of no more
than average learning, and of rather less than average
vigour ; backward at games, unable to stand up for
himself, hindered by self-consciousness, and sick with
longing for the love and the comfort of home ; hard
to understand, but easy to bully. He was at first
utterly wretched : one of his letters home was so wild
that his people came tearing back from Innsbrück,
travelling night and day, fearing they knew not what.
Shrewsbury left him an accomplished scholar, a lover
of Greek and Latin, with a keen sense of criticism and
of style. It put into him self-confidence, ambition, and
the enjoyment of accurate work. It did not stop there ;
for it taught him how to make friends, how to exercise
his singular power of drawing men to him. And, of
course, while the school-life was going forward, the
home-life was not standing still, but was steadily
becoming more and more delightful. The anxiety
and the want of money were at an end ; each year beat
the record in social and intellectual distinction ; the
home-life was going full speed ahead, every day of the
holidays bringing pleasure to him ; and the quantity
and the quality of pleasure to be got out of Harewood
Place are not to be had in every house in London.

Thus he received the double blessing of happiness at school and at home. Shrewsbury and London, like the mirrors of a helioscope, winked at each other in the sunshine ; and the news was always good, and the sun was always shining on both places.

He was at Shrewsbury from 1864 to 1869 : two years under Dr. Kennedy, and three under Mr. Moss. He began in Shell form, and it appears that he did not, for the first year or so, appreciate the beauty of the classics ; for Mr. Burbidge, one of the masters, writes : " He was a boy of the Lower Sixth at Shrewsbury when I became a master there, and he was generally regarded as a very painstaking and conscientious plodder, but without any suggestion of brilliancy in his work." But, once he was in the Upper Sixth, he discovered what it is to have the real scholarly love of Greek and Latin.

Nine years ago, in that admirable book *Between the Acts*, Mr. H. W. Nevinson described Shrewsbury ; he went there the year after Paget left. He writes of the school in its old home, not on its present grand estate above the river :—

Of course, we had Latin too (as well as Greek), and up to the Sixth form our time was equally divided between the two languages ; but Latin, as being easier and rather more connected with modern life, never ranked so high. Latin prose, it is true, was thought more of than Greek prose, and no doubt there was some instinctive reason why. I suspect that in reality it is the more difficult ; for it was the unconscious rule of our ancient tradition, that of two subjects the more difficult was the better worth learning. . . . Our sole duty was to convert, with absolute precision, so much Greek into so much English. No possible shade of meaning or delicate inflection on the page was allowed to pass unnoticed. The phases of every mood with all its accompanying satellites were traced with the exactitude of astronomy. No one cared much about beauty of language provided the definite meaning was secure. Yet beauty sometimes came by chance, just as happiness comes ; and I first learnt what style is from the renderings of the head-boy when he mounted the "rostrum." . . . The school breathed Greek, and through its ancient buildings a Greek wind blew. To enter head-room—a dim, panelled chamber which the Upper Sixth used as a study—was to become a scholar. I doubt if good Greek verse could be written anywhere else. Winged iambics fluttered through the air ; they hung like bats along the shelves, and the dust fell in Greek particles.

Other subjects besides Greek were taught, but nobody learned them. Mathematics were held in scarcely less contempt than French. A boy who really knew any mathematics was regarded by ourselves and the masters as a kind of freak. There was no dealing with him. His mathematical marks got him into forms beyond his real knowledge—his knowledge of Greek. He upset the natural order of things.

. . . Our one lesson on Sunday was a difficulty to the masters. Of course there was the Greek Testament to fall back upon, but its Greek was so easy and so inferior to ours that it became a positive danger. We were sometimes given a Latin catechism, but that also we had to read with caution lest it should influence our Latin prose. Once we waded through Dr. Westcott's *Gospel of the Resurrection*, a supposed concession to those of us who were going to Oxford. On Sunday evenings we learnt cantos of the *In Memoriam* by heart, and explained them next morning by suggesting how they might be turned into Greek or Latin lyrics. Then the real labour of life began again with Greek, and so the weeks rolled on without a change.

Once, it is true, our greatest master got an afternoon hour for the teaching of wisdom to the Sixth, and we really tried to listen, for he stood six feet four and had been captain of football at Oxford. But it was no good. Wisdom was far too easy and unimportant for us, and we let her voice cry in vain.

Mr. Nevinson is not perfectly accurate over the *In Memoriam*. It is true that the Sixth did, now and again, turn a measured length of Tennyson into the likeness of Horace : but nine Sundays out of ten they learned the *In Memoriam* for its own sake, and they took more than two years of Sundays over it. The reference to " our greatest master " is to Mr. Gilkes, now Master of Dulwich College ; he used to take the Sixth, once a week, over passages of Plato, giving them their first notion of philosophy ; and a great pleasure it was to them. But these excursions into Tennyson and philosophy were after Paget's time.

All his life he was thankful, and had good reason to be thankful, for what Shrewsbury did for him. It built Greek and Latin into the very structure of his mind, till they were to him almost like food and warmth to his bodily life. He could not get on without them ; he could refrain, as a matter of courtesy, from quoting them to less fortunate people ; but there they were, always, deciding the choice of his words and the turn of his sentences. Sometimes, in the simplest talk, he seemed to be visualising Greek and Latin ; he dropped into them in his familiar letters, like Silas Wegg dropping into poetry ; he made puns of rare excellence in them. He would send his love, in Greek or Latin, with his presents on birthdays or at Christmas. Among some books which he thus gave, thirty or more years ago, are Shelley, the *Bab Ballads*, and *In Memoriam*. He wrote in the Shelley, Φωνῶντα συνετοῖσιν ; in the *Bab Ballads*, Βαβαῖ βαβαῖαξ ; in the *In Memoriam*, Ὁ δὲ θεὸς διὰ πάντων τούτων ἕλκει τὴν ψυχὴν ὅποι ἂν βούληται τῶν ἀνθρώπων, ἀνακρεμαννὺς ἐξ ἀλλήλων τὴν δύναμιν, *Frater fratri, Oxoniensi Oxoniensis*. He composed, for a book on the surgery of the chest, this dedication :

Magistris meis omnibus, Primo praesertim omnium et summo Patri dilectissimo, Imo de pectore refero gratias, libellum dedico ; and he suggested, when his friend Dr. Prout restored the stonework of a well at Binsey, this inscription : *Prout fuit Prout fecit.* In the year of his death he wrote, in a book for his grandchild, *Franciscus sexagenarius Francisco nuperrime dentato.* The dedications of three of his books are as follows : The first, to his father and mother, *Parentibus dilectissimis, Disciplinæ, exempli, amoris, Proventum hunc quantulumcunque dedico.* The second, to Dean Church's memory, *Quem dedit Dominus, quem recepit, Ricardum Willelmum Church, Lucem, firmamentum, desiderium dilectissimum, Amore prosequor.* The third, to the Bishop of Lincoln, *Reverendissimo in Christo patri, Edwardo episcopo Lincolniensi, Qui libertatis defensor, obedientiæ exemplar, Uno caritatis tenore Per æqua per ardua conservato, Vitam Christianam quam pulchra sit, quam potens, declaravit.* He used Latin in his private notes for prayers and sermons, and recommended this use to a young man preparing for ordination. In Cathedral, when he was Dean of Christ Church, he was careful to follow the second lesson in Greek, and he would even, so far as he could, follow the first lesson in Hebrew. It all goes back to the time when Shrewsbury made a scholar of him, critical of every syllable and accent, every hair's-breadth of construction : no wonder that he got to love the place and was grateful to it, and in his later life sent three of his sons there, where he had learned the habit of work. Toward the end of his time at Shrewsbury, when he was reading for a junior studentship at Christ Church, he would work till one or two in the morning, lying in a blanket on the floor of the dormitory, comforting himself with a glass of port daily allowed to him on the score of his

health, and screening his candle with an old biscuit-tin,
lest he should be detected in this exemplary wrong-
doing.

Mr. Moss has very kindly written the following
account :—

When I was appointed Head Master of Shrewsbury School
in the middle of 1866, my distinguished predecessor, Dr.
Kennedy, handed over to me a Sixth form containing several
boys of exceptional ability, and among them the future Bishop
of Oxford, Francis Paget.   F. Paget was then 16 years old,
and in the lower division of the form.   G. H. Whitaker,
destined one day to be Senior Classic and (later) Canon of
Truro, was head-boy.   He and a few others left in October
1866, to enter upon their University career, and I then
examined the rest of the Sixth form to decide in what order
they should be placed.   I have the marks before me as I
write.   W. E. Heitland, the well-known scholar and historian,
Craven Scholar in 1869 and Senior Classic in 1871, was at the
head of the list with 919 marks ; F. Paget, who was two
years younger, obtained 480 marks, and was placed 13th.
In the annual examination of April 1867 he gained two
places, being 11th.   In April 1868 he was 8th, the first
two being those brilliant scholars Mr. T. E. Page, the editor
of Horace, and the late Mr. R. D. Archer-Hind (then R. D.
Hodgson), the editor of the *Phaedo*, Fellow and Lecturer of
Trinity College, Cambridge, for many years.   In April 1869,
F. Paget was second in the examination, being again beaten
by T. E. Page.   About this time he was elected a Junior
Student of Christ Church, Oxford, and began his residence at
that University in the following October.   As was only to be
expected, he had improved vastly between October 1866 and
April 1869.   His marks had gone up from 480 to 882, and,
when examined in detail, they show that, especially in his last
year, he took a keen interest in the form-lessons, and that his
powers had developed steadily until, for a boy, he was a first-
rate scholar.   I do not think that when he was at school,
though he sometimes wrote very fair verses, Verse Composition

was his *forte*. I am confirmed in this impression by an anecdote which he told in my presence to guests assembled in the Hall of Christ Church when he was Dean. After he had made complimentary remarks about other guests, he said some kind things about me, and added laughingly that even then he had not quite forgiven an observation I had once made when looking over with him a set of original Latin hexameters on some subject or other. "These verses," he alleged that I had said, "remind me of the style of a leading article in the *Daily Telegraph*, only they are not so poetical." Of course I was wholly unconscious of having ever said anything of the kind. But this little story corroborates my belief that the singular — the almost unique — grace of expression which delighted his hearers in later years in his speeches and sermons was not foreshadowed, when he was a schoolboy, in his Verse Composition.

His letters home from Shrewsbury to his elder sister are of a very different style from his classics. He could not be learning everything at once, and he was learning his Greek and Latin at the expense of his English. He must pay the price of scholarship; his classics were out of proportion in his school-life, and in the early years of his life at Oxford; they were too much his masters, not enough his servants. Shrewsbury taught him neither English literature, nor the history of his own times, nor a word of natural science; and it left him to find out for himself the beauty of art and of Nature. He did teach himself, with the help of the choir-master, a little music, and became *choregus*, responsible for the singing of the chants and hymns, such as it was, in the school chapel; for the annual school concert, and for the "chorusing" allowed, near the end of each term, in the dormitory: but this music was not of a very high order. Still, he made the most of it; and he and another boy once had a friendly contest over the rival merits of Gregorian and Anglican chants, each writing parodies against the other.   But the fact remains that his Greek and Latin tended to exhaust the soil in which they flourished.   His letters home are clever but without style ; he is experimenting how to write English, and the earlier experiments are not successful.   He invented, his first term, a fantastical, mock-heroic sort of letters, with long strings of Aristophanic adjectives.   This invention was partly due to the influence, in those days, of *Artemus Ward* and the *Ingoldsby Legends* ; but most likely it was a relief from the unhappiness of the term, and he wrote his mock-heroics to keep up his courage, as a boy might whistle going down a dark lane at night.   Next year, 1865, he writes more quietly :—

I have joined the choir !   Unprecedented success !   First appearance in public !   I perform on a weedy, little treble which just manages to make a very little noise but is rather shaky on its legs & easily upset by any high note.

A week later, he writes of his father, dangerously ill with pneumonia :—

Thank God that your last account of Papa is so hopeful a one.   Nothing could be kinder than the manner of the Dr. & Mrs. Kennedy.   They really were as kind as if I'd been the one boy in the school and my troubles were their own.   I had packed my things, & was sitting very sorrowfully in my study intending to start in about a quarter of an hour when a boy brought me your telegram.   Did not I rush into the Dr., & he was so glad, & so indeed was I.   Thank God that he is better, & now, I trust, on the road to recovery. . . . I do wish, though, that I were at home, as I might be of some use in writing letters & going errands & taking the little boys off your hands, & besides that I should always know how Papa was & not how he had been.

The home letters written during 1866–67 have not

been kept. By 1868, his letters are not yet clear of slang and extravagance, but they are no longer childish. His mind is greatly exercised over matters of Church doctrine and ritual. It was the time when "the Ritualists" were being attacked and defended in every newspaper and at many breakfast-tables. The home-life at Harewood Place, so far as the sons and daughters were concerned, began to be, and for a few years was, deeply committed to disputes on these lines or just off them. In these lengthy family arguments, which were not without heat, he was quick and skilful, sometimes angry, always serious.[1] They taught him how to arrange and produce his facts and evidences, how to hold his ground in the give and take of a debate. There was too much of them; but they were good exercise and discipline for him at this time of his life. The position which he then took, more than forty years ago, remained, in its general outlines, his position when he was Bishop of Oxford; but the changes in the work of the Church, and in him, between 1870 and 1910, are so great, that nothing is gained by defining his "position" when he was at Shrewsbury. It is more to the point that he and two other boys used daily to meet and read the Bible together. There is more of him in that than in these tempestuous, half-jest, half-earnest letters.

Papa has actually cured that arch-heretic & contemptible pettifogger, —. There's a perversion of talent. . . . *Floreat Salopia!* I've just found out that the Rev. G. Nugee, rector of Widley & Wymmering, Hants, is a Shrewsbury man. For further particulars read your Church Times. As you speak disparagingly of the Church Times, I send you, for your *private*

---

[1] The disputing was not always on the affairs of the Church : memory recalls him, a few years later, no less in earnest over Fichte and Hegel, and over the ethical teaching of George Eliot.

edification and reading, an article therefrom. I think if you read it calmly you'll agree with me that nothing could be *less* bigoted, uncharitable, or unwise. . . . I've got a footing in Cæsar's household ; I've planted good seed in the kitchen-garden of heresy ; *feci, solus, Franciscus Pagetus* ; I've given one of Dr. Littledale's tracts to Mr. Fisher, the mathematical master, & I think he'll read it. . . . Judgment is given in Flamank *v.* Simpson & Martin *v.* Mackonochie combined on Saturday 25th inst. Will you please get me the 2nd edition of the John Bull [1] which, I am told, will give the judgment in full, and send it to me by post on Saturday night. . . . I'm so glad you like Mr. Rivington. You've gone up ten degrees in the thermometer of my favour.

He draws, in one of these letters, a rough sketch of the thermometer of his favour (March 26, 1868). Below zero are Calvin, Macaulay, Spurgeon, Colenso, Stanley, the publishers of the *Rock* and the *Record*, and " the aggrieved parishioner who put his hat in the font." Above zero, and rising thence to 100°, are Dr. Jeune, Anglicans, the Bishop of London, the Bishop of Durham, Cranmer, Luther, High Church-men, the Bishop of Oxford, and the publisher of the *Church Times.* At 100° are Ritualists. Above boiling-point, out of reach of the ascending mercury, are Dr. Pusey, Mr. Richards, Mr. Rivington, Mr. Mackonochie, and the Bishops of Salisbury and of Cape Town. Highest of all, and right off the scale, is All Saints, Margaret Street. Later (November 22, 1868) he assails the Prime Minister :—

He is unchanged in feelings (if he ever has any), & takes the first opportunity & the surest way to bring his charge to ruin. Sooner would I back John Bright in the total abolition of the Queen & the House of Lords, sooner would I vote for President Beales & Citizen Bradlaugh, than support Disraeli.

---

[1] This paper must not be confused with a paper of to-day which has the same title.

He knows as well as I do who are the real supports of the English Church. Unless some other leader can be found for what I suppose will soon be the Opposition I'll never say another word in support of the Conservatives. Oh it is cruel to see self-denying hard work & earnestness passed over in this way.

Shrewsbury left him in these matters of controversy to find his own way, and was content and more than content with his Greek and Latin, and with him. It gave him that inestimable blessing—the pride of scholarship. It threw in, one might say as an extra, a decent measure of proficiency at games ; and it brought him independence, and a sufficient range of interests and of friendship. The general tone of the School, with the strong Welsh element in it, was rather rough ; the learning was Athenian, but the daily life, with its prevailing indifference to the refinements of food, dress, and so forth, was Spartan. Paget, by what we call temperament or nature, was fastidious, precise, formal, elaborate in his attention to his surroundings ; and this exclusiveness put him at some disadvantage. Happily, it was too strong in him to be " knocked out of him " ; rather, it gathered strength by a kind of reaction. And this reaction was slightly in excess ; he became toward the end of his time very punctilious in his manners, unduly careful of his appearance. "Paget was never in too much of a hurry to be polite," it was said of him at Shrewsbury ; but he carried his politeness now and again further than the occasion demanded.

There remain two letters home to his sister, a year apart. On March 8, 1868, he writes to her that he is working hard, even getting up early to work :—

And now for some good news. *Imprimis*, last week Gilkes went up to Ch. Church to try for a studentship there. The studentships are not only open to all competitors, but also to men in the second year. Notwithstanding this, Gilkes, who is only 18, & has never been in for an exam. of the sort before, came out *first of all*, & got the first studentship. His going up to Ch. Ch. is now settled. Secondly, Hallam, who two years ago was head boy here, has got the Craven University Scholarship at Cambridge, for which there is immense competition, & which it is a glorious honour to get. *Floreat Salopia.*

Forty years ago Shrewsbury sent many more boys to Cambridge than to Oxford ; and it is probable that Paget would have gone to Cambridge—for his elder brother, now Sir John Paget, K.C., was at Trinity Hall, and his uncle, Sir George Paget, was Regius Professor of Medicine at Cambridge—if it had not been for this lead given him by the present Master of Dulwich College. In February, 1869, he went up for a junior studentship at Christ Church. There were twenty-nine candidates, and he came out first. He writes to his sister, February 22 ; he is just back from the examination :—

I got down here quite safely & comfortably, with the exception of the fact that a hopelessly drunken man got in at Wellington, & in the course of about 12 miles he shook hands with me four times, declaring on each occasion that I was a "puffick genelman." He made some very valuable but slightly erratic remarks on the subject of human life in general and his own experience of it in particular, but soon relapsed into a state of slumber and pudding. . . . The fellows clapped me tremendously as I came into breakfast this morning. You can't think how nice it feels being congratulated by all the masters & fellows & everybody. I do feel so happy.

CHAPTER II

In October, 1869, he went to Christ Church. His rooms were in Meadow Buildings, on the first floor, at the St. Aldate's end: staircase vi, 4. He had these rooms till he went into lodgings in 1873; and, during 1872–73, his brother, now Bishop of Stepney, had the ground-floor rooms just under them. He got a kind welcome from his father's friends in Oxford, Sir Henry Acland, Professor Rolleston, Mr. Coxe the Bodleian Librarian, and Mr. Symonds. He writes home, his first term, to his elder sister,[1] telling her all his news. He has been to breakfast with Craufurd Tait—" no small honour for a freshman "; and Dr. Liddon has called on him, and found him dressing for football: " I bowed and apologized myself backwards into my bedroom, from which I emerged an altered being.

---

[1] All through his earlier life he made her his counsellor. In 1882 he writes to her, thanking her for all that she has been to him, " ever since the days when, I can remember, I used to wait, in the dim foreshadowings of penitence, to tell you rather than anybody else when I had been naughty—I can recall the whole scene sometimes, even the very vagueness of my fear and sense of need "; and he reminds her, on her birthday, of " the old childlike birthdays, for which one used to wake with a joyful and presumptuous sense that it was one's own day, specially devoted, somehow, to the gratification of all one's own tastes in sweets and domestic pre-eminence." In 1885 he praises her kindness " ever since you were my 'sister-confessor,' & I used to cry in the nursery till you came, because I felt wicked. I think there was something very typical in those nursery consolations, which I remember very vividly."

Photo. Hills & Saunders.

ROSCOFF, 1873.

However, yesterday we had a very pleasant and amusing breakfast, & have, I think, settled most of the important questions of the day." He finds Sunday dull, for want of something to read : " Why doesn't somebody write a decent Sunday novel ? I think the state of our Sabbatical literature is disgraceful. I can find nothing between *The Sunday at Home* and *Hare's Sermons*. I'd try *Pilgrim's Progress*, only Giant Pope has failed to frighten me." [1] He is reading steadily— " I'm very glad to say that I have kept up and improved my average, so that I have worked a little over seven hours every day since my Matric." — and he is not afraid of being ploughed for Responsions, but he will be glad when he is through : " It makes one dizzy to look over a precipice, even though one has not the smallest intention or expectation of tumbling over, simply to think what a mangled corpse one would be at the bottom." He writes also of the floods, and of a disturbance made by the idle set : " We are daily expecting the floods up here ; when they do come, I believe, the only dry spots in the place are Gilkes's head and the University sermon. . . . At 3 o'clock last Monday morning, there was a grand row, commencing with a trio for a French horn and two bugles ; the performers then got together a considerable band, who broke a lot of windows & wrenched away about ten of the letter-boxes at the foot of each staircase, which they then deposited in the fountain in Tom Quad. Altogether I should think it was a very pleasant & reasonable amusement."

Christ Church, forty years ago, under the rule of one of the greatest of all Deans of Christ Church, was

---

[1] In the later years he took great delight in *Pilgrim's Progress*. When he was Bishop of Oxford, he would read aloud from it to the candidates for ordination.

a very beautiful and magnificent place for a young man to be living in ; it was indeed a more pleasant life than words can say ; but it was rather too full of good things. There was not much hard work, and there was very little understanding of the value of money. It was nobody's business to teach undergraduates what they ought to pay for their incessant purchases. The usual grocer charged four-and-sixpence a pound for tea ; the usual confectioner charged half-a-crown for sending in a plateful of thin bread-and-butter ; and a man was at Oxford to learn many things, but not the price of tea and bread-and-butter. Thus, apart from any deliberate extravagance, hospitality was a costly affair ; and it would have been, somehow, wrong to enquire closely into prices, or to buy anything but the best. And this indifference to the price of bread-and-butter might tend to make a man indifferent to the fact that many people have no butter with their bread. It was not the way of Christ Church, forty years ago, to be greatly exercised over poverty, drink, social unrest, democracy, and other " storms that rage outside our happy ground." It was Matthew Arnold's Oxford, full of beauty, full of magic, full of sentiment : Oxford before the days of University Extension Lectures, College Missions, and Christian Socialism. There were no Nonconformist Colleges, and no Colleges for Women. There was no desire that the working-man should see what Oxford had to show him, or hear what Oxford had to tell him. The raw brickwork of Keble, and the new Museum, and the Parks, had a strange, uncomfortable air ; they hardly seemed to belong to Oxford. The æsthetic movement was gaining ground : it led, in the end, to great things, but some of its followers took themselves too seriously over small

things.   It was enough to make any young man
exclusive, forty years ago, to be at Oxford ; and, for a
time, the change from school-life to University-life, for
Paget, was even more than he needed ; for he found
in Christ Church, on a grand scale, those opportunities
for ultra-refinement which Shrewsbury had afforded
him on a small scale.   At Shrewsbury, it had been a
pleasure to him to be fastidious ; at Christ Church,
it came to him in the light of a duty.   He was over-
anxious about the look of his rooms, the correctness of
his tastes, the choice of his acquaintance, and so forth.
Shrewsbury had made him a Latinist, Christ Church
made him a humanist.   At school he had taken his
work on the lines of Browning's Grammarian ; at Oxford
he took it on the lines of the Renaissance : one is
reminded of the bearing of the young men who look-
on, in the old Italian pictures, at the Nativity, or at
the Death of Dido.   But, under all that now seems
trivial or unworthy of him in these years of his life, lay
the foundations, his Greek and Latin.   In other fields
of thought he is still experimenting, feeling his way,
half-jest, half-earnest ; but the Greek and Latin stand ;
he is on solid ground.   Even as a freshman, he was a
notable figure at the House for his masterful hold on
scholarship, his ambitious work, his sense of style
in writing.   Christ Church men, at this time, were
inclined to speak lightly, with a touch of jealousy,
of Balliol men, calling them sons of Belial ; and he
had the honour of representing Christ Church, in pride
of learning, against Balliol.

His first Long Vacation, 1870, was spent with his
people at Penmaenmawr.   It was the year of the
Franco-German War ; and he was all for France.
He read steadily during the Long, and through the

winter of 1870–71 ; and in March 1871 he gained the
Hertford Scholarship.   He writes to his sister :—

The news was not more unexpected to you than it was to
me, & when dear Mrs. Liddell came in & told me, I didn't
know what to do. Oh, I am so happy. I couldn't sleep
much last night from sheer bliss, & I've got a delicious head-
ache to-day from the same cause. They rang the bells for me
yesterday, and, I need hardly add, the ringers came to dun me
this morning, & made me sign my name in a book, in which
I saw also " H. P. Liddon," " A. P. Stanley," " B. Jowett,"
" S. Wilberforce," & lots of others, after whom I was wholly
ashamed to put " Francis Paget." Among heaps of other
congratulations I have had a most kind note from Mr. Palmer,
telling me that I am the first Hertford Scholar the House has
had since 1842, when Goldwin Smith got it. I am to dine
at the dear Deanery on Sunday, & with my tutor Sargent (to
whom I owe more than I can tell you in a letter) on Tuesday.
Please don't think me too conceited : I cannot help telling
you all this because I think it may please you. *P.S.*—There
were two or three Balliol men in.

In the Easter Vacation, he went to Paris with a
friend, and saw what the Siege and the Commune
had done to wreck Paris. In June, he gained the
Chancellor's Prize for Latin Verse, and a first-class in
Moderations. The subject for the Chancellor's Prize
was photography—" Sol Pictor " ; and he took for
his motto the line out of the Georgics—" Sol tibi
signa dabit.   Solem quis dicere falsum Audeat ? " [1]
With admirable judgment and daring, he wrote, not
in the style of Virgil, but in the style of Lucretius :
and it is remembered of him, that he wrote the latter
part of the poem quickly, as it were against time : but
he is doubtless right in saying that the poem, as a
whole, was *noctes multas vigilata serenas*.   It sounds a

---

[1] Sol Pictor. Carmen Latinum in Theatro Sheldoniano recitatum die Junii xiv.
mdccclxxi. Francisco Paget, ex Aede Christi. Shrimpton & Sons, Oxford, 1871.

hard task, to put photography into Latin hexameters.
Two good passages in this *Carmen Latinum* are the
invocation of Lucretius, and the description of the
spectrum :—

(1) At tua vementer virtus hortatur et urget
 Exemplumque tuum, sapientum octave, Lucreti,
 Quos Graii memorant longeque ex omnibu' princeps.
 Qui reserare olim divinis versibu' quisti
 Et mundi rationem et foedera naturai,
 Multaque vulgâsti non ante audita Latine.

(2) Nam quaecunque cluent aliquo fucata colore
 Cum niteant, sive herba decens seu purpura vestis
 Sive imbuta auro pavonum saecla corusco,
 Naviter hoc nescis quo pacto fiat et unde.
 Quod vincam fieri per lucida tela diei.
 Quae tibi simplice cum videantur corpore et uno
 Constare, atque oculos claro candore ferire,
 Septenis doceo radiis consistere creta ;
 Candidus unde tibi fulgor compostu' refulget.
 Miscetur primus violae color, inde profundi
 Caeruleus, glaucus porro, viridisque relucet ;
 Aureus addit se quintum, rubet igneus ardor,
 Denique puniceum tribuit rosa roscida fucum.

He spent the Long Vacation this year (1871) with
his people at Lucerne ; with excursions to the Rhone
Valley, and to Einsiedeln on the day of the great
pilgrimage. It was the rule of these family holidays,
that the sons should read on them ; and he read five
or six hours daily. In the Long Vacation of 1872, he
was at Geneva and Chamonix. His letters from Christ
Church to his sister, during 1870–72, are for the most
part airy and off-hand :—

I think society is in much more danger from capitalists
than communists. . . . I have come to the conclusion that
old china & a good conscience are, after all, the chief requisites

for a happy life. . . . I am going to dine, or more probably
to feed, at ——— this evening : the entertainment begins at
half-past four, with Chapel : then a lecture on Missionaries :
and then "to dinner with what appetite we may." . . . The
debating Society met in my rooms on Friday last, and I supported Egerton's motion for the disestablishment of the English
Church. I have offered to bring forward a motion at the
Society : "that the time has come for the re-establishment of
the English constitution on a republican basis." I don't think
it in the least ; but I think I can make out a very fair case,
& I mean to argue it out on the most conservative grounds.
. . . There is no company so pleasant as that of a gentle-
manly don. . . . I was so delighted the other day, on looking
at the *Ingoldsby Legends,* to find that I think them detest-
able, whereas three years ago I thought them most brilliant.
. . . I am sorry you have begun with the New Testament in
your Greek studies : for the English translation is a thousand
times more charming than the original. I will bring you the
Phaedo of Plato when I come home, which, with the aid of
a translation, you will read quite as easily as the New Testament, and I think with far more pleasure. Don't you think
it would be well if you always wrote to me in Greek, I to
you in French ? whereby we should mutually improve.

So the letters run on, half-chaffing, half-serious.[1] By
1873 he was coming under deeper influences ; for he
was reading hard for his degree, and Literae Humaniores
had got hold of him. It is said that the fineness of his
Greek and Latin was for a time impaired by his wide
reading of other subjects. It would be more to
the point if one could give an exact account of his
mind toward these subjects ; but memory can hardly be

---

[1] There was a fashion, about this time, for "character-books," in which people
wrote half-chaffing half-serious "confessions" of their likes and dislikes. On
April 12, 1873, he wrote, in a book of this kind, that his favourite hero in real life
was Strafford, and in fiction Colonel Newcome. His favourite heroines in fiction
were Mrs. Casaubon, Lady Castlewood, and Romola. His favourite motto was
Sceptra fide, frenis plebs eget, ara metu. Opposite the question, Person most disliked ?
he wrote εὐφημεῖτε εὐφημεῖτε.

trusted so far back.   Forty years ago, Mill and Herbert
Spencer were important books for Greats : T. H. Green
was teaching at Balliol, but was not widely known to
undergraduates outside Balliol.   It is possible that
Paget gave too much attention to Spencer, and not
enough to Green's philosophy.[1]   In that wider circle of
books which are not " read for Greats," one remembers,
about this time, his delight over Morris's *Earthly Paradise*, and over the metres of Swinburne, and his preference of anything in French to anything in German.

Best of all, in 1873, he found out the happiness of
reading-parties ; and got from them, for the next nine
years of his life, what neither home, nor term time, nor
both of them together, could give him.

His first reading-party, July 1873, with Scott
Holland, Herbert Barnett, Herbert Hope, and F. A.
O'Brien, was at Roscoff, on the Brittany coast.   Mr.
Hope has kindly written the following account of
this party : " We lived in a little hotel, quite small,
and we shared a sitting-room, but took our meals with
the other visitors in the old-fashioned way at a long
table.   The other guests were middle-class French
people.   We all did our reading independently.
Holland, I remember, read Renan.   I had finished
my schools, and read some French and some political
economy.   The rest of the party were, I think, reading
for the schools.   All the morning we read : in the
afternoons we wandered along the shore and scrambled
on the rocks.   I think we all used to attend mass in

---

[1] In a letter home, nine years later, April 1882, he describes a meeting held in
Christ Church to interest men in the newly-founded Christ Church Mission in
Poplar : " Holland spoke better than I have ever heard him. . . . He spoke of
Green, and what Green had taught him and others, of the work to be done, and how
no tangle or complexity need hinder or delay it : and then how in such work as this
he felt that he was with Green still, and living the life that Green had helped to
teach and show him."

the village church on Sundays. I can remember no
conversations amongst ourselves, or discussions, or
consideration of views! although I believe we did not
cease to talk and laugh the whole time that we were
out of doors."

In a long Sunday letter home, July 13, Paget describes a little adventure, which they called "O'Brien's
water-party" :—

We have had a small adventure. This morning was the
most unmistakably rainy time we have had : but after
morning service we started for a long & wet walk. We
went as hard as we could for about five miles, when we came
to a narrow strip of land joining, at low tide, some splendid
big rocks to the rest of the shore. Across this we hurried :
for we knew that the tide was coming in, and we wanted to
get to the end of the promontory. When we got there, it
was glorious : the weather had mended, and we were perched
on a huge pile of granite with a fierce, hard sea roaring under-
neath and throwing spray all round us. Then we turned to
get back ; and tumbled across the rocks to our isthmus. But
it soon appeared that we had stopped too long, & loved the
sea, not wisely, but too well ; for our neck of land was now a
strait of about a hundred yards width, and there was nothing
for it but to wade. And wade we did, with a vengeance ; for
the water was up to our necks. . . . Then came the walk
back of about five miles, with every rag on one a perfect
sponge for moisture ; and then *table d'hôte*, with an appetite
which the Gauls must have thought little short of savage.
Altogether, I think the incident has at least established our
nationality. Our *table d'hôte* has received a very charming
addition in the person of an elderly lady from Paris, unaccom-
panied save by a gigantic Pyrenæan hound, whose otherwise
remarkable appearance she has enhanced by shaving him all
over, as clean as a whistle. The dogs here are numerous and
fantastically christened ; nor is there one among them whom
I should describe as belonging to any one breed rather than to
any other. Their names are Tapinaud, Robinard, Frédégonde,

& Diaoul (the last is Breton for Diable).   We also believe that
there is a pig called Gobinaud.

The maid-of-all-work has just been in to tell us that the
Vicaire has *grondé* her for not going to confessional : that by
reason thereof she trembles with rage : and that she will leave
Roscoff to-morrow.   However, Holland explained that in that
case we should be so desolated with grief that we should all go
away at once, & that M. le Vicaire would infallibly find her
out wherever she went to ; so she has agreed to stop.

They are immensely droll people about here, & religious
and royalist to a man.   The important pilgrimage has not yet
come off ; but they had a little one the other day, trudging
six miles there, and six miles back, to pray for a king. . . .

Mr. O'Brien remembers, of this reading-party, that
" You had to drive some sixteen miles from the station
at Morlaix to the hotel (des Bains) at Roscoff : and the
Englishmen felt rather sorry for the lean but willing
horses that made up the team of the *Entreprise Baude.*
About the courtyard of the hotel assembled rather
curious dogs, which sometimes went off together hunting." It appears that Courteau, Finette, and Diane
must be added to Paget's list. " The *patron* was a rather
excitable sporting sort of man called Le Gad. The
person who looked after us was a very cheerful middle-
aged woman called Marie : she greatly admired the
black hair which then adorned one of our party, whom
she named something like *Laga Dhu.* Some of the
seafaring folk of Roscoff used to sail over with potatoes
and onions to Cardiff, and the boys seemed proud of
the English that they had picked up : they would look
in at the window of the ground-floor salon, and say,
' One, two, three, four, five English '—once, at least,
adding ' pigs '—and they were struck with the size of
our Liddell and Scott.   Some of our companions at the
table d'hôte—the Lyonnaise, the Marseillaise, and the

Lady from Brest, as we called them—with the elderly
rédacteur of a country paper, used to flop about in their
bathing-dresses and compare notes afterwards of their
efforts. 'Mais vous avancez?' 'Ah oui, j'avance.'
'Oh moi, je n'avance pas.' The Oxonians, though
more adventurous in the water, were not, as a party,
good at modern languages. . . . The most distant and
memorable of our excursions was to Guingamp, for the
Pardon : but Paget stayed by himself with his books.
Next term, we had an entertainment in his rooms, in a
style as near as possible to our *déjeuner* at Roscoff."

In October, 1873, Paget went into lodgings, at 90
St. Aldate's. He writes to his sister, Oct. 26, of
Dr. King's preaching :—

One is so ready to praise even moderately good sermons,
that one has no words left to extol such preaching as his
according or nearly according to its deserts. He speaks
without either notes or hesitation. . . . I think that a liberal
High Churchman is the very best thing that the world, or
even Oxford, can show ; and to see an elderly canon, perfect
in every detail of culture, standing up to say such things as
King said this morning, is a most happy confirmation of one's
faith in humanity, present and future. . . . It is hard not to
write about my sentiments with regard to Greats, and at least
equally hard to express them. I am a victim to mental
indigestion, very full & very ignorant. However, Tuesday
three weeks, & it will all be over. *Nov.* 23. I wish you
were at Oxford to-day, for I never saw the place look so
lovely, with a glorious sun and the sweetest of west winds. I
have been busy idling the last three or four days, and am
pretty well tired of it. This afternoon I am going to walk
over to Cuddesdon for chapel, dinner, and compline—my first
initiation into these mysteries. I had a charming note
yesterday from Dr. Pusey, about my going in for the clerical
studentship. I will show it you when we meet. I think he
can put more perfection into fewer words than any one I know.

In December he got a first-class in Greats, and was elected to a clerical Senior Studentship at Christ Church. He writes to Herbert Hope, Jan. 16, 1874 :—

I had the closest possible shave for my First, being involved in the greatest peril by my Roman History ; and there was a very small field for the Studentship ; so that even if I had not a more-than-Socratic conviction of my own ignorance, I shouldn't have much to plume myself on with regard to the examiners. . . . You and I, as a good, safe second, and a very shabby, rather fraudulent first, shake hands over a mere arbitrary line, inserted according to the fancy and digestion of the examiners. . . . I mean to go up and read like blazes for some time to come ; and you shall, on equitable terms, defend the widow and orphan till you reach the woolsack. I very much wish I could have gone to Algiers : nothing could have been proposed more temptingly ; but I have already had too long a holiday, so that I seem to have forgotten all I ever knew, and Plato & Aristotle sound like more utter strangers than ever.

The holiday, to which this letter refers, was with his friend Lord Antrim in Ireland. He writes to his sister, Jan. 4 :—

The cold is so clean and natural that one quite enjoys it after the piercing dirt of London. To-morrow we are to go out shooting, and I have given Antrim so honest an account of my merits as a sportsman that I think I look forward to the amusement rather more than he does. *Jan. 5.* This morning we went to look at salmon, and new buildings, and so forth ; and after lunch Antrim and I went out to shoot woodcocks— a delightful sport, affording the greatest amount of walking with the least occasion of making a fool of one's self. I reaped the reward of my preliminary honesty in not caring at all whether I hit or missed.

Other letters to her, about this time, are concerned with two of her many protégés—one is a tailor's son with a great passion for learning, and one is a clever,

lazy, young ne'er-do-well.   For the tailor's son, he
sends her, on Feb. 2, a translation of one of Plato's
Dialogues—

> . . . and this your studious friend is very welcome to keep, if he
> likes it ; for my Jowett suffices me.   I should have thought it
> better to begin with some account of Plato, rather than with
> his own writings, for the greater part of his meaning is lost
> unless one has learnt what he came to supersede & to preface ;
> and if the young man would care to know anything of this I
> will gladly lend him books about it.   But perhaps his hunger
> is for the raw meat.   If the book I send fails to stodge him,
> there is plenty more where that comes from, but I fear he
> cannot appreciate Plato without some knowledge of the
> questions he had to answer.   *Feb.* 25.   Your young tailor
> was a trifle unfortunate in his selection of the quinque-
> syllabic firework which he let off at you the other day, for
> Plato wasn't a Peripatetic at all ; and I am afraid the
> remark shows, as you may tell him, by way of tit for tat, a
> lack of philosophic synopsis.

The clever, lazy, young man gets very different
treatment :—

> Finding him in (I believe he was only just out of bed, at
> ten o'clock) I packed him off at once to the British Museum,
> having administered to him a long lecture on the text that
> it's better to be useful & commonplace than anything higher
> and better.   Perhaps, if his mother were rather more wealthy,
> his surrounding might, while we deliberate, be made rather
> brighter ; and the enclosed may help towards this.   Don't let
> any thoughts of expense stand in the way of helping him, if we
> can.   You know I'm quite rich now. . . . I have had two
> invitations for the next two Vacs—one, to go to Paris for a
> course of French sermons during Passion week ; and another, to
> go on a reading-party with Holland & Fremantle in Cornwall.

This was the fateful Newquay reading-party, July,
1874, after which five of them had typhoid fever.
Among the members of the party were Scott Holland

and his brother Spencer, Stephen Fremantle, Francis
Paget and his brother H. L. Paget, Lawrence Hardy,
F. Greenwood, and Edwin Birch-Reynardson : later,
Mr. and Mrs. Arthur Acland joined them.   Newquay,
in 1874, was hardly more than a fishing - village.
Fremantle died of the fever; and Paget was very
dangerously ill.   When he was convalescent, he went
to Brighton with his mother ; here the news came to
him of Fremantle's death.

It is not open to doubt that this illness had a very
great influence on the course of his life.   The five
years, between October 1869 and October 1874,
brought him many gifts ; but it is probable that the
two which were most important to him were Scott
Holland's friendship and his own coming near to
death.

To his Elder Sister

Eotham House, New Quay, July 1874.—Our ways here are
very simple, and the small things which relieve our work
are too small to travel.   We bathe early, & then drink
our coffee or porridge ; then, in lieu of prayers, Holland and
Fremantle read us a little service in the church, in which
the pastor has given us free right of grazing; then we
read till breakfast, and again after breakfast till early dinner ;
after which we divert ourselves till high tea.   The little
service in the mornings is very nice & happy, for I think
family prayers without family associations, and with no strong
characteristic save a smell of coming bacon & coffee, are an
uncomely function.

The people about here are charming, quite as nice as those
we met at the Land's End and Penzance.   It's a wonderful
place for dissenters.   It seems that there was a total gap in the
Ecclesiastical History of Cornwall between St. Augustine and
John Wesley, and the local theology is based chiefly on the
tenets of the later divine.   Our cook (who really is very fair
for a shilling a day) astonished Fremantle, when he was making

D

benign arrangements for cold dinners on Sundays, by saying that "sometimes she went to church, sometimes to chapel, but not often to either."

We are getting on enormously with our Hebrew—so well indeed that Fremantle, who preached us a *capital* sermon this morning, actually referred us to the original language. It sounded so funny.

New Quay, July 23.—My life in London has shown me a hundred new charms in the country, which I think I never understood till this summer. I have seen colours and outlines here that made me groan for the very existence of cities, and weep for all that dwell in them. Evening after evening we sit in the verandah looking over the sea at great cliffs dim with soft light ; & we have waves sometimes that toss their spray well up the black rocks, so that it seems to hang from the bits that jut out, and then falls slowly and lightly back. And I have had one or two talks with Holland, and he has preached us the best sermon I have heard for a long while : and in many ways I have had "a good time" . . . . Arthur Acland and his charming wife have come to complete our number, and I hear that the general belief in the neighbouring villages is that Eotham House is tenanted by "Mr. and Mrs. Acland with their twelve sons." We have taken to playing hockey on the sands, and the natives have challenged us to play them, eight a side.

New Quay, August 2. . . . A place called Trerica, to which I went with the Aclands, an old Elizabethan farm-house, built by the Arundels, and still haunted by the ghost of the last wicked earl, who murdered his wife there, and who haunts the lane outside, because the horses would not draw his coffin to the churchyard. Now, the place is only a big farm belonging to Sir Thomas Acland, but it is quite perfect, undiluted George Eliot ; and one detail came out after another, the old-fashioned garden, the great hall, with a glorious window of twenty-four lights, the music-gallery, the state drawing-room, never used now, but with the *Book of Beauty* open on the table to look fashionable, the haunted room that the maids won't go by, the clipped yews, and the magnolia trees, and last of all, just such

a tea as comes into the *Mill on the Floss*—I never so happily
realized favourite books as then. . . . I wonder whether you
would read some German with me, really, this autumn.   If so,
would you mind our trying Neander's *Church History*?   I'm
afraid I shall only read it very slowly, but I think it's the best
way to begin on a reasonable book.[1]

Christ Church, Oct. 16.[2] . . . You know what Holland
is to me, and how high his love stands in the long list of God's
gifts to me. . . . I felt when I was ill, and I think any one
must feel in an illness so full of what we call risks as typhoid
is, that every day I lived, and every hour, was God's direct,
unaided, uncovenanted gift to me, and, if He should help me
to live well, then to you and to all who prayed for me.   I
know this is true of all times & of all men ; but in a fever it
comes out so plainly : you see, doctors only watch one (nursing,
such as I had, is another matter, for it comes of love, and so is
very near to prayer), but doctors look at one and tap one, and
that is almost all ; they only watch what God will do ; and at
an ill look or a wrong sound they would give it all up, one
knows.   And so one could not help seeing what one forgets,
or at least what I had forgotten, in the stupidity of health and
strength ; and I used to feel that nothing but prayer and media-
tion was between me and God's anger ; and to prayer, yours
and mine and the much-availing prayer which you won for me,
God granted my life.   I knew all along that there was nothing
for it but to pray. . . . I shall not try to thank you ; perhaps,
as it is life that you have helped so much to get for me, even
my gratitude must depend on how I live.   *Oct.* 27. They
have asked me to take some work at Keble, and I have promised

---

[1] In this letter he mentions the offer just made to him of a Fellowship at
Hertford College. "Of course I can settle nothing without my father, though one's
first impressions are that nothing in Oxford can take one from Christ Church.   But
the letter has only just come, and I am quite in a state of solution.   I will write to
my father about it, or else come home and talk about it with him."

[2] He writes the same day to his friend, Miss Mary Lawrence, who also had had
typhoid fever.   "I think there is a great happiness that comes out of illness and
almost accounts for its being in this good and charming world, it so helps one to
feel with people.   I am glad that I was ill before you, and am less of an 'outsider'
to all trouble than I was last August. . . . Brighton gave me the impression of how
grievously the earth is cumbered ; I never saw so many people so idle before."

to do it, almost solely that I may get to know more of some of the best people and the best work in Oxford. I am to lecture there once a week on Composition; I only hope I haven't sacrificed the interests of the Keble men to my own. People are so very good to me, and things go with me so much as I have hoped they might go, that it almost scares me; it is so terribly undeserved. But George Eliot says, "When a man gets a good post, most of the deserving comes after"; and I pray that it may be so.

CHRIST CHURCH.   TOM QUAD.

CHAPTER III

From twenty-four to thirty-two, his life was divided
between Oxford in term-time and London in vacations ;
with reading parties, and holidays with his people. His
letters recall his keen enjoyment of these holidays, and
of the home-life in London. Men who were with him
at Christ Church, and saw much of him, will remember
what he was like at this time. His face was beginning
to lose the look of youth, and to be thin and strong-
featured. He had the gift of good health, and he set
himself not to be nervous over the affairs of his body :
he had to learn this wise indifference—it did not come
without learning. For his recreation, he could row
and ride fairly well, he played racquets well, and he
could walk all day long, and enjoy every mile of it.
His rooms, on the first floor in Peckwater, staircase
II, 4, were almost ultra-refined. He had a notable
library, including two or three yards of prizes : it
filled one side of the large oak-panelled study, with
its three tall windows into the Quad. Over the
mantelpiece was a mirror, framed in carved chestnut
wood from the old Jacobean choir-stalls in Cathedral ;
Dean Liddell had condemned them as " the unsightly
carving of the Second Charles." The bric-à-brac on
the mantelpiece had come, some of it, from Sir James

37

Paget's home in Yarmouth.   The high standing desk,
at which he used to work, lasted him all his life.   Of
his pictures, some were destined to be outgrown ;
among these were Greuze, Meissonier, Reynolds's
Ladies Waldegrave, and a rather half-hearted picture of
a thread-like bridge between earth and heaven.   Others
remained in his affection to the end ; among these
was a copy of Giotto's "St. Francis preaching to the
Birds."   For Giotto's sky was so generously blue ; and
St. Francis was like Stephen Fremantle.   Beyond this
large and beautiful room where he worked, and now
and again gave a little dinner-party, was a small room,
which he seldom used for himself, but it served to
complete his hospitality.   One can imagine a stranger
in these rooms, thinking them too fine, too æsthetic,
for a young cleric.   But the rooms saw what the
stranger did not ; the steady and precise work, the
grave attention given to pupils, and the frequent
prayer and self-examination.

It is certain that he found great happiness in these
eight years at Christ Church.   He had, as people say,
everything to make him happy.   It was his good
fortune to be working under Dean Liddell, and to be
a member of Common-Room with Liddon, Holland,
Dodgson, Bayne, and H. L. Thompson.   Outside
Christ Church, he had many friends in Oxford ; above
all, the Warden of Keble and Mrs. Talbot.   Outside
Oxford, he had London, with Harewood Place at the
height of his father's fame ; and, for work in London,
he was beginning to be sought after as a preacher.
Especially, he used to help in the work of St. Andrew's,
Wells Street.[1]   In 1878, he was appointed to be one

---

[1] He writes on December 27, 1877, to his friend E. Milsom, asking him whether
he would be inclined to take work in London.   "The work would be at a church

of the examining chaplains to the Bishop of Ely : and his first book, *Concerning Spiritual Gifts* (Parker and Co., 1881), was a series of four addresses to candidates for ordination in the Ely diocese. In 1881, he was appointed Select Preacher at Whitehall, in the Chapel Royal, which now is the National Service Museum.[1]

But toward the end of these eight years he began to see that he had lived long enough in Oxford. Partly, by his strict allegiance to Dr. Pusey and Dr. Liddon,[2] he was getting out of touch with other members of the Governing Body of Christ Church : and in 1882 this rift was suddenly widened. Partly he felt, and had for many years been feeling, his ignorance of the facts

---

which is, I think, almost perfect in its order and system of life, and under a vicar such as would that there were a thousand in the English Church ! Nor could I easily exhaust the praises of those who would be your fellow-curates. I should be very glad, for your sake, for my own, and for that of work which I love, if there were a hope of your coming." December 31 : " I wrote on behalf of the vicar of St. Andrew's, Wells Street ; my brother is a curate there, and I too, when I am in town, hold myself almost one of the staff. I know no church with which I feel more fully and happily sympathetic. In ritual, in system of parochial work, in teaching, in personal tone and character, in relation to the many poor of the parish —in all these St. Andrew's is, I think, very good : I hardly know of anything which I should venture to judge a fault in it."

[1] He writes to Stephen Paget : " I was very doubtful what to say ; but my father, & King, & Liddon all thought that I ought to do it, so I have written to say I will. I don't much like it : first, because it will hinder one's preaching at places where one would be much happier and might do more good ; and, secondly, because there seems an uncomfortable flavour of courtliness about it, which it is sickening to bring into contact with the thought of preaching. But on the whole it seemed right to try ; and what I want to do is to write a string of sermons more or less on the general evidences, especially on the antecedent probabilities, of Christianity ; not that I am so foolish as to think that I can say anything new, but only to try to go over the things which I find myself always forgetting, & which I find help in remembering. It seems so hopeless to write twenty sermons with no connection, ἐξ ὧν οὐδὲν γίνεται τέλος ; and perhaps some of the very few people who come there may have had less time for reading than I have had."

[2] Pusey, on one occasion, being unable, from ill-health, to preach the University Sermon, bade Paget read it for him. Paget told Liddon that he dreaded it : he quoted *Parturiunt montes, nascetur ridiculus mus.* " Not at all, dear friend," said Liddon, " not at all. They will see a mouse go up into the pulpit, and there be delivered of a mountain." " You must allow," said Paget, " that it would be very painful for the mouse." " Yes, dear friend," said Liddon ; " painful, but glorious."

of poverty, his inexperience of parochial work ; and had come to dislike the closeness of the air of his life, and the measure of conventionality in it. Partly—whether he felt it or not—it is not good for a man to be alone. So, in 1883, these years came to an end. Here they are noted, year by year, from 1875 onward.

1875

In the Easter Vacation of this year he went with his friend Cholmondeley to Belgium and Holland. His letters home on this holiday are the first record of his enjoyment of the old masters ; for, so far as memory can be trusted, he had not hitherto paid much attention to them. On June 9, he gave the Commemoration address, in Christ Church, on Lord Grenville. The reading party, this year, was at Mortehoe, North Devon. On July 24, he went to Cuddesdon Theological College, to prepare himself for his ordination.[1] On August 25, he made his first confession. On Sunday, September 19, in Cuddesdon parish church, he was ordained deacon by Bishop Mackarness : he was chosen to read the Gospel at the ordination service. His first sermon, a few weeks later, was at Shotover, near Oxford, in a little temporary church, built there for men working in some stone-quarries.

The oration on Lord Grenville shows him already, at twenty-four, able to write pure and noble English. This annual oration is given in the Chapter House, at the time of the Gaude, by a B.A. student of Christ

---

[1] Eight years later, in Sept. 1883, he writes to a friend who is just going to Cuddesdon, " I think that it has a power of help in it which no other place can quite rival : and I shall, I hope, never forget what it taught me and what I owe to it. I do hope with all my heart that you may find there all that I found of help and good." He was ordained priest, by Bishop Mackarness, on Sept. 23, 1877.

Church, on some famous Christ Church man.   Lord
Grenville, when he was Chancellor of the University,
founded the Chancellor's Prize for Latin Verse ; and
it was for this reason, doubtless, that Dean Liddell
bade Paget write on him.   The present Dean has
kindly allowed the use of the manuscript.   The
opening paragraph is as good as any lover of good
English can desire :—

It is a Breton custom that when the great feast of St. John's
Eve comes round, when the bonfire is lighted, and the long
procession of Priests and Choir with the banners and the relics
has gone slowly down the hill to the village, that then seats
are set beside the bright embers for those whose bodies are in
the Churchyard, "that they too may look on at the dancers."
And we, each year, when we leave our Chapel and meet again
in Hall, are wont to call to our high Festival some ghost from
the quiet dead, some one of those who in past time went out
from this House to serve their country well in Church and
State, whose memory is our heritage.   This evening I am
bidden to raise among us the form of one who sought no
shelter from the storm which broke on Europe at the end of
the last century : that in him we may see how a Christ Church
man stood in the rough shock of new and old : that we may
remember the power of the place in which we are set.

And there are other passages worthy to be recalled
here, for their style, and for the insight which they
afford into his mind :—

In the crisis of the French Revolution, a few days before
Louis the Sixteenth was recognized by the post-master of
Varennes, and brought back to Paris, to insults, to death ;
when Lord Cornwallis was fighting in India against the Sultan
of Mysore, and no one could dare to forecast the events of a
single day, Lord Grenville was called to the grave and almost
intolerable responsibilities of the Foreign Secretary.   Hitherto
he had fought for Pitt in the battles of Parliament : now he
was bidden to stand out as England's champion in the wide

arena of the world, where friends and foes changed and mingled
in bewildering complications. . . . The story of his toil is now
the story of the world ; and, without claiming for him a
genius such as was that of his great chief, I believe that if it
were possible for history to rise to the height whence things
are seen as they are, in their true proportions, and the mountain
does not hide a world behind, Grenville's share in the labour
and heat and glory of that long administration would be seen
to be wider and even greater than Pitt's.   The epic grandeur
of the duel between Fox and Pitt—

> Like Titans, face to face,
> Athos and Ida, with a dashing sea
> Of eloquence between—

this has drawn the eyes of an age, which looks more gladly
on passion than on work, away from the real battle, which was
waged not in the House of Commons against a restless
Opposition and a divided Court, but with the weapons of war
and diplomacy in the field of Europe.

" The height whence things are seen as they are, in
their true proportions "—" An age which looks more
gladly on passion than on work."   It is not likely that
anything in his later writings excels these two phrases.

To his Elder Sister, 1875

1. *Bruges and Ghent, March* 31.—We have had a great
day for the opening of our unenlightened minds, for we have
seen the Memlings and the Van Eyck.   One has always been
inclined to fancy that the perfection of detail must involve
something short of perfection in the general design and feeling
of a picture, as though no one could hold fast to a great
conception throughout all the labour of painting jewels and
clothes, and every detail of line and substance in faces more
complex and deep than life itself.   And yet this is what
Memling has done.   I have never seen such a picture as the
' Adoration of the Magi ' ; we could hardly get away after an
hour at the Hospice, and we both long to go again, and

I could write platitudes about it by the sheet. I think the black Magus is the most wonderful and glorious : I have always thought that negroes were all on a dead level of Indian-rubber-like ugliness and dullness, but this is a black saint and hero, full of grace and beauty and dignity. But all the faces were perfect in their way, and made me very angry with most modern painting. . . . And then the little peeps of distance, behind the manger, are so thoroughly *in* the picture, neither throwing it out, nor swallowing it up.

As to the Van Eyck—well, I've written so much about Memling, that I've no room left : and perhaps this is pretty nearly what I felt when first I saw it ; as though I hadn't any place to put another great picture in, this one day. But as we sat there (with the old man sleeping peacefully in the corner of the chapel) the picture seemed to get into one much more, as though to-morrow one might understand it better. To-day I felt rather 'as if something were going-on,' but I didn't quite know what.

2. *The Hague, Sunday, April* 4.—We were shown into a vast and conspicuous pew in the Groote Kerk, so that for very shame we were obliged to stop for an hour and a half, and lustily to take part in a psalm and a hymn, out of a big book, with music ; keeping our countenances as best we could. There were two sermons and three collections : these last being effected by means of a long butterfly-net thrust irrepressibly under one's nose ; I now see the advantage of a coinage with an infinitesimal unit. . . . It appeared that there were about thirty Dutch babes to be admitted, by ' Het heilige Doop,' to the ' Gereformedte Kerk.' We saw three or four of them 'Sprankelt mit Wasser,' & then slipped out, encountering a last collector at the door.

3. *Christ Church, April* 25. — Nettleship and Barclay Thompson have been lashing into my piano for the last two hours, with fugues & concertos, and reviving some of the pleasures which you and my mother have given me & taught me to enjoy. . . . Our match yesterday ended admirably : the students beat the second eleven in one innings. Of my own special achievements therein it would be egotistic &

undesirable to speak. *June* 6. As the clock struck twelve last night I wrote the last words of my speech. It will want some revision and probably some pruning, but it's an immense relief to have come out at the other end of it. I was so keen to finish it last night that I did not go to the great party at the Museum. I hear there was an enormous, unreasonable crowd : two teaspoonsful of Royalty to several tumblers of University ragtag & bobtail. One can hardly move for princes, & I suppose we shall have another disgraceful scene in the Cathedral this afternoon. On Friday I lunched *tête-à-têtes* (is that right?) with the Warden & Mrs. Talbot, the two best people I know, almost. I always come away from their house as full of good resolutions as if Dr. Pusey had preached me three sermons on end, all about myself. I hope, if all is well, to leave Oxford on Thursday, and to row from Reading to Eton with Holland, Houblon & Maule. *June* 10. Last night I had to make my oration before about a hundred old Dons, &, most terrible of all, the great Gladstone himself ; so you can conceive my state of mind since Sunday. I think the speech went off all right : C—— came up & spoke to me very politely about it, & Mowbray, and, best of all, the Dean, patted me on the back in their speeches after dinner. Gladstone came to give the Dean his portrait,[1] and made a glorious speech after dinner.

4. *Mortehoe, July* 18.—We have just come in from a regular Sunday walk : wilder, dirtier, wetter, pleasanter, and more lawless in its trespasses than any I've been before. We came out at last right under the windows of the only magnate in the neighbourhood, & regained the road along his drive. Last week we went to the very most beautiful place I've ever seen : the end of the next point westward of this : thronged with gulls & cormorants, who sailed past us by the glorious jagged cliffs, & over the dear sea. And then coming back I had a long, helpful talk with Holland, and refreshed my poor seedy little soul. I don't know what I should do, or what I should have been, without him : he is so high, and yet so easy to get at : his whole life seems like a

---

[1] The portrait by Mr. Watts, which is in Christ Church Hall.

rendering of Christianity into the simple language of daily
work & rest, ennobling them just as the Bible ennobles
common English.   I shall never be able to bear any fruit
worthy of his friendship : it must always be an unrequited
culture, for which a better soil would have borne a hundredfold.
It is all right about the testimonial for my Ordination.   That
dear old Dean set all rules at defiance, & not only wrote the
Bishop such a letter that he had consented to do without the
usual document, but wrote to me at the same time most
charmingly and freely, opening his wide old heart, about
Gladstone's article, and the troubles of the Church : such a
good letter.

5. *Cuddesdon, Aug.* 1.—I think it would do me good,
some Lent, to submit myself to the wholesome discipline of an
epistolary fast, a total abstinence from the enjoyment of letters,
relieved perhaps on Feast Days by an occasional bill.   I am
sure that the passion for being written-to grows on me, and
that every year ' postums ' becomes more & more the arbiter of
my day.   Perhaps I would begin the discipline now, and ask
you not to write to me, if it were not that I feel here just at
present as tho' I could not do without the link my letters
make with all that is really near to one ; so that writing home
& hearing from home are the only chances I have of free &
intimate & natural talk.   But I am sure that it is good for
me just once to get out of the quick, bright, unreflecting life
of Oxford and of our home, the life that is much rather in
others than for others, and to try for once to live by rule and
in comparative solitude.   Perhaps, by God's help, I may be
able when I come back to make a higher use of all the happiness
of the vivid life which I have not appreciated before.   *Aug.* 24.
. . . I think I am right in adding this, to be told to no one.
To-morrow I hope, by God's help, to make my first Confession
—perhaps my only one, for I am not clear about the duty &
safety of using so solemn a help save at *great* crises, when one
hopes really to begin a new life, nearer to God than one has
been before ; far nearer I trust mine may be.   Will you pray
very earnestly for me ?   *Aug.* 27. I cannot try to thank you
for your prayers for me on Wednesday. . . . I think I could

never tell you the joy which Wednesday brought.   Everything
seems different, aye and is different.   I am happier than I have
ever been before ; so that it seems as though I had hardly
known what happiness could be before now.

After his ordination he set himself a rule of discipline ; and he finds fault with himself, that he is
" such a bad hand at fasting : so greedy, and fanciful,
& easily beaten."   He also gave up going to theatres.
In a letter to a friend, he writes of his dislike of " the
apologetic look, and a way of getting into the back of
the box," which he has noticed, he says, in some clerics
at the theatre—" I should not like to feel as I have
seen them look " ; his fear of offending other people,
in the Scriptural sense of the word ; and his resolve
that nobody shall have occasion to call him, what Mr.
Herbert Spencer had called a well-known cleric, " a man
of the world."   But he is judging for himself alone—
" In all matters such as this I shall try to make up my
mind simply with regard to myself, and until that is
perfectly clear, far clearer than, I think, it can ever be,
to have no opinion at all concerning any one else. . . .
Perhaps when I am Archbishop of Canterbury I may
have to consider further whether my presence might not
' raise the tone of the stage,' but at present the question
is not so complicated."

1876

Early in 1876 he was appointed to be a Tutor.
The following account of his way of teaching is from
an article, by the present Dean of Christ Church, in
the *Reading University College Review*, Dec. 1911 :—

My first acquaintance with him was in the days of his
Tutorship.   I attended lectures of his on Sophocles, Demos-
thenes, and Juvenal, and I went to him privately for composition.   I was not assigned to him as pupil, and I did

not know him at all well at this time. His method in
dealing with composition was very new to me. He was immensely laborious, and appeared extremely diffident of the
accuracy of his memory and of his judgement. He constantly
verified his suggestions by the use of the dictionary, and rarely
condemned any phrase or word as unclassical without such
verification. Moreover, he did not, as a rule, make any
attempt to remodel the composition before him : he produced
a 'fair copy,' either by himself or by one of the great masters
of Latin and Greek composition, which he asked one to copy.
I had been accustomed to very different methods. The Head
Master of Westminster, C. B. Scott, was a great scholar, from
the home of so many great scholars, Trinity College, Cambridge. He had an enormous memory which he trusted absolutely and with complete justification. If he formed an
unfavourable view of a composition, he communicated it
without delay, assigning unanswerable reasons. He then used
to take the composition before him, and turn it into something
that satisfied him, explaining, as he went along, the changes
he introduced. To a person accustomed to these methods,
Paget's diffident laboriousness, taken in connection with his
great reputation as a scholar, was somewhat disconcerting : it
seemed a curious way of being always right. I have been
reminded rather vividly of these impressions by reading some
of the comments upon him at his death. I think that the
difficulty which some seem to have found in his manner was
due to the combination in him of diffidence and self-repression
with the capacity of singularly clear vision.

The July reading party this year was at Bettws-y-
coed. He writes to his sister, on July 14 :—

I am devoting to letter-writing the most beautiful afternoon
that has ever lit this marvellous place. We look across the
little village with its lazy blue smoke to soft hills, shaggily
coated with pines, except where a great grey rock sets off a
patch of purple heather ; & the whole air seems astir with the
boyish life of the little streams that come down the three valleys
and meet at our feet & begin to talk of the sea, & the cliffs

that will meet them at the Orme's Head. I mean to find a Welsh Saint (I don't think there've been any for some time, but perhaps they may have been a nicer people once), and keep his day by going over to Dwygyfylchy. (That looks taily enough.)

He very nearly got killed, on the last day of this reading party. The young men were clambering about the Swallow Falls, and he fell in, and his foot was badly crushed by a piece of rock which fell with him. He was for the moment in great danger of drowning : and this narrow escape from death made a very lasting impression on him. Happily, with good care in London, his foot healed well : " Mr. Callender and Mr. Marsh are quite enthusiastic over the progress of my foot. I am said to be healing ' like a prize-fighter,' in whose unworthy flesh, it seems, the power of recuperation is almost idealized "—and he was able to join his people at Innsbruck, and to get his first sight of the Dolomite Alps and of Venice.

In December of this year he preached for the first time in St Paul's. He writes to Herbert Barnett, who had asked him how he fared :—

St. Paul's, last Sunday, was wonderful. I only wish I could have taught the people a fraction of what I learnt myself. . . . The whole thing made one feel how, as a nation, we have the Lord for our God. I never feel more glad for England than in St. Paul's. And then I was awfully nervous and not very well, and it was so marvellous to feel God's strength helping one through, so easily that one hardly believed it was all finished when one came to the end. I fancy everybody heard me all right. But what I felt almost as much as anything else was the need of a better background to one's sermon, the miserable discrepancy between one's daily life and what one had to say. I am sure that, if one has not the purifying action of parish work, one must live with more regularity and concentration if one is to preach without unreality. There is a fearful burst of egotism ; but you provoked it.

1877–1878

Two undated letters, written about this time, may come here. They are concerned with disappointment, and with pain :—

1. I think, as I look back over my life, that there is hardly a single thwarting of my wishes, hardly a single instance where things seemed to go against me, in which I cannot even now see, that by God's profound mercy they really went for me all the while ; so that if I could have looked forward only so far as the time now present I should have longed for & welcomed all those things which I have feared and grudgingly accepted. . . . There is nothing that God does not work up into His perfect plan of our lives : all lines converge, all movements tend to do His will, on earth as in Heaven.

2. As to the effect of. pain on us, will you let me tell you what I have found ? In old times, whenever it came, it was my lord & master so long as it stopped with me : but I do believe that now, and since Cuddesdon, it has far less power *against* me. I think it is far less able than of old to make me *worse*, less able to come between me & God, making me ill-tempered, and dark, & miserable.

Over these years, memory is vague as to the exact order of the reading parties ; there was one at Porlock, one at Thirlmere : and there were " holy parties " after the reading parties. Canon Holland, in the *Commonwealth*, September, 1911, recalls the happiness which came of these parties :—

. . . He loved the play of happy companionship. He was a master in the art of personal chaff. And all was so clean, and delicate, and fastidious, and good-tempered. There was never a shadow upon our joy in being together. And this joy of comradeship was carried on, with ever deepening satisfaction, into endless Reading Parties, in spring and summer. . . . And into all of them came his dear presence, and in them all I hear still the sound of his gaiety and the play of his wit. And

E

through them all our intimacy deepened, and the powers of the world beyond began to work, with fuller force, upon the lives that were now together committed to the ministry of the Spirit and the service of Christ.   Out of such days of companionship as these, life receives its imperishable endowments, of which no after years, with their harsher obligations and uneasy troubles, can ever rob us.

After the ecstasy of the Reading Party, Paget would come on to the more sober felicities of what we ironically named the "Holy Party." It was simply the habit of a gang of us young Donlets to occupy some small country parish for a month, do the duty, read, discuss, say our offices and keep our hours together. Talbot, Gore, Illingworth, Richmond, Arthur Lyttelton, J. H. Maude, Robert Moberly would be there,—with Lock, or Cheyne, now and again. We would work, and play, and talk over the possibilities of an Anglican Oratorian Community, and be exceedingly happy. We would think whether anybody could be found to meet Dr. King's demand and write a new *Summa Theologica*. Who would do it? Perhaps Swallow, the learned Cuddesdon chaplain? "No," said Paget, "not quite. It is not every Swallow that can make a Summa." Or we would devise an office to be said in term by weary hard-run tutors. "Yes," said Paget, "and the antiphon would be *She tired her head*." . . .

To his Elder Sister

Christ Church, Jan. 26, 1877.[1]—It is very charming to be back here—the men are so pleasant, and the work, for the most part, full of interest. Is it not strange how one finds one's self verifying, one by one, the maxims which in one's youth one could only receive with an incredulous wink? I really do not think that until this year I ever believed that the highest pleasure could be found in work ; rather deeming that the principle was all very well for those who had nothing but

---

[1] He has been under the care of his dental surgeon—"My pen must return thanks for kind enquiries on behalf of my mouth. It has gone on splendidly, with a noble indifference to the decrease in its population, and the remnant of the garrison has risen to the occasion, and do their double duty without a murmur."

work to enjoy ; but I think it's dawning upon me, without any fading away of other pleasures, that there is a most real delight even in the work itself—it's rather shocking to be finding it so late.

To Herbert Barnett

Peasemore Rectory, Newbury, Aug. 19, 1878. — Is not Mozley splendid ?   We read him out loud every afternoon, and talk about him, and every day one gets to wonder at and delight in him more.   *The Book of Job* is splendid, and *Blanco White* climbs to the most sudden and brilliant heights. *Arnold* we were a little disappointed with, save for some splendid bits—one about Hurrell Froude, never to be forgotten. My father is delighted with the *Argument of Design,* and more than ever believes in Mozley and Pusey as the great prophets of the age.

It is *very* good, I think, being here ; our common life is very helpful, and we read very fairly ; only I always long to be in a town, and last night when I went over to the great parish church at Newbury, with its quick, vigorous, flashing service and crowd of people, I began to wonder how any one can talk so much of " quiet country parishes " with such delight. Houblon seems getting on very well here, and the services at the two churches which he has left to us are enough to keep us busy on Sundays.   But the people don't seem sensitive enough to get all the good that might be got from such work and such character as his.

Did you know that the Bishop of Ely has made me one of his examining chaplains ?   I am more grateful for it than I can say ; it will be such a help to me, I think, to be brought near to ordinations, and constantly reminded of those greatest days in my own life.   And it is wonderful to follow Fremantle here again, as, in outward things, I have so often followed the lines of his life.

To his Elder Sister

Christ Church, Dec. 2, 1878.—This is the saddest bit of the term, the bit in which the attractions of a curacy at St.

Andrew's seem almost overpowering, for the schools are on, and I know that half of the pupils I care for most will be ploughed & miserable. The dreary list has begun with K——, who, after really working hard, has failed again, and must go down with wrath in his good heart, thinking that we are all ungrateful for the real help which his good sense and kindliness have given us. I suppose he will go straight into business, but it is very sad.

And the Commission[1] have been dealing very roughly with us, so that it is hard to feel very hopeful about the future : Liddon is almost desperate and Dr. Pusey most sadly prophetic. I suppose one always overrates both the evil & the good of one's own time ; but it does seem as though the Church was practically set aside in Oxford by the changes which the Commission are making here and elsewhere. I do hope we may skirmish a bit, at least in Christ Church, & carry on a sort of guerilla warfare, especially if all our enemies will marry, and live a long way off, with multitudinous families.

1879–1880

In 1879 it appears that he was invited to offer himself for the Wardenship of Radley. He writes, on November 7, 1879, to Herbert Barnett :—

The choice has really been taken away from me by the unhesitating advice of those whom I was bound to consult, and all but bound to obey. They see far more clearly than I can that there is work for me in Oxford, and that it would be wrong to leave my present place to be filled, perhaps, by some one definitely anti-Christian (this reason I can feel to be strong and clear) ; and my father, by writing that he greatly doubts

---

[1] The 1877 Parliamentary Commission. "Though the constitution of Christ Church was not altered so far as concerned the ownership and administration of the property, yet very considerable alterations were introduced in relation to the tenure and emoluments of the Studentships, and the College is now ruled by statutes which became law in 1882. The senior Students, again (as before 1858) termed simply Students, were divided into two classes, official and non-official, with different conditions of election and tenure ; the junior Students became scholars, and some changes were made in the tenure of their scholarships." (*Christ Church*. By the Rev. H. L. Thompson. Robinson & Co., 1900.)

whether I am fit for a Head Mastership, makes me hope that in declining your father's trustful offer, I am doing what is really best for Radley.   I pray God it may indeed be so. . . .

The reading party, in 1879, was in North Wales; the family holiday was in the Austrian Tyrol and Italy.   In 1880 there was a reading party at Clovelly, a " holy party " at Hoar Cross, a visit to Lord Antrim in Ireland, and a family holiday in Yate, Gloucestershire.   On this holiday there was a family reading of *The Tempest* : Sir James took Prospero ; Sir George Paget was Gonzalo, the " honest old Counsellor " ; Francis Paget took Caliban, and the intellectuality of his Caliban would have surprised Shakspere.

Over the plans for the Clovelly reading party, he writes to J. W. Williams, now Bishop of St. John's, Kaffraria, who had met with some accident : " Please do not think of staying away, even though both your arms, and legs, were to be in slings for the whole time. There will be lots of quiet things to do, and ' little Italian meals ' to eat with a spoon, and one can read very well with one hand.   So please come, and you shall have any of our hands that you like."   A few years later, he writes to him, in Cape Colony, recalling the reading parties—" pleasantest memories of real hills, and rivers like alabaster, and bathes like nothing else in the world."

One point may be noted here, as to his method of advising and helping younger men.   He was not much older than they, but he was responsible for them as their tutor.   Looking back, in 1882, over this part of his life, he writes to one of them of the " retrospect of so many, so very many failures and neglects.   In plain truth—*quae facienda erant, omisimus ; et quae non facienda erant, admisimus.   Tu autem, Domine, miserere nostri.*" When one thinks of all that he was at Christ Church in these years, the words seem to need " a grain of glorie mixed with humbleness " ; for some people so make it a point of honour to allude to their own shortcomings, that they are in danger of falling into a conventional way of talking. With him, at this time, to find fault with himself was not only an act of religion and a point of honour, it was also an act of courtesy and an exercise of influence. By his formal delivery of judgment against himself he was asking the younger man to accept his guidance. It was a very gradual and rather complex way of giving help ; but it was profoundly sincere, and it achieved its purpose. He never could fly at a man's soul as a moth flies at a lamp ; he must approach it with almost tedious gentleness, almost exaggerated deference. It looked like timidity, it might even look like flattery ; nor was he immune by nature against the desire to please. The *maxima reverentia* which is due to undergraduates may perhaps be carried to excess ; and it is possible that he would have gained, not lost, by a more off-hand, downright directness. He came to a man's conscience as he would come into a sick-room, treading softly, and bringing flowers. In the later years he knew well, none better, how to look and what to say over some grave offence ; he could wither a man ; only, for that, the offence must be grave indeed. But in the earlier years he took infinite care never to be abrupt or overbearing ; and he sought access to younger men by confessing himself to them. But this deliberate humility was something far higher than a calculated move in the business of " getting at the men " ; it was of the very essence of his honour as a gentleman, his religion as a Christian. The mere sense

that he had the advantage over the other man tended
to send him down on his knees to him ; the greater
the contrast between them the more he felt the need
of self-abasement.   The other man, not knowing him
well, not knowing him by heart, might be at a loss to
understand him, might think him merely affected and
elaborate.   And all the time Paget would be remembering him in his prayers, and full of anxiety for his
spiritual life.

He did his best, likewise, to keep in touch with
his pupils after they had left Christ Church ; to follow
them in thought, in their diverse ways of life ;
to please and amuse them with long letters, often
written very late at night, but always full of the news
that they would be wanting to hear, always quickening
in them the memory of Oxford, and the power of
Oxford over them.   He would play at being an undergraduate again, in his letters to them.

To Lord Victor Seymour

Belluno, Italy, Aug. 20, 1879.—I have been a real brute
in not writing long ago, & I have no excuse, unless it be that
since I came abroad an idleness has seized on me of which an
Italian might be ashamed.   And they are — about here at
least—the most idle dogs, lying about in the shade at all hours
of the day while their wives slave for them. . . . And then
my father's wonderful vigour for walking & climbing makes
it very hard to get a letter written.

For we've been delighting in splendid weather among the
Dolomites, & walking nearly twenty miles most days ; so that
in the evening one is too sleepy to bore any one but one's
family & too tired to be coherent.

And lastly—tho' my letter must not be made up of excuses
for delay—I should have written sooner, I think, if I had had
nothing but what is easy & pleasant to say, in most sincere
thanks for your letter & its welcome kindness, and for all that

you added to the pleasantness of July. But I feel that there is something else to be said, & that I may say it wrongly or unwisely : please forgive me, dear Seymour, if in any way it vexes you, & forgive me whatever fault of mine it involves. July *was* very pleasant, full of the ease & friendliness which make reading parties what they should be, & have made them among the happiest times of my life ; and I am very grateful indeed for all the kindness & brightness & goodness which made the time go so delightfully ; and yet there was a blemish which made me anxious while we were together, & just touches the memory of the month,—for I think that some of us, and you especially, did less work than ought to be done on a reading party. I could not help thinking that if one barely keeps up four hours a day in Wales, where rival attractions are so very few, one must do less in Oxford, where everything crowds in on the afternoon & evening, & even the morning has its temptations ; & I am sure that very few men have ever got honours on four hours a day of work. Going in for honours must mean a difference both in the amount & in the manner of one's work ; one must do more & do it more keenly, really urging one's self at the work, throwing one's self into it, and making it one's own :—thinking about it sometimes when one is *not* doing it, & thinking of nothing else when one is. And then one must either get up early or else sit up late, in order to get those fresh hours of morning or night in which one really learns, and lays hold of things ; and altogether, I think, one must in some degree discipline one's self, and use some measure of hardness, if one is to be an honours man. There must be something like *military* discipline in every life which is worth living, & in every course which has an end worth thinking of.

I am afraid that all this sounds unattractive : please forgive me if I have thought or said it harshly or unnecessarily or rudely : I have had it in my mind a long time, & I should feel untrue to my office and to our friendship if I did not try to say it somehow. It may seem so unattractive as to make you ask whether it is worth while to try for honours ; but I *do* hope you will try, for I think that the work for honours may be full of all sorts of good for you & the beginning of a vigorous and fruitful life.

It is a great thing to have found out before one leaves Oxford the happiness of working more than one is forced to work : it is almost necessary, when one looks to ordination, to learn that nothing worth doing is to be done without self-denial. I should not venture to write thus except out of the consciousness, most real & deep, of my own failure in industry, & how terribly I have lost in strength and usefulness by not having worked more, & more intensely than I have done ; with the knowledge, too, that all that has been best and happiest in my life has come by work.

Please read this patiently, dear Seymour, & kindly, believing that in this, and in all else, I long to be, very truly yours,

FRANCIS PAGET.

We have come in for the autumn manœuvres of the Alpine division of the Italian army, the "crack regiment," as one of the officers, who had stayed at Aldershot, told us, of the whole lot. They look splendid men, but *very* dirty, and march excellently. They start every day at four in the morning : and manœuvre all over these, their native mountains.

To HERBERT BARNETT

Harewood Place, Jan. 11, 1879.—I verified Mrs. Barnett's prophecy by leaving my umbrella somewhere at or near Glympton ; I think it had enjoyed itself so much that it refused to come away. If you find it, and if you remember, and if Dr. Pusey preaches again, and if you come to stay with me, and if you bring it with you, and if by chance we meet during your visit, will you give it me back ? Meanwhile I think I had better get another. . . . *P.S.*—Guess how much that umbrella cost ? It came from what's-his-name.

Harewood Place, Dec. 16, 1879.—I am very grateful to you and to King for trusting me with the inscription, which I will gladly set about writing ; I hope I shall not make any howlers : I think of beginning, *O Vice-Principalis, Tu, quantus es et qualis, Cur, cur abire malis In partes Orientalis ?*

Will something like that do ?   *Jan.* 8, 1880.—I finished the inscription long ago, and sent it to Henry Thompson for his cold and classical criticism, and he has not yet sent it back. Do you think it will do thus ?   *Virum in Christo reverendum, E. F. Willis, Patriâ exulantem quo plures Patri reducat, Doctrinae, laborum, amoris memores, Dono, precibus prosequuntur amici atque discipuli de Cuddesdon.*   (*Reduco* and *prosequor* are used like this in regard to exiles :—I am not sure of better authority than Terence for *patriâ exulari.*)

Yate House, Yate, Glos., Aug. 17, 1880.—I have just come away from two months' reading, first with boys, in a party of eleven, at Clovelly, and then with dons, in charge of a very little parish, at Hoar Cross.   Clovelly was delicious, even better than Roscoff, in some ways ; and for the beauty of the place, beyond any we have ever been at : we lived in five little cottages, like the Fathers of the desert, only I expect that we made more noise than was usual in Nitria.   At Hoar Cross we were very happy, though our parish work was a sham, for most of the time there was only one old woman to visit and she was stone deaf and begged us to go away. . . . Please give my love to Gore, and tell him that I wish I were at Cuddesdon among the *fortunati nimium* who attend his lectures, and that I think C——[1] missed him very much at Hoar Cross, and was driven, for lack of his company, to browse disconsolately but continuously among the gooseberry bushes at the end of the gardens, in the intervals of wild orgies upon ginger-bread biscuits, potatoes, and marmalade.

Christ Church, Oct. 26, 1880.—

My dear Mr. B.	I've a lecture at six,
What a pleasure for me,	So the time we will fix
To give you to-morrow a little high tea !	At seven o'clock, and not one minute past :
Just one little dish,	And if on the way
With two little fish,	You can manage to slay
Potatoes and toast—that is all there will be.	Just one little sparrow, we shan't break the fast.

---

[1] A very learned member of the Hoar Cross party, who had adopted a vegetarian diet.

To Stephen Paget

Christ Church, Nov. 9, 1879.—I have a hope that you may care for a few lines of Oxford news, even tho' they are written at the tired end of a most happy Sunday. The heart of the day for me (& not, I hope, for me alone) has been Holland's first sermon, as Select Preacher. I cannot tell you what it was, how it has even changed my hopes and fears about Oxford, and deepened my love for him. It seemed to me easier, because more thoroughly planned & built up, than any I have ever heard him preach ; he had brought all his strength under control, without sacrificing anything of its fulness and freedom ; and I think that for depth of thought & sympathy and true philosophic power, it went beyond all words. I cannot tell you how thankful I am for it—how hopeful that it is the beginning of much that he will do for us all, here & elsewhere. I will send it you when it comes out in the Undergraduates' Journal. The Church was quite full, & the very men one longed to see there. The Fifth went off very well, and so did a great many fireworks. When we came back from Chapel,[1] Peck was really beautiful, with red lights and countless most lively crackers, & roman candles. It was impossible to go straight to one's rooms without saying anything, so I boldly made a raid on Foljambe & Lawson, who were so good as to flee : so solving my wonder what I was to do next. We have been very quiet before and since the Fifth : so that I was quite glad of the vivacity of that night.

I am afraid Graves & Webb have been disappointed in not getting pupils ; but I do not think there have been any to send them : the Pass-coaching business is all taken up by experts ; and Honour-coaching for Mods. is almost extinct. Cowell seems very flourishing & happy ; and he, with Webb & Vincent, is using his " Culture Term " for the learning of German.

Christ Church, Feb. 1, 1880. . . . The Shakespeare Society is very promising, and is getting into more shape : we are

---

[1] There was at this time a short service in Cathedral at 10 every night.

less afraid of our own voices and of one another ; in fact there are germs of gesticulation, reminding one of the Dædalean period of sculpture. *Whitsunday.*—I am only writing in the hope that you may care for a little Oxford shop. And yet, as I wonder what there is to tell you, it seems as though there were very little which must not seem unreal and very trivial in comparison with the great things which you live and work among : a row in Peck, or the screwing-up of a Proctor, makes us talk and look grave; but I thought, when I was in London last time, that you must have sprung clean beyond the interests of a life which is mainly concerned with such things, and wonder how we can see anything but childishness in them : that from the standpoint of your present work, and from the midst of its intense and worthy interests, all but a few features of Oxford must look very dream-like and over-rated : while the few things which remain, or perhaps grow, in reality, are not those of which it is easy to talk or write. If once one gets outside it, Oxford life must look most artificial & confused : I often think that to the man who sees his work, clear and single and engrossing, before him, we must look just like ants on a broken hill, running about with great things in their mouths, and nowhere to put them. *November 9.*—I found at the beginning of the Term a demand for a Juvenal lecture : so I have been grinding at that with ever-increasing admiration for Mayor ; and reverence for Juvenal. I do think that there is something very great & noble, at times even awful, in his pure indignation : and as one reads him carefully one feels the extraordinary strength of the motive which never flags or wavers through lines & poems in which every word is burdened with meaning and purpose. And I believe that, with all his insight and indignation, he is never scornful—never pessimist —never irreverent towards mankind : — he seldom or never confounds the sinner with his sin : & that must have been hard to avoid, when one was writing of Tigellinus or Domitian.

1881

Many events, and many letters, come into this year. It may be well to begin with three letters which are concerned with the very serious "row" in Christ Church, in the summer-term of 1881. The matter was so grave that Dean Liddell withdrew his permission for the Christ Church Ball. Happily, on full enquiry, it was found that the offenders were, some of them, not Christ Church men ; and the Ball was allowed to take place.

To his Younger Sister

Christ Church, Feb. 13.—It has been a delightful Sunday, for Sumner has been down here ; and we have had a walk, and many talks such as are most delightful—it is a wonderful happiness to get readily so near to any one as one does to him, and to find how all his success has only made him more admirable and sincere and simple. . . . Great things are brewing here : a possible Concert to be given by the Christ Church Musical Society next Term ; but, more probable and more magnificent, a real Christ Church Ball, to be given entirely by House men, & *in the Hall.* If it really is fixed you must of course come down. . . . All the people here who have been to Rome this Vac. talk of it so that I feel inclined simply to bolt off, & defy the consequences & the Dean. Short of that, have you ever seen Wells ? I have to go down there in the Vac., and it would be delightful if we could make my work an excuse for another lesson in Architecture, and love the beautiful with economy. This is a dull letter ; no wonder the stylograph has written it so badly.

To Stephen Paget

Christ Church, Whitsunday.—It was a horrid trouble ; all had seemed so happy and friendly here that we had got, I suppose, foolishly confident, and dependent on the *entente cordiale.* And so when it even seemed to be broken up we were all miserable to a degree which now one can hardly understand ; everybody looked white & overwrought, and dear Holland was more wretched than I have ever seen him. By the time I got down all debates were over and all conceivable rigours decreed, and we all marched into Hall, and the Dean made a dreadful speech. And then began for me a series of interviews which set me up again ; for one found out little by little how free the row had been from all deliberate ill-will against any one, how heartily the men disowned all that seemed worse in it, and how very much was due to some rowdy strangers who had come in simply to make a row—whom would that we could catch. And so each day helped one to look at things more happily ; and by Monday, when the Ball was re-sanctioned, I was another man—and ashamed of my dejection. . . . B—— has appeared, having gone round the world, but he talks of it so dully that I think after all it must be flat.

To his Younger Sister

I write, my dear Mary,
To say that, contrary
To all expectation
And vaticination—
Since the men have explained
That their loyalty remained
Unshaken, throughout
What looked like a rout :
Since peace is restored
With a general accord ;
Since the Dean is appeased
And the Censors are pleased
To put by-gones away—
On the first-mentioned day,
The twentieth of June,
To some frivolous tune,
We will open the Ball,
If you please, in the Hall.
So pray believe me,
In haste but in glee,
As always, to be
Your devoted, F. P.

The reading party this July was at Holne, Ashburton, North Devon. From Holne, he writes to Stephen Paget that one of the party has been learning to swim, and now, with Holland and Gull, *flos ille gregis*, as supporters, "can float like S. Catherine in Luini's picture" ; another has brought a horn with him, "which was rather a blow at first" ; another, an old Salopian, "is admirable, with Gilkes peeping out at every crack in his constitution." At the end of July he was in London during the International Medical Congress, of which his father was the President. He writes to Miss Lawrence : "I think I never shall forget how my father has borne himself through it—his untouched simplicity, and quietude, and ease, and his wonderful gentleness to us all at home." In August, he and H. L. Thompson had a little holiday abroad, and saw Dresden and Nuremberg. In October, he went to Ireland. A man had been getting money out of people, representing that he was " Sir James Paget's second son " ; and Paget went for the purpose of proving his own identity. He might have got off going, but he did not like to put his convenience above a matter of justice.

To his Younger Sister

Holne, Ashburton, July 21.—The Mods. list has been our great excitement to-day, and made me very, very happy, for I never thought that we should get four Firsts ; and there is only one approach to a disappointment in the whole list. It seems to open up a new hope for one's work, and—what is a worthier ground of delight—a better prospect for the House.

We saw a wonderful thing yesterday : for we drove over to Princeton in the hope of seeing something of the great Dartmoor Prison. We got hold of the Deputy-Governor, and, to our surprize, he most kindly took us himself all over the place. I think I shall never forget it. They have at present over a thousand convicts there—none for less than five years, about 40 for life ; and as one went from one place to another and saw hardly anything but the dreary repetition of the same heavy, hopeless look on the worst type of face, one felt as though there were depths & possibilities of darkening for a man's life which one had never realized or thought of before. There is no cruelty in the place, nothing arbitrary, no real hardship ; but relentless order and utter bareness and steady mechanism about every detail, with constant watch over every movement and hardly a chance of speaking to any one. Not a man has escaped since the prison was built. Still, they are fairly fed & cared for ; they can gain some privileges by good conduct, and all learn & practice some work.   It is only the *utter* loss of freedom that seemed pitiable & beyond what one had realized, and only the uniform lowness of the faces that made one wretched.   You should see their Chapel!   Hideous in itself, with little perches all about for the Warders to sit on and watch their prisoners; & a place at the end where about 20 of the guard sit all through service with loaded carbines. It was rather weird to read on the walls such texts as, "I will fill this House with Glory."   One felt that the Chaplain must be either a Saint or a Warder.

Dresden, Aug. 13.—I feel as though I had seen hardly anything but the one great picture, the San Sisto, as though it stood quite alone among great and beautiful things, one highest thought, given to one man to express, and which no words can reach.   It is the purest and loftiest work I have ever seen, so that I cannot bring it into relation with any other picture I know, or see at all how Raffaelle came to paint it.   We must hope to see it together some day, and help one another to understand more about it than I do yet.   I feel there is a movement about the Blessed Virgin's figure, an impression that she is coming towards one, which no copy has ever given me, and that in our Saviour's face there is a look of active thought, and of royalty, which make it quite different from the expression of mere abstraction.   But the whole picture lies far beyond my knowledge.   Let me get over the confession that I am utterly unconverted by the Correggios.   I was unfortunate in beginning with one in which a blooming and clearly conceited young man, who would, I know, be very popular if he were at Christ Church, is doing duty for S. John Baptist.   This threw me off, and I have not quite recovered, but I am very happy.

Ballyboat Court House, Newry, Oct. 5.—I am waiting here with my pseudonym, poor fellow, sitting opposite to me between two policemen, and "with gyves upon his wrists." I don't know him, but he is a very nice-looking fellow, well and quietly dressed, with a quiet nervous look, not very sorrowful, I am glad to say, but distressed-looking rather.   He might almost be an undergraduate, but he is much more like a smart confectioner at Oxford, named Forrest. . . . (*Later*) The prisoner, whom the magistrates (three solemn old boys) gravely address as Mr. Paget, has just made an appeal for dismissal (Lord Kilmorey being late), in a tone of such complete impudence that I don't a bit mind giving evidence against him.

At the end of this year, the Christ Church Mission was founded in Poplar, under the charge of his brother H. L. Paget, now Bishop of Stepney. It began in a very small way—just a ground-floor in Follett Street, two rooms knocked into one to serve both for church and school-room, and a little house for H. L. Paget in the East India Dock Road. Francis Paget, at this time, was at Nice with his father, who had been ordered South after a dangerous illness.

To Stephen Paget

Dec. 13.—One thing my father may have forgotten, since he tells so little of himself, that he seems already clearly and considerably better and stronger. And this gain of his in health and strength is the best part of all our happiness, and the part which we all can share, by the East India Docks as well as by the Port of Limpia, where the ships have lateen sails and freights of Italian marble. . . . *Dec.* 21. — I might really help the happiness of your Christmas if I could worthily tell you how wonderfully well and constantly happy my father is, sleeping soundly through the night, reading Victor Hugo with an untiring alternation of interest and disgust, talking with us all more delightfully than ever, and heartily & freshly enjoying every pleasure and beauty of the place—from the glory of scenery and sunlight to the astonishing variety of our meals,—or again how my mother is clearly gaining health & strength from the perfect quietude and ease of the living here, without a thought of the housekeeper's room, and in quite a lotus-eater's indifference to weekly bills. . . . I am ashamed to be so long among more delights than I can tell or appreciate. I try to read dull books, but somehow the mornings go as they never went before.

F

To Stephen Paget, 1881

March 16.—I do believe that you have partly misunderstood the meaning of the Holy Communion. Certainly it should be, it must come to be, the most intimate act of love between man & God ; but it has also, surely, two other aspects at least, for which one should cling to it through years even of uncertainty. First, it is offered to us as the vehicle of a spiritual Presence coming to work in us & for us, bound by no laws save those of Spirit, and so able to act as mysteriously as love (which indeed it is). It is not primarily laid upon us as a duty, but let down to us as a hope ; in it God meets us while we are yet a great way off, and teaches & changes us in ways we do not stop to notice & could not, perhaps, understand. . . . And, secondly, it is the great means whereby we all realize our unity and fellowship one with another, in which we try to put aside for a little while our own special needs & difficulties & peculiarities, & throw ourselves into the wide stream of life with which the world is moving towards God. . . . For these two uses I would cling, I believe, to the Eucharist, by God's grace, through the loss of almost all else, even though mists and doubts were thick about me. I would rather miss many matins than one quiet and untroubled Celebration in the early morning. . . .

Just let me say one more thing. I can well believe that your present circumstances are *most* full of difficulties in regard to the realization of Christianity & the growth of its power on you. First, because you are living mostly with men of your own age, many of whom, I suppose, have not yet felt all those varied experiences of anxiety & sympathy & love & sorrow which go so far to make up the data, the material of faith, and who are all busily, constantly engaged with a life of more than sufficient interest—they have emerged from all dependence upon others, while they are not yet clearly responsible for others—as a father for his children, a tutor for his pupils ; & it is such responsibility which forces one to give the full weight to all the issues of life. And then your own life is, is it not, full from morning till night with an unrivalled stream of occupation & excitement ; and while these are new & always changing, there must be, I should think, a difficulty in gathering from them, as they hurry by, the spiritual help & light which, later on, they all may bring to you. God, I doubt not, is in them all, in all your work; but He is in its very depths; and while it is all new and changing & rushing on day after day, it must be hard to get below its surface; it may be especially necessary to seek in prayer, & to wait in faith, for the light which you will presently see in all your life.

Sexagesima Sunday.—As I read Pompilia at breakfast I made up my mind that I must write to you, even though my letter should clash with that hasty breakfast which, like Juvenal's peacock, *crudum super omnibus aufers* down to the Hospital.

And in the course of the morning I made up my mind what I would write. For Holland preached the 'Varsity Sermon, and it was such as I have never heard, I think, even from him; lifting one's thoughts more firmly, and as if more easily, into the higher air of his own soul; holding more steadily, and telling us more plainly and irresistibly, the spiritual things which seem to grow before his sight even while they escape his words. Indeed, it was such a time as one cannot forget, such as one longs to share with all whom one loves. May I try to tell you, while I remember it, just something of what he said? I shall enjoy trying, and you need only read my letter when & as you like.

He took for his text, " What man knoweth the things of a man, save the Spirit of man which is in him? Even so the things of God knoweth no man, but the Spirit of God." He started from Renan's epigram that no man can be the critic of a religion save he who has believed it once, and believes it no longer; and his subject was the work of the critical reason in regard to religion. His central point was that which, I think, he never leaves—the mutual interpenetration of reason and emotion, of light and love—that the act of faith is the act of the whole man, and that we come to know God as by His grace we live according to that which we already know of truest and best. And so the purely external criticism of spiritual things appears as doomed to error by its own profession of externality; it declares at the outset that it has no knowledge of the experience which is the essential matter of

religion; and the very indifference which it calls impartiality
is the confession of its inadequacy for understanding the
subject.

From this central point he went out to claim for reason, in
its critical exercise, the power, the right, the duty of dealing
with the subject-matter of religion, basing this, much as Caird
does, I think, on the necessary rationality of human emotion;
reason can understand, must explain emotion, because it has
been in it all along. But then he brought in a new line of
thought—new at least to me—the unutterable *vastness* of the
task which thus lies upon reason, the immense and varied
and delicate mass of feeling which she has to deal with in
religion. And he helped one to see this by the analogy of
music; how all the incalculable wealth and intricacy and force
of thought which moves in a great piece of music is, after all,
less in volume, as it were, and not more, than one single
emotion in one human heart; how we find one joy, one sorrow
of our own, expressed, but not more than expressed, in all that
marvellous mass of art: "we are surprized, we are not sur-
passed": we have emotions in us, every lover, every mourner,
has passions which are not spoken yet; the experience of our
own life is more than all the fulness even of music.

But if in music form is only given to a part of our emotion,
what a task lies before the reason when it turns to find itself,
to trace its forms in the *religious* feeling, to criticize & reduce
to order the passion wherewith the Saints have given themselves to God. For here is an emotion so wide, so vast, so
masterful, so sufficient & satisfied, absorbing, and triumphant,
that for its sake men have sacrificed every other desire of their
heart, and loved here so that they desired no other love. If no
art can exhaust or explain the everyday devotion with which a
man loves his friend or his child, how can reason lightly, easily,
quickly, without training thro' a life of purity & prayer, grasp
& formulate & express the infinitely manifold tide of feeling
with which the soul of man throws itself before Almighty
God?

. . . You will guess, perhaps, one reason why I could not
write to-day to you as one often does. I have thought that
you must be feeling sad about Cotton's death, & the gap in

that happy, blameless colony of Christ Church people. And
so I could not easily write what might jar on you ; it was
much easier to write even remotely of the thoughts which
alone complete the fragments of this visible life. *P.S.*—I
suppose there is no chance that you would come down on
Saturday & hear Laurence Holland read Antony and Cleopatra ?
It would be delightful if you could.

1882

This year the new statutes, drawn up by the
University Commission, came into force.   Hitherto,
there had been a large body of senior students.   The
great majority of them held clerical studentships, and
must resign them if they married.   Under the new
statutes the name " senior students " was abolished.
The senior students were simply called " students,"
the junior students were called scholars, and
the number of the clerical studentships was greatly
reduced.   In 1882 three of the senior students had
resigned their studentships ; but, under the temporary
provisions of the new statutes, it was open to the
Governing Body to re-elect them to " official " studentships.   One of them had written a Hibbert Essay,
containing statements as to the Resurrection which
were not in accord with the teaching of the Church :
and the question was brought forward, whether he
ought to be elected : for, if he were elected, he would
be not only a lecturer but a tutor.   If, on the other
hand, he were not elected, he would be deprived of
that recognition of his work to which he was entitled.
Pusey—it was his last attendance as a member of the
Governing Body—and Liddon strongly opposed his
election, and he was not elected.   Paget, though a
tutor, voted against the tutors, and with Pusey and

Liddon. This event brought a long period of dissen-
sion into the work of the House. The tutors had
been to all intents and purposes unanimous. It was
they who ought to decide and arrange the teaching;
and they had been outvoted by the exercise of "outside" influences. The teaching in Christ Church of
Greek History, for honours in Greats, had been
seriously impaired; for some years, no permanent
appointment was made for this subject. There came
a long time of division in Common-room, even a time
of ill-feeling; and, when one of the Censorships fell
vacant, Paget's candidature was strongly opposed, and
Holland, against his own wish, was elected to that office.

A very different event, in April, was a meeting in
Christ Church to interest men in the work of the Poplar
Mission. There is a letter in July to Lord Victor
Seymour, who was working there :—

> In all the retrospect of the past year there is nothing at all that
> makes me so happy, & thankful, & full of hope for all that I
> love best, as the growth and work of the mission; and I think
> that for years to come the thoughts & feelings which it has
> given me will make me better and stronger and more trustful
> towards God and men.

An earlier letter to him, Feb. 23, was just written late
at night to amuse him, at Poplar, with news of Christ
Church :—

> I am sorry to say that the week has not been one of un-
> broken peace; for on Monday night certain persons were
> seized with an insane craving after the fire-engine; and as the
> door was locked they tried to open it with violence and a pick-
> axe: a purpose which they gave up when Salwey appeared, and
> ran them to ground on Liddon's staircase. There was a gloomy
> interview at the Deanery next morning; and two would-be
> firemen are gated for the rest of the term. It is a great bore—
> for though they meant it quite humorously it is misunderstood,

and upsets harmony. King was going by just after, with a
Greek cleric who was up here ; and who, as he saw a large
party hurrying through Tom, and was told that they were
students, said that it was very late for them to be coming back
from Lecture ! The Torpids began to-day, Phillips stroking
our first ; and I suppose one must be thankful that both first
and second kept their places. I could not go and see them,
for Holland and I were engaged in licking Lyon and Greenwood at racquets. The Christ Church entertainment (to the
college servants) went off capitally on Saturday, with a big and
enthusiastic audience, who were especially delighted with
Adderley's performance of the Farm-yard.

In April, on the day of Mr. Darwin's funeral,
he writes to George Romanes :—

I have been thinking to-day of the great national solemnity
in which you are taking part : there is all through the sorrow
much to be thankful for, I think ; for I do hope and believe
that the great scene and the deep and universal mourning may
mark and perpetuate, or increase, a degree of brotherhood, of
mutual forbearance and mutual help, among all of us who,
however poorly, seek the Truth, such as one longs and prays
for every day, with, thank God, a continually-growing hope. I
think we did not so understand one another, or hope for it,
thirty years ago.[1]

In Holy Week, he gave four addresses at the mid-
day services in St. Paul's. (*The Redemption of Work,*

---

[1] *To Stephen Paget, April 23.*—" Romanes has told me very much about Darwin,
whom he seems to have known very nearly. It is indeed an immeasurable loss : a
great, pure mind taken out of sight as the pattern of study : and all of us poorer,
unless we can imitate something of the simplicity and humility and self-forgetfulness
which made him mighty and noble as the *minister et interpres Naturae.* Are you not
thankful to have seen him once ? " This one occasion was when Mr. Darwin had
come to lunch at Harewood Place. In the course of the talk mention was made of
Herbert Spencer, and Mr. Darwin said, " I never read a page of that man's books
without thinking, Well, here's work for a man for a hundred years to find out
whether it's true." He told also, laughing heartily, how he had been wrong, and
his gardener had been right, over a fact in botany : " It serves me right," he said,
" for meddling with things that I didn't understand."

Parker & Co., 1882.) This year, also, he gave the
Bodleian oration in Oxford.[1]

In July, to Holland and him, after the conflict of
opinions at Christ Church, came the happiness of the
reading party at Helmsley in Ryedale :—

It is a wonderful country, with the most splendid surprises
of beauty : dales as rich as a Tyrol valley, hidden in the most
varied woods, and full of flowers : while here and there one
comes on a panorama of moorland and hills rolling away as
though there were not a town within the Continent. And
the people are capital : clean and busy and capable, most
unbubulcic. We are the oddest party, far more heterogeneous
than we have ever been before ; but we get on so far splendidly.
We work like troopers : chapel every morning at 7.30 ; breakfast at 9.15, and back to work at 10 ; so that at present we
all do about eight hours : except the Invalides, headed by
W——, who reads the profoundest works for the shortest
periods of time. Gull and Phillips go at it like breaking
stones, with relentless energy.

He was himself among "the Invalides" for the
latter half of the reading party.[2] During August, he

---

[1] Canon Driver, Regius Professor of Hebrew in Oxford, has kindly sent a note
on this annual Oration. It was founded by Dr. John Morris, Professor of Hebrew
in 1629–1648. It is given in Latin, by an M.A. of Christ Church appointed by the
Dean : in honour of Sir Thomas Bodley, and "as a panegyric and encouragement of
the Hebrew studies." In Paget's time, it was given in the Library, before the
Curators alone : but recently it has been given publicly, in the Convocation House.
The day is November 8, when the Curators make their annual visitation. It is said
that Mark Pattison, hearing Paget's oration, said "Who is this reactionary young
man, who writes such good Latin ? "

[2] He amuses himself, in bed with a bad throat, by sending to his younger sister
a little poem, " On my first Yawn." It begins well—*Hail, dozy-fingered Yawn* ; and
there are fine lines in it—*Sleep is not sleep unheralded by thee* ; and again, *That open
diapason of the jaws* ; and again, *The eddying gargle's undiminished rill.* He imagines
the Yawn, now here, now there—

> Nor seldom in some unattractive den,
> Some Academic haunt of dons and men,
> While the poor patient Tutor lectures on
> Magrath's Selections from the Organon,
> And conscientiously fills up the hour,
> Even the bashful freshman owns thy power.

was now in London, now at Crayford in Kent, where
his people had taken the vicarage for the summer.
From Crayford, he writes to Miss Lawrence : " I was
in London a few days ago, and felt its real empti-
ness when I saw Mr. Meredith staring earnestly at
some light suits in a ready-made tailor's in Regent
Street." From London, Aug. 12, he writes to his
elder sister :—

No trace of my small illness, save the ignorance which that
fortnight might have disturbed and which is still unruffled. It
was a bore to lose half one's reading-party, but the boys were
so good to me, and my little doctor so charming a friend, that
there was plenty of pleasure in the trouble. I think my
mother is happier at Crayford than I have ever seen her anywhere. It is to me very pathetic to see her delight in such a
place, for it shows how she must hunger for the country half
the time she is in London, since Crayford in itself is hardly
inspiring and distinctly suburban. . . . I am all alone here
and so mercilessly garrulous, but I know you will bear with
me. I wonder how long I should love London, if I lived in
it, as I love it now. There is hardly a place from which I am
not glad to come to it, and it is a real pleasure, even in this
desolate, carpetless house, at ten o'clock at night, to think that
I am in London ; while, at Oxford I could almost envy the
stokers on the up-trains. It seems to me the one place I know
where the atmosphere tastes stronger of action than of criticism,
where most people do their own work instead of finding fault
with others ; & certainly a London street is a much happier
looking thing than an Oxford one. I suppose it is because
Oxford is still " in a state of transition," but somehow I doubt

---

Some too, on Sundays, for the servants' sake,
A large and early dinner dare to take ;
Then seek the Parish church ; and, lo ! thy flight
Is with them ; and before the sequence trite
Of firstly, secondly, and to conclude,
Is well begun, with interruption rude
From mouth to mouth thou bear'st thy voiceless news,
The chartered libertine of private pews.

whether the coming events will be much brighter than the shadow they have cast before them—a sufficiently gloomy and angry shadow.

But his heart was full, this August, of something better than Oxford politics. On September 8, the greatest blessing of his life was given to him. "An entirely wonderful thing has happened; a sheer, unhindered blessing such as no words can tell and no life be long enough to show one's thanks for. I am engaged to be married to Miss Helen Church." It is thirty years since they were engaged; it is twelve since she died. "I think of her," says one to whom she was *animae dimidium meae*, "as of the sun shining warmly and gently on a June day. She filled our lives while she was here." She was a daughter of Dean Church, and was born at Whatley, Somerset, in 1858. Her father, in a letter written when she was about three years old, calls her "Helen always merry, always hungry, always in mischief." There is a story of her, when she was a young girl, riding after the hounds, and getting thrown, and her beautiful hair all coming down; and the young men in the field, at the sight of her, straightway fell in love with her. All through her girlhood, over and above her unending delight in riding, skating, dancing, tennis, and holiday-making, there was her diligence over her music and Italian, and her pleasure in them; her admiration of all the good in people; her perfect gift of love and reverence for home; and her simplicity, as if she had come out of a poem by Wordsworth. Her father was her teacher, and his friends were her friends. At the time of her engagement, she had lived twelve years in the country and twelve in the Deanery of St. Paul's. It was said of her, and well said, that she was like the

Demeter in the British Museum ; she had the same outline of the features, the same poise of the head, the same quiet, noble look in the forehead and the eyes ; and the beauty of her face was set off by the beauty of her fair hair. It made one feel more of a gentleman to see her come into the room—*Vera incessu patuit dea.* Her voice was pleasant and musical, alike in speaking and in singing, and she had been taught by Sir John Stainer to be a good organist : she could even play the great organ of St. Paul's. Among her many virtues, one thinks first of her sincerity. She gave to everybody an immediate sense of truth, such as we have when a sum comes right. She could not be disloyal or disingenuous ; she had no use for any sort of trick or artifice ; it was not in her to act or pose or rehearse effects. She called homely things by their right names, not holding herself too good for dull work ; and she ruled her household affairs carefully, with pride in them, like one of Homer's women. As her face recalled the Demeter, so her spirit seemed to recall the heroic age. Or put Florence for Oxford, and she might have been Romola, but that she had more sympathy, more humour. For her steady acceptance of facts did not prevent her from being so in love with life that acts of kindness came natural to her, and she could no more leave off being generous than she could leave off breathing. Only, in the later years—if one can speak of later years, where death came so early—she must have found it hard sometimes to hold on to her love of life ; for she had lost her father, her brother, and one of her sisters ; and there were times of heavy anxiety, and always the rush of Term, the care of her husband and the six children, the incessant hospitality, and all the burden of her woman's kingdom in Oxford. Yet, to the very end, she kept the radiance and the vivid beauty of the earlier years ; and when she died the greater part of the beauty of Christ Church, for some of us, died with her.

BROMSGROVE CHURCH.

CHAPTER IV

Soon after their engagement, he and Miss Church decided that their first home should not be in Oxford. He had been long enough, indeed he had been too long, without a parish of his own : he needed to get away, out of Oxford, out into the open, there to find his way, as it were, across country. To their great happiness, the living of Bromsgrove, Worcestershire, was offered to him. He writes, on January 8, 1883, to Lord Victor Seymour : " I want very much to be the first to tell you of a great bit of happiness which has come to me. . . . The Dean and Chapter of Worcester have appointed me to the vicarage of Bromsgrove. It is a large parish, 4900 people : I should never have dared to seek, or even to desire, so great a charge ; but it has come unsought, by the free act of those who have the responsibility of choosing. There is a glorious church : in good order : and the people seem very ready for any work which, with humility and by God's help, may be done there. So we shall be married, I hope, very soon after Easter : for just before the suggestion of Bromsgrove came, Holland's acceptance of the Censorship left me free to leave when I wished ; and I go back on Friday for my last Term in the old place." On January 10, to

Herbert Barnett : " There are other things about it—
such as the Trusteeship of the School and the patron-
age of three livings—which increase the responsibility :
and I do feel very deeply how little I have learned to
use such a position. But I have learnt some things
at Oxford, which can be used, I know, in every field
of work ; and I am sure that God will help and teach
me ; and the new work will begin with a new help
and blessing of my life which seems, as I look forward to it, to raise and brighten everything."

On February 9, he writes to James Adderley, now
vicar of Saltley, Birmingham, advising him as to the
choice of a profession. The letter is a good example of
his care for his pupils, and comes well here, at the end
of his seven years' work as a College tutor :—

Thank you very truly and heartily for all the trust and
friendship of your letter : indeed I am very grateful for it. I
am sure you will not blame me for having waited one day
before trying to answer it :—I think there is no graver thing
in the world than venturing to advise any one in the choice
of his profession. I do wish that we had had a talk : it was
wrong of me not to manage it ; but those first days of the
Term were full of work.

Of course, dear Adderley, I feel with you that God may be
served and His glory advanced in any calling :—perhaps pre-
eminently in those which are not usually sought for the
highest motives or pursued with an unselfish aim. But if one
has the desire to serve Him—the desire which can and will
be fulfilled, if one holds it fast, in any profession—then there
comes the question—in what way can I, *being what I am*,
serve Him best? And the answer may come, I think,
in various ways :—to some by the irresistible pressure of outward
circumstances—some men have no choice, they *must* use
the one opportunity which comes to them :—to others again
by the clear, steady sense of a divine call and ordering of
their life to *one* line, outside which they would feel miserable

and disloyal :—to others again, to many, I think, by the recognition that in one profession all, or almost all, their best gifts and faculties will find scope and use :—to others by a convergence and mixture of motives which they may at first only be able to trust tentatively, but find continually stronger and clearer as they go on in obedience to this guiding.

But I believe that for most men who are free to choose, the indication of the right choice comes by a sense of fitness for one profession above all others :—a belief that they will in it do as much as they can of that which they can do best. I do not think that any one can choose with any heart a profession in which many of his best powers will be unexercised or repressed : nor can he be happy in it : for a large part of him will be doomed to inaction ; and inaction for a healthy man is miserable. And positively too, I think a man may fairly feel himself called to the life which will exercise and satisfy his best energies, his highest desires.

So I should believe that if a man feels in himself a wish to take orders, but doubts whether he is called by God, the best test is that he should, not suddenly or in one day, but quietly and naturally, try to see what desires he has, what kind of enjoyment and gratification he expects in life, what sort of things he already does with pleasure, or is beginning to find pleasure in. The love of worship, care for the poor, sympathy with sorrow, the sense of a great debt of gratitude to Christ for all He bore for us, and a loving desire to serve Him and to help those for whom He died :—these are feelings which find exercise and rest and delight in the life of a Parish Priest, and, by whatever unworthiness & uncertainty they may be hindered, do seem to mark a man out for that life. And if he has these, or feels them growing in him, then I do believe that there is no happiness or blessing comparable with that which he will find, in spite of all failure and weakness, in the life of a clergyman. And if he has these, if he can be fairly sure of them, if they are strongest in him when he is most himself, then I do not think he needs be afraid that he is being misled by any side or subordinate motive which may tend in the same way. They are only incidental, and will not stand the tests which bring out the strength of these.

I can quite understand that you may find it hard at once to answer these questions to yourself—that you may want time. But I do not like the idea of your taking any other profession for the present : it is so hard to find any satisfactory course.

I am sure that staying up here to coach is a bad plan : it is such a desultory, irresponsible life—so easily drifting into superficial and inadequate work.

A tutorship away from here is rather better, but not much : and I do not think that you would like it. I really believe that if you wish for time to test yourself to get sure of your own wish and calling, it would be better to go into the Sollicitor's work, with the understanding that at the end of a definite period—say three or five years—you shall reconsider your position, and if then you feel clear for the ordained life, leave the law and take Holy Orders. I think that you would lose less and be more likely to gain in strength and clearness thus than by any life which you felt to be merely a life of hesitation on the edge of your choice. I do not know how far this is possible :—but it is what a man who is coming to be my curate at Bromsgrove has done : he was a Sollicitor up to 25 & then went to Cambridge, to take a degree and be ordained.

Of course I only suggest this in case you feel that you must take some time to know yourself better (—a hard knowledge for us all to gain—) before you choose.

God bless you, dear Adderley, I shall very often pray for you.—Yours affectionately, FRANCIS PAGET.

Bromsgrove, fourteen miles from Birmingham, comes into Domesday Book, and was a busy town when Birmingham was a little village, on the other side of the Lickey Hills. King John granted it a market : it returned two members to Parliament, under Edward the First : it was a centre of the cloth and linen trade, in the time of Henry the Eighth. Later, to its sorrow, it saw less of cloth and linen, and took up with the trade in hand-made nails : the work is done at home, in little forges built up against the cottages : women do much of it, and it is laborious, ill-paid, failing work. "It is a dying industry," writes Mr. Noel Paterson, the present vicar, "owing to the introduction of machinery ; the young people preferring now to work in factories which have sprung up in recent years." The parish church, one of the finest in Worcestershire, recalls, by its architecture and its monuments, the great traditions of the town. "It is really splendid : I saw it with a little sunshine on it : and I think I have never seen a parish church which I would choose before it. Even St. Mary's at Shrewsbury is, in some ways, less likely for worship"—so Paget wrote home, after a preliminary visit. Later in life, he said that he had felt so nervous, as he walked up from the station, that he nearly turned back. Even after a year's work there, he was hindered by his inexperience : "I feel so empiric, so deficient in never having been a curate. But it is too late now : and one can only go on, & trust that good is being wrought out of it all, and pray that the blunders & the presumption may be forgiven : and that at all events one may be saved from the folly of being content with one's self ; wondering all the while at the abundant happiness that continually refreshes one, day after day."

Before leaving Christ Church, on March 1, 1883, he writes to Victor Seymour :—

It is very strange to feel that I can count on my fingers the days of my stay here : that I have only eight or nine more lectures to give. It will be very sad to go away, and I dread rather the actual good-bye to the place—it has been to me so full of kindness and friendship. But I have, thank God, a most happy hope for the other end of my journey. It has been a peaceful & prosperous term : notable for the glory of the

Torpids, our two boats having made between them ten bumps. Then we were only just beaten to-day for the Football Challenge Cup: and we seem likely to have two men at least running at Lillie Bridge. So we are sitting up.

On March 9, to J. W. Williams :—

I never thought last year that I could ever think of any one going to the Riviera without a little envy : but—strange to say—I would not change my Easter Vac. for all the villas that have been built since the time of Mæcenas.

On March 17, he was inducted into his living by the Archdeacon of Worcester, and on Palm Sunday, March 18, preached his first sermon in Bromsgrove. On March 28, he and Miss Church were married in St. Paul's. Dr. Liddon married them, and Dr. Talbot, then Warden of Keble, took part in the service. Sir John Stainer wrote a special anthem for the occasion. After a short honeymoon in Devonshire, they took up their work in Bromsgrove. He had the help of two curates : for, beside the many services in the parish church, there were two mission-rooms, one two and a half miles from the town, and the other at Sidemoor, in the nailers' district.

They had to be very economical : for he only received two thirds of the income of the living : besides, they were always spending money on good works : so that he said, years afterwards, laughing, that if he had stayed much longer at Bromsgrove he would certainly have been ruined. Strict and anxious economy was new to him. They started a pony-cart—what could better ensure efficiency without extravagance ?—but the pony-cart had to be put down. He writes in 1884 to J. W. Williams, on the duty of enquiring before alms-giving :—

At Oxford we had not, or fancied we had not, time for this : & our neglect of it forced us to choose, I think, between the dangers of undue giving and undue refusing. If one can enquire and will do so with a kind and charitable heart, the case is somewhat changed. At Oxford there was little exercise of compassion in our daily work, & so a greater danger of growing hard than we ought to find among the blessings & privileges of a parish priest's life. At Oxford most of my giving was divided between subscription-lists and beggars : but now, by God's great mercy, one's heart must be daily touched and quickened by the knowledge of real needs.

But it is probable that he was less circumspect than he thought. For there is the story of the woman who put all her ornaments on the parlour table, and declared that the brokers were in the house ; whereby she got a sovereign from the vicar, and another from Mrs. Paget. And there is the story of the old woman who, seeing him come striding down the road, bet that she would get half-a-crown from him by pretending to be ill ; and she did. These things will happen. A graver story—he kept a token of it, to the end of his life, in his study—is of a woman who threatened to kill herself, and he watched over her, all night, in her cottage. And to these stories may be added a wise saying, which remained in his memory. He had congratulated a poor old man on his recovery from severe illness, and had got this answer, " Well, I don't know about that, sir : I expect I shall just have to do it all over again."

In November, 1883, he writes to Romanes, thanking him for some game—" somehow you must have found out that yesterday evening was the date of our first dinner-party, and that your gift would arrive just in time to relieve the administrative mind, and to give distinction to our feast "—and he goes on to tell of his work : " We are most happy here : with any amount of work to do ; and work so various and engrossing that it seems to have an unfailing refreshment in it. The sadness is the deep poverty of the place : the poverty of a failing trade : for most of the people work at hand-made nails : and their average earnings are about eight shillings a week :—nor is it easy to see how a fresh trade can be at present introduced." He invented a new sort of Christmas present, a box of best assorted Bromsgrove hand - made nails, with hammer and all complete ; and was eloquent over the inferiority of machine-made nails : but he could not fight Birmingham.

He and Mrs. Paget did "any amount of work " : night-schools, classes, visits, choir-practices, two ser- vices daily, and four on Sundays : a letter from her, October, 1883, gives a formidable list of their duties : the wonder is, that out of it she could capture time for reading—" I have just attacked a four-volume Life of Bach, in German." He was at this time preparing more than a hundred and thirty candidates for Confirmation. He writes, on the day after Christmas Day :—

Thank God, yesterday was a happiness beyond words : for I think nearly all our newly-confirmed came to the Holy Communion :—there were 165 at the early celebration, and 72 afterwards at mid-day :—so that I do trust that, by God's great goodness to us, we have got a start from which we may look forward.

In 1884, on Good Friday, he writes :—

We have had great encouragement in the week-day services : the people have come so very steadily, in very good numbers, & listened so thoughtfully : and we have had the church crammed each Sunday night : which is also good, so far as it goes : but it means less, I think, than the other : the especial blessing having been in dear Ottley's sermons this week :—I do

think everybody must have been helped by their beauty &
simplicity & strength.

In March, 1884, their first child was born to them.
He writes to Lawrence Hardy, asking him to be a
godfather :—

You and I have known one another many years, and shared
very many thoughts : and our friendship has been to me a
steadily deepening source of happiness and of entire trust.
And we are anxious that among the chief and nearest influences on our boy's life there should be the example and advice
of those who will give him wider views of life than are apt to
be given by the daily talk and interests of a parish priest's
home : we want him to see from the first how much bigger
a thing Christianity is than that clerical aspect of it to which
he is born.   I think that the children of the clergy sometimes
suffer (either by narrowness, or by the reaction from it) from
hearing & thinking too much of a clergyman's life.

In August they took a short holiday, and stayed
with Lord Blachford and Dean Church at Ivy Bridge.
He writes to his younger sister :—

I don't think you can be happier than we are.   I do long
indeed to be with you all : I grudge a year that goes by
without a week spent with my father, & in learning from
him : [1]—but barring that, I could not find a wish in my heart.
It seemed clearly right to come away for a little bit : for the
dear wife was looking very white and tired with the great
heat, and I was longing (& probably my people were also)
for one Sunday without a sermon : (Butler used to say that,
for his people's sake, if he could not get a holiday he would
bury himself in his own garden for a month :—)   And so on
Monday we started, & slept at Hereford.   There Ouseley

---

[1] In 1885, he writes to her of his father's influence as "the continual influence
of one of the very greatest & best & most disciplined men in the world" ; and
in 1898 of "the counsel and encouragement that, among human helps, has meant
most to me."   In 1892, to C. C. Brookes : "How wonderful fathers are when they
are like yours and mine."

showed us all over the beautiful little Duomo, with its variety
of interest, from suspected Saxon to some of the best Per-
pendicular I have ever seen : and then we went on to Ross,
Chepstow, & Tintern : & so here. . . . And you know
this place : and can imagine what it looks like in this glorious
sunlight.   It is a wonderful happiness to be here : & if ever
one turns away from the delights of every sense in the garden
& the park, there is the great happiness of talking with the
Dean & Lord Blachford :—a happiness which I never felt so
much as now, when most of one's work is in contact with
simple minds, to whom, with all their goodness & moral
elevation, words and thoughts suggest nothing, awake nothing,
beyond their immediate, inevitable meaning.   It is a delight to
get again into an atmosphere which seems alive & teeming
with analogies for every thought ; & to be with minds on
which words fall & ring & spring up again like gold.
You won't misunderstand me, as tho' I were depreciating
the helpfulness of patient, dutiful people everywhere : you
know that : only this is another delight, and, I think, a
right one.

In September, came what Bromsgrove, doubtless,
had not seen for very many years : an ordination
service in the parish church, a new curate for Bromsgrove being one of the ordinands.   At Christmas
came a great rush of festal affairs : E. F. Sampson,
who was there, writes that

. . . the way the vicar and Mrs. Paget threw themselves
into all kinds of entertainments for all the various sections of
the people was quite magnificent.   She was a wonderful help
at all this work.   I have sometimes, perhaps a little im-
pertinently, wondered what the vicar's home balance-sheet
looked like : but nothing could make him stint his generosity
to everything and everybody in the parish.   I went down for
Holy Week, 1885 : I remember now the evensong on Easter
Day, the lift and power of it all, as the *O filii et filiæ* was sung.

Two letters, in 1884, to Victor Seymour, are con-

cerned with the death of his father, and with a plan for
a day of retreat :—

Jan. 26.—. . . I was very grateful to see that you were
with him, and that you could celebrate the Holy Communion
for him :—I have come to know more and more how near
God is to us, how the things that are not seen seem almost to
break through the veil of the visible, in such a service : how
our Blessed Lord will indeed come forth to enter in and to be
with His servant through the valley of the shadow of death,
that he may fear no evil, while the Eternal Light and Truth is
leading him to the holy Hill and to God's dwelling : and so
He giveth His beloved sleep : taking them to the quiet place
where they may wait for us, till His mercy may bring even us
too to His welcome, to the love which fears no end.   I am so
thankful that in the sorrow you were granted one of the
greatest blessings of our Priesthood :—that God made you the
minister of that great gift to the best father, I should think,
that any son ever had. . . .

Aug. 4.—I am very greatly looking forward to the day : for
I think I never felt the need of such help so much as now.
The practical side of one's life gets so grievously out of all
proportion to the thoughtful side : and though God's Grace
keeps one up & carries one on, still it seems like tempting
Him when one prays & thinks so little as I have been doing.
I wonder whether it will be a life-long effort, a life-long
theme of regret, that one gets (or makes) so little time for
prayer—at all events it must not be less than a life-long effort :
one must never acquiesce in it, I feel quite sure.

In August, 1885, there is a letter to him, con-
gratulating him on his engagement :—

. . . It is *all* true, dear Victor : all that fills your heart
now, all that you are thanking God for : all the wealth of
hope that changes and enlightens the very thought of living,—
all is true and sure :—only it will grow and deepen as the years
go on, with a grace and power not of this world : you will
find yourself loving and rejoicing with a strength and restful

happiness which will seem always new : and as this great gift of love enables you for every duty of life, as it leads you on to further depths and heights both in your manhood & in your Priesthood, so too, be sure, the love itself will grow beyond all that you can ask or think, teaching you fresh truths of Him who gives it you, the author & source of all pure noble love. May He continually & most richly bless you, and her who is to share your life & work & to make your home.

Early in this year, when Dr. King became Bishop of Lincoln, Paget was appointed to succeed him in Oxford as Regius Professor of Pastoral Theology, and Canon of Christ Church. It is certain that he would gladly have stayed longer at Bromsgrove. He had gone there, with some nervousness, to work that was new to him : and they had made him welcome. It had been almost like a holiday ; like the delight of waking, after the long journey, and finding himself, at early morning, past the frontier, and in Switzerland. There was nothing, in all Bromsgrove, which had not a voice for him : the whole place gave itself to him, and he to it. He noted for observance the chief dates of this short space of his life : the days of his institution and induction, and of his bringing his wife there ; the first day in their first home, and the three last days there ; and, with these, the days on which he received and accepted, in February, 1885, Mr. Gladstone's offer of the work in Oxford. On March 19, he writes to Lawrence Hardy :—

   . . . I do dread the great responsibility of such high and delicate work. And it will be a great & deep sorrow to leave this dear place :—people have been so wonderfully kind & trustful, & worked with us so generously, that I don't know how we shall dig up all our roots. But there are some big bits of happiness in the thought of being at Oxford again :

—high among them the happiness of hoping that our friends really will come to see us now sometimes.[1]

Your godson is dethroned : or at least has only a divided empire. For on Thursday, to our great joy, a daughter was safely and happily born to us : & Richard, mon roi, no longer reigns alone.[2]

On June 27, at a presentation meeting, he spoke his thanks—" I came here to my first parish. I had nothing to tell you save God's Truth as I believed it, as I through His mercy had lived by it, as I by His grace hope to die in it. Your love, your generosity, your unearned thanks, these will be to me as a life-long reinforcement of that Truth of God in my mind." A few days later—in a letter to Victor Seymour—" It was *dreadful* leaving Bromsgrove on Monday : I did not know how tight my heart was fixed there." From Christ Church, on October 6, just before Term-time, he writes to Mr. Webb, Vicar of St. Andrew's, Wells Street, promising to preach there :—

I know you will be charitable to the hastily-written discourse of a Freshman-Professor, in the scurry of his first term. . . . We are very well, thank God, babes and all :—only waiting rather anxiously for the bell to ring and the curtain to go up for the First Scene of our new life here.

To the end of his days, he was thankful for the friendships and the experience of these two years. Again and again, he harks back to them : " all the

---

[1] *To Herbert Barnett, March* 17 : " Mind you are always coming. I'll never preach for you unless you lunch with me." *To James Adderley, March* 25 : " Though the house can never be what King made it, still we do want to keep it always open to those whom he would have delighted to welcome :—& it is one of the very best bits of the prospect to look forward to seeing often the old friends. —Besides, you must come & tell me all about Bethnal Green, & give me tips for my lectures."

[2] *To his elder sister, March* 20 : " Bromsgrove feels a glow of self-congratulation over my son & daughter :—as one of my dear District Visitors said to me to-day, ' It gives universal satisfaction.' "

kindness & sympathy which God gave us there . . . that true-hearted place . . . the place in which I spent the happiest bit, I think, of my life." Of Mr. Prosser, the surgeon, he writes : " No one ever finds out more than a very small fraction of Mr. Prosser's good deeds : but one cannot go at all among the poor without learning something of the work he does and the generosity he shows." To Mr. Wilder, he writes : " Here is my young master's photograph, which I promised to send you :—I think he looks as though he would do credit to his birthplace . . . and I trust that I never shall forget what Bromsgrove taught me." His last visit there was in July 1909, for the sexcentenary festival of the church : and as he went away, he said, " I always feel when I come to Bromsgrove that I'm coming home."

Helen Beatrice Paget.

CHAPTER V

It did not take him long to make his way in his new work. Among some of the Christ Church tutors, there was still a feeling of resentment against his action in 1882 ; but among undergraduates, many of whom had been schoolboys in that year, events so remote were of no great interest ; and his work, first and foremost, was for them. Besides, it was done not for Christ Church alone, but for all Oxford. These six years were full of home-love and friendship : and he and Mrs. Paget found a welcome everywhere in Oxford. Four children, during these years, 1885–1891, were born to them.

Mr. Douglas Maclaren, vicar of Salcombe Regis, has kindly written the following account :—

There are certain versatile people who, in new situations, seem to develop qualities so completely new that each fresh task or call as it comes seems to present to one almost a new person. If the man in question is a student and is suddenly set in a position of authority, he will begin to display a talent for administration, of which his friends will say that "they never imagined that he had it in him." If he is thrown among simple people, he will show himself so perfectly at home with their primitive and simple ways of thought that they themselves find it difficult to believe that he is really a man of learning. If, once more, he is followed inside his own front door and you hear him talking clever nonsense with his children round his study fire, and then compare him with the serious teacher or the able administrator, you say " He seemed *then* an entirely different being."

Of Francis Paget I think the opposite was true. Any who knew him as the scholarly preacher, as the head of a great College, and as the hard-worked Bishop of an unwieldy Diocese, and who then saw him in his own home or had him as a guest in a country parsonage, felt indeed that in him was a rare " diversity of gifts," but the recollection of him which would remain would not be that of a man who showed many different and contrasted sides of himself in succession—not of one in whom different characteristics lay side by side, as it were, in strips, and were brought out as occasion required—but rather the image of him which fixes itself in one's mind is that of a person in whom the various qualities so ran into one another and overlapped, that the same man, and the whole of him, was thrown into everything he did.

This is what makes it hard to speak of Paget in different capacities. One cannot keep the various aspects of the man, or of his work, distinct. Work of many different kinds did, of course, come to him ; but a man's work is ultimately what he himself is, and Paget, more than most people, was always the same man. Hence, one has some misgivings in trying to separate his work into several strands.

As Professor of Pastoral Theology, Paget was one of a very few theological lecturers at that time, whose influence followed undergraduates any distance outside the lecture room. As a lecturer, Paget found waiting for him a great opportunity which he was able to take and use. In the theological faculty five and twenty years ago were to be found some weighty and honoured names, but, with some very rare exceptions, it can hardly be claimed that they were seductive lecturers. Their lectures were attended either because prudence seemed to indicate that it would be a good thing to go and listen to a man whom one was likely to meet as an examiner in the Schools, or because a certificate of attendance at certain courses of lectures was required by Bishops from candidates for Holy Orders. It has to be confessed that if no question of a certificate had been involved, the attendance at some of these lectures would have been very thin. Men may have been mistaken in the estimate they formed of their value; but what the estimate was can be fairly gathered from the fact that it was by no means an unknown thing for men to provide themselves with books which they would produce and read during the lecture, with very little attempt at concealment, and very little pretence of listening to the lecturer. No doubt it was disrespectful, but only those who themselves passed through that particular fire can realise how strong the temptations to this discreditable fault actually were. In the case of Paget's lectures, however, men came with their eyes on something more than a certificate. They came because they felt that the lectures were worth attending—the proof of it being that when the course was at an end men would present themselves, of their own free will, to listen to a second, or a third. And certainly they were worth it. Perhaps the first thing about them to strike a hearer was the extreme care which had obviously been given to the preparation of them. This was one of those features characteristic of all that Paget did. It was felt or seen in everything, from his personal appearance upwards. In his lectures it was especially apparent. Indeed, the criticism which the undergraduate mind was likely to make was that they were, if possible, too thorough. In lecturing, for instance, on Hooker, "with special reference to Book Five," Paget, I remember, began the course by several introductory lectures, giving the historical setting, in England and on the Continent, into which Hooker's great work had to be fitted. He went on to devote three or four more to a summary of the first four Books, defining the positions reached and emphasising their importance. He reached the fifth Book only at the end of the course, and delivered a second supplementary course in the afternoons, in which he dealt with the actual subject itself with the same careful thoroughness. In the same way, it was a favourite dictum of his that minute criticism of the New Testament was not of necessity fanciful; and his lectures on the Pastoral Epistles were examples of the same extremely thorough and exhaustive method. He would stay for a considerable part of his hour over a simple word, discussing its history and etymology, and comparing the use of it by classical writers with that of the New Testament. Perhaps this extreme attention to detail sometimes tended to give an important place to what was certainly only secondary in St. Paul's own mind; and the minute analysis which he was in the habit of giving to a short Epistle was apt to be a little bewildering, and to give an air of complexity and artifice somewhat at variance with the simplicity of its real nature. But, after all, where is the commentator or the expositor who perfectly fulfils his true office, which is to make the salient things salient and not allow the trees to conceal the wood?

A second feature of his lectures, I should say, was his obvious enjoyment of his subject. It is a common and depressing experience to attend lectures which, the lecturer gives you to understand by his manner, are delivered not because he is interested in his work, but because he has to do it. Paget always conveyed the impression of lecturing because he liked it. In different forms this, again, was a "note" belonging to every part of his work. In the case of his lectures, this sense of enjoyment which he displayed ran back, I imagine, very largely to the work and care involved in the preparation. Certainly it served to establish a *rapport* between himself and his audience, and made them feel, as he evidently felt, that the lectures were not a bore.

Then, the lectures were well delivered and put into that graceful English which seemed to come naturally to him whether in sermons or lectures or letters or private conversation.

As illustrating the manner in which Paget and his lectures may be said to have got into one another, instead of remaining strangers, it will probably have been pointed out by others that some of his subjects left a palpable mark upon him. There must be many who remember the enthusiasm with which he would speak of Hooker's conception of the nature and the range of Law, and the feeling with which he would quote that splendid passage on the majesty of Law which forms the close of the first Book. It was from Hooker that Paget

strengthened—if he did not gain—that severe view of insubordination and disregard of law which he showed more than
once in speech and action during his Episcopate.

I said that Paget's work and influence as Professor did not
stop short at the lecture room.   He let himself be approached
privately, in his own house, by undergraduates having questions
to ask or wanting advice.   In these personal interviews there
came out, in another form, the same quality which was felt in
his lectures.   Just as he appeared to find an actual pleasure in
lecturing, so he contrived to give the impression that he liked
being made use of privately—even when he was busy with
work of his own.   Nothing that one remembers or thinks of
in connection with him, stands out more clearly than that.

In his lectures on Parochialia he used to warn men that the
parish priest in his visiting, more especially in his visiting of
the sick, should never let it be felt that he was in a hurry, or
that he had other things to attend to which were more
important.   It was a piece of advice which he never failed to
practise in his reception of the men who found their way into
his study.   He never let them go away with the unpleasant
feeling that he regarded the interruption they had caused as a
nuisance.   He would be as cordial in his greeting as if their
coming meant a pleasant quarter of an hour for a man who
either had nothing at all to do, or who was glad to have an
excuse for putting aside something that interested him less
than they did.   It was a conspicuous triumph of sympathy
and patience.   Paget was a man who knew the value of
method : he worked and lived to a great extent by rule : he
liked to have a programme for the day and to keep to it.   But
he never made the mistake of letting his rule or his programme
become inflexible.   He never allowed them to forget their
place and become his masters instead of being his servants.
He *liked* an interruption probably no more than any other
student, but I never knew him resent one.   He seemed to feel
that the Professor was made for the undergraduates, not the
undergraduates for him.   It is not necessary to say that they
discovered this and that they appreciated it.

One thing which may have made it easier to him than it

would have been to others to deal thus gently with intruders was his unusual power of taking up his interrupted work exactly where he had laid it down. He said once that his father was remarkable in that respect. As one who sometimes has had to suffer from vexatious interruptions, I have often envied him his willingness to endure them and his peculiar gift of picking up a broken thread and getting his iron up again in a moment to exactly the same heat as before.

It was in his first term as Professor that I began to know him. Every one agreed in saying that, apart from the directly formal work belonging to it, there was no place in Oxford harder to fill than that made vacant by Dr. King's resignation. Perhaps no one could have exercised the same influence on undergraduate life in quite the same way ; but, if not in the same way then in a way not very greatly different, Paget soon began to tell on undergraduates socially.

The Pagets' house in Tom Quad was a place to which men liked to go ; and from the number of men who were to be met with at their luncheon parties—not in droves, but usually only two or three at a time—one could see that Paget was beginning to have a large undergraduate acquaintance, outside his own College.

It was, I suppose, after he had been made Dean that Oxford society awoke to Mrs. Paget's great excellence as a hostess, but the undergraduates discovered it long before. Occasionally Paget would go for an afternoon walk with some one of them.[1]　Not often, I think : as a rule he and Mrs.

---

[1] Mr. Michael Wood writes from Greys Rectory, Henley-on-Thames : " I remember how, after a walk with him—when he was Professor of Pastoral Theology —I asked him, just as we reached Tom Gate, a question on behalf of a friend of mine, who wished to be ordained but had scruples as to his own motives, afraid that he might be allowing the advantages, which ordination might confer, in the worth of a certain position, to draw him on, where he ought to hold back. I remember most distinctly Dr. Paget's look and expression—though I suppose it is twenty-five years ago—as he turned beneath Tom Tower, and the substance of what he said as he expounded ' vocation,' showing that *all* the circumstances of one's life were part of the Call of God, and that there was a vocation to every kind of life, according as a man considered that he could serve God best as a doctor, soldier, lawyer, merchant, or whatever the profession might be. Also, I remember that he said, ' None of us, to begin with, is fit for any post : we only become more so by God's grace '—or words to that effect."

Paget spent the two hours or so that he allowed himself in a walk together.

There are one or two things which we used to notice about Paget's conversation on these occasional walks or at his own table. I think it is J. S. Mill who says that a man's mental capacity can best be judged not by his conversation on his special interests, but by his talk on general subjects. If this is true, Paget's must have been a very first-rate mind. Perhaps the best way of expressing the feeling he produced is by saying that he seemed to be a kind of embodiment of what he has said in his well-known sermon on " Leisure Thoughts." He speaks there of the kind of things with which the mind may legitimately occupy itself when it is " off duty." St. Paul, he says, in the verse which that sermon takes for its text (Philippians iv. 8) suggests a " large and noble list " ; and the things which Paget talked of in his leisure moments—natural scenery, and the objects seen along the road, athletics and new books, the prospects of the man he was walking with, not very much of other people unless they were public men, and still less of his own family and himself—showed what a large range of interests he had, and how bright and wholesome was the air in which he breathed. He was playful and full of good stories and enjoyed a new one when he heard it, but even when he was in his lightest moods one caught oneself remembering what he used to say, in his Lectures on the Pastoral Epistles, of the word σεμνότης, and of the place of what he called " gravity " in the clerical character. He always seemed to—

> Have among least things an under-sense of greatest.

No one, probably, could speak half a dozen words to Paget without noticing his eager cordiality. Perhaps his *empressé* manner sometimes led men to make the mistake of thinking that any one so sympathetic as Paget obviously was, could be easily " managed." The mistake if it ever was made was certainly never made by the same man twice. In his College and in his Diocese it was very soon discovered that behind his ready sympathy there was a very firm will. In the lecture room, as I said, he drew an attentive audience, but one is not detracting from the merit of the lectures themselves in saying that it would have gone ill with any man who had tried to read even Paget's beloved Aristotle whilst he himself was lecturing on Hooker or on the work of the Parson in his Parish.

Strangers, or people who knew him only slightly, may have wondered perhaps how much of genuine interest lay behind his sympathetic manner. Those who came at all close to him would have been able to set such doubts at rest. There are some—there must be many—to whom Paget endeared himself most of all by an affectionate interest which stood the test of time. He was once speaking to a bride whom he was to marry the next day to a young clergyman who had been a pupil of his two or three years before. "Don't forget," was the sane and judicious advice he gave her, "that your chief business has to be your home. You are to be a wife first, a clergyman's wife only second." Fifteen years later he happened to meet her father in a Devonshire village. "How is E. ? " he asked at once, calling her by her Christian name ; and he showed as he went on to talk that the wedding with all the incidents and details belonging to it was still fresh in his mind.

Paget used to hold devotional meetings for undergraduates at " Bethel," a small chapel at the end of his own garden. The services, he used to say, were intended for those who had come up to Oxford with the hope or wish, "however faint or vague," of being ordained, or who had found the hope since they had come up. The order of service was very simple :—a hymn, a few collects, an address, a second hymn, and a closing collect. Paget would be vested in cassock, surplice, and stole, and would generally take a single subject or book every Term. The Creed, the Lord's Prayer, the Beatitudes,—I have notes on all of these taken down from his addresses at " Bethel. " Sometimes he took one of the works of the Fathers. Many, no doubt, will remember hearing him speak of St. Chrysostom's *De Sacerdotio*, or of St. Gregory's *Pastoral Charge*, or of St. Bernard's *De Consideratione*. He never for long lost sight of the purpose which the services were especially meant to fulfil, and his ways of trying to keep alive and to strengthen that wish or hope, "however faint or vague," were wise ways.   No one ever felt more strongly than Paget that the call to the ministry was the call to the happiest as well as to the hardest life. "The life of the Parish Priest," he often said, "should be a life of perpetual youth."   He knew, as well as any one, that it has its disappointments—disappointments which are very real. But few teachers have been able so to impress on others by their words and their own living example that even the disappointments and "tribulations" of the ordained life are "tribulations" in which it is possible for plain men to "rejoice," and that it has its profound and blessed consolations.   He had little sympathy with the teaching of some whose preparation of candidates for Holy Orders is largely made up of warnings as to the difficulties and disillusions which will form the chief portion of the history of the man of God.

After the service—it lasted about 45 or 50 minutes—the undergraduates were invited to meet him and Mrs. Paget in her drawing-room, where they had coffee and talked a little. But the things that Paget used to speak of at "Bethel" left men but little inclined to talk of common subjects.

There is nothing to be added to this account of his use of his professorship.   It remains to note some events of these years of his life, and some of his letters to his friends.

1885–1887

A holiday letter, dated thus—*Tarascon (chez M. Tartarin) Sept.* 24, 1886—was written on his way home from Arles :—

It is quite hopeless to write to you about it, because you've been there: and it would be quite as hopeless to write to Nell about it, because Nell hasn't.   But I thought you might like to have a line to say it's all still there.—We walked along the bank of the Rhone, where it sweeps round in that splendid curve, and then struck down the Rue de l'Amphithéâtre, and came to that, the first of our sights.   Of course it cannot rival the beauty & preservation of Nîmes : but one part of it I never shall forget :—my father doubts whether you saw it four years ago :—the ring of dungeons, without a glimmer of light, behind the inner ring in which the wild beasts were kept :—the dungeons serving for the victims, whether captives or Christians, who were to be given to the beasts. There was something very vivid in the old man's description—meeting at many points the early Acta Martyrum so far as I know them —of the way in which *ces misérables* were led out in full sight of the wild beasts, with only a grating to keep them back, into the great space of the Arena with the 25,000 faces watching to see them die : how then the gratings were shifted, and the beasts allowed to see their prey : and then again the gates of the inner gallery opened to the Arena, & then, I suppose, all was soon over. One tries, in vain, I think, to measure by any strain of one's own will that one has ever come near knowing or can even imagine, the effort of resolution that must have been kept up in days & nights spent in the dungeons. We went on to the beautiful ruins of the theatre—as Greek & bright as anything one has ever dreamt of : — just like what Alma Tadema tries to give one :—the only bit of really Greek work, I think, that we have come across — (& certainly the faces of the women at Arles explain why they should have everything as Greek as it could be in so late an age). There was a perfect sky behind the two faultless columns — (how true Browning is about it all). . . .

Next year, 1887, when holiday time came, he had to be in residence in Christ Church : and he consoles himself by dating a letter to Romanes, from Oxford, thus :—

A villeggiatura near Abingdon, Aug. 19.—I am here, " called back " into residence : but I go out to Boar's Hill this evening : for my wife & bairns are still staying there. We had a thunder-storm which nearly shook us out of our skins on Wednesday : I never have seen the like of it in England—a really wonderful pageant, both for sight and sound. It was pretty to see our children's simple enjoyment of it, without one touch of fear or uneasiness.

In September, from Ely, he writes to Miss Lawrence :—

Your tour sounds wholly delightful. I could build a beautiful Castle in the air (such as Mr. Bodley himself might not scorn for its architecture & adornment) by imagining how great a pleasure it would be if Helen & I could meet you somewhere.

This year, he published a collection of sermons, preached, most of them, at Whitehall, St. Paul's, and the University churches of Cambridge and Oxford, under the rather cumbrous title, *Faculties and Difficulties for Belief and Disbelief.* He writes to his elder sister :—

June 13, 1887.—I was very unhappy about the book : so sincerely & deeply dissatisfied with it that I tried hard to get out of my agreement with Rivington's, when the time of printing began : but some one whom I always trust advised me to go on. . . . I have never seen Oxford look quite so glorious as it has looked in this surprize of summer. To-day I rowed Helen down the river : and then this evening we dined in the garden : & watched the Cathedral spire glow with a deepening & then waning flush as the sun went down, & then flush up again with a wonderful after-glow.

Of letters of advice, in 1886–87, one is to Victor Seymour, concerning a lady who had asked that the surplice should not be used when the Holy Communion was given to her in her own house. The letter mentions two reasons for the use of the surplice, then a third :—

You say, "if I give in to one I shall have to give in to another " :—so that I gather you think it would be talked about, & she might be led to speak or think of it as a victory or a

score, that she had made you come without your surplice :—
& this, of course, would be very bad for her, as well as,
probably, for others. These reasons would, I think, allay in
me any fear that I was acting hardly if I simply pleaded in
such a case that I was bound by the provision of the Prayer
Book & the universal custom of the Catholic Church : and
that I could only be very, very sorry for her affliction in having
so peculiar a temperament and nervous system : entreating
her, of course, to try by all means to overcome her prejudice.
I believe you will be stronger in your position by taking this
line :—tho', of course, it may be misrepresented. Still it will
only be misrepresentation such as steady and loving work will
always counteract.

Another letter is to a lady, concerning the use of
confession :—

June 18, 1886.—I will try to tell you quite simply what I
believe to be the truth about the matter of Private Confession.
First of all I believe that no one ought to be urged to use it
against the judgement of their own conscience : and further,
that it ought never to be represented as necessary to the
highest life : I believe that people may attain, & that many
do attain, to the highest level of the religious life without ever
using it. If we gather up in thought the sins & failures of
which we know that we have been guilty, & with the sorrow
for them in our hearts join in the General Confession of the
Daily Service or of the Holy Eucharist, God sends to us His
full forgiveness, & the sins are blotted out for our Saviour's
sake. The access to Private Confession, the gift of Private
and Special Absolution is offered as a help to those whose
conscience is still troubled & unsatisfied. As Hooker says :
" If peace with God do not follow the pains we have taken in
seeking after it, if we continue disquieted & not delivered
from anguish, . . . it argueth that our sore doth exceed our
own skill, & that the wisdom of the Pastor must bind up those
parts which, being bruised, are not able to be re-cured of
themselves."

So I should never advise to Private Confession any one who

was happily & trustfully serving God without it:—I should never deter from it any one who was in great & heavy trouble, & who believed that thus relief might come.

I believe that it has been provided in love & mercy to be a means of help & comfort & strength, not an added duty or burden : that it should bring gladness to those who need it, & not suggest perplexity or disquietude to those who can with a good conscience work on without it.

May I add a word of caution which probably is quite unnecessary ? Please forgive me if it seems intrusive ; I was grateful for counsel *something* like it. It is that if ever you should, under any circumstances, be led to the use of Private Confession, you should first tell your husband, & ask his leave.

Another letter is to James Adderley, who in 1887 was Head of the Christ Church Mission in Poplar :—

Oct. 14, 1887.—I think that one may quite rightly appeal to a Secularist, disbelieving Christianity, on the ground of the secular effects of Christianity : pointing to what it has done, (proving that if only Christians were true to it, it ought to have done and ought to do far more than it has done,) for common life, as a great power of beneficence even in the limited sphere with which he, as a Secularist, is professedly concerned :—one may say to him, " here, in this field about which you are anxious, for the amelioration of which you plead & work, Christianity has had, is having, must, we believe, always have, an incomparable effect for good :—does it not then, if you are a sincere Secularist, demand your attentive, respectful, hopeful study ? "

But I should feel bound to let him know my entire conviction that these effects are essentially due to something beyond the moral & social conceptions which may be admired in Christianity :—that they are wrought by a power resting on historic and supernatural facts and drawn from a supernatural Source :—that they can never be secured or sustained apart from the Incarnate, Crucified, Risen, ascended, ever-living Christ, the Son of God.

And so I should wish him to know that I should anticipate

disappointment & failure in the case of any individual or society where the secular usefulness of Christianity was held and admired and trusted in severance from its Supernatural and Sacramental character.

It is, I believe, the one best guide for present conduct, the one best agent in social and secular life : but it is not, I believe, either one or the other if Christ be not risen, and the Spirit be not given :—and I should feel bound, for my sake and for his own, to let a man know the whole of that belief.

I quite agree with you that the question is much better considered apart from persons whose conduct it concerns : besides, I really have no personal knowledge of him of whom you write.—So on that side of it, I would only say *generally* that I do think *proportion* in teaching is essential to the presentation of the truth : and that every year I get to trust more deeply and thankfully and entirely those who maintain above all the true proportion between the things that are welcome & the things that are unwelcome, the things that make people look pleasant & the things that make them look puzzled or annoyed, the things that get applause & the things that get silence, or hisses.—I mean men like the Bishop of Lincoln and the Dean of St. Paul's, and Gore.—It is a rare strength that grows in them.

1888–1889

In January, 1888, he gave six addresses, in Eton College Chapel, to a meeting of Public School Masters (*The Hallowing of Work*, Longmans, Green and Co., 1888). It was in this month that 'Mrs. Paget's only brother died : and the dedication of the book is *Fratrem carissimum F. J. C., Amicorum, veritatis, virtutis amantissimum, Pietate prosequor.*

In March, Bach's Passion Music was given in Cathedral : " It is strange, I think," he writes to his elder sister, " that any one should doubt about the rightness of such services. For by the stillness of the huge congregation, & that inexplicable sense of reality

which one sometimes has so clearly, one felt very sure
that the people were learning :—that the endless record
of the Passion was meaning more for very many of
them than it had meant before." He goes on to
thank her for not sending him a birthday present : " I
am so rich in tokens of love & kindness, I have so
many things all about me to delight my eyes that I am
ashamed sometimes when men come into my room :—
it looks so opulent."

There are two letters, in the autumn, to Miss
Lightfoot, who was at this time in charge of a Nursing
Home in London :—

1. It was a real pleasure to hear of your work, while we
were abroad :—it all sounds so straight and true and business-
like and right :—there must be a wonderful sense of being on
the spot when one is dealing so directly with clear & unmis-
takable needs.—And, through all the over-tiredness and bothers
and bad times, there is a surprising gladness and refreshment in
it, is there not ?—I always remember an essay of Hinton's, in
which he talks of "others' needs" as the great power for
reconciling pleasure and goodness :—we want to be good (so
far as we can) and we want to enjoy ourselves :—& the
moment we set ourselves elaborately to work out goodness we
seem to be turning our backs on pleasure : & if we plan for
pleasure we seem to turn our backs on goodness :—but in
"others' needs" we find them both, reconciled & bound up
together : and then it's all right : we begin to discover the
happiness that leaves no bad taste in the mouth afterwards :—
the happiness that goes on growing to the end of life—and
further still.—I'm so sorry : I never meant to write a sermon :
—it's the unrecognized influence of Sunday,—or something in
the ink. We walked out to Boar's Hill to luncheon to-day,
& saw the children, & made a great noise in the garden :—I
incurred all sorts of perils by eating all the white (or rather
dingy) currants which Richard and Beatrice were so good &
polite as to pick for me. The real strain on parental affection
was when Edward brought one, quite squashed in the transit.

—Richard is very proud of his discoveries in agriculture : but he got out a little as to the hay :—" They put it into carts, you know :—& then—don't they make it into bread ? " He was very pleased with himself, for knowing that potatoes do not grow in the same way as gooseberries, & that it is idle to look for them under the leaves of the plant.

The Bishop of Oxford is dying, if indeed he has not already passed away. We shall miss him very much : he is so constant, and true, and affectionate, & frank :—it has been, I think, a very noble & dutiful life. I am very thankful indeed that Bp. Stubbs succeeds him :—I don't think they could possibly have made a better appointment :—it is a great blessing for the Diocese, & for the Church.

2. With regard to attending at the celebration of the Holy Eucharist without communicating, I suppose one would make some distinction between (1) the attendance of those who seldom or never communicate, & (2) the attendance of regular communicants, who have made their communion already that day, or very lately. About the former I have never felt quite happy :—and I see that Mr. Keble was strongly opposed to it :—he wrote " I cannot deny that I have a strong feeling against the foreign custom of encouraging *all sorts of persons* to ' assist ' at the Holy Eucharist, without communicating."—(Letters of Spiritual Counsel, p. 263.) About the latter, I do not feel any scruple. For—

(*a*) It seems at first sight reasonable & likely to be helpful ; & it is found by very many to be a real help & happiness.

(*b*) It has the sanction of many ages, both in the Eastern & in the Western Church. Archdeacon Wilberforce goes so far as to say that it is " a custom which has existed, as it would seem, from the very commencement of the Church " (I doubt whether quite so much as that can be proved), "and which was for the first time forbidden, through the influence of the Zwinglian party, at the end of fifteen centuries and a half." Wilberforce on the Doctrine of the Holy Eucharist, p. 412. Certainly the general feeling of the Catholic Church has sanctioned & approved it.

(*c*) I do not think the Church of England anywhere forbids

or discourages it.—The service does indeed at some points imply communicating. But this could not be otherwise—for of course the *complete* act contains *both* the Pleading of the Sacrifice & the reception of the sacrament : and the service is framed for the complete act. And so, since this could not be otherwise, the Prayer Book does not seem to me in any way to censure or discourage the partial use of the service at times by those who are really in the position, the "status" of communicants.—And it seems striking (though I should not lay quite so much stress on it as Archdeacon Wilberforce pp. 378-380 does, for it is not directly relevant, cf. Luckock on the Prayer Bk. p. 100) that the express bidding of non-communicants to depart, which was inserted in the Prayer Book of 1552, was tacitly cut out in 1662. One wd. certainly think that if the English Church were set against all non-communicating attendance, something to shew this wd. have been inserted when the words in question were cut out. More clearly significant in the same way is the *failure* of an attempt made in 1562 to get the presence of any non-communicants forbidden.

Thus I feel free to do what I find, (as I should expect to find it) very helpful. Mr. Keble says, in the letter from which I have quoted before : "I cannot deny that there may be any number of cases in which attendance without communicating may be morally & spiritually (I could not say, sacramentally) beneficial." And it is just this moral & spiritual benefit which, I think, a regular communicant may thankfully & happily seek at a High Celebration, without necessarily communicating. There is the blessing of knowing that our Blessed Lord is there in a most especial manner—achieving the great mystery of His Love :—there is the blessing of joining one's self with the very highest, and most glorious, and upward-soaring act of worship that a human being can approach :—there is the blessing of uniting one's poor, weak, faltering efforts of prayer, (for one's self, for one's friends, for those who are in trouble or temptation, for the whole Church,) with the divinely-appointed pleading of that One Sacrifice which alone gives power to all prayers :—there is the blessing of blending one's dull & cold thanksgiving with that Perfect Sacrifice, that everlasting utterance of Praise and Love before the Throne of God.—These are real and great blessings, are they not? And so, while I always feel that the Act is not full & complete without communion, I have no hesitation, (when, for any reason, I do not mean to communicate,) in seeking through non-communicating attendance the joy & refreshment which may be found in the partial, the imperfect Act. Only, I should be careful to remember that it is imperfect : that it lacks something which belongs to its entirety : & that even one's pleading of the Sacrifice is, so to speak, closer, higher, nearer, fuller, at those Celebrations at which one also communicates.

I fear I have written this clumsily and obscurely. But I send it, sincerely trusting that you will be so very kind as to tell me quite frankly if it puzzles or distresses you in any way.

Praying that God may guide and gladden and bless you in your work, & in your worship, & in all your ways, I am, yours most truly,   F. PAGET.

One other way in which, I think, one may sometimes be very thankful for the opportunity of a second Celebration, is that one may try to remember, & be especially careful about, anything in regard to which one lacked time, thoughtfulness, or earnestness at the First Celebration :—one can renew one's sorrow for sin, one's hold on the assurance of God's Mercy :— one can plead for those whom one could not plead for earlier : —one may fill up something of all that was lacking in one's thanksgiving.

In 1889, *Lux Mundi*, "a Series of Studies in the Religion of the Incarnation," was published (John Murray, pp. xxiii + 525).[1] It was edited by the present Bishop of Oxford, who in 1889 was Principal of Pusey House. "The writers found themselves at Oxford together, between the years 1875–1885, engaged in the common work of University education ; and

[1] A full account of *Lux Mundi* is given in the Life of Dr. Liddon, by Canon Johnston, Principal of Cuddesdon Theological College (Longmans, 1904).

compelled for their own sake, no less than that of others, to attempt to put the Catholic faith into its right relation to modern intellectual and moral problems. Such common necessity and effort led to not infrequent meetings, in which a common body of thought and sentiment, and a common method of commending the faith to the acceptance of others, tended to form itself." (*Editor's Preface.*) The honoured names of the contributors who "once enjoyed this happy companionship" are Holland, Aubrey Moore, Illingworth, Talbot, Moberly, Arthur Lyttelton, Gore, Lock, Paget, Campion, and Ottley. Paget wrote the essay on Sacraments. One passage, in this essay, may be put here, not only as an example of the style of his writing, but as a record of his philosophy :—

The life we have to order is a twofold life, it moves through a twofold course of experience : the facts, the activities in which we are conscious of it, are of two kinds ; and men ordinarily distinguish them as bodily and spiritual. Some such distinction is recognized and understood by the simplest of us : it is imbedded beyond possibility of expulsion in all language : stubbornly and successfully it resists all efforts to abolish it. We know for ourselves that either of the two groups of facts may stand out in clearer light, in keener consciousness, at certain times : we may even for a while, a little while, lose sight of either of them and seem to be wholly occupied with the other : but presently the neglected facts will re-assert their rights : neither the one group nor the other may long be set aside without risk of the Nemesis which avenges slighted truths—the Nemesis of disproportion and disease. We may confuse our sense of the distinction ; we may shift or blur or bend whatever line had seemed to mark it : we may insist on the qualifying phenomena which forbid us to think of any barrier as impenetrable ; but we cannot so exalt or push forward either realm as utterly to extrude, absorb, or annihilate the other : we cannot, with consistency or sanity, live as though our life were merely spiritual or merely bodily. It is as impossible steadily to regard the spirit as a mere function or product of the body, as it is to treat the body with entire indifference, as a casually adjacent fragment of the external world. But further, as the distinction of the two elements in our being seems insuperable, so does their union seem essential to the integrity of our life. Any abstraction of one element, as though it could detach itself from the other and live on its own resources, is felt to be unreal and destructive of our proper nature. . . .

If we try to imagine our life in abstraction from the body we can only think of it as incomplete and isolated ; as impoverished, deficient, and expectant. And certainly in our present state, in the interval between what we call birth and death, the severance of the two elements is inconceivable : they are knit together in incessant and indissoluble communion. In no activity, no experience of either, can the other be utterly discarded : "for each action and reaction passing between them is a fibre of that which forms their mutual bond."[1] Even into those energies of which men speak as purely spiritual, the bodily life will find its way, will send its help or hindrance : sickness, hunger, weariness, and desire : these are but some of its messengers to the spirit, messengers who will not always be denied. And in every conscious action of the bodily life the presence of the spirit is to be discerned. The merely animal fulfilment of merely animal demands, devoid of moral quality, is only possible within that dark tract of instinct which lies below the range of our consciousness. When once desire is consciously directed to its object, (wherever the desire has originated and whatever be the nature of the object,) a moral quality appears, a moral issue is determined : and the act of the body becomes an event in the life of the spirit.[2] . . .

Thus complex are we,—we who crave more light and strength, who want to find the conditions of our health and growth, who lift up our eyes unto the hills from whence

---

[1] Lotze, *Microcosmus*, bk. iii. c. i. § 2.
[2] Cf. T. H. Green, *Prolegomena to Ethics*, bk. ii. ch. ii. §§ 125, 126.

cometh our help. It would be interesting to consider from
how many different points of view the complexity has been
recognised, resented, slandered, or ignored ; and how steadily
it has held its own. It may need some exercise of faith (that
is to say, of reasonable patience amidst half-lights and
fragments) to keep the truth before one, and to allow it its
just bearing upon thought and conduct, without exaggeration,
or self-deception, or one-sidedness ; but there is neither health
of body nor peace of mind in trifling with it.

In February of this year, he and Mrs. Paget were
helping in the work for the Bishop of Lincoln Fund.
He writes, on February 8, to Mr. A. J. Butler,
thanking him for a donation : "I have always had a
great respect for Gallio. I am sure that he would
have seen at once that the Public Worship Regulation
Act was a most unstatesmanlike measure : and
certainly he would have used 'a short & easy method
of dealing' with the Bishop of Lincoln's prosecutors."
In a letter to him on October 29, he says : "Yes, we
ought all to be better men than we are at Oxford,
seeing we are made to read Aristotle at some time of
our lives. If only one could keep it up steadily, and
then go on with just a few of those whom he helped to
know & to be great, one might some day learn to think."
Of two letters to Miss Lawrence, one is in May, in
"the rush of warmth & light & fragrance that
came with these first days of real spring"; the other
in December, thanking her for a photograph of
Browning, "helping me to know something of the
fire and intensity that come out in the great poems,
and that made his simple geniality and kindness so
beautiful. It seems a singularly noble character to
recall—with its magnificent courage and vigour and
brilliancy in work, its unfading devotion to one love,
its constant care for the gladness of other people's

lives. I am very grateful for the privilege of having known him ;—& grateful to those who have helped me to know him." There is a letter to Miss Lightfoot : " It is wonderful that one should be allowed to help people at all. It was a real privilege & refreshment to come to the Infirmary :—and I hope I shall long remember many things : the bright look of the Wards, and the sort of healthy glow about the place, and Jack, and the little service in the evening. I'm sure moral fresh air does much more for one than physical :—and it's so good to think of afterwards " : and a letter to Mrs. Romanes, on some reference to Pascal : " I meant to refer to his statement of the present evidence of a Fall—not to his representation of man's state before the Fall. There, I should think, his words need much explanation, and guarding, and probably some qualifying ;—but the words which I was thinking of were rather such as these : ' sans ce mistère le plus inconpréhensible de tous, nous sommes inconpréhensibles à nous mesmes. Le nœud de nostre condition prend ses replis et ses tours dans cet abisme ' etc. Evolution would account for the dispassionate and even cheering sense of imperfection : but we want something to account for the very different, the dismal and sickening sense of sin." And there is a letter, November 14, the forerunner of other letters of friendship, to Dr. R. W. Dale ; thanking him for the gift of one of his writings, and saying—

I trust that I may with humility take the word "Evangelical," in a very real sense, to designate the conception and hope of my work : and you have suggested to me point after point for self-examination in regard to it ; so that your words will often help me, I hope, to test my loyalty and to be ashamed of my falterings in the service of our Lord, and in the preaching of His truth. . . . I need not speak of our divergent convictions upon some great matters : for I have only to write of my true thankfulness for the clearness & wisdom of the voice which comes to me across all our differences. . . .

In October, 1889, he writes to Victor Seymour :—

I think I can quite understand the sort of feeling out of which you write about the things people say in regard to Rome. One is often made miserable by the sayings of more or less prominent people ; but so one would be, I expect, in any community in which life was astir & active.

And I think the most remarkable thing is this : how in spite of all the poor and disappointing and jarring things that are said by English Churchmen, there has been going on such a steady increase in the prevalence & recognition of the truth :—how wonderfully, for instance, at the last Lambeth Conference, the historic ground was taken, and the principles of the Catholic Church accepted as ruling in all that was resolved. The slack hazy sort of pietism which was thought quite becoming & respectable 20 years ago was simply no-where. I do not think there could have been a more encouraging token of the way in which, beneath & together with all the obvious gains of our day, there has been also a real advance in the realisation of Church principles & of that which they involve and preclude.

I think that the impression which a Roman sometimes gives one of being " pre-eminently a witness to & supporter of his Faith " is due to various causes.

In part & with some it may be and is, I thankfully believe, a just impression, due to a man's having really a very deep & vivid sense of the Unseen :—& so far as it is this it seems like the impression one gets from men of holiness and unworldliness in our own communion :—from the Bishop of Lincoln, or from Lord Halifax or from Father Benson.

But in part & in many cases, I expect, it is due to the fact that Romans stand apart in religion from ordinary society :—they are exceptions here, and they feel it, & make others

I

feel it. An exception attracts notice : & attracting notice makes a man into a witness, whether he knows clearly to what he witnesses, or no.

Abroad, I think, that impression of witnessing is not nearly so strong. And then this comes in : that the Roman has secured compactness for his religious teaching : he has made it portable, & easily producible : he has a concise, positive, unhesitating answer for every question : and that gives a sort of independence.

But at what a cost ! and with a result how unlike the bearing of frail & finite beings in the presence of the Infinite Truth ! There may be much that is striking in the easily-recognised adherence to a concise body of dogma, a compact scheme, an authority within four walls :—but it is loyalty to every fragment of truth, to all its dim revealings, wherever they are vouchsafed, patient and faithful waiting, acceptance of all the discipline of incompleteness, that God looks for, I believe, from us, as our part, our service, for the truth's sake, while we are here.

Twelve years later, in 1901, soon after Mrs. Paget's death, he writes, to one of his own people, of a friend who, after a heavy sorrow, had been received into the Roman Church :—

One must think of the restlessness that may come with the monotony of sorrow :—of the not unusual craving to get from religion something that religion is not meant to give, but rather to strengthen us to go on without, till the reality that the craving misconceives is given us :—and then, of the arduousness of waiting on the gradual & fragmentary disclosure of sheer truth : — the patience and temperance and self-possession that that life-long task demands. These are the qualities of the " elect," like Helen, and her father, and ours :— and they bore with the dimness, and were content all their life long to hunger and thirst after righteousness:—and now —well, may God grant us to stumble on somehow in the way they held, that we may be as they are, and with them.

1890

In September of this year, came the death of Dr.
Liddon ; and, in December, the death of Dean Church.
Under Dr. Liddon's will, Dr. Paget was made a literary
executor, with Dr. Gore and the Principal of Cuddesdon :
and for a time he helped to edit Dr. Liddon's *Passion-
Tide Sermons*, and his *Life of Dr. Pusey*.

He was elected, this year, to the Hebdomadal
Council.   He was occupied, also, over plans for
University Extension ; and over the writing of the
" Essay concerning Accidie" for his forthcoming book,
The Spirit of Discipline.

He and Mrs. Paget got a fortnight, in July, in
France : he writes, from Caen, to C. C. Brookes, of a
curacy at St. Pancras, where his brother was vicar :
" All is going, I think, very hopefully at St. Pancras :
and there certainly are opportunities of almost endless
work and influence there.   And I trust and believe
that you and my brother will get on very happily,—he
is, so to speak, my very brotherest brother " ;—and from
Christ Church, in August, thanking him for a book
and some roses : " I love books : and certainly I am
a lover of roses, ignorant but devout :—they always
seem to me to belong to the brightest days in all the
year—days like this, when one knows not how to be
thankful enough for light and colour—and for the
power of enjoying them.   My heart always goes
right along with Newman's thanksgiving for the
blessing of friends :—& it is marvellous, what friends
God has given to me."   From Roscoff, revisited on
his holiday, on July 17, he writes to E. Harding Firth,
encouraging him over the new and uphill work of a
country parish :—

It does indeed sound like going straight at it :—and quite surely all the hindrances and discouragement must yield in time. . . . People's hearts are won more wholly because they have held out longer. It will come presently, that wonderful answer of gratitude & trust : and when it comes, all disappointment or irresponsiveness before will be almost forgotten.

But please do not run risks of getting overworked, overstrained. These Sundays are a tremendous pull on a man's strength : & if you have to do the whole day's work, it ought to be strictly on the condition that you take a real & complete holiday on one day in the week :—one day in every week. Do plan for that :—remembering that you cannot tell what God may have in store for you to do in the years to come :—we none of us know : & we ought just to be doing what we have to do as well as ever we can, & not forcing more work out of ourselves than we ever were meant to yield. We mustn't spend our capital of strength : because it isn't ours. Please think of this, & be prudent.[1]

See how I preach on the last day of a fortnight's pleasure-making. Mrs. Paget and I have been travelling about in Normandy and Brittany. It is a privilege to be among these Bretons :—they seem so strong and kindly and frank & faithful. Our best happiness has been here. For 17 years ago Holland and I were here with a reading-party : & we made friends with three small boys here, brothers : and yesterday I found them out, & we have had two delightful visits to their home :—& they are all doing well, one on the railway, one as a blacksmith, one as a ship's carpenter : and there was a wonderful glow of happiness in their welcome, and in finding them so good and genial. Certainly there is no beauty in

---

[1] One remembers him, as an undergraduate, advising a younger brother, at school, "never to work *invitâ Minervâ*, or against the grain." There is a good reason for this bad advice : he knew that mere "sapping" would raise the quantity, but lower the quality, of a boy's Greek and Latin. He was easily made anxious, it may be over-anxious, lest a friend should break down under his work : and he bore in mind what Wilfred Brinton said, that a man ought to keep some strength in reserve, believing that there was a big job waiting for him, and that he must be strong enough to tackle it when it came. One remembers him, also, speaking with great dislike of the phrase "dying in harness" : but that was thirty years before his own death.

nature or art comparable with the beauty of a simple, loyal character :—nothing so refreshes one, so makes one thank God for His goodness. . . .

In August, the Dean and Mrs. Paget attended the funeral of Cardinal Newman. They had enjoyed the privilege of a visit to him, not long before his death.

On September 19, he writes to Victor Seymour, of Dr. Liddon's death :—

I do trust that God in His mercy may beckon to the front, with Holland and Gore, some who may bring there for His special service gifts of mind and heart, and strength and readiness, such as I am very, very far from having. But we can all help :—and He will show to each one of us our task : and one's great hope is that the very sense of loss and need may be turned by His grace into an increasing strength and earnestness, and sense of brotherhood in a great cause. There seems so vast a hope in sight—though not, it well may be, for our time : —but so vast that we may well thank God if when we come to die we have only kept it, by His help, unimpaired for those who come after us. But there is need of much patience.

We shall miss dear Liddon in our home most sadly. He and Gore always used to come here to tea on Fridays, to our great delight : and he was always, I think—& love immensely to think—very happy here, & felt at home. It is very hard to realise that we shall not see him next Term : and then he and Aubrey Moore were *the* two people in Oxford to whom one turned most trustfully to talk over anything :—it does seem so dreadful a void in that way.

On December 11, he writes to him, of Dean Church's death :—

One was always so absolutely certain of his insight & justice & generosity in judgement : I can recall no single point at which I ever had even the slightest wish to choose another course than that which he thought best : and he was so brilliant and humble and strong and unworldly. One must try to remember it all as vividly as one can, & to let it tell on one, by God's grace, always. I should so like to have a good talk with you about him, some day.

And, on December 30, to E. Harding Firth :—

I do wish you had known the Dean. There was in him such a wonderful mixture of calmness, balance, patience, justice, with fire and enthusiasm : a mixture of severity with tenderness :—of the characteristics of the thorough scholar with the characteristics of the true parish priest. You can imagine what a privilege it was to be with him, to turn to him in difficulties. I love to think how happy he was at Whatley : and few things have touched me more than the many signs of gratitude and affection that came out from all the people there —from people of all classes—in regard to him. There was a thoughtfulness for little details in the services there on the 15th and 16th which told how lasting and how delicate is the gratitude of the simple and the poor.

There remain, for 1889–90, his letters to Romanes. One, in October 1889, is to thank him for some game : "This is indeed enough to make anybody ashamed of himself : the least sensitive of bacteria might blush to the roots of his hair :—I neglect your medicine and you provide for my meat. Thank you very, very much for an example of forgiveness and four brace of partridges." Another, in January 1890, is to thank him for what he had written of Aubrey Moore :—

It seems to me equally just and delightful :—and I am deeply thankful that it can be said, & should be said, & so said, & by you :—no one, I think, could so well recognise that especial distinction of dear Moore's mind and work.

I have only two very trifling suggestions to make, using the privilege you have given me.

I doubt whether I should have used the word "immense" in speaking of his stores of knowledge. It is so very strong a word :—the word one might use of Dr. Döllinger or of Lord Acton :—I feel as though it were hardly possible for any man at Moore's age quite to warrant it : though certainly I have known no man come so near warranting it as he and Gore.

Secondly, do you think the different groups of men here are "sharply" divided? There is a certain division : and there are some who make it sharper & harder than it need be : but I should have thought that there was *little* of the bitterness, or determined & unenquiring hostility, which most people associate with a "sharp division" in a community. I think too that the division is not really between *lay* & *clerical* : that is hardly the true "fundamentum divisionis."

But these are very little points : & I may be quite wrong about them. . . .

Other letters are concerned with the issues involved in one of Romanes' sonnets, and with his address at Toynbee Hall :—

Nov. 4, 1889.— . . . I am somewhat more confident in my uneasiness about the MS. sonnet on St. Mark xiv. 9.[1] It is a minor point that. . . . What I feel more deeply is that loveliness and beauty make no difference at all in the aspect of sin . . . & there is nothing that I should more desire to bring home to people than that beauty and gracefulness & strength & intellect do not take away from sin one atom of its vileness :— that Napoleon the 1st, or the most beautiful of sinners, is as unseemly & hideous a spectacle in the light of truth (supposing the moral conditions to be the same) as any sodden drunkard or broken-down & battered misery that slouches about White-chapel—perhaps far uglier. . . .

Nov. 9.—Thank you with all my heart for the kindness of your letter, and for all your patience with me.

I will not venture upon the great question as to the relation between the morally and the poetically beautiful :—but this much I cannot help thinking, or easily forbear saying : that when poetry handles distinctly moral facts it must take them with their moral associations & affinities. "Sin," if the word

---

[1] " Verily I say unto you, Wheresoever this gospel shall be preached throughout the whole world, this also that she hath done shall be spoken of for a memorial of her."

means anything at all, has an essential antagonism to holiness & purity, to moral beauty : and it has certain well-known effects & tendencies in the character of the sinner ; and these cannot be ignored in any treatment of it.

I think the analogy of bodily disease is just. I suppose there are skin diseases in which the colour of the diseased part is, in itself, a fine colour : but no artist could, on that ground, make a picture of the eruption : (I am wilfully revolting, because it is just the common & necessary loathsomeness of corruption that I want to bring out :) the artist would be hindered by the inseparable associations of disease, & the tendency to death :— and sin seems to me to be precluded in just the same two-fold way from artistic treatment. It is intrinsically vile and deadly : and art can do nothing with it. If anything is to be made of the visible beauty which incidentally is linked with sin, it can only be by drawing the mind away from the sin (as, in Hood's "Bridge of Sighs," by the intensity of pathos, though, personally, I do not wholly like this) : the effect is blocked and arrested as soon as the mind is directed to the sin. Most of us know too much of sin to be capable of enjoying an artistic presentation of it.

I think that I feel this especially in regard to a scene taken from the Bible. For there sin is held relentlessly in its true aspect : one cannot forget for a moment what it is. And in that scene, too, one is led to think of the two figures, & how sin seemed to them : & one wonders whether its artistic treatment would have seemed stranger to Him who was to die for it, or to her, who was, perhaps, to see Him die. . . .

Jan. 14, 1890.—I hope you will not think me impertinent if I write a few words of gratitude for the happiness which I enjoyed in reading to-day even such account of your address at Toynbee Hall as the *Times* gave me.

There is always a risk of impertinence in thanking a man for what he has said : for of course he has said it because he saw it, and thought he ought to say it, quite simply. But I may just thank you for the generous willingness with which you accepted such a task :—and for the light in which you looked at it :—as an opportunity for saying so ungrudgingly, so

open-heartedly, that which is dear to you about our Lord.
This must be, please God, a real bit of help to others ; and I
trust & pray that it may return in help to you.   Men of
science sometimes tell us what they think we may reasonably
teach :—but a new hope comes in view when, as men of conscience, they stand forth themselves to teach, and to bear their
part in the great moral conflict of the world.   I cannot help
being very deeply grateful for this.

But how dark you were about it ! I should have been
furious if I had been in London, & not there.   So perhaps
my domestic measles have saved our friendship, though they
have robbed me of this evening's pleasure. . . .

1891

Early in this year, *The Spirit of Discipline* was published : a collection of sermons, to which he added, at
the end of the book, an address on Bishop Andrewes ;
and, at the beginning, an essay on Accidie,[1] " the sorrow
of the world."   He had preached, in Oxford, on " The
sorrow of the world worketh death," and had quoted
what Dante, Chaucer, Cassian, and St. Thomas Aquinas
say of the sin of " gloom, sloth, and irritation " : but
his own description is doubtless as good as theirs, or
better.   Accidie is—

The mood of days on which it seems as though we cannot
genuinely laugh, as though we cannot get rid of a dull or
acrid tone in our voice ; when it seems impossible frankly to
" rejoice with them that do rejoice," and equally impossible
to go freely out in any true, unselfish sympathy with sorrow ;

---

[1] ἀκηδία, acedia, or accidie. " Concerning the orthography of the Greek word
there can be no doubt.   The Latin form here given is that employed, *e.g.*, by
Cassian and by St. Thomas Aquinas, and justly defended by the Benedictine Commentator on Cassian : in Cic. *ad Att.* xii. 45, the Greek word is used.   The
English form, while, in common with the Italian, it conceals the derivation of the
word, has the decisive sanction of Dr. Murray's Dictionary, *q.v.* ; cf. also Ducange,
q.v." (a footnote in the essay). The 12th impression of *The Spirit of Discipline*
was published in 1911.   The essay and the sermon on Accidie have lately been
published as a separate book, under the title *The Sorrow of the World* (Longmans).

days when, as one has said, "everything that everybody does seems inopportune and out of good taste"; days when the things that are true and honest, just and pure, lovely and of good report, seem to have lost all loveliness and glow and charm of hue, and look as dismal as a flat country in the drizzling mist of an east wind; days when we might be cynical if we had a little more energy in us; when all enthusiasm and confidence of hope, all sense of a Divine impulse, flags out of our work; when the schemes which we have begun look stale and poor and unattractive as the scenery of an empty stage by daylight; days when there is nothing that we *like* to do—when, without anything to complain of, nothing stirs so readily in us as complaint. . . . It occurs to one at once that this misery of accidie lies on the border-line between the physical and the spiritual life; that if there is something to be said of it as a sin, there is also something to be said of it as an ailment. It is a truth that was recognised long ago both by Cassian and by St. Thomas Aquinas, who expressly discusses and dismisses this objection against regarding accidie as a sin at all. Undoubtedly physical conditions of temperament and constitution, of weakness, illness, harassing, weariness, overwork, may give at times to such a mood of mind and heart a strange power against us; at times the forces for resistance may seem frail and few. It is a truth which should make us endlessly charitable, endlessly forbearing and considerate and uncritical towards others; but surely it is a truth that we had better be shy of using for ourselves. It will do us no harm to over-estimate the degree in which our own gloom and sullenness are voluntary; it will do us very great harm to get into the way of exaggerating whatever there may be in them that is physical and involuntary. For the border-line over which accidie hovers is, practically, a shifting and uncertain line, and *possunt quia posse videntur* may be true of the powers upon either side of it. We need not bring speculative questions out of their proper place to confuse the distinctness of the practical issue. We have ample warrant, by manifold evidence, by clear experience, for being sure for ourselves that the worth and happiness of life depend just on this—that in the strength which God gives, and in the eagerness of His service, the will should ever be extending the range of its dominion, ever refusing to be shut out or overborne, ever restless in defeat, ever pushing on its frontier.

And he goes on to say how accidie may be fought :— by sympathy with real pain and sorrow ; by occupation over such work as does not depend on the weather of the mind—" the comparatively featureless bits of work, the business letters, the mechanism of life, the tasks which may be almost as well done then as ever " ; and for a third way—" it is strange, indeed,—it would be inconceivable if it were not so very common—that a man can look back to Calvary and still be sullen."

This sermon, to his great surprise, was talked-of far and wide. He had come across " accidie " in his study of Dante : and books, as they will to him who loves them, had led him on and on. Reading his translation of Cassian, we understand his delight over the minute account, by a hermit of the Thebaid, of that state of mind which Oxford is apt to dismiss with a monosyllable of slang. So he preached on accidie : and people forthwith realised, like M. Jourdain, that they had long been subject to it without knowing it. Here was an adventure : it had its humorous side : the jest was made, that he had " invented a new sin for undergraduates." Then he wrote the essay, a monument of his learning, an example of what it is to be a theologian. The text of the essay rides high on a tossing sea of foot-notes ; Greek and Latin and French and English authors are quoted : to take our own poets only, one would say that he had read everything, from Chaucer to Stevenson. And all this wealth of references is felt, rather than displayed : it enhances, not hinders, the strength of the essay. No amount of footnotes can stay the advance of such sentences as this—"The inmost quality, the secret history, of a selfish choice or a sullen mood, and the ingredients of a bad temper, are, probably, nearly what they were in quieter days ; and there seems sometimes a curious sameness in the tricks that men play with conscience, and in the main elements of a soul's tragedy."

In the Easter Vacation, he and Mrs. Paget went to Costebelle, to her mother and sisters. In July, they had a fortnight at Brixham ; he seems to be alluding to Brixham in the preface to the seventh edition of *The Spirit of Discipline* :—

There is, I think, in the spiritual life an experience somewhat like that of which a trawler in the west of England told me. He said that sometimes through a dark night, when on the deck the air is dull and heavy, and there seems to be a dead calm, there may be wind enough astir, not many feet above the sea, to catch the topsail and carry the sloop along ; so that at daybreak it is found farther on its course than the men, for all their keen sense of seafaring, had ever thought it could be.

Among the letters of this year, one in July is to Dr. Dale, on his illness : "I shall be, please God, thinking of you every day in the way which I know that you would wish. It must be a refreshment, I think, in your illness to know how very many, in England and elsewhere, are so remembering you before Almighty God." One is to Mr. E. V. Hall, on the rules and management of Confraternities : "I am very sorry that the Confraternities are causing you especial anxiety. I think it is often the case that after schemes have been at work for a few years they do thus threaten to flag, and need special measures for their re-invigoration. I remember hearing the opinion of a Parish Priest of great experience, that it was generally about the 5th year that tried an institution. So perhaps one must not be surprised or discouraged when these crises come." One is to Mr. Firth, promising to be godfather to one of his children : "and I will pray for him, and remember him from time to time in the Holy Eucharist, and be thankful if ever I have the chance of doing him any service." One is to Mr. A. J. Butler, a long letter on some passages in Dante ; and one in September is to Miss Lawrence, on Mr. Lowell's death :—

I had met him several times, at your house and at my father's : and it was impossible not to feel something of the rare & beautiful qualities which were in him. I think I shall always remember him as one in whom one saw the simplicity and strength and brightness and kindliness of a really poetic mind : —all touched with a certain sadness, which made one sure that he would be very gentle to one in any sorrow.

On October 21, he writes to a friend, of Dean Liddell's retirement :—

We are all very doleful just now, over the prospect of the Dean's leaving us at Christmas. It is impossible to say how great the loss will be : he has been so generous & wise and so absolutely & in all things trustworthy :—& I owe him more kindness than I can say. We shall feel sadly impoverished without him.

Then came his appointment to be Dean Liddell's successor. He writes, on October 31, to Victor Seymour :—

It is a most grave and solemn thing to be taking up the dear old Dean's work :—I have looked up to him with such constant reverence & honour : and then the work, as one tries to think over it, seems so vast and complex :—it is very strange to me still. . . . And please remember that you have promised to ask me to preach for you. I want to come & I shall come with a clear conscience if I have something to do. Only it must be in the vac.

To Lawrence Hardy, on November 14 :—

It would be so terrible to fail, in any way guiltily, the place which is so very dear to me, and to which one owes more than one can ever measure, of one's training, happiness, light, friendships, and much else. I do earnestly trust that I may have strength & wisdom to work very diligently & patiently & sincerely. Thank you especially for what you say about my wife and her share in the work. Yes, there I am quite hopeful and un-anxious :—and all the wonderful kindness of friends has been a great source of encouragement since the news.

To F. A. O'Brien, on Advent Sunday :—

I can only say to myself again and again that the true strength is made perfect in weakness : I can only long and pray that God will give me grace to work diligently and unselfishly, in humility and patience; so that He, in His mercy, may somehow use me for His service. I can never forget, nor cease, I trust, to be grateful for, and to be helped by, the wonderful kindness which has been shown me since my designation to the Deanery: it has been very, very wonderful: and it has been a most real and generous encouragement. And now I have the happiness of knowing that I am to hand over my present work to a really good man : to one who will do much to recall and revive all the work of 1873–1885. It is a delight that Moberly is coming here : there are depths and reserves of strength in him which will do splendid service.

He was installed as Dean of Christ Church, in Cathedral, on January 21, 1892 ; and in March went into residence in the Deanery. "Chaos has come," he writes to one of his people, on March 22, "for all our furniture is ʻon the moveʼ : and one feels how much is taken for granted in ordinary life."

THE DEANERY DRAWING-ROOM.

THE DEANERY STUDY.

CHAPTER VI

THOSE fortunate young men, who are now at the
House, should study H. L. Thompson's *History of
Christ Church* : that they may learn the greatness of
the place where they have the honour to reside, and
all that it means for them to be able to put *ex Æde
Christi* after their names. And when they come to
read of Christ Church under Dean Liddell, from 1855
to 1891, they may find themselves wondering what
further work was left for his successor. Liddell had
succeeded that mighty scholar Gaisford, who for a
quarter of a century, from 1831 to 1855, had stood
out against reform. " To all external interference with
the University and its colleges Dean Gaisford offered
a stubborn resistance. To the inquiries of the first
university commissioners he alone of all the heads of
colleges would vouchsafe no reply of any kind. He
acknowledged none of their communications." Reform
from within was no more acceptable to him than interference from without : and he strictly maintained, in
Christ Church, the observance of rank and wealth.
" There was a distinction, between the richer and
poorer members of the society. This was an article of
faith with him. The servitor, however learned and
meritorious, must never be raised to the rank of

student.   The two orders must never be confused."
He was indifferent, whether Christ Church, as compared with other colleges, did well or ill in the
University examinations, which were a new thing in
his time : "he cared little for distinctions gained outside the walls of Christ Church, and did not encourage
the competition for them.   One result of this old-
fashioned attitude was that the position of Christ
Church men in the class lists, which up to this time
had been singularly high, quickly changed after he
became Dean."   And he did little for the fabric of the
House.   "On the buildings, scarcely any money was
spent during the whole of Gaisford's long reign."

Then, in 1855, came Dean Liddell, and with him
the Augustan Age of the House.   He had been a
member of the first University Commission : and he
steadily guided and brought to fulfilment the administrative changes of 1858, 1867, and 1882.   He exercised
a profound influence for good, not over Christ Church
alone, but over all Oxford.   He was the first Dean
since Aldrich to be Vice-Chancellor of the University.
He exalted Christ Church to a position which Gaisford
had not dreamed of.   Yet, as one stands to-day in
Tom Quad, and looks toward the Deanery, one thinks
first and foremost not of him as administrator but of
him as architect.   Everywhere, in Cathedral, in Hall, in
Tom Quad, in Meadow Buildings, one is reminded of
him.   The fine staircase in the Deanery, the "Lexicon
staircase," was built by him, and paid for out of the
profits from "Liddell and Scott" : the way down from
Meadow Gate to the Barges was made and planted by
him.   If any undergraduate will spend a few afternoons,
with the *History of Christ Church*, over the buildings of
Christ Church, he will learn much English history, and

he will learn what Liddell achieved for the beauty of one of the most famous of all colleges.

Thus, when Dr. Paget became Dean, there was no such opportunity for him as had been given to his predecessor. He was debarred, by the completeness of things, from the happiness of completing them : he could not leave Christ Church even more beautiful in 1902 than in 1892. No change in its administration, no sign of his love of its buildings, is associated with his name.

This limitation of his opportunities cannot be reckoned as a grievance : but he had no lack of more positive difficulties. The departure of Dr. Liddell was for him the loss of the best of all his advisers in Oxford : there was none of the Governing Body who could be to him what Liddell had been. Besides, for the first year or so of his office, the Governing Body, though it welcomed his appointment, was not always able to give him that immediate support which alone could make every stroke of his work tell : and he was more hindered than helped, now and again, by so many wheels within wheels between him and the under-graduate members of the House. One is tempted to think that it might have been a good thing, if he had been able to have the management of certain affairs, for a year, more to himself.

And it must be borne in mind, that neither the Head of a College, nor those who are in authority under him, nor any other power on earth, can prevent the coming of trouble, if there happens to be a bad set among the undergraduates.

It is the custom, that matters affecting the general discipline of the House should be dealt with by the Dean and the Censors, without any obligation to

K

consult the tutors ; except in matters where scholars, or others on the foundation, are concerned. The two Censors, at this time, were unlike in length of service, influence, and temperament. Besides, though a Censor be well-nigh perfect, yet, by the nature of his office, he is not always acceptable to impulsive undergraduates. Should he upbraid, they do not vow that he'll prevail. And if there should be a bad set among them, the Dean and the Censors, when things go wrong, may have to bear more than their share of the reproach in Oxford, and outside Oxford.

Early in 1893, the Dean was very dangerously ill. During his long illness and convalescence, Archdeacon Palmer, by the rule of the House, was his official representative : and neither the Archdeacon nor the Junior Censor, at this time, had a very intimate acquaintance with all the details of administration. Thus, affairs came the more heavily to the Senior Censor : who, though he incessantly desired the welfare of the House, had not, as mathematical tutor, much opportunity of meeting the general body of the undergraduates. The Dean's illness ensured a quiet period, and was an occasion of hearty sympathy : but it did nothing to prevent the troubles which were ahead.

Toward the end of 1893, the Duke of Marlborough gave a great ball at Blenheim, to which he invited many undergraduates. There was a rule in Christ Church against giving leave of absence for the night on such occasions. This rule had been made in Dr. Liddell's time : but a ball at Blenheim was an occasion of such magnitude as to raise expectations that leave would be given. It is probable that the Dean, if he had been free to do what he liked, would have waived the rule and let the young men go. The question was endlessly discussed : and there is reason to believe that one or two misunderstandings occurred over it. Finally, the rule was upheld, and leave was refused.

On the night of the ball, some of the men painted the walls of Tom Quad with gross abuse of the Dean and the Senior Censor ; there was also much painting of doors and so forth ; and the bell-rope of Tom was cut. It is hardly open to doubt that the offenders would have been caught—for the offence must have taken some time in the doing—if they had not bribed one of the porters. It was easy to discover from whose rooms the paint had been supplied : and the owner of the rooms was told that he would be sent down for a year, unless the whole matter were put in the hands of the Dean, and all names given up. The offence was grave indeed : the general body of undergraduates was very angry at the defacement of Tom Quad with bad language : and, as the way through Christ Church is open to the public, the inscriptions had been displayed to all Oxford. It seems certain, that the men would have submitted, and the whole affair would have been properly dealt with : but the father of one of them got hold of them all, and set them against surrender. They withheld the submission which they seemed about to offer : and the young man was sent down, leaving behind him no chance of peace. If it had not been for the father's interference, the whole trouble might have come to an end then and there. During the Lent term of 1894, there was no great disturbance, but there was no settlement : and there was more than enough of surmise and gossip. The Dean was supposed to be favouring persons of wealth and position ; and all kinds of ridiculous notions were abroad about him.

In the Summer term of 1894, there was a dinner of the Bullingdon Club : and, that evening, nearly all the windows in Peckwater were broken. To add insult to injury, they were broken by men from other colleges, whom the Christ Church members of the Bullingdon Club had brought in with them into Christ Church after the dinner. Neither the authorities, nor the general body of Christ Church men, were going to stand this sort of thing. The authorities, therefore, sent down, for the rest of the term, those members of the Bullingdon Club who had brought in the men who broke the windows. This was the right course. It is true that some men, who probably disapproved of the disturbance, were involved in the general sentence : but this could not be helped. They need not have been involved, if the leaders of the disturbance had so chosen. The defence was, that the disturbance was not premeditated. This defence did not meet the facts of the case. It was perfectly well-known, in Christ Church, that a "row" was to be made on that day : indeed, one member of the club had prudently kept away from the dinner for that reason.

After this storm, the air slowly cleared. The Senior Censor felt himself at liberty to resign his office : and the powers of the Censorship were exercised in a way to disconcert its opponents. One more demonstration was made against the authorities, in the Eights week ; but it did not come to much. A correspondence in the *Times* was started, on the side of the men who had been sent down : there was a letter signed with many distinguished names, and there was an article finding fault with the Dean.   This one-sided correspondence was the last episode : and Christ Church, henceforth, was at peace.

It is probable that the Dean's position would have been less difficult, and less exposed to criticism, if he had not felt bound to consult so many advisers, and to take into account so many opinions beside his own : indeed, one thinks of him, at this time, as occupied with the hearing of "things which must not be repeated to anybody," and aware of things said against himself, which were repeated to everybody. And this oppressive sense of too much talk flying round and round Christ Church must have deepened in him that scrupulous regard for the privacy of private affairs, which in later life was almost a passion in him.   He guarded ordinary confidences as if they were confessions : he recognised no line between one sort of secret and another.   He had a phrase, *Sub sigillissimo* : and he would say, "This must be *sub sigillissimo*," or, "Mind, this mustn't get out through a crack anywhere."   There is a good phrase, in one of his letters : "Dead secrets have sometimes more liveliness than we think."   He liked to say that he had inherited his father's power of keeping secrets : and, writing in 1900 to one of his brothers, he says, "One of the very few things I know is how to hold my tongue, I hope."   It is almost the only place, in the many hundreds of his letters, where he puts in a good word for himself.   And of all the many kind things said of him, none was more to his liking than what was said of him, many years ago, by the present Dean of Christ Church—that telling a secret to him was like posting a letter in a broken lamp-post : you could be quite sure that it would not get any further.

After all, the misdeeds of one set of men in a college, and the difficulty of dealing with them, must not be exalted to the level of tragedy. There is always, over Oxford, a tendency to make too much of troubles of this kind. As a youthful contributor to the *Oxford Magazine* well said, in November, 1896, "One cannot walk through Peck with a cigarette alight but rumour next morning proclaims some desperate arson." Minor offences, against himself, the Dean could take lightly enough. For example, some undergraduates put a badger in the Deanery garden ; and the Dean was made anxious, because one of his gardeners was bitten : otherwise, he did not appear to be greatly moved by the presence of the badger. And the graver acts of disorder, the offences against Christ Church, were the work of a small minority, who were so far unpopular with the majority that they would have fared no better if their sentence had been determined not by the authorities but by a vote of the whole House. He never doubted that he was on the right lines : he knew for certain that his ideals would come true.

Of all that was written of him after his death, there is one letter which describes, in ten words, how he regarded his duty toward Christ Church. Dr. Sadler, sometime student and steward of Christ Church, now Vice-Chancellor of the University of Leeds, writes, on December 18, 1911 : "Hardly a day passes without my thinking of him. *He raised administration to the level of a pastoral office*, and to discuss political questions with him was to be shown what one ought to try to do before forming a judgment upon any problem of government."

In Dean Liddell's time, if memory may be trusted

to go back thirty-five years, the average undergraduate
did not expect the Dean to know or care much about
him.   It was enough for him, that the Dean was there :
he was immensely proud of being at Christ Church :
he did not think himself interesting to the Dean :
indeed, he enjoyed the Dean's remoteness as part of
the size and magnificence of the House.   To be
invited to the Deanery was a social distinction, and a
great happiness : but he was under no delusion that
the Dean wanted to see him : rather, it contented him
to feel that the Dean was indifferent to his presence.
At the end of each term, he handed in his epistle at the
door of the Deanery—*Termino jam rite peracto,
veniam abeundi petit favoris tui studiosissimus*—with a
clear sense that Latin was the proper language.   It
hardly entered his head that the Dean could be concerned over the spiritual affairs of each undergraduate.
Something of the immortality of Christ Church seemed
to him to belong to the Dean of Christ Church : he
could not associate with that splendid figure the idea of
infirmity and failure, nor imagine another Dean, any
more than he could imagine another Christ Church.
The bond, such as it was, between the Dean and him
was, truly, nothing less than all Christ Church : and
he thought of the Dean as caring for all Christ Church,
not for him.   There is much to be said in favour of
this old-fashioned sort of loyalty : but it is not the
only sort : and, with the general widening of the ways
of Oxford, the time came for something else.

As Dr. Paget, on his appointment, had no further
to move than out of one door, and in at the next, so
he brought to his new work that anxious thought for
each man's individual welfare which he had exercised as
Professor of Pastoral Theology, and had taught others

to exercise. "He raised administration to the level of a pastoral office." And, as time went on, he and Mrs. Paget—he could not have done it without her—did, in a very remarkable way, gain and keep the direct personal friendship of undergraduates. None of them could fail to see that he was longing to be of use to each of them : that he would give the very best of himself to any man who would let him : that he was always looking to the words *Cor ad cor loquitur*. Men who were at Christ Church under him remember how the Deanery, on Sunday afternoons, would make welcome thirty or forty undergraduates, come for this reason and no other, that they liked coming : they wanted to get to know the Dean, and they admired Mrs. Paget. He drew them individually to himself, and he did it without manœuvring round them : simply, it became an easy thing, to call at the Deanery ; and men who would not go there might almost be thought "unusual" by their friends, or accidious. Nor was it only the undergraduates, to whom he gave personal service and friendship : he took equal care to befriend all the servants of the House, its porters and scouts : and, outside Christ Church, he set himself to know and make friends with the Christ Church tenants ; and visited the many farms and estates which paid their rents to Christ Church, as to a company, not expecting more than a formal acknowledgment. Among other works of personal influence were his work for Reading University College, and for the Christ Church Mission ; and his chaplaincy of the Oxfordshire Yeomanry. Besides, he had his share of the burden of all administrative affairs, both as Dean of the Cathedral, and as Head of the College, and his share of all the many charities, hospitalities, and solemnities of Oxford society ; and he was a member of the Hebdomadal Council, and of the Lower House of the Convocation of Canterbury. But, of all memories of this part of his life, the clearest now is the memory of the Deanery at the time of the South African War, in which so many Christ Church men were fighting, and of Mrs. Paget's death. If evidence were needed of his love of Christ Church, it is in the fact that even after her death he wished to stay on there. And this love of Christ Church was far deeper than mere attachment to a place. He was proud of Christ Church, past all telling ; proud that the late King, and Queen Alexandra, and our present King and Queen, and Mr. Gladstone, and other great personages, came there, and visited the Deanery ; proud of every distinction gained by Christ Church men, in the Schools, or on the river. Only, along with his enjoyment of the honour and glory of Christ Church, his delight in its beauty, strength, tradition, and place in our national history, went his religion, every inch of the way, and every hour of the day. And it was vital to his religion, that he should desire to be *servus servorum Aedis Christi*, the servant alike of Christ Church and of each member and servant of Christ Church.

1892–1893

On his appointment, an address was sent to him from the Christ Church Mission : and, on February 7, he writes to James Adderley :—

First of all, above & in all, I am thankful to Almighty God, Who has put such thoughtful kindness and generosity into the hearts of his Servants . . . and then all my gratitude to my brother, for all he has been to me since we were

children, is carried forward and deepened : for I know that it
is to his thorough, self-denying, happy work at the Mission
that I owe whatever of personal regard, beyond the thought of
Christ Church, is borne to me at Poplar.

And then, dear Adderley, I must say one word of truest
thanks to you, for all the help that your loving toil has won
and is winning for us all, and for the Church of Christ. I
have always felt that it would be impossible to measure the
good that from the Christ Church Mission flows back to
Christ Church. But of course I feel that now with fresh
vividness and thankfulness. I must try to show my gratitude
better than I can tell it, as time goes on : and in one way
especially, remembering in my prayers and at the altar those
who have shown me such wonderful & true kindness.

In March, he writes to Miss Lawrence, thanking
her for the gift of Lowell's published letters :—

Do you know the phrase of "a man's conversation in his
shirt-sleeves " ? It is only, I think, the most cultivated, keen,
delightful, & kindly minds that can afford to be discovered
so talking, & that are found then as charming & unfailing as
ever. And Mr. Lowell's mind was, I think, just of that
order :—and so I am sure that I shall find in these beautiful
volumes—into which I have begun already to dip—that rare
and great enjoyment which great men can give at their ease.

In May of this year, Reading University College
was founded. The work of University Extension
lectures in Reading had started in 1885. Mr. Butter,
Mr. Sharkey, and Mr. George Palmer had taken part in
it ; and, about 1890, the Reading University Extension
Association had been formed : President, Mr. Walter
Palmer, and Hon. Secretary, Mr. Theodore White.
On May 21, 1892, the Dean wrote to Mr. Walter
Palmer :—

SIR,—You are, I believe, aware that the governing body of
Christ Church have, with the consent of their Visitor, recently

appointed Mr. H. J. Mackinder, M.A., University Reader in Geography, to be a student of Christ Church for three years.

This appointment was made by the governing body in pursuance of their desire to establish a connection between Christ Church and one of the University Extension centres, with a view to giving system and completeness to the educational work at that centre.

It is unnecessary for me to say anything of Mr. Mackinder's qualifications for the furtherance of this desire and intention. Those who have studied and supported the work of University Extension know the zeal and care which he has given to it, and the welfare which has attended his labours.

Reading has been selected as the centre to which his work, in pursuance of the design which I have indicated, shall now be offered. This selection has been guided not only by the position of Reading as the most important and oldest centre of University Extension in the Oxford district, but also by the evidence which the town has already given of interest and enterprize in the work, and by the belief that an especial opportunity is there open for such help as Mr. Mackinder will be able to afford.

I trust that you will judge it right to welcome the action which has thus been taken ; and I greatly hope that it may be of service for the advancement, the co-ordination, and the deepening of study.—I beg leave to remain, Sir, yours very faithfully,   FRANCIS PAGET,
                                    Dean of Christ Church.

At the annual general meeting of the Association, May 27, Mr. Walter Palmer read this letter, and Mr. Mackinder and others spoke. The offer was very gladly accepted : and Reading University College was constituted, with Mr. Mackinder as Principal. He held office till 1903, when he was succeeded by Mr. W. M. Childs. The Dean of Christ Church was appointed Visitor of the College : and, on Michaelmas Day, 1892, he declared it open. To the end of his life, Reading had a great hold on him : and the names which everybody associates with Reading are the names of some of his friends.

On October 24, 1892, in the Sheldonian Theatre, Mr. Gladstone gave the first Romanes Lecture, on Mediæval Universities. He and Mrs. Gladstone stayed at the Deanery, and met Lord Acton there, and many other friends of the Dean and Mrs. Paget. Two days after the Romanes Lecture, Mr. Froude gave his Inaugural Lecture.

To George Romanes

Oct. 3.—It was immensely good of you to write to me your own self : & it was a great pleasure to read your hand-writing again. Nor must you dispraise the said hand-writing, for I read it as easily as gladly : & that is saying a great deal.

But, dear Romanes, glad as I was to get your letter, I could not but have a great sorrow for the cause which, you said, made you write it yourself. For I fear I read in your letter a disappointment as to the result of the rest that your eyes have had. Of course I have been thinking of you very often—every day, I think—& constantly I have been wondering how your sight was faring, & longing for good news of it : and now I cannot help fearing that the benefit of which you are as yet conscious is less than we all hoped it might be. . . . It will be indeed a relief & happiness to us all when you can give us some bit of clear good news.

And meanwhile, whenever you are at Oxford, you must let us try our very best to lighten (be it ever so little) the prolonged trial.

I know that I can never do more than next door to nothing. And indeed it really is a favour & a bit of help for myself that I have to ask. One of the ways in which I go down the hill is that I am always filching for some other use the time I ought to give to the reading of poetry, or the poetic in some form. That is one way in which those who are born men may come to die grocers. So it will be a real work of charity, a missionary enterprise, if *often* you will drop in at the Deanery, and say that the moment has come for one to leave off writing letters, & read some Browning, or whatever it may be. It may inconvenience you : but you must reflect that it is for my good.

Dec. 21.—I am ashamed that my hearty good wishes should be late ; but perhaps they may have something of that privilege which falls to the last comers at an afternoon party—the chance of saying a word quietly when the crowd is passed. And so they may gain your ear for the assurance of my trust . . . that your recovery of health may be one of the happy things that 1893 is hiding for us :—one of the things that will help to make it a praise-worthy year, for you & for your home & for your friends.

[Other Oxford events, 1892.—In February, there was a performance of the " Frogs " of Aristophanes, by the Oxford University Dramatic Society. On March 16, Professor Freeman died ; and Mr. Froude was appointed to succeed him. In March, there was a great meeting at Balliol, in support of Toynbee Hall, at which Canon Barnett, Lord Herschell, and Mr. Asquith spoke ; and, in May, a meeting at Exeter, in support of Oxford House. The Newdigate Prize, this year, was won by a Christ Church man, Lord Warkworth. Mr. Harwood succeeded Dr. Lloyd as organist to Cathedral. This year, died R. L. Nettleship of Balliol, and Campion of Keble.]

At the end of the year, the Dean and Mrs. Paget paid a visit to her mother and sisters at Costebelle : and, on the journey back (Jan. 1893), were exposed to bitter cold. A day or two later, he was taken very dangerously ill, with acute abdominal obstruction. He was attended by his lifelong friend Sir Thomas Smith, Sir William Broadbent, and Mr. Julius Sankey. There was no operation. His father was present at the consultations, but could not bring himself to take his part in them : mostly he kept his room in the Deanery :

and, every morning, was careful to telegraph a report to
His Majesty the late King, and to Mr. Gladstone.   It
goes without saying, that the Dean was a good patient,
" a patient without exception."   For the first few days,
it was more likely that he would die than live : there
is a story of Sir Thomas saying to Mrs. Paget,
" My dear, your poor husband is very ill, very ill
indeed : now, you just run away and have a good cry."
It would be hard to say which of the two was the more
admirable through these days, the patient or his wife.
In the preface—dictated to Mrs. Paget on February 3—
for the fifth edition of *The Spirit of Discipline*, he
alludes to this illness :—

I am ashamed that I have let various hindrances, with bad
husbandry of time, delay my revising this book for a new
edition, and writing a fresh preface for it, until an attack of
illness has made the work impossible within the set time.   I
am sorry for this, because I wanted to do justice, if I could, to
the suggestions which friends have given me about the sin of
Accidie, and about its name.   This I cannot do at present ;
but one thing I may do, with some special fitness : I may own
once more my gratitude to all those—known by face, by name,
or by kind words that bore no name—whose friendship and
help have been granted to me through this book.   For the
thought of their kindness, very poorly deserved and very
generously bestowed, has often been bright among all the
welcome forms that move about in the quiet spaces of illness
and of convalescence.

This year, they took a cottage, " Priest Leys," at
Lane End, near High Wycombe ; and had the use of
it for the next few years.   It was a bare little dwelling-
place, with poor furniture, and no " improvements " ;
but it stood high, on a common, with beech-woods for
neighbours : and they lent it more than once to some
invalid friend.   Great was his love of the beech-woods :

and, in defence of the "naked house," he quoted Stevenson's *The House Beautiful* :—

> Yet shall your ragged moor receive
> The incomparable pomp of eve,
> And the cold glories of the dawn
> Behind your shivering trees be drawn.

He writes from Priest Leys, on August 5, to the Rev. G. S. Barrett, of Norwich, thanking him for his book, *Religion in Daily Life* :—

. . . A friend of mine said to me once about my father-in-law, after an University sermon at Oxford : "Well, at all events he has one great quality as a preacher—he makes one thoroughly uncomfortable " ;—and I am thankful for some thoroughly disturbing words of yours. And I am thankful, too, with all my heart, for the resolute gathering of all daily life, of all its relations and opportunities and tasks and phases and problems, into the light of our Lord's teaching, to be ruled by His demand and estimated by His standard :—together with the recurring witness to the gladness of a disciplined life, the rest that is hidden in the strenuousness of obedience. . . .

I write from a very small cottage which we have taken, on the top of a hill among the beech-woods of this beautiful county. We can just pack all our party into the limits of our cottage : and the air and the views and the walks through the woods are most delightful and refreshing : while there is a real element of pleasure in the wide contrast with our normal conditions ;—for our cottage has not even a door-bell. On Monday I go to stay for a week with Mrs. and Miss Church at Hursley Vicarage, Mr. Keble's old home. It is wonderful how the place matches with its associations, and how much of the ἦθος of the Christian Year seems still to haunt it.

To George Romanes

Oct. 14.—I could not say this morning all I wanted to say : partly because of my clumsiness in speech : partly because of a certain reverence, a dread of pressing in and hurrying where God, Who knows all, is working as He sees best. But I want you, if you kindly will, to accept and to take abroad with you the picture I am venturing to send :—a picture of the central & supreme example of patience. Dear friend, whenever I try to think of Him, it deepens my trust and thankfulness in regard to your life, so far as in your goodness to me you have let me enter into it. There are very many, I think, who are much nearer to Him in heart & life, and in all that, we believe, He most regards, than consciously they themselves know. He said that there will be many hereafter who will think they never saw Him when all the while they were ministering to Him :—and then again it is not His way to break the bruised reed or quench the smoking flax :—nor to ignore the ventures of belief because of the unbelief that, not crushing them, yet checks them back from thorough freedom & clearness & happiness.

To desire to be like Him : to love the lives & ways that take their character from Him : to follow the example of His patience & humility : to prize the fragments of the knowledge of Him : to refuse ever to give up hoping that the fragments will some day grow & expand & blend into the whole :—surely these are acts of faith from which He never will withhold His blessing—the blessing of perseverance here, of peace here or, if not here, hereafter.

So it all comes back to the old lesson of looking up, and holding on, "till the day break & the shadows flee away." And whenever the thought of venturing forward in the acts and ways of faith seems to grow in your mind, I should believe that there are deeper, stronger, broader tides of life & growth beneath that thought than, perhaps, the faculty of logic tells of. . . .

Nov. 24.—I hope you will forgive the uncomeliness of a letter written in a train, as we creep along on a branch line through a frosty mist to go & visit a Christ Church tenant. It's a bit of my work over which I am inclined to laugh at my Cockney self as we walk about fields and farm yards and our talk is of bullocks :—but I think there is some gain in getting

to know personally those to whom Christ Church must sometimes seem rather a remote & mysterious corporation. . . . It
will be a most happy Christmas this year if it comes to us on
a flowing tide of steadily good news of you. . . Caird will
bring to Oxford a great reputation and a very powerful and
philosophic mind :—I think that 20 years ago, when he came
back for a term and lectured in New College Hall, he was a
most brilliant and quickening teacher : and what I know of
his writing seems to me high and thorough and masterly.

Dec. 23.—It has been a great happiness to get of late
steadily better news of you :—all the Christmas cards that
overwork all postmen would not equal a really good account of
your progress : and all the Christmas bills that come to more
than was expected could not check the delight of hearing that
the progress was steadily maintained.

You will have seen that Robinson Ellis is the new Professor
of Latin :—a Professor who severely and indisputably knows
his subject, & might be honoured with a Grammarian's
Funeral.   But I hope that for many years before that he will
be honoured by a fair attendance at his lectures.

Richard has come home from School, greatly the better for
his first Term there . . . advancing in civilization according
to Mozley's definition of it as the art of maintaining an
interesting conversation.   The sonnet is most beautiful, dear
Romanes : and I will guard it most carefully.

[1893.—In February, the O.U.D.C. performed
" The Two Gentlemen of Verona."   On March 1, a
meeting was held in the Sheldonian in support of the
Radcliffe Infirmary ; Lord Salisbury, Chancellor of the
University, presiding.   On May 18, the Romanes Lecture was given by Professor Huxley, on " Evolution
and Ethics."   In June, Mr. Bryce gave his valedictory
lecture.   Dr. Gore, this year, accepted the living of
Radley ; and Dr. Ottley succeeded him as Principal
of Pusey House.   In October, Manchester College
was opened.   This year, died Jowett, Henry Nettleship,

Professor Pritchard, Mr. J. A. Symonds, and Mr. T. C. Edwards-Moss.]

1894

To George Romanes

March 15. — Do you remember, some time in the last century or in the last but one, (so it seems to me,) sitting with me on a sunny, grassy, flowery, cricket-thronged slope above Grindelwald and expounding to me a certain high opinion which you had formed of Mrs. Church :—which high opinion was afterwards, as I recall, a matter of much gratification to her eldest daughter ?

How little we thought how much you would come to see of one another ! It has been a great happiness, in the midst of all anxiety, to know the happiness "produced" (in Euclid's glowing phrase) "ever so far," in both directions, by your companionship this spring. Indeed I often reflect on the sagacity with which you chose your best man [1]—(that was in the century before the other :—) for of course you took " him " in a large sense : & your prophetic eye discerned in those who should afterwards go with him a deservingness which the bare article quite lacked.

What an emphasis gets on to kindness as life goes on ! Indeed it seems as though the emphasis of life in general shifts :—we begin by recognizing that there is a moral & spiritual import attached to the things & experiences of sense : we come rather to think of those things & experiences as attached to the moral & spiritual import :—*that* emerging into such greatness, such evident possibility of inconceivable development. It is a great help, I think, towards understanding the quiet decision with which St. Paul & St. John speak of things seen and unseen, & of the relation between them.

---

[1] At the Romanes' wedding-breakfast, having to make a speech, he quoted Lamb's apology for his black clothes at a feast :—the fable of all the birds invited to the linnets' wedding, " at which, when all the rest came in their gayest feathers, the raven alone apologised for his cloak because ' he had no other.' "

Far off as one is, one seems to get a glimpse of what was always in their minds.

Gore turned up in the last week of Term : really, I think, well again and very cheery.   He is the ideal traveller : for he "hides not himself" from his fellow-men, whatever tongue they speak, but boldly makes friends with them, and talks of all sorts of things with them ; he always makes me utterly ashamed of the "separate compartment" character of all my travelling.

We went to London yesterday & saw my people.   They are tired, I think, and wanting to get into the country for a bit :—but my father looked very well.   He met us at the New Gallery ; where there are indeed treasures :—the Botticelli belonging to Lord Rosebery, which might make him happy even with the member for Northampton.

To F. E. Jones [1]

Aug. 29.—I know it is a grave and long task that is before you.   But you are young and strong, thank God : and you know the sources & the secrets of true power in working for the souls of men : and that no task is too hard for love, with the patience that love gives.   I hope you may work for many years there : & I would venture to suggest (—I know you will pardon me—) that it would be well to have a long perspective, as it were :—to work as one who need not hurry things, who does not expect to see much happening for a good while. If only one can have courage & faith & patience to go on pouring toil into the indisputable ways of doing good, grinding away at the things that no one can fail to recognize as one's duty, then as years go on, after a longish spell, one may look back & wonder to see how much has come about incidentally that one hardly thought of.   All sorts of people will be ready to be kind : & that is a blessing : but of course one has to work on & on & on that kindness may be turned into trust : & it is right that one should have to.   I remember how the Dean of St. Paul's, not very long before he died, lifted up his

---

[1] Mr. F. E. Jones had been appointed to a living in Devonshire.

hand, & said to me—"Patience, patience, patience" :—just that—& I fancy that often when one is tempted to think that one has been patient long enough, the real need and demand are only beginning.   Those are really endless tasks ;—to keep up patience, to make allowance for the differences that there are among people, to toil to enter into people's minds & ways. *Oct.* 31. . . . I quite agree with you about the Municipal dinners and functions.   I should go, and try to do it all as well as I possibly could :—thinking over speeches beforehand ; & also trying rather hard to be at one's best, so as to be free to be quite genial & cheery & at one's ease, just because of the depth & freshness of one's sense & recollection, please God, of the greatest things :—just as a Retreat ought to make one brighter & simpler & readier & pleasanter for the ordinary uses of society.

Other letters of this year are concerned with books and their authors :—

1. *To A. J. Butler.*—My paper (at the Oxford Dante Society)[1] was a venture, not to say an audacious one ; for I have nothing like the knowledge of Dante which warrants a man in talking about him ; and I have often thought that I ought to withdraw from the Society, into which I got, if not on false pretences, at least on hopes which never have been verified.   The excuse for my venture in the paper was that the moral problem had greatly interested and puzzled me ; and so I am especially grateful for your letter and the evidence of your interest.   I think there are a good many ethical fragments that get less than justice done them because people cannot reduce them to order & so dislike thinking about them.

2. *To J. Polehampton.*—The two characteristics of the Christian attitude towards sin defined by Dr. Liddon and evinced, I think, by Mr. Browning are negative characteristics—the abstin-

---

[1] Dr. Moore, Principal of St. Edmund Hall, kindly writes, that the Dean was elected to the Oxford Dante Society in November 1890.   On May 30, 1894, he read a paper on "Dante's conception of the Vigliacchi in Inf. III."   On Nov. 28, 1898, he read a paper on "The Permanent Import of the De Monarchiâ."   He proposed to read a paper in 1903, but was unable.   He resigned his membership in February 1904.

ence from ever making light of sin, and the abstinence from ever treating it as invincible. My ground, therefore, for the assertion which I ventured to make about Mr. Browning's attitude towards sin is rather in his writings as a whole than in particular passages; it is that I cannot recall any poem in which he does make light of sin or doubt that men should fight against it hopefully. I remember that one, who knew Browning better than I can claim to, confirmed me in the main in this; only doubting (so far as I can recall) whether in "The Blot on the 'Scutcheon" there was not a slight declension from the position I had claimed as Browning's. For the positive bits of his teaching about sin I should turn, I think, to the Pope's soliloquy in the "Ring and the Book," to "Gold Hair at Pornic," to "Easter Day," to the "Epilogue";—though in this regard also it is to his general tone, of bracing courage and hopefulness and conviction that it is all worth while, that I feel the greatest debt.

3. *To Dr. Dale* (thanking him for his book on *Christian Doctrine*).—Your book on the Atonement began my long debt to you; and this has often recalled what I learnt then. But in another way it takes its place in my mind & gratitude with your book on The Living Christ and the Four Gospels. For in both, I think, there has been granted you the courage & the skill to share with others (as few writers do, or perhaps can do), the strength & patience that experience brings—Δι' ὧν πάσχει πεισθήσεται—I have just come on these words in a book by Professor Kirkpatrick:—and they are being verified, I trust, hour after hour, in one life after another. And through personal contact & teaching & influence the conviction of the truth spreads from soul to soul:—but rarely, I think, with real & living force, through writing.

4. *To T. Norton Longman.*—I can well understand (so far as understanding is possible in such matters) what you have felt & feel about Froude. He struck me as having a very rare kind-heartedness and simplicity and charm: & he was very singularly kind to me, though it was only since he came back to Oxford that I had the privilege of knowing him at all, and only very seldom that we met. It is, I think, among the penalties of a

hurried life that are real (as compared with the penalties one fancies or makes for one's self,) that it is so difficult to use as one would the chances of getting to know those whose friendship might give one real happiness & help.

[1894.—The play performed this year by the O.U.D.C. was "The Tempest." On February 14, the University sermon was preached by the Archbishop of Canterbury ; and the Lord Chief Justice attended it, as a Judge of Assize.[1] This year the University Galleries received the Combe Bequest. On May 2 the Romanes Lecture was given by Professor Weismann. The Chancellor's Prize for Latin Verse, this year, was won by a Christ Church man, Mr. J. S. Phillimore. Dr. Lang was appointed vicar of St. Mary's. A Board of Studies was constituted for the School of English Literature. The new building of the Indian Institute was opened. Sir Henry Acland resigned the Regius Professorship of Medicine. This year died Froude, Romanes, Walter Pater, and Sir Charles Newton.]

1895–1896

On January 7, 1895, his mother died, after a short illness.

To his Elder Sister

Jan. 19.—How hard it is to realize that not three weeks have passed since the beginning of the New Year. But days and weeks have little to do with the intervals great changes

---

[1] The *Oxford Magazine*, Oct. 4, 1896, speaking of Archbishop Benson's death, says : " His last appearance here was not one to be forgotten, the occasion of his preaching before the University and Lord Coleridge, acting as Judge of Assize, in St. Mary's. The whole scene, with the two processions ingeniously arranged by the Vice-Chancellor, Dr. Boyd, the conjunction and appearance of the two figures, both looking their part to perfection, will never be forgotten by those who saw the scene."

make. It is more like turning over a page, and finding yourself in another book. *March* 20.—I suppose that to think of any true love that has been granted to one must be to think also of the poverty of one's response : just as one must think in regard to the greatest Love of all, that which is the source & life of all love. But it was given to you, I think, to realize and answer our mother's love, & to gladden her by your answer, as very few children do. . . . It is a great puzzle to me how she could ever think of me as she did. But love such as hers has a strange way of arraying with its own colours those on whom it is spent.

It was about the time of his mother's death that his *Studies in the Christian Character* were published :[1] a collection of sermons, with an Introductory Essay, dated All Saints' Day, 1894. This book needs more than a passing notice, and something is said of it in another chapter.

[1895.—Performance by the O.U.D.C. of "The Merchant of Venice." Mr. York Powell appointed Regius Professor of Modern History. Dr. Burdon-Sanderson appointed Regius Professor of Medicine. In February Mr. Marriott succeeded Dr. Sadler as Secretary to the University Extension Delegates. In March the new buildings of the Oxford Eye Hospital were opened. Appointment of Dr. Gotch to be Waynflete Professor of Physiology. Appointment of Dr. Sanday to be Lady Margaret Professor of Divinity. In May Mr. Holman Hunt gave the Romanes Lecture, "On the Obligations of the Universities towards Art." Mr. Courthope appointed Professor of Poetry. Mr. Lock appointed Ireland Professor of Exegesis. In November, Archdeacon Palmer died : and Dr. Randall, Bishop of Reading, succeeded him as

---

[1] *Studies in the Christian Character.* By Francis Paget, D.D. Longmans, Green & Co., 1895. Pp. xxxvi + 258.

Archdeacon of Oxford. Mr. Wooldridge succeeded Professor Herkomer as Slade Professor of Fine Arts. This year died Lord Selborne, Lord Randolph Churchill, Dr. Dale, Canon Heurtley, Alfred Robinson of New College, and C. W. Boase of Exeter.]

At the Christ Church Gaude in 1896, the new Doctors of Civil Law, who had just received their degrees at the Encænia, dined in Christ Church Hall : among them were Lord Morley, Mr. Joseph Chamberlain, Sir William Richmond, Sir Archibald Geikie, and Dr. Anton Dohrn. The Dean, of course, presided, and proposed the health of each of these distinguished guests. Mr. Chamberlain stayed at the Deanery.

On November 26, 1896, the Princess of Wales, with Prince and Princess Charles of Denmark, and Princess Victoria, visited Christ Church.

[1896.—The performance by the O.U.D.C. this year was "The Merry Wives of Windsor." In January, Mr. Sidney Owen succeeded Mr. Hassall as Junior Censor. In April Dr. Lang went to St. Mary's, Portsea ; and was succeeded, as vicar of St. Mary's, Oxford, by Mr. H. L. Thompson : and Dr. Field was appointed Warden of Radley. On December 2 there was a great meeting of the Christian Social Union in Christ Church Hall, at which Dr. Westcott spoke on International Arbitration. Carfax church, this year, was pulled down, to widen Carfax : its walls were bought, and the stones numbered, and it is now the chapel of Mrs. Scott Malden's school in Brighton.]

1897–1898

To Charles L. Jelf

First Sunday after the Epiphany, 1897. . . . They understand it (Christmas) better, I expect, in Saxony than in
France :—though one thing has always greatly delighted me in
the village churches in France at this time of year :—the way
in which they set out the whole scene of the Nativity on one of
the side altars :—the children, apparently, bringing their own
dolls when there is not money enough to buy appropriate
figures.   I have seen the queerest dolls bearing their part, in tall
hats & Parisian costumes :—& in the church at Toulouse I
remember a large china pug-dog, looking surprized to find
himself there.   We spent our Christmas at Oxford :—the carols
in the Cathedral were, I thought, more beautiful than ever :—
and we had a very pleasant choristers' party, just before the
boys went off for their holiday.

I wonder whether the opportunities of music at Dresden are
now what they are in the summer.   I always remember a
restaurant on a terrace by the river where we used to dine and
listen to very good orchestral music.—I remember the hush
that fell on the place when the best music was played.[1]

I quite agree with you about the San Sisto.   To my mind
it is one of the very greatest pictures I have ever seen : no
familiarity with reproductions of it lessens the wonder of the
original :—and in the original there is an impression of moving
or floating forward that no reproduction gives :—and the background throbbing with light & praise is wonderful :—I hope I
may see it again some day : and also that marvellous little

---

[1] He had been in Dresden sixteen years ago, in 1881 : see p. 64.   There
is a letter from him, on Aug. 14, 1881, to his elder sister, telling her of a Sunday in
Dresden : Mass at the Hof Kirche, a long walk out into the country, evening
service at the English church, and dinner at the Café Belvedere—" where a splendid
band plays the best music every night.   It is wonderful to find how completely one
forgets oneself :—and how soon it seems natural to be sitting in a room filled with
smoke, blazing with gas, and ringing with music while one eats one's delicious little
dinner, and only now and then a vague thought of Oxford or Whitehall comes
across one, to make the present enjoyment all the more quaint and refreshing.   It
is great fun."

Dürer of the Crucifixion, with the strange sense of storm & awefulness about it.

July 27. . . . I have a happy recollection of many of the pictures at Munich : and I delighted in Regensburg : but Prag and Nürnberg are the towns that stand out beyond all in that district for me : I don't think I shall ever forget the days I spent in them :—one evening is pre-eminent, with a walk all round Nürnberg, in quite perfect light.—I hope you will keep a good bit of affection for Bruges ; and there above all for the Memlings. Do you know the great Van Eyck at Ghent ? Last year I had a good study of it, for the third time of seeing it :—and I do think it is one of the greatest pictures I know.

On May 12, 1897, His Majesty the late King, then Prince of Wales, visited Oxford ; and opened the new Municipal Buildings, and the Sarah Acland Nursing Home. He stayed at the Deanery, and dined in Hall ; and afterwards was present at the reception given in the Town Hall by the Mayor of Oxford. It was a moment of some anxiety to the Dean, when a crowd of undergraduates suddenly asked and obtained leave to drag the carriage from Tom Gate to the Town Hall. An excess of loyalty, at a later hour of the night, brought several of them into collision with the police.

"The honours of the Schools last summer," says the *Oxford Magazine*, October 20, "were certainly with Christ Church. When we remember her achievements on the river, we must certainly congratulate the House on a most successful year."

[1897.—Performance by the O.U.D.C. of the "Knights" of Aristophanes, and "The Taming of the Shrew." In May, Mr. Coles succeeded Dr. Ottley as Principal of Pusey House. The Romanes Lecture was given by Lord Morley, on Machiavelli. In June, Dr.

Woods, President of Trinity College, resigned office, and was succeeded by Mr. Pelham. Appointment of Mr. J. A. Stewart to the Professorship of Moral Philosophy. This year died Dr. Wilson, Professor Legge, Mr. Stone, and Mr. Francis Turner Palgrave.]

To E. Harding Firth

Dec. 15.—I am indeed glad and thankful that you have the prospect of a settlement for home and work :—a field of your own, with all the deep and special interest that means. I could wish with you that the flock were rather more :—but my father-in-law had little more than half the number at Whatley : and it never failed him, I think, for diligence or interest or affection or happiness.—And you have the love of books to fill all the space that you can find for them in your days :—and for your children I think there can be nothing happier or healthier than such scenes of home & work and kindness as they, please God, will have around them. . . .

We are all well, thank God, at the end of a very busy, happy Term.—Mrs. Paget & I have come here (Bonchurch, Isle of Wight) for a few days of rest between our Term & the children's holidays :—two boys back from school ;—and Bernard on the verge of being our third school-boy.

To Stephen Paget

Dec. 26.—We had a very happy Christmas Day : and we made a great noise at early dinner.[1]—I had three other books, besides yours :—the great new edition of Pascal's Pensées, from Mrs. Church and Mary, with two wonderful pictures of his mask, giving me quite a new idea of the face :—The 2nd series of the Golden Treasury, from the children :—and (a few days ago) the very first printed edition of St. Augustine's Confessions,

---

[1] It was not often, at the Deanery, that the children were allowed to "make a great noise" : he took his work too gravely for that. There is a story, that on one occasion he went up to the nursery, rather angry at the noise there, and found that the chief offender was not the children, but Lord Rosebery, who was playing with them.

—a most beautiful volume,—from Strong. So my library is manifoldly enriched. I do hope one of the children may love books.

To Bryan T. Holland

March 22, 1898.—I am always glad and thankful when men look back over their time here as you do. For though just now it makes for you the pain of feeling that the time has come to an end, it means also that you have gained in the years you have spent here much that you will never lose : friendships & associations & memories & powers & ways of looking at things, such as will make a life-long difference to you. I do not think that you need fear that you will ever really lose your hold on Oxford & on the House. And the way of keeping it up must be to come & see us at the Deanery now & then.—How would it be to begin by coming next Term for the Sunday in the middle of the Eights ? I gladly send the photograph : and Mrs. Paget promises that she will as soon as possible get and send you one of hers.

[1898.—In January died Dr. Liddell and Mr. C. L. Dodgson, "Lewis Carroll." In May, Mr. Gladstone, and Sir Thomas Dyke Acland. In June the Prince of Wales opened the new buildings of Reading College. At the Encænia, the Duke of York received an honorary degree. The play this year by the O.U.D.C. was "Romeo and Juliet." The Romanes Lecture was given by Sir Archibald Geikie. Proposals were brought forward for the establishment of a School of Agriculture. Professor Weldon succeeded Sir Edwin Ray Lankester as Linacre Professor of Comparative Anatomy. This year Christ Church acquired the Cardinal's hat bestowed on Wolsey, and hung it in Hall.]

1899

In May of this year he published his *Introduction*

to the Fifth Book of Hooker's Ecclesiastical Polity.[1] In 1888 the Clarendon Press had published, in three volumes, *The Works of Richard Hooker, arranged by John Keble.* Seventh edition, revised by R. W. Church and F. Paget. In the Preface to this 1888 edition, Dean Church wrote: " The printer's copy from which Book V. was printed, with Whitgift's signature and corrections in Hooker's handwriting, procured for the Bodleian by Mr. Coxe, has been collated by Dr. Paget, Professor of Pastoral Theology, with the first edition. An account of this MS. will be found prefixed to Book V." The Clarendon Press, when they were publishing this 1888 edition, had suggested to Dr. Paget that he should prepare a separate edition of the Fifth Book of the *Ecclesiastical Polity,* apart from the other Books : and he had undertaken to do this. But, as time went on, his material grew to the measure of a separate volume, apart from the text of the Fifth Book : and the Clarendon Press issued the text of the Fifth Book by itself, as a companion volume. This Introduction has been called, by a good judge, the best of all his writings. It is dedicated *Dilectissimæ Conjugi.* There is a letter from him to his father, dated May 24, 1899 : " Dearest Father, I hope to send you to-morrow with true love what I have written about Hooker. I wish with all my heart that it were worthier to be sent to you : but I know that, for love's sake, you will find kind acceptance for it."

In the preface, he thanks Mr. Doble, Dr. Bright, Dr. Moberly, and Mr. Hassall, for their help in the work : and he goes on to say :—

---

[1] *An Introduction to the Fifth Book of Hooker's Treatise of the Laws of Ecclesiastical Polity.* By the Very Rev. Francis Paget, D.D., Dean of Christ Church. Oxford, at the Clarendon Press, 1899. Pages x + 265.

. . . . I thought the work I had undertaken would be finished in two or three years. I should exceed even the licence enjoyed by egotism in a Preface if I tried to tell the hindrances or own the faults which have nearly stretched the two or three years into twelve. I will only say that there have been hindrances as well as faults : and that I think the misfortune of having to lay one's task aside, and let it lie untouched, for weeks and months of business far removed from it, can only be realized through experience. The references that seemed securely luminous, the plans one thought one had thought out, the fragments that had promised to cohere, relapse into obscurity and confusion : time after time one has almost to start afresh, with a dwindling capacity for freshness, and with a growing dread of blunders : since it is hard to make sure of thoroughness and accuracy where work is intermittent and lacks the long spells of thought and study that have the best chance of getting at the truth. And so it is with uneasiness and a sense of manifold failure that I send out this volume. But perhaps it may help some one else to do what I meant to do.

I have been revising the proofs through days of hot debate and much anxiety in the Church of England : and here and there passages in the book have seemed to me to bear somewhat plainly on the present troubles. And so it may not be impertinent to say that I am not conscious of having written a single sentence with any such reference in my mind. Whatever lessons or warnings the words convey rise simply, I hope, out of the past, where any one, I think, may find them.

In Commemoration week, on June 19, the Duke and Duchess of York came to Oxford, and stayed at the Deanery ; and were present at the Christ Church Ball. Lord Kitchener, Lord Elgin, Mr. Cecil Rhodes, and Sir Hubert Parry were among those who received degrees at the Encænia.

During the Vacation, he was engaged over a new edition of his book, *Faculties and Difficulties for*

CHRIST CHURCH. COMMEMORATION WEEK, 1899.

Belief and Disbelief. He writes to Mr. Longman, in August, from Hyde Farm, near Bideford, saying that he had carried this bit of work with him abroad,— " but it was fine weather, and a holiday of much walking : and I failed to do my duty."

On Saturday, December 9, the Colours of the First Oxfordshire Light Infantry were received in Cathedral, to be kept there till they should be reclaimed after the War. At the service for their reception, he said :—

Captain Watt, officers, and men of the Oxfordshire Light Infantry :—I accept thankfully the trust with which you and those whom you represent have to-day honoured us. The Colours shall be kept here with honour and reverence until you return, please God, in safety—and God grant it may be ere long—to reclaim them from us. Meanwhile the Colours will not be idle or without meaning. For you will know that they are securely guarded in this House of God and reverenced by us as by you : and to us they will be, I trust, a constant help, helping us to make our prayers for you more constant and more earnest, and helping us also to keep before us that standard of duty and obedience and courage and soldierly loyalty which is the secret of an honourable life, whether it be for soldiers or civilians. And now I would bid you—you and those whom you represent—good-bye and God speed. You go to serve a Queen who loves her people, and has never failed to do her utmost for their welfare and happiness. You go to serve a country dear, most dear to us, a country of which we are all proud, as, thank God, a country that has ever held high the standard of honour, and liberty, and justice. And you go to face the risk of that for which all wise and brave men, be they civilians or soldiers, must try, in the fear and love of God, to prepare themselves. God grant to you and to us so to live day by day that we may not be afraid, if it be His will, to die, so to live that life may be indeed worth living, so to live that the fear of death may seem as nothing to us in comparison with duty. God be with you now and always. You and we are in His hands : and may He, in His love and mercy, help you and us according to our several callings to do His will. . . .

"I write in heavy-hearted times," he says to Mr. Jelf, on Dec. 19 ; "God grant us soon the better news for which we hunger." He goes on to speak of Mr. Jelf's school at Folkestone :—

. . . I am indeed interested to think of your work, & of its prospects. It seems to me that in no part of education has there been more marked advance than in the work of preparatory schools : and it is splendid to see now what they do for boys : how real and wise a preparation they make for the life of a Public School. It is wonderful to me to think how far readier my boys are for that than I was at their age. It is a great blessing :—& I think that if a man will live wholly for his work at a Preparatory School he may do untold good.

I expect you are right about the *talk*, the "shop" of athleticism :—it is that much more than the actual athletics that upsets the proportion of things and gives boys misleading ideals.

With the end of the year, on Saturday, December 30, 1899, came the death of his father : "one more of those partings which bring on the loneliness of later years,— the years in which one has to do without the counsel and encouragement that, among human helps, has meant most to me."

[1899.—In February a meeting was held, with Professor York Powell presiding, to inaugurate Ruskin Hall. The Romanes Lecture this year was given by Professor Jebb. Sir William Anson was chosen to represent the University in Parliament. Sir John Stainer resigned the Professorship of Music. This year died Ruskin, Sir John Mowbray, and Sir Monier Monier-Williams.]

1900

To T. Norton Longman

Jan. 8, 1900.—I have thought of a project which I am anxious in the first instance to put before you. It rises out of my desire to do all I can for the funds in relief of the misery caused by the War. I have been for some years Chaplain to the Oxfordshire Yeomanry, and in that office have preached a sermon each year on the Sunday in their training. These seven sermons, though not a series, would form a coherent volume. My thought is to publish them immediately . . . with an agreement, & announcement, that all the profits, accruing either to the publishers or to the writer, should go to the Transvaal War Funds.

This little book, *The Redemption of War*,[1] was " dedicated with respect and gratitude to Colonel Viscount Valentia and the Officers and Men of the Queen's Own Oxfordshire Hussars by their Chaplain." To the second edition, a few months later, he added some short addresses given in Cathedral to men going out to the war—the 40th and 59th Companies of the Imperial Yeomanry, and the Imperial Volunteer Company of the 1st Oxfordshire Light Infantry.

In these addresses—which were spoken, not read— he seems to be feeling not only admiration, but downright envy, of men on active service. For example, some passages in his address on Sunday, February 25, 1900 :—

Lieut. Hext, officers, and men of the 59th Company of the Imperial Yeomanry :—In a few days you will be going towards the front ; and it may be to go on right up to the front. And I trust that we may humbly believe, and that you may humbly

---

[1] *The Redemption of War.* Sermons preached in the Cathedral Church of Christ. By Francis Paget, D.D., Dean of Christ Church, Chaplain to the Queen's Own Oxfordshire Hussars. Longmans, 1900. Pages xv + 87.

M

say in your hearts, that it is God who has called you to go.
For you go in obedience to your Queen, for the sake of your
country, to do your duty.   And that means that the powers
that be, the powers that are ordained of God, have called for
some to go, and you have said that you will : and it means that
the land which gave you birth and nurture, in time of need has
called for help, and you have said you will give it : and it means,
I trust, that conscience has said to you that you should go, and
each one of you has answered, " Then I will."   And I do not
think that one can be far wrong in saying that when a man
hears the voice of his Queen, the voice of his country, and the
voice of his conscience, he hears, in no obscure way, the voice
of God.   And therefore it is that I trust that we may humbly
believe that it is God who has called you to the front.   He who
certainly and wonderfully has been speaking to England through
these months of trial, He, we believe, has spoken to you, and
you have had grace to hear and to obey. . . .

Be sure of this, that He Who has called you, He Whose
voice you believe that you have heard, He Who has given you
grace to obey, will give you grace also to go through with it.
That is the one thought I would ask you to take with you
from this service : To remember that people in every age, all
down the centuries, people in all ranks and conditions of life,
and in all sorts of trials, have set their seal to this truth, that
if God gives a man a thing to do or bear, He gives him strength
to do and bear it.   Only, my brothers, hold fast by Him.   Try
through all the stress to keep near to Him. . . .

And so good-bye and God be with you.   You go to serve
a country that through these months of trial has shown itself
more great and more dear than we perhaps ever knew it to be.
You go to serve a Queen, who uses the greatest position in the
world just to think and watch and work for her people whom
she loves.   And you go to join and to back up those who have
been doing nobly and bravely.   May God go with you and help
you in all things ; may you go, sheltered and guarded by the
love of God the Father, Who created you ; and in the power
and grace of God the Son, Who redeemed you ; and upheld and
guided and helped by the indwelling of God the Holy Ghost,

Who sanctifieth you.   So we commend you to the love of God, which passeth knowledge, and which is the fount of all the love and loyalty that we can know.   To His love we commend you, through Jesus Christ our Lord.

The sermons to the yeomanry are no less full of his pleasure in speaking to soldiers.   Sometimes his theme is arms, sometimes the man.   One sermon is on St. Louis of France and his wedding-ring with *God, France, Margaret* on it—loyalty to God, country, and home— and "let us be sure of it, there is no disloyalty more dreadful than disloyalty to one's home : let us pray God to keep us, in His love and pity, absolutely clear of it."   In another, he tells the story of Sir Philip Sidney's death :—

So he lay there, simply, dutifully doing all that he was told, even when he had begun to feel fairly sure in his own mind that it was not much use ; until, after about a fortnight, though his surgeon still spoke hopefully, he *knew* that he was dying ; and then, without ceasing to obey the surgeons— "continuing," it is said, "a patient without exception"— he did this.   First summoning to his side those who best might help him, he sought in prayer, with deep humility, God's forgiveness of all his sins, for Christ's sake.   Then, after a long silence, he asked those who were by him to talk to him about heaven, so that he might fill his mind and heart, as it were, with thoughts of that.   Then he sent for his will, that he might add a bit to it, and leave something to every one, of whatsoever sort, who had been kind to him during his illness.   Then he asked that music might be sung to him ; he had always loved and studied it, for he was a man of the finest culture, a scholar and a poet, as well as a great soldier ; and one song especially he asked for, a song that he himself had named.   And so, quietly, bravely, brightly, he moved on towards death : to which, indeed, he had come now very near. But before he died he said good-bye to his younger brother, who was most dear to him, and whom he had helped very lovingly and wisely ; and, as he bade him good-bye, he asked him to love his memory and to cherish his friends ; " But, above all," he said, " govern your will and affections by the Will and Word of your Creator." Then, as the poor lad broke down altogether, he gently told those who were by to lead him from the room ; and very soon the end of all the suffering came, and the soul of Philip Sidney passed out of this world.

In another he tells of a Brixham fisherman's death :—

About ten days ago I had a letter telling of the death of one whom I may claim as a friend—a fisherman down in the West. He was young and strong and capable and vigorous ; it might have been easy for him to think that he would set about being religious later on ; but, thank God, he thought, and had long thought, otherwise. It was about the last week of Lent, and his vessel was ready to go out to sea. He had to work hard for his living ; it was fair weather ; and a week's fishing meant much to him. But he had set his heart on not missing his Easter Communion ; so he waited, only for that. Easter came, and he received the Holy Communion of the Body and Blood of Christ in the little church he loved. Then he put out to sea ; and those storms of Easter week came on ; and he has never come home, nor ever will come to his home in this world.—It is a simple story, of a common sorrow ; it was written to me the other day quite simply by another fisherman with whom he worked. But it is in lives like his that the reality of a man's answer to the love of God comes flashing out.

To Miss Lawrence

Feb. 14.—I have long thought with special honour of the profession of a soldier : it seems to me a profession in which great qualities find a high & simple use : and so the sermons in the little book meant much to me as I tried to write them, while at the same time I feared I might be presuming and blundering about things that lay apart from my own life, and " great matters, which are too high for me." I cannot tell you how the reassurance you have gained for me has touched me : or how grateful I am for the kindness which has brought the little book, by Lord Wolseley's generosity, to those whom I most long to help in any way.

Falmouth, March 27. . . . . all the charm of the Riviera, with the added happiness—which has never meant so much to me as now—of being in England. I feel as though all the experience of the past five months had wedded me afresh to my country "for better, for worse, for richer, for poorer," to love, honour,—and obey.

To Leonard Noble

May 18.—You and those who are with you will be so much in my thoughts when I go to Banbury on Sunday for the Church Parade that I must write a few words by this mail ; though I have to ask you to put up with a dull letter.

Lord Wolseley, who was a friend of my Father's, is coming to-morrow to stay with us : and Colonel Norris has asked him to go over to Banbury on the Sunday, to see the Yeomanry & lunch at the Mess : and he has consented.—It will seem strange to me to be there and to be speaking to the men, while you are all away : it is those who are in Africa who are our teachers now :—and I do hope we may all be the better for their teaching. Butler's letter has brought home to me more than ever the privilege of being linked with the Yeomanry.—How I wish I had been with you that Easter day ! It made me very heavy-hearted to think of you being there without a Chaplain :—and though I was not worthy to be there, I might somehow have been of some use—at every Celebration we remember "as in special duty bound" the officers and men of the 40th Co. of the Imperial Yeomanry. . . . I am glad to say that we are going to keep Commem. very quietly this year :—putting by our festivities till you come home, please God, to share them.

Yesterday and to-day we have been hungering for news of Mafeking's relief.—The whole place is ready to break out into flags and rejoicings :—and we have warned the bell-ringers to be ready :—and people flock to look at every telegram that goes up.—Butler said the 22nd : so I am not letting myself be too hopeful this week.

This spring is late and slow. . . . The Eights begin next week, and Christ Church ought to go up : for we have two 'Varsity oars in the boat.

Sept. 20.—It must indeed have been a heavy, weary time at Heilbron :—all the harder to bear because the glow and stir of enterprise was not there to make things seem lighter. But it was borne in a noble cause :—and, thank God, all that was borne for that cause has not been in vain :—and I hope we may now feel that we are not far from an honourable peace, with a good promise of stability in it.—It is wonderful to look back over the ten months and to think of all that men have done & borne for England since those heavy days. . . .

To C. P. S. Clarke

Sept. 19.—I am very glad indeed that the Retreat was as you describe it. I think that the revival of Retreats is one of the clearest gains granted the Church of England in our time : and I think,—so far as I can see,—that the true use of them comes by such ways as your words point towards.—And surely the Retreat & all that struck you in the streets of Poplar on Saturday might have their reflection in the Transfiguration and the scene that was going on at the foot of the mountain : the excellent glory that St. Peter would have lingered in, and the havoc of a human life that men were, or seemed, helpless to mend. That parallel holds, I think, constantly : and I suppose there has never been an age of the Church in which those who wanted to serve Christ have not felt the strain of it. It is sometimes a tremendous strain. As one thinks of the truth that God has granted one to see, and then looks out at the world as it is, it may be, in Newman's phrase, like looking in a mirror and seeing a face not one's own.—But there, in the midst of that havoc, lies one's work :—and in one's work, please God, the way of holiness. He careth for us :—and in slums, or even letter-writing and meetings, I trust, He will not let us suffer in the end by trying to work on at the business He has given us.—"Inasmuch as ye have done it unto one of the least of these"—no monastery can lead men straighter to their Lord than those words promise that they shall come who try to help the poor & wretched & outcast of this world.

On account of the War, there was no performance this year by the O.U.D.C., no Commemoration festivities, and no honorary degrees at the Encænia. [The Romanes Lecture was given by Dr. Murray : the School of Geography was established : Mr. Oman was appointed Chichele Professor of History : Mr. Hatchett Jackson was appointed Radcliffe Librarian. This year died Prince Christian Victor, Sir Henry Acland, and Sir William Hunter.] For Christ Church, the year began with the sending out of men to the War and ended with Mrs. Paget's death. She had worked hard all the year : had collected more than £400 for the Imperial Yeomanry Hospital Fund : had added to all her other work innumerable acts of charity and of sympathy : and the mere sight of her did good. She had lived fifteen years in Oxford : and her presence there had been more of a blessing than ever, in this last year of her life. On Thursday, November 15, she was taken ill with acute meningitis. For two or three days she was in suffering. She was attended by Sir William Broadbent, Sir Victor Horsley, and Mr. Sankey. No operation was possible : she passed into unconsciousness, and died on Thursday, November 22. On the Monday, her body was carried into Cathedral by eight junior members of the House— J. M. Thompson, E. de G. Lucas, E. K. Talbot, R. E. More, W. R. B. Riddell, J. B. Aspinall, Lord Helmsley, and R. L. Charteris—and was buried in the little grave-yard beyond the cloisters. At the Communion service in Cathedral, that morning, the Dean celebrated ; and added her name after the words

"We also bless thy holy Name for all thy servants
departed this life in thy faith and fear." During
her illness, he wrote with his own hand the bulletins
which were put on the door of the Deanery. All
Oxford was thinking of her, and went into mourning
for her. In Christ Church, as Dr. Talbot said in
Cathedral, her death "was felt with real and aching
pain by seniors and juniors, residents and non-residents,
the servants as well as the members of the House" :—

Am I wrong in thinking that in the heart of many a House-
man for many a year one of the forces that will make for
purity, and tenderness, and simple conscientiousness of daily
living, and self-forgetfulness for others' sake, will be the un-
effaced picture of her who was indeed the lady of the House
during their undergraduate days ?—the memory of a life with
the dignity and freedom of entire simplicity, with something
in it still of the brightness of a girl, but enlarged by the
tenderness of mother and wife to take in every gladness or
sorrow of others' lives. They will remember, perhaps, the
atmosphere of a presence into which nothing unclean, or unworthy, or ungenerous could dare to come ; though everything
that was natural and fair found ready welcome, and each was
taken at his best. . . .

> A creature not too pure and good
> For human nature's daily food,
> And yet a spirit still, and bright
> With something of angelic light.

I could say more, and you will remember more, of quiet
daily duty done at a constant cost of strain and toil ; of the
determined, almost desperate, effort to leave no lives within
this place outside the circle of courtesy and friendship ; of the
constant care and friendship towards those who, as the world
speaks, were beneath her in station—the servants of the House
and their families ; of the eagerness of heart with which she
followed the war, felt for those who suffered, sent her letters of
bright sympathy to House-men at the front ; worked at the

head of what Oxford did for the wives and children of its soldiers.

In memory of her, an inscription, written by the Dean, was put in Cathedral :—

IN PACE DOMINI REQUIESCAT
HELENA BEATRIX
FILIA RICARDI WILLELMI CHURCH
FRANCISCI PAGET UXOR
SUORUM ET ÆDIS ISTIUS IN DEO
AMANTISSIMA
NATA FEB. XXII A.S.   MDCCCLVIII
OBDORMIVIT NOV. XXII A.S.   MCM
DOLORIS MAGNI BREVE MONUMENTUM
UNA CUM DECANO DISCIPULI POSUERUNT.

On December 1, he writes to C. P. S. Clarke : [1]—

There are many things I have to thank you for, dear Clarke :—one specially rises in my mind :—your share in the happiness of the Devonshire holidays,—and especially of this year's. For it meant so very much to her that the holidays should " go well " :—you know the endless trouble she took about it :—and it always was a delight to her to look back and see that things had " gone well "—and this year, I think, they were the happiest holidays we had had :—and you had had a very large share in helping them to be so :—and I am very grateful when I think of it.

The following letters to Stephen Paget refer to the *Memoirs and Letters of Sir James Paget,* which the Dean was helping him to edit :—

11, *Downing Street, July* 11, 1900. . . . What a standard it raises ! Again & again, as I read, it struck me that the story was dwarfing or over-topping the stories of other men's lives, just as his photograph goes ahead of all the other portraits you can bring near it :—by the force of sheer simplicity. Other men may have rivalled him here & there :—I can think of no one who seems to have reached equal excellence at so many

---

[1] Mr. Clarke had been with them at Hyde Farm, as a holiday-tutor for the boys.

points :—but what I am sure of is that I have never seen or read of such power used so simply, so freely. It is a magnificent story. . . . The Memoir seems to me one of the very finest and most valuable bits of work I have ever read :—I expect even those who knew him will be surprised at what it tells & at the way it is told :—I did not think Autobiography could be so good.

. . . In one point I think the recurrence of the story [1] has led to a bit of disproportion. I think that in the Life too large a part of the horizon is covered by the difficulties about money & about getting on at the Hospital.—You will say at once that these did cover at times almost all the range of outlook.—But I think they produce an erroneous effect in the story :—the Memoir has spoken of them with reserve as well as strength :— and I think that one must be careful not to let the recital of them give any impression of harping on the same string.—I wish we could talk of this : for I have expressed myself badly, and may be misunderstood : but do not decisively misunderstand me till we can meet.

Hyde Farm, Aug. 10.—It troubles me that you have dealt so severely and trenchantly with what you had written : and as I think of it all being cut about I feel a distress like that of a carpenter who sees fine wood-work being re-arranged. . . . I have been writing letters all the morning : and so write stupidly and illegibly :—but I will think more & try to write better. *Aug.* 19.—I quite agree with you in not caring for isolated letters to "swells." What I should hope for would be a few letters showing how absolutely people whose trust means much trusted him :—a few letters, perhaps, showing the reasons which underlay certain characteristic rules of his :— & a few letters to people who had asked his guidance about questions of professional or private conduct. *Aug.* 27. . . . My impression is that my mother's part would be shown most truly and characteristically, not in a separate chapter, but in the emergence here & there of what she was.—A deep, vivid

---

[1] The book begins with a Memoir, written by Sir James Paget himself, and goes on with a Life written by his son. The Memoir is chiefly concerned with the earlier years, and the Life goes over these years again.

trait seen briefly often tells more than anything else the power of such a life :—and the chapter wd. be so hard to keep right as to be almost impossible. I think you are right in avoiding the 1st person, if you can.—I believe I have never used it in any review or article I have written : but with different reasons for the avoidance. *Sept.* 2.—I want you to consider, some time, the insertion of a deliberate bit about his theology. I do not mean his religious life : that was like his love of my mother : a thing to come out rather than to be told :—though there was a certain characteristic note of it that ought, I think, to be secured somewhere, somehow. But his theology was a part of his mind and thought which was remarkable, and might, I think, be described without any risk of dragging things private into publicity. His lifelong study & brilliant appreciation of Pascal, Hooker, Butler, Mozley, the Cambridge Platonists (I think), was a thing to be noted : and it made him a real teacher in that field.—I am not really a theologian :—but whatever approach to theological insight I may ever have had is very largely (mainly, I think), due to his guidance. *Sept.* 11. . . . I can see the necessity of saying " my father," " my mother." —After all, the avoidance of the first person is but a means to an end : & one must not imperil the end to keep it up. One thing I feel it is hard for you & me adequately to guard against :—to wit, lest the disclosure of affection should lose force by frequency.—His tenderness & love were wonderful : and the wonder of them can only be felt in the book if it *flashes* out ; and that must not be too often. I do not know how to express what I mean :—but it is something like a phrase I read a few days ago, " une lumière uniforme ne va pas au rayon." There must not be too many affectionate letters or passages : lest the revelation of his heart should lose the concentrated force which reaches a reader's heart.—Bah ! how clumsy one is. And I do not mean that I think there are too many :— only that it needs great care that there should not be :—and that I should like you to keep this care in the front of your mind. *Sept.* 12.—Looking this morning through last night's letter, & talking a bit with Helen, I am inclined to suggest being on guard against letting the home-life *predominate* in the general impression of the letters, so as at all to draw away your emphasis & your readers' attention from the great height & importance & distinction of the work, professional, scientific, public.—You see, I tell you all my scruples, for you to deal with as you like.

Christ Church, Nov. 15. . . . I am glad it all goes into one volume : for two men, I think, will read one for one who would read two :—though the book anyhow is secure of its demand. I have never sent you the bit about the theological reading :—I am heartily ashamed. I have begun to work at it : but I got stuck for lack of time :—I will hurry up, to the best of my power. Some of us entertained a lot of the Colonial troops at luncheon in the Hall to-day : and very interesting it was.—A great many of them seemed to me singularly fine, straight-looking fellows, with a good blending of discipline & independence. Helen has, I am sorry to say, an attack of neuralgia, and went to bed early. I trust she will be better to-morrow, and able to write her judgement as to A & B. . . . *P.S. Nov.* 16.—Helen is, I am very sorry to say, no better : and I have sent for Sankey. So, I send my letter : not liking to keep it back for her verdict, which cd. hardly come to-day. But, lacking her verdict, it shd. be tentative.

On the day after Mrs. Paget's death, he writes :—

Nov. 23.—I have only time at 11.50 for a word to tell you that Mary Church and all the children are, thank God, well : —I don't think that Mary is really or harmfully over-tired.— And we never can come near forgetting your goodness to us. Still the face is so beautiful and noble and quiet & untroubled.

To Stephen Paget, 1901

Feb. 15.—What you told me (of Queen Victoria's Funeral) is the first thing that has made me wish I had been there :—the thought of seeing even great and noble sights seems strangely faded and lifeless in my mind just now :—but I do wish I had been by you there. . . . You have made me bold to send you a little paper on Ruskin.[1]—It was all done before "the time the

---

[1] He wrote this paper for the Birmingham Ruskin Society, of which he was President.

storm fell upon " me : & reads strangely now :—but you will
allow for that. . . . I don't think much of my value anywhere.
—But, so far as I can see, there is more chance of my being of
just some service here than elsewhere :—so I hope I may go on
here so long as I have strength for the work, and so long as
there seems the power & opportunity of doing good, or making
it easier for others to do it.—It is your postscript that provokes
this outbreak of egotism. *May* 4.—It is a real pleasure to
think that you and Nell are in Venice. . . . When I used to
go abroad, or indeed anywhere, part of the pleasure was to try
to be surprisingly clever in finding something really original
and delightful for Helen.—I can never now spend any money
in this way :—so will you spend a little for me : and will you
buy something that it gives you pleasure to buy for Nell, or for
Ellie & Molly ?—If you will do me this kindness, you will find
about a hundred francs waiting for you at Thomas Cook's &
Sons. . . . Above all, don't think of answering this letter :
nothing spoils a holiday so much as letter-writing.

In May 1901, he was appointed Bishop of Oxford.
When the offer of the appointment came, he asked
that he might be allowed to stay on at Christ Church.
Then Lord Salisbury sent his chief private secretary to
him, to urge him very strongly to accept. About the
middle of May the appointment was made public. " I
believe it is right," he says, on May 23, to Stephen
Paget, " and that is infinitely the greatest thing :—and
when one is once clear about that, many points emerge
in it to be very thankful & hopeful about. But it is,
every way, more than one can speak of." On St.
Peter's Day, June 29, in St. Paul's, he was consecrated
by Archbishop Temple : the assisting clergy were the
Archbishop of Cape Town and the Bishops of London,
Bangor, Ely, Lincoln, Rochester, St. Albans, Stepney,
Reading, and St. Andrews. The sermon was preached
by Canon Scott Holland. On July 1, he did homage

and was invested as Chancellor of the Order of the Garter.

For his last sermon in Cathedral as Dean of Christ Church, he took the text : " And Jacob awaked out of his sleep, and he said, Surely the Lord is in this place ; and I knew it not. And he was afraid." At the end of his sermon, he said :—

I am speaking here for the last time as Dean. Within a little while I shall have done with the great trust that I have borne here : I shall have left it to be taken up by one to whom I yield it with thankfulness and joy : one who will, I know, dedicate to it wholly himself and all his gifts. So, speaking for the last time, I have tried to tell the chief truths that I seem to have learnt here. I have not spoken to you of my gratitude for all that you, elder and younger alike, have been to me : for words sound poor and dull when I try to think of that, and of all that has been granted me in the House, and in the University and City of Oxford. I have not said how sorry I am for my mistakes and faults : partly because you have shown me that you have put them out of sight, partly because what they really need is God's forgiveness, and God's over-ruling. And I have not tried to say good-bye. I have simply wished to gather up for you and for myself the lessons that seem to rise out of the years that I have spent here. First the duty of reverence and loyalty towards Christ Church. Then the duty of reverence and gentleness towards all, with that charity which suffereth long and is kind, and hopeth all things. And then the lesson of that plain, upholding trust that if a man will only try to do his best, and to keep clear of worldliness and selfish plans, and to cast out the love of praise and power, seeking and relying on God's Grace, then, in spite of all his weakness and blundering and failure, God will somehow find a use for him, and somehow bring things right after all. For He in very truth, without Whom nothing is pure, nothing is holy, is and will be the strength of them that put their trust in Him ; even though the trust with which they cast their care on Him may be indeed but a very poor answer to all that He has taught them of His Love.

In July he was in Switzerland, with his friend Dr. Woods, now the Master of the Temple.

To his Elder Sister

Mont Prosa Hotel, July 21.—I have been walking through scenes that have brought back the old Lucerne holiday of 1871 : and I cannot help writing of them. Do you remember that magnificent round, planned with all my father's enterprise and holiday sumptuousness ? I can almost see the carriages waiting for us at Fluelen, after the journey up the Lake :— and a strange bathe at either Andermatt or Hospenthal :—and then the meeting with Mr. Gilson Humphrey at the Rhone Glacier ; & the " short & easy method " the waiter took with the flies that blackened the ceiling at the Hotel. It is hard to realize that 30 years have passed since we were all here together : and yet, if some one told me that all that time belonged to some one else's life & not to mine, I could almost believe it :—so much has come, and passed, since then.

But *here* we were not : for Woods & I struck off from the old route at Hospenthal this morning, and came up here. . . . Very few tourists stay here now, I think ;—they all go through the 20 minutes stuffiness of the tunnel, instead of the two days glory of the Pass. . . . It is the most wonderful refreshment, to be quiet, and to walk day after day through fresh and beautiful country. I trust that a fortnight hence I shall come home, please God, readier for a year's work, if all be well, than I was a week ago. I do not think I have ever needed a holiday more : & it is an unspeakable blessing to have it.

To Miss Lawrence

Hyde Farm, Aug. 26.—I left the Deanery about ten days ago : you will guess that it was rather heavy-hearted work, going. But, for one thing I cannot be thankful enough : and that is, for all the goodness & kindness of my successor there. It is a real happiness to look forward to his work and influence there. . . . No chance of settling into Cuddesdon till October.

To Stephen Paget

St. Lawrence Vicarage, Reading, Oct. 12.—What a brute I
have been ! But indeed life has been very difficult : with the
rush of work, the ceaseless demand, the responsibility, the
homelessness. I don't think I should mind being hard worked :
but to be always behindhand is a trial. However, one can only
do one's best :—and there are many bits of happiness to be
thankful for. I will write to Longman to-night. It has been
a real delight to see the reception given to the book :—I have
heard but one opinion of it :—I feel very proud of it. *Oct.* 23.
—They have to-day made me an Honorary Student of Christ
Church. No honour in the world could ever mean to me what
that does. I wish I could tell you more of what it moves in
my heart.

After Mrs. Paget's death, her sister, Miss Church,
devoted herself to the children, and to the care of the
household.

CHAPTER VII

" STUDIES IN THE CHRISTIAN CHARACTER "

A VOLUME of sermons, in the hands of a man who never knew the preacher of them, may be very dull ; but the nearer the preacher was to him, the nearer the sermons are. They bring back his friend, the way he took things, his judgment of people and books and pictures and music, even the sound of his voice and the look of his face ; the book is read for the reader's happiness in recalling what his friend was to him. These sermons by Dr. Paget were preached, most of them, between 1891 and 1894, to undergraduates, in Cathedral, or in the University church. Some of them, doubtless, were written under pressure of other affairs : but the Introductory Essay was written with the utmost care, and every word of it weighed. It begins with a definition of the Christian character as " the coherent group of traits evinced in lives surrendered to the rule of Christ with reliance on His grace." The subject, he says, seems to get less than its due share of thought :—

To turn one's mind to it in some of those free spaces which all the overcrowding of one's days may still leave open (unless one has the folly to enclose them for the cultivation of anxiety when it is out of season) ; to give one's unclaimed thoughts to the recollection and study of the most Christ-like characters, the most unselfish lives that one has known;—even this, besides raising greatly the value of one's leisure, would tend to discoveries well worth making about one's self and about others, and might lead one on to the discernment or surmising of truths far beyond all price.   But it would be well to devote something more than such leisurely and occasional thinking to the scrutiny and examination of the Christian character.   It would be well to make it the subject of the strongest and most persevering attention that one is able to use; to study it as men study the things they are most bent on understanding and least ready to think they understand; to concentrate on it efforts of thought resembling as nearly as possible the accurate, sustained, and irrepressible inquiry by which a great scholar or physician labours on in silence towards that victory of penetration which releases light.

Beyond its " broad and obvious notes," we may find in it " strange reserves of strength, wonders of tenderness, adjustments of ministry, details of beauty and wisdom, refinements of loyalty, secrets of endurance and of self-sacrifice."   The study of it, for Christians, is a safeguard against formalism: for it " stands in ceaseless witness against all stopping short or swerving off from the highest endeavour, the central calling of the Christian life."   It appeals, also, to those who disbelieve or doubt the Christian faith:—

The share borne by the Christian character in the appeal which Christianity can make to those who are doubting its truth is, perhaps, larger in the actual experience of men than it seems in the formal statement of evidence.   For in many cases it is at once haunting and uncontentious; it is associated with thoughts and memories which are rightly dear to men; it is apt to speak to them most clearly when they know themselves to be at their best.   And so its hidden energy on the side of faith is probably far beyond its prominence in argument; it goes about the world as one of those secret forces of beneficence which are behind the surprises of goodness, and which, if they were made visible, might decisively reinforce a great deal of threatened and imperilled hope. But there is one signal service which the appeal of the Christian character is peculiarly apt to render in the cause of faith. It is often the only power which can confront the steady, surreptitious, miserable pressure with which the sins of Christians fight against the work of Christ. It may be that the contest between these two forces covers by far the greater part of the whole battle-field ; and that, while critics and apologists, with their latest weapons (or with the latest improvement of their old ones), are charging and clashing amid clouds of dust—with the world still thinking that here at last is the real crisis—the practical question between belief and disbelief is actually being settled for the vast majority of men by the silent and protracted conflict between the consistent and the inconsistent lives of those who alike profess themselves Christians ; the conflict between the contrasted experience of Christ's Presence manifest in goodness, and Christ's Name dishonoured in hypocrisy, or blindness, or indifference. In many lives faith must have to hold on somehow through an almost overwhelming weight of discouragement in the hourly experience of the ill-temper, or injustice, or worldliness, or self-indulgence of religious people —it may even be of some who are actively ministering in God's Name ;—and the one stand-by and stronghold through that dismal onset of unreality may be the known reality of the Christian character, the personal conviction that there are some at least on whom the grace of God is not bestowed in vain, in whom it does achieve its distinctive and transcendent work—the Mind of Christ.

Even if it were rarer than it is, it would still be a reality, a fact to be attended to and accounted for :—

Rarity, apart from the probability of false or erroneous recording, does not prove casualness or insignificance ; and nature would supply analogies for any amount of sterility and waste in the sphere of grace. But somewhat more than this may without fear be claimed, when the character appears not in a few scattered cases here and there, but as a vigorous,

enduring, and coherent element in moral history; submitting
to the changes of human life that it may subdue what is
unchanged in humanity; stooping, as it were, to conquer;
adapting itself to different nationalities and generations, yet
proving presently to have adapted their inner life to its inner
substance; suffering some harm at times, as everything must
suffer that is projected boldly into the tumult and treachery of
the world, yet recovering its health as if by the power of an
endless life; moving like a great river, now broader, and
now deeper, through the ages since Christ came; referred
and traced to Him, as its one Source and Principle and Guide
and Strength, by the accordant voice of all in whom its might
and beauty have been manifest.

And, the more it is studied, the heavier is the strain
on any explanation of it apart from the Christian
faith :—

There is always danger of misrepresentation in the attempt
to present a view that is not one's own; but it does seem clear
that those who deny the Divinity of Christ must think that
the Christian character was introduced and realized and pro-
pagated and maintained under strangely incongruous and
uncongenial conditions. It certainly does not look like a
character that has started up out of an enthusiastic delusion,
an exaggerated and misguided devotion, a fanatical misunderstanding of a teacher's meaning, a credulous fostering of
irrational hopes and fancies; still less can the thought of it
be brought into connexion with any wilful or self-deceiving
fraud. For it is not out of such darkness and disorder, by the
working of natures so perverse and unhealthy and unreasonable,
that such a type of moral excellence as this could spring up
and endure—a type in which humanity attains its best harmony
and strength, and renders its most reasonable service. The
sobriety and usefulness of the Christian character; its quiet
and wide attractiveness; its unconscious skill in prompting
others to do right; its readiness for adaptation to new
demands and opportunities in shifting circumstances and
strange countries; its peculiar balance and blending of traits

which are generally found apart, and thought to stand in
contrast ; its steady health and freshness ; its hidden stores of
strength and charm and wisdom and refreshment ; its power
to help all men at all times ;—these are distinctive qualities
which seem to thrust away the suggestion of an origin in
delusion, or misunderstanding, or extravagance, and to claim
for the character that bears them a direct line of kindred with
some perfect type of manhood, some true idea of what man
might and should be, some thought about him in the mind of
God.

Then comes the question whether, in national life,
it will ever prove antiquated, or ineffective, or out of
touch with the social order :—

The resourcefulness and triumphs of the Christian character
in the past seem a real ground for courageously refusing such
an apprehension about the future.   Time after time that
character has addressed itself to new and great tasks ; it has
accepted strange conditions ; it has confronted vast demands
with the fearless confidence of treasures that are infinite ; the
fierceness of man has turned to its praise, and his frailty has
been ennobled by its tenderness ; nations most unlike in temperament and ideals have alike been purified, exalted, hallowed
by its discipline ; it has put forth new powers of beneficence
and sympathy and attraction in the presence of new perils and
opportunities ; at times it has assumed an aspect men had never
seen before, so that those who came to fight against it saw in
it what they could not but revere and love.   While the character which has so told upon the past abides in unspent energy
and promise, while the tradition of the saints is still sustained
and clear, it is faithless to despond about the future.   Already
the Christian character has seemed to be feeling its way
towards new ventures of self-devotion and new renderings of
old virtues in adaptation to the new wants of modern life in
England.   Already thoughtful and impartial students have
suggested that Christian self-denial and sympathy and brother-
liness have told during the last fifty years in a real mitigation
of those crises and conflicts through which great changes

penetrate the fabric of society and affect the relations of its parts.

But it must have a future, not only in the course of society, but also in the individual life. And, unless it be prophetic, in each life, of some final and unimaginable likeness to Christ, then the Christian may be suspected —" and the suspicion is not strange ; for words which may well account for it are freely said by Christians, and still more freely sung"—of reckoning on a rather mercenary and selfish sort of heaven. But, as a matter of fact—

The sort of men Christ's servants come to be, the traits they take and perfect as they move towards death, are a fair token what it really is that they hope to find beyond death. Few things tell on character more surely and precisely than the goal on which the heart is set and the temper in which that goal is sought. And certainly the Christian character, as it appears in Christ-like lives, does not look at all as though it had been formed and fostered and determined by a mercenary attention to a selfish aim. For the faculties and the capacity that grow in those who try to be true to Christ in daily life are strikingly ill-suited for the opportunities of enjoyment which might be imagined in a heaven of selfishness. Christians do not grow in the capacity for selfish pleasure, nor attain an exceptional power of relishing to the utmost a separate and individual gratification. The faculty which they develop is the faculty of self-denial ; of glad, unhindered self-forgetfulness for others' sake ; of delighting in goodness and eliciting what is best in others ; of simple, cheerful, unclouded self-surrender. These, and such as these, are the powers that accrue to those who choose the Christian life ; and it is strange if the way along which they are acquired is a way of self-seeking ; strange if, in striving towards a paradise of selfish pleasure, there is formed a character which would be as wretched there as a selfish character in the heaven of the saints. Surely it is a very different sort of aim and quest that is betrayed in the development of the Christian character and in the lines on which it presses forward ; its preparation through the discipline of this life is for something else than what is here called pleasure or success ; the faculties that are strengthened with its strength must have a work surpassing all our thoughts, and the capacity it brings can never be satisfied with aught that is created. For, in truth, the Christian character prophesies of this—that God has made us for Himself ; and that there is neither rest, nor goal, nor joy for man, save in His Love.

The sermons for which he wrote this Introductory Essay illustrate, again and again, his ideals of life ; for example, the following passages :—

The Simplicity of Goodness

What men call simple goodness is, under very complex conditions of work, not so simple or obvious a matter as it sounds. Behind the simplicity of the result there are qualities, both moral and intellectual, which are among the greatest attainments of a human nature. They may be attained through moral discipline ; but none the less may they outstrip in a common field of exercise the mental gifts which men rate highest. The unembarrassed insight which goes straight to the real character of an action or suggestion ; the just imagination which can enter into another's position, and transpose without altering the parts of a transaction where one's self is interested ; the kindly shrewdness which is never credulous and never cynical ; the strength of mind that can resist the temptation to be clever ; and, above all, that sense of things unseen which makes palpable the folly of ever fancying that there can be through evil a short cut to good ;—these are some of the faculties which are required and exerted and developed in that simple goodness which is enlightened and sustained by trust in God ; that consistent and unwearied doing good, that purity both of purpose and of method, which is the distinction of the souls that humbly and sincerely rest on Him.

Forbearance

Who are we, what is our insight into other men's hearts, that we should foreclose the time of their growth ; that we should call for speed, when God, it may be, is patiently disengaging their minds from difficulties that we have never known ; that we should let ourselves resent their present refusal of that truth which, perhaps, they are already preparing to welcome later on with a depth, an intensity, a thoroughness of acceptance far beyond all that we have ever rendered to it ? If we realize at all the height and greatness of the truth, its hidden depths, its distances of unapproachable light, its divineness and awefulness, we must know ourselves to be incapable of judging how Almighty God may lead men on towards it ; we must feel that it would be strange if all men could be led alike, or if we could always tell how others are dealing with their opportunities. God may be leading them by a way that they know not ; and they may be humbly, anxiously struggling on ; trusting, perhaps, with a hope they hardly dare to put into words, that the light is surely growing somewhat clearer, steadier around them than it was ; that they are somehow nearer to God, or at least not further from Him than they were. And who can tell how He may help them through the reverent and hopeful patience of those who feel the sacredness both of truth and of each human life ? Who can measure the responsibility of trying to force on the decision, to presume the issue ? It is easy to affix a label, to pass our own audacious verdict, to imply that hesitation can be no longer possible or honest ; easy, but very little like His way Who, when men would not receive Him, turned simply, silently to go elsewhere ; refusing to bring things to a crisis, or to let hope go because it was deferred ; giving people time, and waiting that He might have mercy on them.

Nor is it only in the great matters of belief and unbelief, of acceptance and refusal, that we may learn this lesson as to our bearing towards our fellow-men. The example of our Lord, as He humbly and calmly takes the rebuff, and turns to go to another village, may help us in the ordinary ways of ordinary daily life. The little things that vex us in the manner or the words of those with whom we have to do ; the things which seem to us so inconsiderate, or wilful, or annoying, that we think it impossible to get on with the people who are capable of them ; the mistakes which no one, we say, has any right to make ; the shallowness, or conventionality, or narrowness, or positiveness in talk which makes us wince and tempts us towards the cruelty and wickedness of scorn ;—surely in all these things, and in many others like them, of which conscience may be ready enough to speak to most of us, there are really opportunities for thus following the example of our Saviour's great humility and patience. How many friendships we might win or keep, how many chances of serving others we might find, how many lessons we might learn, how much of unsuspected moral beauty might be disclosed around us, if only we were more careful to give people time, to stay judgment, to trust that they will see things more justly, speak of them more wisely, after a while. We are sure to go on closing doors of sympathy, and narrowing-in the interests and opportunities of work around us, if we let ourselves imagine that we can quickly measure the capacities and sift the characters of our fellow-men.

Confession of Dependence

Dependent upon others we all are : the most resolute, the most masterful, the most eminent, the best equipped of us, as truly, as inevitably dependent upon others as the weakest and the least resourceful ; though we may be able somewhat longer to defer the confession of the truth. And who can measure what we miss and mar while we refuse to own our dependence and our need ? For it is not only that we straiten and impoverish our own life, and grow colder and harder and more lonely in our fancied self-sufficiency ; we are also driving others back from the joy they might have found, we are repressing instincts and ventures through which God would have had them move forward in the twice-blest exercise of charity. It is a dreary wintriness that settles down upon the life that would be wholly independent ; the life of one who shuts out sympathy and service and compassion ; who uses reserve not for self-discipline, but for self-exaltation—not as distrusting himself, but as trusting no one else; who hides his sorrow not in patience, but in pride. For there is "a time to keep silence, and a time to speak;" and God, Who seeth in secret, and Who knows our wants and fears, and what we are in our strength and what we may come to in our weakness and old age—God, Who has given men the capacity for pity and generosity and helpfulness, never meant us to imagine or pretend that we can get on by ourselves, that we can do without any to comfort us, that we can take our life apart and never own that we are dependent upon others.

Honouring all Men

It is a blundering and shallow study of experience that gets from it a disbelief in goodness and a scornful view of men. We may wonder at the strange physical theories which, in bygone ages, the facts of nature were supposed to warrant; and yet the facts of life are still misread with quite as much partiality and eccentricity; men say that they have learnt by experience convictions quite as far removed from truth. We may have much to discover of the depth and awefulness of sin; of the weakness of will, the deformity of conscience, the hardheartedness that sin can work: but it will be our own fault, I think, if we do not also find with increasing clearness, and read with steadier certainty, the tokens of the power that is ever beating evil back; the power that reasserts through human goodness man's true claim to honour; the power that bears in itself the pledge of final victory, that must "triumph because of the truth." The scenes and incidents of life through which we may win our growing knowledge of that power may be very different. Sometimes we may see it far off, sometimes very close to us; now in brightness, now in sorrow: but the chances of seeing it come, I think, to all; and they are the truest opportunities that life brings. In all, for instance, that we may come to learn through the experience of illness, the fresh discovery of kindness, patience, generosity, gentleness, self-forgetfulness in human hearts shines out with a distinctive brightness; a brightness which should grow towards that perfect day from which, in truth, it comes. But howsoever

we are led to know of the hidden work that is fashioning the
wonder of goodness in the hearts of men and women, that
knowledge surely may light up for us the bidding of the text
and rebuke us when we forget it. We may gladly and
sincerely "honour all men" as we meet them and deal with
them even in the hurried and conventional ways of ordinary
life; since in all that secret growth may be astir, and we
may be nearer than we can imagine to "the Spirit of glory
and of God."

Courtesy

Upon each one of us there lies, then, unceasingly this
absolute demand of self-respect. It is the safeguard of all that
we are set to offer for the glory of God and for the good of
men. And courtesy, I believe, is nothing else than sympathy
with the self-respect of others. It is just the touch of help, the
appointed service, which each one of us may render to others,
and may receive from others, in regard to this profound condition of man's welfare. There are many forces that imperil
self-respect; it is undermined by sin, it is mocked and
threatened by temptation, it is discouraged by the experience
of failure : only the grace of God, forgiving and renewing us,
suffices wholly to repair and reinvigorate it. But amongst the
means He uses to protect us from our own despondency, to lift
up our hearts, to give us hope and courage to regain lost
ground, none, I think, is surer or more blessed in its work
than courtesy. It helps men to sustain their self-respect by
the quiet, frank, unquestioning respect it shows them ; and it
helps them to recover self-respect by presuming that they have
not lost it. It moves along the level ways where most of life
goes on ; it generally has to do with those comparatively little
matters which make up most of life ; but in those level ways,
amongst those lesser things, it is analogous to that assumption
of high spiritual capacity which calls out in all men the very
best that they can yield ; it may even seem a reflection of
God's goodness in trusting us that He may make us trustworthy. Yes, in all relations and over almost the whole field
of conduct, it has power to help men in regard to that which

most concerns the integrity and independence of their life. It
abolishes no distinctions and is checked by none ; no one is too
humble to show it or too high to be helped by it ; its silent
prompting lifts in all the tone of thought and purpose ; it is
never out of place or out of reach ; and there is nothing more
beautiful than the courtesy of the poor, unless it be the courtesy
of the suffering and of the dying. We may often think how
little we can do to alleviate the troubles, the disappointments,
the mishaps of this world ; but things are bettered not only by
the effort that is directly set to better them, but also by the
virtue of every life that is informed and harmonized by a steady
sense of what is due to all men. And it may be that much of
the strength which is generously devoted to good works would
vastly gain in efficacy if with it always went the grace of
courtesy ; if everywhere alike, in home, in business, in society,
in beneficence, the considerateness of perfect courtesy never
flagged ; the considerateness that is apt to make men wonder
whether they ought not to be aiming higher than they have
ever aimed as yet.

It may sometimes have come into our minds that the haste,
the manifold demands of modern life, make courtesy more
difficult than it ever was before ; that we can hardly be
expected to be always courteous when we are thus hurried and
hardworked. But perhaps we may be overrating the advantages
in this regard of other times ; and also, if we think what
courtesy requires, we may see that it can never have been easy.
Hurry and worry may tell against it now : but how hard it
must have been when slavery halved its range and hid its true
foundation ; when rough and brutal ways prevailed unchecked ;
when men had not yet learnt or had untaught themselves to
be reverent towards womanhood ; when distinctions of rank
were thought to go right down to the very depth of all relations
between man and man ; when great people actually imagined
that their servants were of a different nature from themselves
and their friends. Surely if there are characteristics of our day
which may hinder, there are others which should help, our
growth in courtesy. But, in truth, it never can by any one,
at any time of life, be easily sustained. For, in the first place,

it will often ask of us some exercise of self-withdrawal, self-denial; some promptness to take the lower or less pleasant part; some carelessness about our own comfort; some perseverance when we are tired, and perhaps when others are ungracious; some resoluteness not to let ourselves off easily. For courtesy requires the generosity of

> The gentle soul, that no excuse doth make,
> But for its own another's wish doth take,
> So soon as that by any sign is shown.

And secondly, like some other excellences of the Christian character, it both requires and engenders special powers of discernment—a delicate and penetrating insight, analogous to that with which the artist reads the mystery of nature, and seizes and translates its beauty, or to that which men may get by long training in some special craft :—an insight often exercised unconsciously, suggesting and directing acts whose grace and power may be felt but never analyzed. And yet, again, it needs that quiet and constant care concerning little things which seems to be in almost every field of life the only way of high attainment. It has been said, I think, that genius is an infinite capacity for taking pains; and certainly, when courtesy attains its highest beauty, there is seen in it at once the painstaking and the brilliancy of genius.

Patriotism

Those who live on long in such a place as Christ Church see how much a great society can receive even from the career of one man, in the three or four years that he spends here, if the temper of patriotism is clear and strong and constant in him; if he will always care more for the place than for his own pleasure or advantage in it. Let no one doubt that there is much that he can either render or withhold here; much that he may do or leave undone, to guard and develop and augment the heritage that has come down to us. The true temper of unboasting patriotism never can be barren or unfruitful, and its fruitfulness spreads far wider than the society it immediately serves. For, in the first place, the feeling of patriotism (like all other feelings) grows stronger and more settled in us by

being carried into practice ; just as men generally come to care
most for the cause which they have best served. And so it is
through the exercise of patriotism in one society that we are
trained to own and do our duty towards another. Those who
are loyal to their school and college will be loyal to their
country ; they will carry on with them to the demand of later
years and the vast opportunities of service in national life the
same quality of public-spiritedness which they have shown here.
And who can say how a nation needs that quality ? Surely
there could hardly be for any country a graver loss than that
which M. Renan seemed—unless I do him wrong—to anticipate
without humiliation or dismay from the advance of reflection
and of egotism : that individuals should grow more and more
incapable of those sacrifices by which nations live. But
amidst all that is intricate and confused and discouraging
around us, in spite of all that may be thought intractable and
ominous in the relations of class with class, for all the perils of
unsettled minds and truths half seen, there still is hope while
men will go out to their work in life with public spirit ;
resolute that their influence, be it great or small, shall always
be, by God's help, for the common good : not for this interest
or that, not for any personal gaining or guarding, but for the
true welfare of their country, so far as they can see it ; without
impatience, or despondency, or wilfulness, or reckless words.
Surely that is the spirit and the temper England wants in men
of every class ; in order that through the oscillation and
conflict, the action and reaction of opinions, in the wide
diversity of minds, things may still be working out towards
good. It would be no light reward of years well spent in this
place, of a frank and generous recognition of one's duty
towards Christ Church and towards Oxford, that one should
be better able to understand and meet aright the wide and
urgent needs in national life. But patriotism, here and elsewhere, has another promise in reserve. For these calls to
public spirit, these opportunities of serving the society in which
we live, are very high among the chances that God gives us of
escaping from self-love. They may work together with such
forces as the experience of sorrow, the witnessing of great

patience, the example of saintliness, the discovery of what suffering can be, to win us from the wasteful, fretful blunder of a selfish life.

Exactingness

There seems to be an especial need in England at the present day for a great increase in the grace of considerateness ; and we well may fear that grave disasters may be brought on us by the exacting temper, if it be fostered and indulged on either side in the great conflict that is going on. There are some who think that the social troubles of our time go too deep to be adequately dealt with by those indirect and gradual methods which Christianity has generally used in the vast changes it has already helped to bring about. I cannot judge as to that. But I think that, as in the maladies of the individual, so in those of the society, at least as much is wont to depend on atmosphere and light as on medical or surgical treatment ; and sometimes even in very grave cases a better air will take away the necessity for an operation which was declared to be the only conceivable means of relief. Anyhow, here is one reform in which every one of us may bear a part ; a reform which must tell with certain and immediate benefit on the narrow circle round us, no less than on ourselves ; a reform which may, perhaps, in the hidden channels of one life's influence on others, as it parts, and parts again, into innumerable branches, tell more widely than we can imagine. Only let us see to it that our lives are among our fellow-men as springs of considerateness and equity, that no impulse of exactingness ever starts from our abuse of the power or authority we hold ; and then we shall be doing something towards the diffusion of that temper which in all societies of men, civil or ecclesiastical, great or small, keeps difficulties from hardening to be desperate ; we shall be working as they should work who pray, " Give peace in our time, O Lord."

Cowardice

No one should think that sensitiveness to fear debars him from the grace and helpfulness of courage, nor that a sanguine readiness to take things easily is any safeguard against cowardice. For this δειλία, or cowardice, like faith, its great antagonist, is not ultimately evinced in feeling one way or another, but in action. It is evinced whenever a man declines a task which he believes, or even suspects uncomfortably, that he was meant to face ; whenever he looks along the way of faith, and thinks it will ask much of him, and takes the way of comfort and security—the way where he can be sure of continuous company and indisputable common sense. It may appear either in action or in refusing to act, according as the demand of faith is for patient waiting or for prompt advance ; but the central wrong of it is the withholding of the service, the self-sacrifice, a man was born and bred and trained to render ; it is the sin of "the children of Ephraim, who, being harnessed and carrying bows, turned themselves back in the day of battle." We can see sometimes in history or in fiction how a man seems prepared for and led up to the great opportunity of his life : something is asked of him, some effort, some renunciation, some endurance, which is not asked of others. He may say that if he refuses he is not making his own life easier than the lives of thousands round him seem quite naturally and undisturbedly to be ; but he sinks thenceforward far below them if he does refuse. No man has a freehold of his gifts : his tenure and their development depend always and necessarily on his using them dutifully ; and the demand of duty has no measure save opportunity : for there are no eight hours' days in the spiritual life.—" Mancipio nulli datur, omnibus usu," is written on every higher faculty men wield. To see a task, to know it for one's own, and to decline it ; to hear, for instance, the deep sighing of the poor, and plan for one's self a leisurely and unexacting life ;—that is to incur the doom of a dwindling power to help and a fading sense of need. " Woe is me, if I preach not the Gospel," every one of us might say for himself, whatever be the form of that Gospel which in his clearest, highest hours he has had grace to take to heart, and through whatever ways of dutifulness, whatever calling in life, he might make it felt in others' hearts. " He was afraid, and went and hid his lord's money in the earth "—that is the record of a coward's life ;

and how strange it sounds, in its bare plainness and severity, when we compare it with that sort of admiration that is sometimes shown for those who might, it is said, have done all sorts of brilliant things if only they had cared to try. But there is a yet severer warning in the Bible about trifling with the opportunities of life and with the call of God. Doubtless men may, with very different degrees of blame and for very different causes, fail to find or do their work in this world ; and the judgment is with Him Who knows all. But what the wilful refusal of a task may sometimes be in His sight, and how He would have us watch and pray and fight against the assaults of cowardice, He has shown us in this—that " the fearful and the unbelieving," the cowardly and faithless, stand first of all in the dread list of those whose part shall be in the burning lake, which is " the second death."

The Misuse of Words

(Our Lord said) that men are held responsible, and shall be arraigned before the throne of Christ, not only for the vile, the lying, the malignant and uncharitable words that they have spoken, but for " every idle word ; " for every useless, fruitless, worthless, unprofitable saying ; for all words without reality of meaning or purpose ; for all silly talk for talking's sake ; for the speeches that, as one has said, " aim at nothing and hit it ; " for all sheer careless waste of the great trust of language. We shall " give account of" " every idle word ; " and it may almost seem as though life, social life, hardly could go on if the thought were laid to heart, if men steadily remembered it. As we try to think of our own lives ; of the way we have talked in the past ; of the things we knew we had better not say, and yet said ; of the casual, heedless way in which we have gossiped with our friends ; of yesterday's talk, it may be, or even this morning's ; of our ordinary habits in conversation ;—as we go on to think of others ; of the laxity, the unscrupulousness, the injustice, which is shocking even to our taste ; of the torrent of talk that is always flowing on in society, in a London Season or an Oxford Term ; of the groups of people that we

O

see hanging about the corners of streets, or at the doors of the houses down some wretched alley, or by the public-house ;—as we try to imagine anything of the idle or worse than idle words that are ceaselessly streaming from men's lips, it utterly passes our power of thought to bring to bear on all this worthless talk what our Lord says of it.   For He—He, remember, Who is to be our Judge—warns us plainly that it is all telling, all leaving a mark ; that somewhere, in some way, the record of it is written and is mounting up ; that it makes traces in men's characters, and is reckoned in the total outcome of their lives ; that they will have to face it all again, and give account of it. As the record of forces that seemed merely transient—of the passage of a glacier, of the waves upon the beach, or even of the drops of rain—may sometimes be found fixed upon the surface which they rudely scarred or lightly, quietly dinted ; so men's idle sayings do not utterly and merely pass into the air : they tell somewhere, they are printed somewhere ; things are not quite as they would have been had the foolish words been left unsaid.   The separate stones in the great pillars of this Cathedral may seem to most of us to be plain, featureless, indifferent ; but on each one of them, which time has not defaced, the antiquary reads the distinctive traces of the tool with which the workman dressed its surface.   The surface is not smooth, and the roughness is not casual ; there is history in the lines, the scratches that we have not noticed.   And so surely must it be with the characters of men, scarred and dinted by their thoughts and words and deeds ; only the marks on them are finer and deeper and more subtle, and time has no power to efface them ; and perhaps men never think how thickly they are being multiplied, and how clear and aweful is the history they will disclose.

. . . The purity, the justice, the precision, the discrimination, the right use of words, is in our work what the like qualities in regard to colours or sounds are to the painter or the musician. Not only in the work of teaching, but in all the higher relations of life, in conference, in counsel, in ruling or judging, in praising or finding fault, in encouraging or dissuading, in asking or in giving advice, the value of our part in life depends, far more perhaps than we are apt to think, upon the use that we have been wont to make, the use that we desire to make, of words. A man or woman with a blurred sense of accuracy, a habit of exaggeration, or of letting prejudice get mixed with judgment, is as much hindered in the service of others, in the advancement of the common welfare, as an artist who has lost the sense of what pure colour means. Surely it is only at first sight that the idle, careless, unscrupulous use of the great gift of speech can seem to us a trifling fault. Think of the injustice, the pain, the anxiety, the anger, that spring up round reckless talk. Think of the confusion and uncertainty that comes by inaccurate repetition of inaccurate reports ; think of the loosening of mutual trust, the loss of real interest, the rarity of thorough sympathy, because one has to doubt the justice, the trustworthiness, of so much current talk ; think of the lowering of the standard of truth. Or think, again, how idle words not only disclose the inner character, but react upon it ; making dull the sense of truth, chilling the chivalry of allegiance to it ; confusing distinctions, blurring outlines ; wasting the strength that should find joy in the sincere and arduous and patient quest of the exact truth. Nor is it a little thing that our own idle words so often haunt and vex us ; that we find it hard to leave off fretting at the folly of our own talk—wishing things unsaid, wondering what harm will come of them. And then, over against this picture of encroaching weakness and slovenliness, let us set the greatness that accrues to those who resolutely keep themselves from idle words ; in whose care the gift of speech comes near to being the power and the light it should be. An old Rabbinical fable tells of one who, when he had died and had been for a long while in his grave, was dug up, and found to be living and untouched by any corruption. And being asked what had thus protected him, he answered, " All through my life I never listened to an idle word." The legend holds a truth. It marks the impenetrable purity, the health and soundness of the souls that stand aloof, distinct from petty, worthless talk. They are rare indeed, such souls ; but most of us, I trust, may have known some to whom, perhaps, we did not dare to tell the idle words that we had heard and

helped into currency with others ; some who have had the
courage to be silent when they had nothing real or nothing
kind to say ; some who have guarded speech for its true use
in giving help or gladness to their fellow-men, and glory to
Almighty God.

CHRIST CHURCH. THE CATHEDRAL.

CHAPTER VIII

THE Oxford Diocese extends over Oxfordshire, Berkshire, and Buckinghamshire. The Census returns for 1901 give the total population of these three counties as 633,393. The Diocese covers 2220 square miles, and contains 31 deaneries and 650 benefices. Until 1836, it extended over Oxfordshire only. In 1836, in Bishop Bagot's time, Berkshire was added to the Diocese: and the Bishop of Oxford is therefore Chancellor of the Order of the Garter, because of the Royal Foundation at Windsor.[1] In 1846, in Bishop Wilberforce's time, Buckinghamshire was added to the Diocese.[2]

The village of Cuddesdon is two miles from Wheatley and seven from Oxford. Between the Palace and the Theological College there is but the width of the road : and the friendship between the Bishop and the College was even closer than that. The Palace is a pleasant old house built in the time

[1] The Bishop of Winchester is Prelate of the Order of the Garter, the Bishop of Oxford is Chancellor, and the Dean of Windsor is Registrar. It is the office of the Chancellor to keep the Seals of the Order, and to seal and countersign statutes, warrants, and dispensations. He also takes part in the Investitures.

[2] See a paper by Canon Clayton, on " The Division of the Diocese," read in 1905 before the Ruri-decanal Chapter at Oxford, and published in the Diocesan Magazine, 1906. Buckingham was formally constituted part of the Diocese some years before 1846, but was not "taken over" till that year.

of Bishop Fell (1675–1686), and added to in the time of Bishop Wilberforce.

The only purpose of this chapter is to collect and arrange, in order of time, some events, memories, and letters, which did not come into the plan of Part II of this book. It may best begin with an account of the Bishop's ordinations, written by his brother the Bishop of Stepney :—

Cuddesdon may well claim an honourable share in the process by which Embertide and Ordination have acquired the solemn and inspiring associations which they ought to have. The annexe by which the picturesque front of the house has been masked bears witness to Bishop Wilberforce's desire to house his candidates for the days preceding their ordination. His volume of " Addresses " is still read, and its severity and penetration, its assertion of high standard and self-surrender, are a protest against levity or self-deception at a critical time. His College on the other side of the road is a monument of his great desire that the less immediate preparation should be as complete as it can be made. " Lay hands suddenly on no man " must have been a ruling principle in his idea of a Bishop's responsibilities at a time when perhaps that special danger was less widely felt than it is now.

Bishop Wilberforce's tradition was fully sustained by his successors, and thus Dr. Paget found when he went to Cuddesdon a place where his own high and clear sense of what an ordination ought to be found a natural and congenial home.

His own past life had done much to fit him for the work of Embertide. As tutor, professor, and

Dean of Christ Church he had come to know undergraduates as few men know them. His own ordination had meant more to him than words can say.
His first confession, his letters tell us, had brought
him an almost rapturous sense of freedom and release.
A short spell of parish work at Bromsgrove under the
happiest conditions had strengthened conviction by
a bit of vivid experience. He had welcomed Bishop
Woodford's invitation to become an examining chaplain,
on the ground that contact with men at the time of
their ordination would remind him again and again
of the wonder and the joy of his own. The readers
of this memoir will very likely have asked themselves
whether, after all, the pastoral instinct, the temper of
the parish priest, was not the inmost of his inmost
heart.

> Decano meo dilectissimo
> Francisco Paget
> Theologiæ pastoralis olim Professori
> Animi pastoralis nunquam non exemplari,

that is how Dr. Bright dedicates a volume of sermons
to him ; and those who were present at the luncheon
after his enthronement in the Cathedral will remember
a speech of Dr. Ince's in which he took pains to assure
the company that their new Bishop could turn a Latin
sentence or tackle a Greek inscription, and hazarded
a fear lest they should regard him as merely a parish
clergyman.

The party that assembles at the Bishop's residence
before an ordination is quite unlike anything else.
There rests on the Bishop the responsibility of a
dominance as to which there can be no mistake. He
is master of the house, and these shy young men are
his guests ; he is Father-in-God, and this is probably

the time of their closest association with him ; for they will see more of him now than most of them will ever see again. At his hands they will receive the grace of their ordination, and something like awe of him is probably at the heart of the more sensitive amongst them. Some perhaps have had or will have an interview with the Bishop which leaves its mark on the rest of their lives.

The tone of a Cuddesdon ordination was perhaps on the whole a severe one. The Palace never lapsed into the easy-going disorder of a country-house. Clearly you must be on your manners. The Bishop's rather elaborate courtesy, his dislike of exaggeration and over-certainty, made men careful what they said ; the burden of solitude, of sorrow, of unshared responsibility was upon him ; and Embertide found him, as ever, struggling with an amount of work so great that he could never satisfy the demands of his own high standard in the doing of it. Σεμνότης, a quality that ranked high in his estimation, was present in all he said and did.

Here as elsewhere he gave himself, body, soul, and spirit, to the work, but he did not give himself away. He was restrained, guarded, on the watch. Books were read at some of the meals ; at others he talked and naturally enough led the talk and kept it in hand. Certainly meals were neither silent nor dull ; but talk was disciplined, and he left untold the wealth of anecdote and experience with which at any other time he would have loved to make men laugh. He came, at such times, from prayer to social intercourse, and went back from social intercourse to prayer again : and the quiet of the place was the quiet in which men are apt to hear the Voice of God.

It was characteristic of him that he made a special solemnity of the taking of the Oaths. He gave on one occasion at least a special address on this subject. The oaths were administered with order and gravity ; and before they were taken he spoke gravely of their importance and meaning.

He did not attempt to define exactly the scope of their obligation ; he dwelt rather on the temper and spirit they seemed to require. He was influenced, no doubt, by the conviction which had grown stronger as years went on ; the conviction that Law in its widest and most solemn sense had become less cogent than it ought to be, and that the weakening of its authority was a serious and ill-boding thing.

Proofs are not wanting to show that he felt as keenly as any one the unsatisfactory character of Ecclesiastical jurisdiction as it stands. He was ready to make allowance for all that : but he did not want men to feel comfortable either in insubordination or in obedience to any self-chosen authority. He would not allow them to believe that solemn words of much loyalty and submission meant little. " Loyalty " was often on his lips, and those who knew him will remember the tone in which the word was uttered.

If in any sense law was in abeyance ; if, for example, the injunction of a single Bishop, or of a number of Bishops, could be shown to be a less binding thing than some form of synodical action ; if the present Courts leave much to be desired, it was a serious thing. It meant danger, not safety. If there were no judge in Israel, it by no means followed that men were to do what was right in their own eyes. He was as restless in the absence of authority as some men are restless under its discipline. A world in which authority was ineffective was to him a dangerous and difficult world. To press forward, as by forced marches, simply because authority expressed itself in a form that might be criticised, was to his mind about as wise as to hurry because it happened to be dark. Any young man sufficiently ill-advised to believe that canonical obedience meant a curious obligation payable only under very special conditions, or that loyalty to the Throne was only a picturesque phrase for covert Erastianism, may well have wondered that his Bishop made so much of the taking of the oaths.

At the ordination itself he did not wear the mitre, he was content with the cope ; and as he came out of his oratory to take his place at the end of the long procession, with the marks of a week of much prayer and spiritual effort clear upon him, with the intense seriousness of his approach to the altar, with the simplicity and sympathy of one who, after all, was at heart a parish priest, men must have felt thankful to have been with him for their Embertide devotions, thankful to be beginning their ministry under such a shepherd of the sheep.

One point in the service was specially characteristic of him. He left the preaching of the sermon to the priest who had given the little addresses on the previous days : but he gave a short address at the ordination, in which he was content to sum up and press home some of the lessons the other had tried to teach.

It was characteristic of him in the idea and in the way in which it was carried out. For very strong in him was the habit of making the best, of thinking generously of the work of other men. He was always ready to value anything that was simple and apparently sincere.

But often the preacher must have been surprised at the form which his words, incoherent and ill-chosen, took when the Bishop, in his humility, began to use them. Love made so much of them : Love made them go so far, that it seemed hardly irreverent to recall that blessing of the loaves and fishes when the utterly inadequate became enough and to spare, " He took them in his hands and blessed and brake."

It was only a detail in the great service ; but it was just like him. For he constantly and as of habit esteemed other better than himself. It was the rule of his life (and it often stood him in good stead) to believe that others intended to say what was right ; and it is pleasant to think that the same critical faculty and command of language which were noticeable elsewhere were gladly and lovingly used to make the best of what another had meant to say.

Mr. S. M. Cooke, one of his examining chaplains during 1906–1911, writes :—

It was the Bishop's custom to have his Christmas ordination at the Cathedral, the Trinity ordination in the church at Cuddesdon, and the September ordination at some parish church in the Diocese. The ordinands were summoned for their retreat three days before the ordination, and he also liked all his examining chaplains to assist him throughout the Embertide.

Though he frequently secured the services of some master in the spiritual life to deliver the addresses to the candidates, he not infrequently took them himself and preached the sermon on the day of the ordination. After attending the funeral of King Edward, he came back to Cuddesdon in the evening, and drew out with wonderful force the lessons which such an occasion impressed upon his own keen docile spirit.

Although the whole mass of diocesan business was being

discharged at the same time, the ordinands knew nothing of this : to them it would appear that he had nothing to do but to devote himself to them, and to lay all his rich experience at their feet. They knew nothing of the immense correspondence which he had got through late at night and during the early hours of the morning : he would be up very early, and, looking quite fresh, would celebrate each day, and during breakfast he would himself relieve his chaplains by reading some portion of the book which was being read at meals, and sometimes he would comment upon its contents. At various appointed hours he would interview all the candidates in turn, and in the afternoon he would take one of them for a walk, or perhaps he would go with one of his chaplains and discuss points of importance relating to the candidates. If some one else was giving the addresses in Chapel, he would always take notes of the addresses. He would, afterwards, spend a considerable time in silent prayer, and go back to his study ready to continue the interviews. After the last service at night he would gather his chaplains round him and discuss the merits of the candidates.

After the ordination, he was still the great, loving force in the midst of us all, more than a head and shoulders above any one of us in ability, in humility, in spirituality, in the power of concentration, in sympathy, in geniality, in simplicity, in tact and foresight. He always desired the ordinands to stay over the day of the ordination, deprecating the immediate return to their spheres of work of those ordained priest. His whole heart was in this as in all his other work, and those who had the privilege of receiving ordination at his hands could never forget all he was to them individually.

A letter has been kept which the Bishop wrote, on Sept. 11, 1905, to one of the candidates for ordination :—

I am very sorry to have to say that your paper on Doctrine is, in my judgment, marred by a serious inequality. The second answer is good : and clearly you have read with interest, and noted and remembered phrases well worth remembering.

But there are some very poor parts in the paper :—a good deal is omitted :—there are careless mistakes in historical treatment : and sometimes you write on great things as though you had not thought out the meaning of the words you use—as though you were writing from a glimpse rather than from a view.

I have, with the examining Chaplains, doubted whether the paper can be regarded as satisfactory : and I have decided that it will be right for you to be examined again before Advent, on the 2nd, 9th, 20th, & 28th Articles. I hope that the result of this further examination will enable me to ordain you in December.

The owner of this letter writes, on Dec. 19, 1911:—

I am sending you the only letter I had from the late Bishop of Oxford, in case you think it worth printing. I have treasured it & read it many times, but I value still more a conversation which I had with him the night before my Ordination, when he said to me, " Promise me you will never write anything without knowing what you yourself mean." I said " I will try." I thanked him for those words a year later, when I was ordained priest, but he appeared to have quite forgotten the incident. I have been grateful ever since for his admonition.

1902

By the kindness of the present Dean of Christ Church, rooms in the Deanery were set apart for his use ; and were always a great help and happiness to him.[1]

On Jan. 11 and 12, he gave four addresses at Haileybury, to a meeting of schoolmasters, college tutors, and lecturers. These addresses were published under the title *Christ the Way*. (Longmans, 1902.) In one of them, he brings together, over the Holy Communion, Thomas à Kempis, Hooker, Dr. Johnson,

---

[1] " The Perch " was his name for them. Members of Loder's Club may recall an evening when he dined with them, and after dinner knocked in at Canterbury Gate with them, as if he were an undergraduate again.

and General Gordon.   In another, he brings together
four witnesses to the complexity of life, the " mystery,
and trouble, and hard questioning, and high purpose
scarcely held through storms of difficulty and distress " :—

I will say little of experience ; for each has his own store
of that, about which another's words may seem exaggerated,
inexact, and, perhaps, provoking.   But think how human life
has seemed to those who, in the great ways of art, have tried
to tell us what they saw in it.   With all the risk involved in
talking of what I do not understand, I will point to three
instances.   We may form diverse estimates of Browning's
work : we may be sometimes baffled by " Paracelsus," and
inclined to despair of " Sordello " ; but does not much of the
difficulty come of this—that he is trying to lead us through
the tangled forest of an inner life, haunted by strange forms
of temptation, lit by wandering lights, amidst broken paths
and clues ; that he is bold enough to hint at significant fragments of experience and character and purpose, of which his
piercing insight makes him sure, though even he may see
them but by glimpses ?   Or think of music, such as that of
Beethoven or of Brahms.   Its theme is human life, and passion,
and resolve, and suffering.   To many it speaks with a wealth
and subtlety of eloquence beyond the reach of words ; and
even those who do not understand it feel that there are great
thoughts surging through it.   And what a vast and stormy
world it is out of which those thoughts rise up !   Or as one
stands before one of Rembrandt's portraits of old age ; as one
looks and looks at the face, harassed, furrowed, worn with all
the cares, the failures, the ambitions, the disappointments, the
decisions, the renunciations, the humiliation and endurance
and discipline of an inscrutable past ; as one guesses at what
had been unlearnt and learnt, lost and won, in the battle of
life,—one may suspect that all the difficulties we have felt, and
far more too, were met and somehow lived through long ago,
and that there are deeper and more subtle tasks for a heart to
deal with than we have yet, perhaps, surmised.

To Stephen Paget, 1902

Jan. 2.—When are you coming to see me? It would be a real touch of holiday for me. And I want to show you this place, and the children, and lots of things : and I want you to know my Chaplain. *March* 5.—I love to think of you and of your work. For me, with gleams now and then of undeserved happiness, I just stumble on from day to day, behindhand with all work, finding hardly any time to read or think,—or to write to those I love : only trusting that out of the hurry some scraps of help for some one somehow may be brought. *March* 17. . . . I am very hard driven : somewhat harder than I could wish : but it can't be helped.— The Bp. of Reading is ill : & I must do all I can :—but I should like a little more time to think. *March* 31.—You will be here for the first Sunday that I have spent at home for three months : and indeed there could be no better gladdening of it.—The place is abounding with primroses & violets :—& Beatrice & Frida are in high expectancy. *April* 18.—It is an absurd trouble :—a buzzing in my ears, for the past week, more or less :—I cannot connect it, as Browning did, with a " Reverend Gentleman " : so I suppose it must be something inside. *April* 20.—The buzzing has quite ceased : and I could hear a pin drop on a feather-bed with all the children talking. *Aug.* 23.—You told me not to write ; which is just like you : and I meant to and didn't ; which is just like me. . . . The loneliness of my life grows rather terrible sometimes ; —the multitude of official relations with people, the very seeing so many fresh people, the responsibilities, the decisions to be made, the rows and questions and anxieties, all make one realize it more. And it is well, I think, that one should : for so it may teach one more of what one has to learn : and that is a long lesson.

Between May 29 and June 19, he held his first Visitation of the Diocese. In June, the Diocesan Society of Mission Clergy was instituted, with Mr. Arthur Phillimore as Warden. The Diocesan

Magazine was first published in this year ; and, in
the June number, he refers to a meeting at Reading,
on May 7, at which " nearly eighty of the Clergy met
to join in thought and prayer about our common work,"
and to a meeting at Cuddesdon, on May 9, at which
" the Archdeacons and all the Rural Deans were so
good as to come and take counsel with me " : and
he asks to be remembered in prayer on the anniversary
of his consecration. In the July number, he writes of
the postponement of the Coronation :—

A vast change it is :—yet through it all the call goes
sounding for the same grace, the same strength of faith. One
had come to see, as one looked into the Service for the
Coronation, how the fulness of faith alone could sustain the
meaning, the claim, the awefulness of the Act : how solemn and
unreserved was the profession of faith involved for a Nation
whose King was to be so crowned. And now this great
demand on faith has come ; the same demand, only in another
way, in altered tones.

This year, he and the Bishop of Stepney had a
holiday together, at the Tosa Falls, the place he most
loved in all Italy. He writes to Campbell Crum, his
chaplain, on July 22, from Formazza, Ossola, telling
him of a walk

. . . down the valley for about three hours,—with early
Italian backgrounds all the way, and the mountains towering
up about them, and the hay just being cut or made, & the
grasshoppers chirping their hearts out,—to the Lago Antillone,
a wonderful little lake, hidden among great cliffs, and bright
with water-lilies :—and then on by a track high up on the
wooded hill-side to a tiny village, S. Antonio, which I
thought looked hopeful on the map :—and most beautiful it
was.—Ever so far away from everything, with its fresh little
mountain-stream, and the children all running about, brown
and " bare-fut " and curious and engaging, and a peasant with

the most perfect manners refusing, almost compassionately, the tip I offered him for fetching the key of the relentlessly bedizened little Church.   Then we scrambled down here, where we sleep to-night, in order to go to-morrow to Crego,— one of the most wonderful Churches I know, for its history & position,—& to Baceno, & then back up the valley to the Falls.—I wish you were here :—yes, almost even though it meant that the 28 letters all came out.—You would love the people & their friendliness : a dear old thing came running down the outside staircase of a "Swiss Cottage" in one village we passed through to-day, full of welcome because three years ago I had been there when her boy came back with a prize from the School at Domo d' Ossola,— and because I had remembered it last year.   I shudder to think of the grammar one talks under these conditions :— Richard's Latin Prose would be Ciceronian beside it.

At the Coronation of King Edward VII, August 9, the Bishop of Oxford and the Bishop of Norwich, as the diocesans of Windsor and of Sandringham, were in attendance on Queen Alexandra.   The Litany was sung by the Bishop of Oxford and the Bishop of Bath and Wells, before the arrival of the King, so that the service might be shortened, to save his strength after his illness.   Mr. J. E. C. Bodley, in his History of the Coronation, points out that, as the Bishop of Oxford had not yet succeeded to a seat in the House of Lords, "for the first time in the history of the First Estate it happened that a bishop not being a lord of parliament took a ceremonial part in a coronation."

On Aug. 16, he unveiled the memorial in Cathedral to the officers and men of the 40th Company of the Imperial Yeomanry who died in the War.   In his address, he said :—

We shall pass away, and others will be in our place, and so all the details of these men's lives will be forgotten : but one

P

thing always will stand out, always will be told, generation after generation, concerning them—they died in the service of their King and country. It is, you know, with the memories of men as it is with the villages with which perhaps many of us are familiar, in which we have our homes. When we are there we see every detail, we mark the corner of every cottage, we know what we shall see clustering over its doors as the spring and summer come on : and even from some little way off we know, as we look back to it, all about it ; we can see every little point of the scene. But if we go miles off, far, far away, and look at it, perhaps, from some hill on the horizon, we see little except just a speck, perhaps just a point in the landscape afar off. But if there is any special mark about it, the big house above the village, or the church tower, perhaps, or the cross or the mark cut in the turf on the hill, we see that, we never miss that, we can look out for that, however far off it may be. And so it is with men's lives and the memories of them. All the details are lost as time goes on and the distance increases, and perhaps they are hardly remembered except just by a few : only, if there has been anything marked, unlike anything else, rising high above the level plains of life in them, then it is remembered. And so it is with these twelve of whom we think to-day. When all else is forgotten about them, when all is forgotten about us, this will be remembered —they died in the service of their King and country.

To one of his Clergy

November 10.—I return herewith the form of service, in which I have made some alterations—some of them merely for the sake of form or clearness. The most important relates to the prayer for the Departed. I can well understand the wish your letter shews ; but I feel that the Church of England, for grounds easy to understand, has used a great reticence & reserve in this matter : & I do not think that a Bishop can rightly sanction for public use the breaking of this reserve. So I have felt bound to alter what you have sent me, before giving to it the sanction which, in its altered form, I gladly give.[1]

---

[1] Prayer enclosed. " O Father, remember mercifully Thy servants who have

On December 7, he preached the University sermon in Cambridge : he writes to one of his children of the beauty of King's College Chapel—" and the whole is lit with hundreds of little tapers : so that there is a dim, soft, unearthly sort of light that goes creeping about the far-off lines of the roof, and meeting the music as it too rises up there :—for it is a most perfect building for sound, & they have one of the most faultless choirs in England " : and the letter goes on :—

I had a new experience on Thursday. For I had some business at the House of Lords : & so I went in to listen to the debate for a while. Of course, I'm not in the House :— but I have a right to go and sit on the steps of the dais on which the throne stands :—it's so funny ; for it seems so casual to go & sit down with one's legs stretched out, or one's knees up to one's chin. And then other people, who have the same right, come & sit there :—Lord Helmsley, & Sir Fleetwood Edwards & Mr. Balfour were among them on Thursday.—I think I should often go, if I were in London & had time.

On Christmas Eve, he writes to Mr. Wethered, of Marlow, on the burning of his motor :—

It is most pathetic :—I think of that beautiful, high-spirited, persevering, delightful thing,—now dashing at the bridge on the way to church, now tearing through the night & glorifying the hedge-rows, now making one forget the existence of a Diocesan Conference, now panting gaily up the hill beyond Marlow ;—and it is heart-rending to think of it in the blaze.— I am truly sorry :—it must have been a great vexation for you, needing all your philosophy. But we shall meet on the 7th, and join our lamentations. And then we must try to plan for your visit here :—if only to give my coachman the unedifying triumph of driving you : I've a great mind to hire a motor

departed hence in the Lord, especially Thy servants whom we remember this day. And grant to us such measure of communion with them as Thou knowest to be best for us, through Jesus Christ our Lord."

from Oxford just for that day, to show him that we are not to be scored off. All best wishes for Christmas and for the New Year, to you and to the babes. I've ordered two of those musical picture-books from Nuremberg already.

1903

To Stephen Paget

Windsor Castle, Jan. 26.—I must write a word or two, before I leave this wonderful place, first to thank you, and then to tell you how delightful and touching it has been to realize afresh what my father's name means here. Of course, I well and surely knew that he had won trust & gratitude & friendship here :—but there is an access of happiness in hearing again & again how he is spoken of. It has been a great privilege to be here, and a wonderful experience of kindness. I preached yesterday, and spent the afternoon among the wonders of the pictures & the library—such Vandykes, & Holbeins, & drawings, & miniatures ! This morning, if all be well, I am to christen the child of the Prince & Princess of Wales.

On March 5, writing in the train to him, he refers to the offer of the see of Winchester :—

Yes, my experience in regard to Winchester has somehow come to be " an open secret." But it has been by no fault of mine : and I am in no way ashamed of my decision : so I do not much mind. I "lay" at Stowe the night before last : a most wonderful place—the biggest, I think, that I have ever seen :—marking, I shd. think, the very highest tide of 18th century magnificence.

To one of his Clergy

Verona, June 22.—Let me thank you sincerely for your letter, and for the trust which you are so good as to show me.

Provided that your father and mother do not withhold their consent to your becoming a Probationer in the Community of the Resurrection, I shall willingly assent to it.—But it seems to me a course which I could scarcely *advise* you to take : partly because it must depend, to so large an extent, on feelings and convictions which only you can accurately weigh : partly because I think that, though you and I have known one another fairly well, I scarcely have the thorough and matured knowledge which one ought to have in order to advise such a course.

I venture to add what will, I am sure, go with your own sense of right :—that in such a matter the greatest deference is due to the wishes of a father and mother :—especially when they enter with sympathy into the meaning and tenor of one's ordained life.—If they now oppose, it well may be that later they will approve : and that the delay they ask may be for the deepening and strengthening of the sense of vocation.

May God guide you, now & at all times, to the knowledge of His Will.

To Bernard Paget

July 20.—I have thought a good deal about the Army Class. I think that before you join it you ought to think over as carefully as you can your purpose of being a soldier. I am perfectly willing that you should hold by that purpose, and, if I live, I will do my best to help you to carry it out. But I want you to be as sure as you can that it really is what you want and intend. If you go into the Army you will have to go with very little money to back you up : and that means that you will have to work hard and long to make your way, and probably to take some of the work which richer men may evade :— possibly rather grim, tedious sort of work, in unattractive places.—Still, if you work hard, and get respected and trusted, and are keen, you may come to be very glad indeed that you joined :—& I shall be very glad too. Only, I don't want you to think that the way into the Army will cost any less grind now than the way into any other profession, or that when you get there it will be any easier or less exacting than any other profession. It may look so sometimes, especially for men with money or influence to help them : but it can never be so for men who have to enter it as you will.

Don't think that I want to discourage you from it :—I don't at all.—I want you to count the cost :—& then, if you really, deliberately choose it, I am quite willing that you should give up the thought of anything else, & join the Army Class.

Nov. 4.—Just a word of congratulation on the success in the runs : I was heartily glad of it :—and I wish you all rightful enjoyment of it. I know you won't think too much about it : because it is not good to think too much about any success, in any way of life. One wants to keep one's head, and to look straight forward, and try to do one's best at the next job, without dwelling on the last :—whether it be in runs, or books. I have been here to-day, for the dentist, and a Meeting : but it has been such a beautiful day, and London has looked so cheery and astir, that it has been quite refreshing.

On Nov. 21, in a letter to Miss Lawrence, he says : "It will be just three years to-morrow since Helen passed away. The years the other side of that day seem to me as if they belonged to another life."

To one of his Clergy

Dec. 27, 1903.—If the parishioner of whom you write has already been admitted to Holy Communion, I think that you may rightly communicate him now. If he has not been so admitted, I think it would be right to ask him whether he is willing, in the event of his life being prolonged, to be confirmed privately by the Bishop of Reading or by me, when next either of us is in Banbury : and if he is so willing, you may rightly communicate him now.—If he is not so willing, I should, in view of the clear words of the Rubric, hesitate about communicating him, unless it is clear that his illness brings him into the peril of death :—if that were clear I should yield to his wish & communicate him.

March 18, 1904.—Thank you very much for a very kind and interesting letter, and for allowing me to see the touching letter which I return.—So far as I can judge, I think it would be quite right for the writer to seek confirmation, and I would

gladly confirm her.   I think we all need often to remind ourselves that the Love of God reaches us and draws us to Him
not because we are what we are, but because He is what He is.
A true sorrow for our unworthiness, & a simple desire to seek
& serve Him,—these by His Grace we may bring to Him : &
these He will not despise :—nay, will surely for Christ's sake
accept & bless.   I will gladly look forward to confirming the
two candidates side by side.

1904

To Stephen Paget

G.W.R., March 31.—I fear I must forego Rome.   The
reasons are several, none of them decisive, but all of some
force.—I ought not to spend the money : for I have been
forced to spend very much lately ; & I shd., for the present
at all events, have to take it out of capital.—I am very, very
tired ; and I shd. rather dread the long journey.—I must get
time to *think* : I am always preaching, talking, writing letters,
& giving out when I seem to have little to give : & it seems
presumptuous to go on like that : I really need to read & think,
even more than to be delighted & refreshed.—And, my freedom
is shortened : I shd. probably have to be back by the 23rd.
These all count for something : and, with long thinking, I
have come to feel that I ought to stay in England.

To Bernard Paget

Good Friday.   The Deanery, Windsor. — I came here last
night, immediately after the last of the Confirmations : and
I gave the addresses at the Three Hours' Service in St. George's
Chapel to-day.   It was a wonderful sight, and the whole
service was beautifully ordered.   I am very, very sorry for
all the sadness that has beset this Term at Shrewsbury.   I can
quite enter, I think, into the sort of feeling, as though
there were always a cloud, always a heaviness in the air.   And
I remember very well the shock that came to us all, the sense
of strangeness, when a boy died ;—it was soon after I started
at School, and it is very vivid to me still.—I think it rather
drew us all together, boys and masters too.

In April, 1904, the Royal Commission on Ecclesiastical Discipline was appointed — " To inquire into the alleged prevalence of breaches or neglect of the law relating to the conduct of Divine Service in the Church of England, and to the ornaments and fittings of churches, and to consider the existing powers and procedure applicable to such irregularities, and to make such recommendations as may be deemed requisite for dealing with the aforesaid matters." The Commissioners were Lord St. Aldwyn (Chairman), the Archbishop of Canterbury, the Marquis of Northampton, the Bishop of Oxford, Sir Francis Jeune, Mr. J. G. Talbot, Sir John Kennaway, Sir Samuel Hoare, Sir Edward Clarke, Sir Lewis Dibdin, Dr. Gibson, Dr. Drury, Prof. Prothero, and Mr. George Harwood. In his letter in the May number of the Diocesan Magazine, he asks for the prayers of the Diocese for the work of the Commission ; and he goes on to say :—

> I foresee that the labour of the Commission is likely to call me away sometimes from work that I want to do and would fain try to do, in the Diocese. I have found in these three years quite as much to do as I had time and strength for : I know, with a heavy heart, that much of it has been left undone, much very poorly done : and I cannot be grateful enough for the generosity and forbearance which have been shown me in regard to it. Now I may have to ask yet more forbearance.

"I am taking a fresh measure of my father's greatness," he writes, on June 30, "as I learn how hard the work of a Royal Commission may be, and think how he bore it."

On August 2, the news was made public, that the decision of the Judicial Committee of the Privy Council had deprived the United Free Church of Scotland of all endowments, nearly £2,000,000, held in trust ; and he wrote at once to the Rev. Charles Watson, D.D., of Northfield, Largs, one of the early members of the Free Church :—

> My DEAR SIR—I hope I may rightly venture to send a few words to tell you how deeply I feel for you in the manifold distress, which this day's news, I know, must cause you, and in the anxiety which it brings about the work to which you have been giving your life.—No words of reassurance and hope that I could write could come near the thoughts which will rise out of your own experience : for there is, I think, no clearer lesson in all the teaching of experience than the certainty that truth simply trusted never fails.
>
> May God uphold and guide and gladden those who have to bear the stress of this grave trouble and sorrow.
>
> Let me be, dear sir, with true respect,—Sincerely yours,
>
>   F. OXON.

Dr. Watson wrote back, thanking him for his letter :—

> . . . Indeed we need much the support of such Christian sympathy. The blow we have received is very heavy, but it is from the Hand of God, and it will not, I am sure, prove destructive. Good must come out of it, good to ourselves in Scotland, but good, I am persuaded, having a far wider range.

On October 13, he gave a short address at the Medical College of the West London Hospital, the chief centre in London of "post-graduate" teaching. This address, to men who had "passed beyond the frigid zone, the gloomy and inhospitable realm of compulsory examinations, into the more humane territory of practical life and duty," is full of happy phrases. "You and I alike have travelled on where men can no longer set us papers, or test *vivâ voce* our skill in the concealing of ignorance." And again :—

Unless our minds are touched with that curious form of disease which is known as self-satisfaction, unless our hearts are seriously unsound, we must have felt, very distinctly and effectively, something of the misery of our own ignorance.

And again :—

We learn and take to heart the need of knowledge as we find how our own self-respect depends upon it : how terrible is the temptation, and how swift and sure the punishment, ot pretending to know ; of being where ignorance is ridiculous and trying somehow to get through as though we knew. I think, but am not sure, that it was Fuller who said, " He is an honest man who when people think he has read two books, says, ' I have read but one.' " It is an honesty so self-rewarding, so certainly the best policy, so plainly making for peace, that one would be surprised to find it rare, if one had not sometimes found it difficult.

And, at the end of the address, he describes the excellence of them who go on learning more and more, who never cease from study, even in old age :—

It is an excellence which was felt and noted long ago. The Greek, indeed, with his quick sense of incongruity, could make fun of the ὀψιμαθής, the "Late-Learner," the pursuer (as Theophrastus defines him) of exercises for which he was too old ; the man who at sixty years of age would study passages for recitation, and break down in repeating them over his wine ; the more than middle-aged man who would practise dancing-steps, whistling his own accompaniment : the prototype of M. Jourdain in Molière, and of Mr. Briggs in *Punch*. But the fault of the ὀψιμαθής was that he had lived long and learnt nothing, not even learnt what learning means ; and so he took up this or that pursuit without any sense that one was really different from another, without any standard of doing well anywhere ; thinking that the neglect of all he should have done in youth could be remedied by the neglect of all he should have been in age. It is a curious character ; it seems to have been a vivid terror to the ancient world ; happily we see little of it now, save for a few traits of vanity in the very foolish, a few specimens of it to be found in clubs and perhaps on golf-links; it has nothing but its name to connect it with the late-learning of which I would speak. That, too, the Greek saw and understood; and into the mouth of the wisest of his wise men he put words which very simply tell of it:

γηράσκω δ' αἰεὶ πολλὰ διδασκόμενος,

" I'm growing old, and always learning much."

It is one of the great secrets of happiness in the later stages of life; but like all the finer traits of character it is seldom to be found in its full excellence save as a continuous and growing note of a life consistent through all its stages. It is the man who has tried, at all events, to be a student all along, who can keep his intellectual interest and freshness, even through great bodily weakness, so long as the power of his will lasts. . . . Your great art can do little for us then. It is in those months and years, and probably also in the years that have gone by just before them, with decreasing occupation and increasing weariness, that the real provision for old age is wanted; and the ingrained habit of study,—the insuperable love of reading, watching, thinking,—is one of the best things that a man can then have. I have seen it so, in more than one instance. I have seen the calmness, the self-possession, the gratitude that may go on unshaken through the long trial of patience, when, with a heart true to the loyalty of a lifetime, there is also a mind that has never ceased from wishing to learn. And I shall always think of that as no small part of the true student's glory, though the best of it, I believe, is yet to come, when at length he has to do with the very Truth, the Light of all we learn in any field of study.

To Bernard Paget

Oct. 9. The Deanery, Windsor. . . . I have had a very busy week, with the Diocesan Conference and a good deal else. The Conference went off very well: and we had a great debate about Education, Mr. Cripps and Sir William Anson leading off. They are both good speakers and debaters, and they really knew what they were talking about.   It was almost exciting to watch them making their points, and to wonder how they would answer, and who would come out best.   It was hard to judge between them in the end.

Mr. Crum and I came here yesterday : I had to preach this morning at their great annual commemoration of Founders and Benefactors :—the list of whom began with a long roll of Kings, and ended with a Verger who, I suppose, had given or bequeathed his savings.

The chair which the Miss Lawrences bought for me at Lynton has come home :—a real beauty it is, quite the best, to my thinking, in all M. Charbonnier's collection.

Nov. 16, 1904.   *Turville Park, Henley-on-Thames* (near Priest Leys).—Here I am staying for one night in the house close by the avenue of lime-trees on the way to North End, where we used to have tea, at the little Inn.—Mr. Fiennes, who used to be at the College, came with me, and we walked the last part of the way, up the hills and through the beech-trees.   It was all wonderfully reminding of old days : I only wish I could stay, and go one of the old walks. . . . Well, it's long past twelve, and I've got to be up early to-morrow : so I'd better do a little more work, and then get to bed.

1905–1906

On New Year's Day 1905, came the sudden death of Henry Thompson, vicar of St. Mary's, Oxford, and sometime Warden of Radley.   He and the Bishop had been brothers-in-law since 1877.

To his Elder Sister

Mortehoe, Jan. 2.—He is spared suffering, and weariness, and old age : and you, in your great love for him, will think much of this, that he is spared the trial of loneliness ; and though it falls on you, you will bear it as for him, since one or other must have borne it.   And through it all you will thank God, not only for those hidden purposes of mercy of

which our knowledge of His love may make us sure in all
things :—but also for those clear fruits of His Bounty which
cannot ever be missed or forgotten : for the character, the
heart, the goodness that His Grace wrought in Henry :—
for the wonderful happiness of so many years : — for the
helpfulness and dutifulness and promise of all your sons.—
And as you thank God for all these blessings,—and even when
your heart fails,—He will help you in your trial and sorrow and
weariness :—I am very unworthy to speak at all of His help :—
but indeed I am very sure of its sufficiency :—there is nothing
lacking, on His side.

In May, he sent to the Clergy of the Diocese a
letter " in regard to the attitude which we should hold
towards the movements of religious revival which are
going forward at the present time " :—

First I must say with what reluctance I use the title *undenominational.* It has been so widely current that we have,
I think, grown hardened to its faults : but they are many. It
is, in mere form, ugly : it rouses at once all the associations of
recently-embittered controversy : it is laden with prejudice : it
savours of this world, and sets people thinking of this world's
warfare and weapons : and, above all, it is unjust to the work,
the efforts, to which it is applied. For it points to them with
a mere negation : and they certainly are not negative : if they
were, they could not have the power that they plainly show.
Probably the last thought in the mind of any one who bears
a true part in a Revivalist meeting, for instance, or who is
truly touched by it, is that the meeting is undenominational.
I wish we could get rid of the cold and dreary word : it seems
to me almost profane to use it of some such movements as I
have been thinking of. But I can think of no other term
which will distinguish and group together those ways of work
with reference to which I want now to get my bearings clear.—
What is my duty towards them, holding the office I hold in
the Church of England ?
   I believe that by the Will of God and under the guidance
of the Holy Spirit the historic Church of Christ has received

and maintained the three-fold ministry, of Bishops, Priests, and
Deacons : that in this three-fold ministry the Church has the
right and regular provision for guarding the tradition of the
faith, for upholding the discipline of Christ, for ministering
the means of grace. . . . I am bound steadily to affirm the
belief which I hold, and steadily to point to the way which I
believe to belong to our Lord's provision for the maintenance
of His Church on earth, and to be essential to the restoration
of its unity, whensoever that may be. I must not do anything to obscure what I believe ought to be clear : I must
never treat as unimportant what I believe to be a note of the
main, the divinely-ordered way by which men may surely
come to the fulness of the Christian life and character. . . . It
is this consideration which hinders me, often with a feeling of
great sadness, from taking any public part in religious movements, such as those which have been stirring hearts and
consciences in London and Wales.

Often, I say, it is with a feeling of great sadness that I thus
hold back : partly because I know how indiscriminately one
will be regarded as merely unsympathetic, as standing quite
aloof, because one will not stand on the platform to which one
is invited.   And all the while I know that I am not unsympathetic : that I should think poorly of anyone who could be.
For here are we, with our great tradition, our historic constitution, our three-fold Ministry ; and what multitudes of men and
women are living and dying quite untouched by all that we
can do or say.   Look at the streets of a big town, for instance,
or at a village green, on a fine Sunday, during Service
time ; or look at some favourite bit of the Thames, under the
same conditions.   How nearly helpless we seem, for all our
equipment, all the integrity of our heritage in the Catholic
Church.   What can we do to reach, to move, to bring to
conversion, those groups or crowds of people who, as the phrase
is, "go nowhere " : for whom Sunday is quite as worldly as
any other day in the week ?   We seem to sit resourceless,
baffled, outside the high, strong walls of the modern fortress of
indifference.   Well then, if anyone comes in the Name of
Christ, to batter at those walls, which we are, steadily and

patiently, I trust, beleaguering, who of us can dare not to wish him well, not to long and pray that he may have strength to succeed? that he and we may see the stones shake, and yield, and give some access at least for the herald of the Cross? Yes; though I cannot do as some, perhaps, would have me, though I cannot take the part which to me would seem inconsistent with my conviction and my office, I can and will do what is, perhaps, much more worth doing :—I can pray that God, Who " fulfils Himself in many ways," may be with those with whom I cannot see my way to go : that He may give them wisdom and gentleness and patience and sustained simplicity : that He may touch the hearts of those who listen, perhaps for the first time, to the message of His Love ; and that He may help me, and all who work with me, to know how we best may welcome and help and shepherd and sustain all those who, touched by that message, may look to the Church as they have never looked before ; that we may not disappoint them ; that we may not miss or slightly use the opportunity of humble, loving, persevering service which He may be preparing for us in these days. . . .

He writes, from Cuddesdon, on May 7, to Campbell Crum. He is able to give a favourable report of the family :—

All very well and cheerful and good here :—and if apple-pie beds are made they are quietly slept in.—To-morrow I go to Lambeth, to stay till Friday :—On Tuesday I may take my seat in the House, presented by Edward of Lincoln and Edward of Rochester.—It was a very good Confirmation, I think, at Beckley : to-morrow I go to Grazeley. The whole strength of the company is dormant : or I should have a tumult of messages to send.

On the death of Mrs. Church, on May 10, he wrote in the *Guardian* :—

. . . Round about her in childhood were the traditional tokens of respect belonging to the position of a country gentleman who was also a country parson, and she could remember how, as her father and mother with their train of children came into the village church and walked up the aisle, the congregation (after the fashion of Sir Roger de Coverley's tenants) rose and stood. But in the true squire the expectation of deference was guarded by the recognition of duty : if others had to " know their place," so likewise had the squire ; and his home was a good school for learning that central lesson that if a thing had got to be done you had better do it, soon and simply. . . . Her mind was as sincere and dutiful and humble as her heart, and religion lifted mind and heart alike to a real and quiet nobleness.

The true praise of such a character is that it wears well, and that praise she plainly earned. Through years of anxiety as to ways and means, and through years exempt from such anxiety ; through abundant happiness and great sorrows ; through the delight of an unbroken home, and through the loss of almost all who were dearest to her ; through the vigour of health and through the slow years of failing strength ; through the long, heart-searching trial of great distress and weariness ; through the last days and nights of restlessness and suffering, she was still herself—patient and true and unexacting, mindful of duty and of God, till it pleased Him to call her from the task which she had glorified by bearing it as a matter of course.

In Reading, on October 23 and 30 and November 6, great public meetings were held in the Large Town Hall, to consider three national dangers—intemperance, betting and gambling, and the non-observance of Sunday. He spoke at each of these meetings. He had already, at the Diocesan Conference, spoken on the non-observance of Sunday, asking those present

. . . to consider whether they had not to face, with regard to innocent recreations, a considerable class of people—he was not thinking now of the very poor or the very hard worked— in danger of a great impoverishment of their life and thought by the dominance of athleticism. It was perfectly true that it might be good for them to have this, that, or the other game on Sunday ; only he did think that a great many people were growing up, in the leisured and moneyed class especially, with a sheer incapacity for being quiet, that they dreaded nothing so much as to be left to themselves, and that they welcomed with a feeling which sometimes seemed to him almost insane anything that would relieve them of the necessity of thinking.

In Reading, on November 6, he said that

. . . He would try and speak as much like a layman as he could : and say how he would look at the matter if he were a very lay layman belonging to the class to which the Sunday Observance movement was especially addressed. As the layman looked at the matter he saw very clearly that Sunday was a very different thing in England from what it was fifteen or twenty years ago. He saw that a great deal of the change had involved an almost unqualified loss ; that there were a great many more Sunday dinner parties, Sunday travelling, Sunday amusements of all sorts, sheer Sunday indolence, and something more of Sunday card-playing. He saw in fact that there was a great deal more Sunday everything, except Sunday worship and Sunday rest. Supposing he was a middle-aged layman and could look back over a fair number of years, he would say—with that timidity which characterised laymen when speaking on great issues—he would say apologetically and rather tentatively that all was not well. He would get as far as that at any rate : but they must remember that a very lay layman had an admirable way of understating what he really meant to say ; he was rather shy about it, especially if it involved great principles ; and sooner than say a single syllable more than that which he was prepared to stick to with his whole heart and to the death, he was apt to say a good deal less. The layman saw, then, that his sons and his daughters were going-in for this new treatment of Sunday, that they more and more frequently and less and less hesitatingly were planning for their own way of enjoyment and amusement on Sunday, and were getting to take it for granted first that others and then that they themselves should do things on Sunday that they never would have thought of doing before. And as the layman

Q

looked on at that, the first thing that he was apt to say was, that it was rather a pity ; for he saw that they were losing so much and impoverishing their own lives ; he would say it rather sadly, rather wistfully as he thought of his own bygone Sundays : was it not a pity ?

For he found it harder and harder to keep himself quite clear of it ; he found that a lot of people were coming to the house on Sundays, and that he could not keep his old hours and his old ways on Sundays, because people took it for granted that he was prepared for a great deal of pleasure and some business on Sunday. While he was longing to get on in the old ways, it was getting more and more difficult to stand apart from the advancing tide of vulgarising the Sunday. He would then get a stage further and say still more sadly and heavy-heartedly that it was not only a pity but rather a bore : it had come to be a real trouble and burden in his own life.

But even the layest layman, even the man who looked on the surface of things, got a stage further than that : for he saw what it meant to his servants and to all who were employed in serving either the pleasure or the business of others. He saw what the river was on Sunday, and the great crowd of people rushing about to waste their own time, and hinder others from rest or prayer. He watched that, and at last his righteous soul got a bit hot on the matter, and he said, "I do think it is a shame ! "

And there they touched the great central meeting-point for them all. Whatever they thought, on whatever principles they approached the matter, whatever was their lot in life, they could all say that it was a shame that any people, who could not defend themselves, should be deprived of the opportunities which other people did not care for. Let them all meet on the ground that it was a downright shame.

To Bernard Paget, 1905

March 13. *Cuddesdon.*—I am heartily glad that you have won the Steeple Chase [1] : it does you real credit : and I congratulate

---

[1] The "Steeple-chase" at Shrewsbury is a long cross-country foot-race, with hedges to break through and pools to wade through : and there are points of honour about it, to make it harder to endure.

you with all my heart.   I care much more about it than most
races, because it means a bit of real courage : and courage of
that sort is a help towards the best courage of all,—that moral
courage which is the central virtue of life.   So I am very glad.
I should like to have seen you coming in first.   *July* 31.
House of Lords.—Edward brought back a delightful account of
his visit, and of all that you and he did.   It brought back to
me the wonderful happiness of the first time I went back to
Shrewsbury as an Old Boy :—quite one of the best bits of
enjoyment I have ever had.   I have been at Eton, for the
Stone-laying of the great Hall they are going to build in
memory of those who fell in the War :—& for the Head
Master's last Sunday.—It was a time I shall always remember.
Sept. 18.   *Lynton.*—I do wonder how it's going (Sandhurst),
and what it's like, and how far you like it, and how far you
dislike it.—I often think of you, and want news of you.   It is
the furthest and the loneliest plunge that you have ever yet
taken.—I hope greatly that you have found some really nice
fellows there.—Anyhow, don't be in a hurry either to make
friends, or to think that there are none to be made.   And, if
you want me to come and talk over things, write and say so :
and I will come somehow, whatever else goes to the wall.
Nov. 16.   *Cuddesdon.*—The Sunday at Radley was delightful :
Humphrey is very happy, and Kemm, who shares the little
study with him, seems quite the right sort, well-mannered and
keen and happy :—and they gave us the most wonderful tea I
have ever seen, with all the things that anybody could enjoy,
culminating in Rahat Lakoum :—all set out on a chair :—and I
got the boys a half-holiday : so I hope they all thought I was
some use.   The air is full of trouble, isn't it ?   In Russia,
things look as nearly desperate as they can be :—one thinks
of the saying about sowing the wind and reaping the whirl-
wind :—the people seem restless, and the rulers helpless, with no
policy & no remedy.   And here, in London, though we are
a long way off that, thank God, still the problem of the
unemployed is very urgent ; and if some try to cut the knots
they ought to untie, the misery will get worse and worse.   I
think things are moving rather quick : and I wish with all my

heart that we could better see to what end they move, or towards what.

To Bernard Paget, 1906

Jan. 16. *Cuddesdon.*—I am very unhappy about the course the Election is taking :—it looks to me like an intemperate sway of feeling, treating great issues in the wrong way : and I cannot bear to see honourable, high-minded, public-spirited men, who have served their country without thinking of themselves,—men like the Balfours, and Walter Long, and Lord Hugh Cecil,—slighted and laughed at.—And I expect it means some angry fighting not far off :—and the loss of some things that have done good. . . . I often wish that I could do more to make the holidays all that I would have them to be. We'll try hard together in the spring and summer, if all be well. *May* 5. *Chesham.*—I have been away from home nearly a fortnight, with Confirmations, the Commission, Convocation, and meetings about the Education Bill.—We had a wonderful meeting at Oxford, with the Town Hall crammed, & a multitude of people standing all the time, & an overflow meeting as well :—and then at Aylesbury we had the same sort of scene. It was very thrilling at times : and I really think that a great tide of feeling is rising in the Country against the injustice of the Bill. It seems to me a most illiberal & arbitrary thing for a Liberal Government or any Government to propose.

To one of his Clergy

March 2.—Since those of whom you write have already been received to Communion, I am of opinion that you cannot rightly refuse them until you have ascertained more of the case than you at present know.—It will make a great difference, in my judgement, if the lady was the innocent party in the divorce to which you refer. I shall be glad to know whether this is so ;—and about how long they have been Communicants ;—and also whether the husband from whom the lady was divorced is still living. Pending enquiry on these points, you ought not, I think, to refuse them, since they have been admitted.

To one of his Clergy

March 12.—The case sounds indeed a very sad case, in which one would desire to show all considerateness to one who has innocently suffered much.   But I always feel that, even when the person who comes to be married after a divorce has been, in the matter of the divorce, wholly innocent, the form of our marriage service does make it very inappropriate that the marriage should take place in Church.   I should *wish* that it should be elsewhere than in one of our Churches: though after such a marriage I have not felt able, if I was satisfied of the thorough innocence in regard to the divorce, to refuse Communion.

To the Diocesan Magazine

June 25.—I hope that, about the time at which these words appear, the Report of the Royal Commission on Ecclesiastical Discipline will be published.   I propose to make it the subject of my Charge in October, when I purpose, if it please God, to hold my Visitation.   So far as I can, if no unforeseen necessity for speaking of the subject comes upon me, I shall defer until then what I wish to say about it, for I am anxious to consider as fully as I can, before I speak of the Report, any deliberate and responsible criticism of it : and I am also anxious that those to whom I speak should have had time to read and to think over it.   I hope that they will read it for themselves, and think their own thoughts concerning it : for then, whether we agree or differ, our minds will be in real contact one with another, with a reality of mutual understanding.   When men have gone through the toil of thinking as clearly and thoroughly and independently as they can, they are well on the way to do justice to the thoughts and beliefs of other men.   It is with second-hand opinions that the blank, impenetrable walls of severance are most readily built.

The Report is unanimous : it is the outcome of a careful consideration of voluminous evidence : and it rests on two years of hard work.   It has a right to claim frank and serious study : and while men are so studying it, those who have the welfare of the Church at heart will pray to Him from Whom alone comes the Grace of a right judgement in all things.

Lord St. Aldwyn kindly writes, on January 5, 1912, as follows :—

What struck me was the extreme simplicity and modesty of his character—(qualities inherited from his father)—the deep religious feeling which governed his every action—his courage in undertaking things very distasteful to his own sympathies, such as the prosecution of some recalcitrant Ritualists in his diocese, because he felt it to be his duty—and his great love for Christ Church : I think he was most reluctant to leave it for the Bishopric ; and, as you know, he much preferred, when Bishop, his rooms at the Deanery to Cuddesdon Palace. His services on the Royal Commission were most valuable. His Church views were a good deal higher than mine, and very much higher than those of some of its members. But his intervention was always on the side of promoting agreement, rather than enforcing his own opinions : and while his speech was most persuasive, his powers of drafting were admirable. He aided us greatly in this way through all our Report: but I specially remember his work on Sections (19) and (20) pp. 32 and 33, which were mainly drafted by him.

When we met, we often discussed Church questions of the day : but I only recollect one discussion, on the admission to Holy Communion of those who had married their Deceased Wife's sisters, or the innocent party to a divorce who had married again. He pressed strongly the objections to this : on the ground, I think, of what he described as the " Law of the Church " in the first case, and of the indissolubility of marriage in the second. Eventually he admitted that he would not reject dying persons, in the second case—which seemed to me to give up his principle : but in the first he wouldn't accept my view that the only "law of the Church " in the matter, to a layman, is that contained in the Prayer book, authorized by Parliament, from which the Table of Affinity is excluded—and that persons married according to the law of the land cannot be described as open and notorious evil livers.

Others will tell you of his work at Christ Church when Dean : I only saw it as an occasional visitor. He had to live down very considerable unpopularity in the earlier part of his work, due, I think, to the mistakes of others : but I doubt if there ever was so admirable and charming a helper to the Head of a College as Mrs. Paget—and long before her death, both of them were appreciated as they deserved.

A good deal of the property of " the House " is situated in my part of England—and he took the greatest interest in its management, and was most popular with the tenants.

On Nov. 13, 1906, he took part in the Investiture of the King of Norway with the Order of the Garter. As Chancellor of the Order, he had the office of reading, at an Investiture, one of the admonitions :—

Wear this Riband, adorned with the Image of the Blessed Martyr and Soldier of Christ, SAINT GEORGE, by whose Imitation provoked, thou mayest so overpass both prosperous and adverse encounters, that having stoutly vanquished thine Enemies, both of body and soul, thou mayest not only receive the praise of this transient Combat, but be crowned with the Palm of eternal Victory.

1907

On Feb. 11, he writes to Mr. F. O. Wethered, asking for the help of a motor on Easter Monday, April 1. Between these two dates, he held 49 Confirmations, in addition to all his other work : and, on the Easter Monday, he attended a Teachers' Conference in Oxford, and the opening of a Memorial Hall in Wycombe, and held a Confirmation at Latimer, near Chesham :—

44 *Queen Anne's Gate, Feb.* 11.—This big sheet of paper looks ominous : but you needn't be afraid of a very long letter : for it's close on midnight. But I have been wanting to write to you,—(I've half a mind to write to Adeline, and sign it

"Peter Pan-Bishop": only that would look like the Pope),—
ever since your kind and delightful letter came. . . . Now
will you tell me quite truly whether the motor will be, without
any inconvenience, free on Easter Monday? I have to be at
a function at Oxford at 10.30 that morning :—I don't expect
to be free till 12 at the earliest: and then I have to get to
Wycombe for the ceremony at 3 :—and then to get on to
Chesham.—I believe the train will get me to Chesham well
enough :—but the journey from Oxford is more difficult. . . .

To J. A. Fuller Maitland

Jan. 23.—There are disappointments that turn sour if one
looks at them : and it is with averted gaze that I think of my
lot on Feb. 8. For it would have been a real joy and refreshment to come and stay with you that night, and to listen to
the Bach Choir :—& I can't get it.—The work which would
have brought me to London is shifted : and that means, in the
niggardliness which besets our day, that I must shift into its
place other work which will keep me away from London. I
am ever so sorry, and a little cross : but most of all grateful for
the great kindness of your bidding. The liberty of old days
seems far away : and one did not know how free one was then.
And in all that one misses now, the free spaces for the enjoyment of the happiness of friendship seem among the things
hardest to forgo.

To Bernard Paget

Cuddesdon, Feb. 5.—I did immensely enjoy our bit of
holiday together : I often find myself wondering when we
may get another bit. I have refreshed my recollection with
the post-cards which your letter triumphantly secured :—(I shall
appoint you First Secretary of State for Foreign Affairs).—The
Rodin group at Calais comes out better than I thought : there
is real power about it: but I wish people would use their
power more modestly. . . . Yesterday at Oxford I saw the
enclosed : and I thought I wd. give it to somebody. Will
you have it? It wd. go under the tightest red coat without
making a wrinkle.

G.W.R., 28 *Feb.*—Waiting in a fog, till the line is clear enough for the train to start :—that's where we are, and may be, I think, for some while.   And a capital chance it is, for writing to thank you heartily for two very welcome letters, and to give you such news as I have.   But it is not much news.   For I've been going to and fro, between Buckingham-shire and London, Confirming, and reading Prayers in the House of Lords.   So for lack of news, I'll tell you a story about a great gentleman.

He's a Navvy : and I confirmed him about two years ago. He's on a job at Nottingham now : and the other day he came all the way from Nottingham to a place near Slough to see the parson who prepared him and some other navvies for Confirma-tion.   When he came in he said " I've got to beg your pardon."   Of course the parson said he didn't think that was at all likely : but the Navvy stuck to it, though he found it hard to say why.   Presently something he said made the parson think that perhaps he had been abusing him or laughing at him, and was sorry :—& he tried to hint towards that. But the Navvy said, " No, it isn't that : but some of my mates pitched into you ; and I didn't stop 'em : so I've come to beg pardon."

And all the way from Nottingham !   What a thing it is to be a gentleman !—And here we are, in the country, & out of the fog, and actually passing the place where I confirmed him.   I remember his face quite well :—I wish he had given the addresses instead of me.   " Abe Hood " is his name, I think :—short for Abraham, you know.   And how delightful he would be to Lazarus !

On Oct. 24, on the news of Mr. G. F. Bodley's death, he writes to Miss Lawrence :—

. . . A great, far-reaching loss :—no one kept the standard of true architecture quite so high as he did : no one had so pure and noble and unfanciful a sense of its beauty and dignity :—no one could make a building speak so simply of the greatest things.

On Oct. 29, he sent a letter to the Clergy of the Diocese :—

I write, in pursuance of what I said at the Diocesan Conference, to put before you the outcome of my thinking over the difficulty in which we all are placed by the recent Act concerning Marriage with a Deceased Wife's Sister.

It seems to me important that we should bear in mind the real nature of that difficulty. It lies in this, that we, as ordained Ministers of the Church of England, are pledged to maintain a standard which, so far as that Marriage is concerned, has ceased to be the standard upheld by the law of the land. From the first, the Church of Christ, in its work for the formation of character and the hallowing of life, has maintained for its members a certain standard of conduct: and we are bound to have a constant regard to that standard in all that we may say and do as servants of the Church. A marriage which, according to that standard, is forbidden to members of the Church, is now by the law of the land recognized as a civil contract. Those who thus marry can now point to the law of the land as sanctioning their union: we must frankly acknowledge that it has that sanction: and we must consider carefully what is now required of us by that standard which does not sanction it, and which we are bound to remember and uphold.

We should, I believe, be obscuring the true mission of the Church if we were to bear ourselves as though that standard could be invalidated, and deprived of its claim within the sphere of the Church's life, by an Act in which the Church has not concurred. At the same time it would seem to me unreal and unjust not to recognize that the change in the law of the land has made a difference, to which we must give heed, in the conditions amidst which the standard has to be upheld, and in the conscientious convictions of many thoughtful and religious men. If we ignore this, we shall thwart the very purpose we would serve: for the nation's life will be unaffected by the Church's standard, unless we take care, in our manner of maintaining it, really to commend it to men's conscience in the sight of God. Further, we must recognize that there have been and will be real points of difference distinguishing diverse cases of marriage with a deceased wife's sister: to treat all such cases alike would be, in my judgement, contrary to equity : to apply to them the censure of the second Rubric before the Order of Holy Communion [1] would be morally indefensible and justly resented.

In view of all these considerations, I have come to think as follows :—

(i.) I shall be glad if, in the event of your being asked to receive to the Holy Communion those who have contracted this marriage, you judge it right to consult me before you give an answer.

(ii.) In the event of your being asked to publish the Banns for such a marriage, or to celebrate it, or to allow it to be celebrated in the Parish Church entrusted to you, my advice, if you seek it, will be that you should refuse.   For I think that such a refusal is a clear and plainly lawful way of maintaining and declaring the standard which the Church upholds : and, so long as the Table of Prohibited Degrees remains unaltered, is printed with the Book of Common Prayer, and is hung up in our Churches, it seems to me incongruous to celebrate in Church a marriage which contravenes it.

(iii.) If one of your Parishioners, who has contracted such a marriage, dies, I trust that you will not, on the ground of the marriage, hesitate to use the Burial Service of the Church.

I do not think that you will blame me for thus tendering to you my counsel in a matter of great difficulty, concerning which we must all do our best to see and hold a right course.   I trust that in all we say and do we may guard unfalteringly the grace of charity, praying God to pardon all that is said or done amiss, and not to let it hinder His Church's work for the true welfare of our country.

Next in order of time comes a letter with a little story of its own.   On a Saturday evening in September,

---

[1] " And if any of those be an open and notorious evil liver, or have done any wrong to his neighbours by word or deed, so that the Congregation be thereby offended ; the Curate, having knowledge thereof, shall call him and advertise him, that in any way he presume not to come to the Lord's Table, until he have openly declared himself to have truly repented and amended his former naughty life, that the Congregation may thereby be satisfied, which before were offended ; and that he have recompensed the parties, to whom he hath done wrong ; or at least declare himself to be in full purpose so to do, as soon as he conveniently may."

going to preach in Old Windsor, he had found himself, at Oxford Station, without his glasses ; the train was due in a few minutes : and a stranger, Mr. Abington, of Southville, Bristol, kindly gave his own glasses to him. Later, Mr. Abington wrote to him, of Mrs. Abington's illness : and the Bishop wrote back on November 4 :—

I will indeed pray God, of His merciful compassion, to lighten the anxiety, to spare the life so dear to you and to your home, and to help and comfort Mrs. Abington in the trial that she is bearing. It is wonderful to know how His strength is made manifest in our weakness : and how the assurance of His love and care for us can calm our trouble and distress. May He send out for you, and for those near and dear to you, His Light and Truth according to all your need.

I keep in my cassock-pocket the glasses with which you helped me out of my perplexity that Saturday afternoon : and so I am often using them in Church : and they will always remind me of a true and gladdening bit of friendliness.

On the news of Mrs. Abington's death he wrote :—

With all my heart I do indeed enter into the sorrow of the great loss of which your most kind letter this morning told me. I am very grateful to you for having written to me : and for having told me of those touching words of Mrs. Abington's : there is true help in all that strengthens our assurance that our Lord is very near to His servants in all time of their tribulation, and in the hour of death.

May the God of all comfort help and comfort you day by day—strengthening you according to all your need : and ever refreshing in you the great hope that bears light into our bereavement : the hope that by His Grace we may be so led through the things of this world that we come to the gladness of a meeting beyond all pain or grief or severance. . . . Indeed I vividly recall our meeting and your kindness.

To Bernard Paget

Keble College, Dec. 20. . . . Surely Kirkpatrick was at

the House, towards the end of my time: and he went out to the War, and then I had a bit of a talk with him at the Barracks that night when they fetched the Colours:—I can see it all now. —I don't think I can be wrong about it :—if I'm right, will you remember me most kindly to him? I go to Christ Church to-night, for the Ordination to-morrow : on Sunday I consecrate the new Church in North Oxford & go to the Infirmary in the afternoon : on Monday I hope to get back to Cuddesdon, & to send you Lord Wantage's Life.

Early in 1908, Bernard Paget went to India : the letters to him, during 1908–1911, are put in a separate chapter.

1908

To C. P. S. Clarke

Jan. 29.—I cannot say I was quite happy about the Cambridge Mission to Reading. I heard that people had been stirred by a procession through the streets, and I do not doubt that here and there good was done: many, I think, were touched by the courage of such a venture : but the meeting at which I was present made me uncomfortable, mainly by its lack of simplicity. I did not feel that the speakers had got away from themselves. I was unhappy at the time, and as I think of it I believe I was right.

Trafalgar Day.—The question about the Bible Society rose the first week I was at Bromsgrove.—I refused, and have always refused, to attend their meetings : because I should have to bear part with non-Conformist Ministers in a joint Devotional Act. But I have subscribed to the Society : because that does not involve the same blurring of distinctions, and because the work of the Society is employed by Missions which I hold in great honour. I have never been really uncomfortable about this line :—but perhaps the new School of " Inter-Denominationalists " (—what a luggage train of a word it looks!—) might make me " feel chilly & grown old."

To Miss Lawrence

Feb. 29. . . . . The beautiful photograph of that keen and

noble face :—& with all my heart I am grateful to you and Mary
for a fresh token of the ever-fresh and thoughtful kindness.—
Mr. Meredith's eighty years may not be a pulpit :—but I think
the picture of him will sometimes preach to me, as it stands in my
study : —it seems to me to tell much of the high, alert, independent mind, unswerving from its standard of true work.   No
one in the world of literature—(I should think)—has kept
work clearer from what Clough calls "the horrible pleasure of
pleasing inferior people."[1]

On March 5, he writes to Mr. Arthur Coleridge,
thanking him for Miss Mary Coleridge's poems :—
"The book has been to me *comes itineris* on many
journeys : and a wonderful companion it is"—and he
praises in it "the courage that looks straight at the
uttermost sadness of life, and understands it, and still
declares hope. As I think over it the thoughts of
great things in music and painting, as well as in poetry,
come back to me : and I think that there are messages
in the book that I shall not forget."   Mr. Coleridge
remembers hearing him preach at Bromsgrove—"and I
then and there registered myself as a student of any
book he had published already or intended to publish."
Later, they met at Evolena—"long walks and talks by
day, ending with real music of an evening ; for
Maitland gave us Bach's Preludes and Fugues"—and
he remembers him saying that if a fire broke out in the
house he would save his children first, and then his
Browning. Evolena comes again into a note which
Mr. Fuller Maitland has kindly written : [2]—

---

[1] The reference is to one of the letters in Clough's *Amours de Voyage* :—"Is it
contemptible, Eustace—I'm perfectly ready to think so,—Is it,—the horrible pleasure
of pleasing inferior people ? "

[2] There is a letter, toward the end of 1909, to Miss Lawrence—he is looking far
forward to a Richter concert—"and when a choir sings with more zeal than
discretion I can murmur to myself that in February I may hear the Beethoven
Mass :—what a joy it will be."

" The Bishop's way of listening to music was a thing I shall never forget. There is a very real music-hunger in all who have ears to hear, but in the abundance of concerts it is an appetite of which comparatively few are ever conscious : in public performances so much of the listeners' attention is absorbed in comparison, criticism, or the attempt to analyse the music as it passes, that there is little room to feel any conscious craving for the sustenance which is necessary for every musician's well-being. Sometimes the almost physical longing for music is seen on listeners' faces, and the joy of awakening it is one of the rarest and deepest that can be given to an interpreter of music. More than half the pleasure of giving music to the poor is that this expression is comparatively easy to call up in audiences to whom concerts are a rarity. But never on any human face have I seen anything like the longing for music that Paget showed with complete unconsciousness of what his expression was revealing. Our first meeting was a casual encounter at the hotel at Evolena, and we had both been separated from music for some little time. The only artistic resources of the inn were a very poor piano and a copy of Mendelssohn's *Songs without Words*. Yet one felt that one was able not merely to give a passing pleasure, but to serve as the channel whereby a deep need of another human soul could be in some measure satisfied. It taught us how important is the function of the listener in every musical performance, and in a very short time the casual acquaintance ripened into a friendship which is now only a mere precious memory.

"Paget's music-hunger was not an undiscerning greed for sound of any kind ; how far he was technically educated, I do not know at all, but his tastes were so definite that they must have had some solid basis of knowledge. To love Bach as he did implies a good deal more than the typical amateur's unreasoned preferences, and the Bishop was warmly appreciative of all music that was good. Music spoke so directly to him, as to one of her own sons, that as a matter of course he was not especially sympathetic to productions in which she must play a subordinate or auxiliary part. Programme-music of all kinds would leave him cold, and towards dramatic music, even that of Wagner, he would have had few leanings, even if circumstances had made it easy for him to attend operatic performances, and if he had shared Wagner's ethical opinions. But in ' abstract ' music no taste could have been more faultless or broader than his ; and one felt that whatsoever he did not like was to be regarded with suspicion on its own account."

On May 25, died Mr. Bayne, the oldest of his Christ Church friends. He left his property, to the value of about £120,000, for the support of Church Schools in the Oxford Diocese, and for the benefit of Christ Church men in holy orders. For many years he had been a generous benefactor to Christ Church, and to the Diocese.

To the Diocesan Magazine

May 29.—Ever since I became Bishop, and, I believe, for some years before, " The Bishop's Special Fund " has really and simply meant one man—the Rev. Thomas Vere Bayne, Student of Christ Church, who passed away, after about sixty years of residence in Christ Church, in the early morning of Monday last. Every year, with a characteristic regularity, he sent me a cheque for a large sum to be thus used, honouring me with his absolute trust as to the distribution of it. From time to

time, more frequently as time went on, he would tell me that
a further sum would be at my disposal by a fixed date. . . . I
think that I have known three gifts which were all his appear
under different designations in one list ; the first, a grant from
" The Bishop's Special Fund " ; the second, a large sum,
anonymous ; the third, a smaller sum, with his name attached
to it, and given, perhaps, because he would not pain or puzzle
a friend by a flat refusal. . . . Just as, when he made some
splendid gift to the place he loved and served with true,
sustained devotion, the offer was announced only as coming
from ' An Old Member of the House ' ; just as, when a cheque
came to lighten some burden of anxiety in a Vicar's home,
those whom it gladdened never knew who gave it ; so all this
thoughtful, steady, loyal, unwearied giving was kept as a secret ;
known only to the few on earth who had to know it, and to
Him from Whom no secrets are hid.

To one of his Clergy

June 18.—Forgive my delay in regard to the Irvingite case.
I do not think that it is right for anyone deliberately to con-
template communicating both as a member of the Church of
England and also as a member of a body which has a ministry
of its own apart from the Church of England.

The position of the Irvingites is so peculiar that I should
hesitate to refuse Communion to one who was a communicant
in that body if he had been already confirmed in the Church of
England.   But it is another matter to receive as a candidate
for Confirmation one who avows the intention of maintaining
the position, which I think ought not to be maintained, *i.e.*
the position of communicating both with us and with the
Irvingites. If I did this, I should be sanctioning what I do
not think to be right.   I think, therefore, that your parishioner
may reasonably be asked to make his choice between
(*a*) Confirmation and Communion in the Church of England
and (*b*) the retention of his present position.

This is, I believe, the logical and consistent position to take
up : but I have to say that it is not the position which would
be taken by some with whom I ordinarily find myself in

R

complete agreement, and from whom I feel some uneasiness in differing. For they would regard the Irvingite position as entirely "sui generis," as unique and eccentric, and unlike the position of any non-conformist body : & so regarding it they would treat it quite exceptionally, and would allow Confirmation and Communion without requiring a separation from the Irvingite body. I feel that there are points which give support to this attitude ; and the course to which it leads is one which I can not in any way condemn. Still my mind tilts on the whole towards the other course.

To one of his Clergy

October 30.—It is, I think, quite right that infants dying unbaptized should be buried in the Churchyard.—The custom of burying them there, with some form of prayers other than the Burial Office, is a right custom :—the Rubric before the Burial Office relating not to the place of Burial but to the Office to be used.

I have no doubt that, in any case of clear & imperative necessity, any person who is present may and should baptize the child. There is no valid reason against a parent's administering the baptism : and it seems to me to be reasonably and rightly urged that a parent who is a communicant should be preferred to any other person who is not.

It would be well, I think, if people were made aware of the duty of baptizing a child who is in imminent danger of dying unbaptized. But I should advise you not to preach on the subject, until you know your Parishioners more thoroughly than has yet been possible : for in more than one way a sermon on the subject might be misunderstood, and misleading.

I should like to see you as soon as we can meet, to talk of this subject, if need be, and of the outlook of your work. . . . May God guide & guard you in your work.

In June of this year, the Pan-Anglican Congress was held ; and, in July, the Lambeth Conference. After the Lambeth Conference, he went with the Archbishop of Canterbury and Mrs. Davidson to

Switzerland. The Diocesan Conference was held on Sept. 30 and Oct. 1. He chose, for the chief subjects of his address, Elementary Education, and the Division of the Diocese : and it was resolved that a special committee be nominated by him, "to report fully, at the next meeting, upon the whole question of the Division of the Diocese, and also to suggest any alternative means by which the burden of episcopal work may be relieved." The resignation of the Bishop of Reading at this time left him henceforward without the help of a Suffragan.

Near the end of December, writing his monthly letter for the Magazine—" It is a genial instinct," he says, " that makes men want to be friends when they come to part "—and so it is with the going of the Old Year :—

There may have been moments when we did not understand one another, or get on well together; but, after all, we are sorry he is going ; we should be very sorry if he thought that we were glad : there is a real regret in our hearts as his motor grunts, and turns the corner, and is out of sight : and before the New Year is well settled in, we find ourselves telling him what a good old fellow, on the whole, his predecessor was.

It is a kindly tendency : and like all kindliness, it makes for truth : and if it errs at all, it errs on the right side. Certainly, our later judgment of the troublous days is sounder than the dejection to which we may have yielded as we passed through them : for now we see much that we missed then. We see, perhaps, for how much of the trouble we should have blamed ourselves : and how much better things might have gone if we had been better and more patient, if we had thought more of others and less of ourselves. We begin to know the worth of the lessons we have learnt : and though, instead of all that we might have secured, we have got but one of the Sibyl's volumes (and that a damaged copy, at the price of a Caxton), still it is a great thing to have got that. . . .

The last of this year's letters is to Canon Fowler, on Dec. 29, enclosing a cheque

. . . for the help of the unemployed and poverty-stricken in Reading :—I will try to give something more later on, if more is needed.

1909

TO ONE OF HIS CLERGY

1. *Jan.* 21.—Provided that due notice has been given to you of the intended burial in the churchyard, in accordance with the requirement of the Burials Act, the relatives have a clear right to claim that the service should be conducted by whomsoever they select, and with such "Christian and orderly religious service" as they think fit. I should advise you, in such a case, to take no part of the service.

2. *April* 28. . . . I will gladly look forward to celebrating at 8, confirming at 2.45, & preaching at St. James's in the evening.—If it is necessary to issue a bill as you suggest, I should prefer that my celebrating at 8 were not mentioned : and I must ask that the 10 o'clock service be described as a choral or sung Eucharist, not as a Missa Cantata. I think that I should rather prefer not having the procession before the confirmation. If all be well, I hope to attend the 11 o'clock service : & perhaps to read the Lessons. I am gladly looking forward to coming. I shall be grateful if in the intervals of the Sunday I may get a quiet time : for it comes at the end of a heavy week. I cannot promise to visit the Sunday School : but I will try.

TO STEPHEN PAGET

March 4.—I could not write on the same sheet of paper concerning April 20th[1] & the Cremation Society. So I send

---

[1] On April 20, Stephen Paget's elder daughter was married to Mr. O. J. R. Howarth. The Bishop married them. The second letter is in answer to a suggestion that the wedding ought to dispel, with colour and music, the "grey streaks" which come into less eventful days. He goes on, in this second letter, to speak of Sir Thomas Smith, who at this time was nearing the end of his life : "Dear old Tom Smith ! I must get to see him : he's been just as good to me as anybody ever was to anybody."

a separate letter.   I agree with you about cremation :—ever
since I attended a funeral after cremation had taken place, I
have wished that the practice might prevail.   But I do not
think that it would be well for me to become a Vice-President
of the Society : partly because I hesitate to ask that any one
body should be cremated : partly because I have some doubt
whether, in view of the history, it is a matter in which
Bishops should take a leading part, and some dislike for
standing alone, apart from my brother-Bishops, unless a very
plain duty requires it.

April 5.—I'm looking forward most gladly to the wedding.
—I'd get myself gilt from head to foot, or lit up with electric
light, or anything else in the world, to give you pleasure.—
The grey streaks come to me,—more often than they should,—
and they're more than streaks sometimes.   But still there
are some people who love one : and there are people to be
helped, and people willing to be taught :—and so, I trust, one
will be brought through, with gleams of light enough :—and
perhaps some surprises of gold and music on the way. . . .
I write in the old home, the Deanery :—more moving to me
than any place in the world, save Bromsgrove.

To Miss Lawrence

April 22. . . . And every day I read a bit of the "Egoist "—
not a very big bit : partly because every word matters : partly
because it is so strangely exciting :—specially, I suppose, for
one who reads about two novels a year.   He is the most
wonderful of writers : piercing so deep, rising so high : forcing
you to see the worst, and then reminding you of the best :
making people talk as no one ever talked, yet making them alive
and intense all the while :—provoking you with his elaborateness, yet defying you not to attend.   It seems absurd to write
of him to you :—but I can't say how he interests me, and
grips my mind.

Between May 25 and July 5, he held his third
Triennial Visitation.   In July, he was at Bromsgrove,
for the last time, and got a great welcome there from

his old parishioners. He writes of one of them, on Sept. 1, to Mr. Noel Paterson :—

A few days ago I was speaking of old Mrs. Mickless to two great friends of mine, and telling of her patient courage and cheerfulness. This morning a letter from them brought the enclosed £5 note : with the request that it may be spent in providing some additional comfort for her through the winter. Will you kindly undertake this ministration of kindness ? With glad remembrance of your home and work, & of all my friends in that true-hearted place.

At the Diocesan Conference, the Report of the Committee on the Division of the Diocese was received and discussed. After the Conference, he had a short holiday, with his daughter Beatrice, in North Italy.

To Stephen Paget

Sept. 3.—I think that you have made it impossible for any sane person to have even the mildest flirtation with Christian Science:—the thing is utterly discredited.—The matter for anxiety now is " Mental Therapeutics " :—about that matter I am very anxious :—for I believe that, in the sense in wh. most talk of it, it is seldom untouched by, or far off from, superstition and quackery :—and I am very much frightened when those who are rightly listened to suggest that the Church should take it up. I do earnestly hope that the Church won't. (I've heard nothing for some while about my poor friend with cancer of the larynx. I will enquire.) All best wishes for your Belgian tour. I wish you cd. get a chance of telling the monarch of that country that I think him the greatest of all scoundrels, hung or unhung. *Baveno, Oct.* 21.—I have read of you charging at " Christian Science " quite like Carpaccio's St. George :—I should like to reproduce the whole picture :—with the tokens of victims all about, to show that it was high time somebody did something decisive.

On October 22, he writes from Baveno to his son Humphrey ; telling of a walk up the Sasso di Ferro—

"and a most glorious walk it was :—with chesnuts, vines, mulberries, beeches, hazel, all sorts of beautiful colours, and all brilliant in the perfect sunlight—I picked a lot of wild pinks and wild cyclamen "—and he encloses his bill for luncheon at Laveno—" I'm afraid you won't make it all out :—but you may observe that the wine cost 2d., and the whole thing under 1s. 3d." He writes to Miss Lawrence, on October 23 :—

I wish you were here ; for I do not think there can be a more perfect sight than the lake & the islands and the hill on the beautiful mornings, with the sunlight streaming over the water, and the most delicate mist in varying degrees giving softness to all the outlines and colours. And autumn has brought a wonderful glory upon the foliage : — it cannot surpass the beech-woods of Buckinghamshire :—but it has a wider diversity. . . . I was amused by the answer of a labourer whom I wanted to photograph yesterday : first he said that he had not time to stand still ; which, considering the general ways of Italians, surprized me :—then he said that he did not want to appear on a post-card, which I quite understood.

To the Diocesan Magazine

Oct. 29.—I fear that in many parts of England the heavy rain and the recent floods are bringing very great anxiety and distress to those whose welfare and work depend upon the land. The sadness of the sight has been vivid to me ; for I wrote the main part of this letter on my way home from Italy ; and I shall never forget the contrast between the glory of sunlight that there had gladdened day after day, and the pelting rain, the flooded fields and hop-grounds and orchards of Kent. I venture to ask all those who read this letter to remember in their prayers the special necessity of our farmers and labourers at this time.

On Nov. 15 he took part in the Investiture of the

King of Portugal with the Order of the Garter : on Nov. 17 he preached in St. Paul's at the London Church Choirs' Festival : on Nov. 18 he spoke at the Congo meeting in the Albert Hall.

Toward the time of the General Election, he sent a letter, on Dec. 20, to the Clergy of the Diocese, with a form of prayer ; asking them to read the letter in Church, and to use the prayer at morning and evening services. " A general election," he writes to Major Leonard Noble, " is a strange process :—with some humiliating elements in it."

1910

On New Year's Day, he wrote his Pastoral Letter, announcing the formation of the Bishop of Oxford's Fund, with Mr. Baverstock as Organising Secretary, and explaining its relation to the great Diocesan Societies, and how it would be administered for the work of the Diocese.

On February 26, the Archbishops issued their Appeal to the Church and People of England on behalf of the Western Canada Fund. The Archbishops, with the Archbishop of Rupertsland, are the Presidents of the Council ; and the Bishop of Oxford was appointed Chairman. It is certain that nothing, even in his own Diocese, was nearer to his heart :— " I do not think that the Archbishops have ever before so called upon the Church and Nation to rise to a great opportunity and meet an urgent need. And I am sure that anyone who takes to heart the facts of the case will be thankful that the call has thus sounded out. The Archbishops tell us plainly what is wanted : and no words could add to the force of what they tell."

On March 3, he writes to Mr. F. O. Wethered, concerning the House of Laymen :—

There is nowhere where sound judgment, free from party-spirit, seems more needed. But the expense of time there is large in comparison with the opportunities of service :—it's a wasteful business, notwithstanding its importance : —and I should think it better economy of your help, if you were to give that up than if you were to withdraw from any considerable bit of Diocesan or County work.

On April 10, to Mr. F. A. O'Brien, concerning his elder daughter's engagement :—

I am glad and thankful that Beatrice will have her own home :—and there is clear, good prospect of its being, please God, a very happy home.—For Jeudwine is a very good fellow, of whose worth and work those who know him best speak with real enthusiasm. . . . So the outlook is bright for them. I shall be a bit—a large bit—the more lonely. But I have lots of work : and I am much away from home : and people are wonderfully kind :—and I am in my 60th year. So I hope that, please God, I shall,—as the poor say—"ruggle on."

On April 27, to Mr. E. F. Smith :—

The talk which we had at Cuddesdon last week has made me full of hope that there is clear and lasting work for you to do, please God, in the Diocese of Oxford : and that we may work trustfully and happily together in those two ways of which we then talked.[1]

On May 20, at the funeral of King Edward VII, the Archbishops, the Bishops of Winchester and of Oxford, and the Dean of Windsor, received the King's body at the West door of St. George's Chapel ; and were before the altar during the service.

---

[1] Mr. E. F. Smith was appointed at this time Warden of the Diocesan Society of Mission Clergy, and Secretary of the Diocesan Union in connection with the Church of England Men's Society.

To Humphrey Paget

Deanery, Windsor Castle, May 20.—I write as we wait here for the great service :—it's a day we shall all remember, I think, as long as we live :—a day such as can hardly have been before :—for no King can have been buried with mourning from so vast a range. . . . I am heartily grieved for the great sorrow that has fallen on Radley.—Hetherington had a special place in my mind & heart :—I'll tell you why when we meet. I am very, very sorry for his brother, & for his father & mother. I have ventured to write to the Warden, sending some words to them.

To the Diocesan Magazine

May 31.—A true-hearted King, wise and just, hard-working for his subjects' welfare, has been taken away from us. We had hardly known the full measure of the affection, the trust, the loyalty he had rightly won from the free people whom he ruled. We knew it when he died : and our hearts were open and eager, in gratitude and grief and awe, to talk and prize the teaching of his laborious life. We could see then the secret of his unrivalled influence—his kindness, his straightforwardness, his generosity, his equity, his loyalty, his patience :—the simplest dutifulness in the highest place, —that arrested us : and we understood that we were being called in those days to do our duty better in all the days to come. We must not forget that clear call, nor be disobedient to it. . . . That constant prayer of his for peace, that Christian love of peace, he seems to call us all to share. Let us set our hearts, with sincerity and steadfastness, to answer to his call. And let us remember this :—that the temper which makes for peace is one and the same in all fields of action. We must be cherishing that temper in all ways at home, if we want to bear our part in averting war. We must be eager and solicitous for reconciliation, for mutual understanding, for generous considerateness, for ungrudging justice in all matters of controversy and debate, if we are to be among the peace-makers of the world. And there is not one of us who may not do something, and perhaps a good deal, to advance in England a sane and peaceable treatment of those difficulties and differences which suspicion, exaggeration, party-spirit and harsh, hasty words may harden into intractable conflict.   Let us, then, quietly do our best to be peace-makers at home first.   There is no better way to show our sense of what King Edward taught us : no better way of serving the country that he loved and served : no better loyalty that we can render to King George, as he, thank God, religiously and dutifully and courageously takes up the burden of his great inheritance : as he comes, in frank reliance on the all-enabling Grace of our Lord and Saviour, to bear rule over us.   God save the King : God grant peace in his time : God grant to him, and to us all, the blessing surely pledged to peace-makers.[1]

At the end of June, 1910, he suddenly had a very severe and dangerous illness (volvulus).   He was attended by Sir Thomas Barlow and Sir Anthony Bowlby : and on July 3, at Welbeck House, Sir Anthony operated on him, assisted by Mr. R. C. Bailey and Mr. W. F. Cross.   It was a remarkable feature of his case, that he appeared, for the most part, to have not more but less than the usual pain and distress of such cases.   On the first day of his illness, after a bad night, he went and read prayers in the House of Lords, and then went to Sir Thomas Barlow, with a half-apology for troubling him.   At the operation, he was more than two hours under the hands of the surgeons : but he suffered no shock, slept for six or seven hours, and had a quiet pulse and temperature.   The second day after the operation, he

[1] A few months later, at the request of an Oxford Committee, he wrote a prayer for international understanding and friendship : — "Almighty God, from Whom all thoughts of truth and peace proceed ; kindle, we pray Thee, in the hearts of all men the true love of peace, and guide with Thy pure and peaceable wisdom those who take counsel for the nations of the earth : that in tranquillity Thy Kingdom may go forward, till the earth be filled with the knowledge of Thy Love : through Jesus Christ our Lord."

said that he thought he would like to read a novel ; and found pleasure in *The Prisoner of Zenda*. Day after day, it was the same thing : he was so tranquil, that it seemed almost as if he were indifferent—not as if he were bearing anything, but as if he were waiting for something very hard to bear : indeed, it was irreverently said of him that he was healing like one of the lower organisms. Grave discomforts, which for a time were the necessary result of the operation, he took with imperturbable courtesy : and, as he accepted all discomforts, so he enjoyed all comforts of good nursing. This peace of body and mind, which he gave to himself in his own illness, he could sometimes give to others. Miss Mayo, the Matron of the Sanatorium at Wellington, writes of him :—

I remember once, some years ago, on a Speech Day, we had a boy apparently dying that day from typhoid fever, which he contracted at home and developed here soon after returning to School. The good Bishop came to see him, but the mother hesitated till I told her she could never say no to the Bishop's desire to see a patient, and so he came to see the poor boy ; who just knew him, for the Bishop had confirmed him the autumn before ; which the Bishop referred to, and with his usual quiet helpful way he said a few prayers, and bid the boy good-bye : and a few moments after the Bishop left the room, the poor boy's first sleep came, and from that hour he began to recover.

So soon as he was well enough to leave London, he went to stay with the Miss Lawrences at Lynton ; and then, with Archdeacon Houblon, to Hindhead.

To the Diocesan Magazine

July 23.—I want to write a few words out of many thoughts of thankfulness that are in my heart. I want to tell just something of my gratitude to those who, during my illness, have been helping me with their prayers.

It has been a time full of mercy and loving kindness. I was, I think, "even hard at death's door," but God delivered me and has led me far on the way of recovery, and I am bidden to hope for a full return of health and strength. And all along I have had round me such care and comfort, such wealth of kindness, far and near, as might gladden any man. Nor has God, in spite of all my undeserving, withheld from me the light of His Countenance.

I long that through whatsoever years He wills I may more simply and more thankfully live for Him in the service of the Diocese, to which indeed these weeks have bound my heart closer than ever before.

To Miss Lawrence

Holy Trinity Vicarage, Barnstaple. Sept. 2. (*On the way back from Lynton to Hindhead.*)—We have all talked of this year's summer as sunless :—for me it has really been through all the past nine weeks sunny with an experience of kindness which has seemed new every morning, and made every day bright— and the kindness which has been about me all along has been the distinctive gladness of the weeks of convalescence :—I shall remember it thankfully and happily as long as I live :—but I can never, dear friends, thank you for it as I would. *Beacon Hotel, Hindhead. Sept.* 4.—The air is full of fragrance and freshness and health : and the views are quite glorious. There are great stretches of heather and gorse rolling up to, and on into, the grounds of the hotel : and, beyond the moorland, ranges of shapely hills, so that, amidst all that you see, you feel that there is far more yet to be discovered,—a reserve of beauty undisclosed. *Sept.* 17. (*A visit, from Hindhead, to Petworth.*) . . . the astonishing wealth of pictures there :— the most glorious Vandykes, and Turners, besides splendid Romneys, & Reynolds :—I doubt whether any one house, save, perhaps, Windsor Castle, & possibly Lockinge, holds such wealth :— we spent a really exciting three hours there.

On Sept. 26, he writes from Hindhead to Mr. W. G.

Boyd, head of the Mission House of the Archbishops' Western Canada Fund, Edmonton, Alberta :—

With all my heart I hope that things are going hopefully with you and with your company. The field into which the enterprise has gone is so vast, the strength we can throw into it seems so scanty, the forces that make for discouragement are so copious, that at times it must be very hard to keep one's heart up. I think I know something of the things that come and shake their fists at one when one is alone :—though I have never had to shake my fist back, & bluff my best, amidst difficulties anywhere near yours.—But those bullying fists retreat, thank God, in a way which makes one feel (in spite of Elia) that a bully is, if not a coward, a poor creature ; and we are granted wonderful disclosures of the goodness & patience & kindness and upward longing that is sustained in the depths of human hearts and hidden by their shyness. . . . We must be doing our utmost to prevent the workers and the work from suffering from wasteful hardships :—hardships such as can be & should be prevented. I hope that we shall have this in the front of our thoughts when the Council meets next month. . . . I have settled into a deliberate conviction that this really is the most beautiful place I know : a conviction which will be indelible until I lose my heart as happily to some other bit of country.

On October 20, from Cuddesdon, he writes to A. C. Madan, in Northern Rhodesia, of his illness—" doctors, and nurses, and colleagues & friends, all at it :— enough to spoil anybody :—and I can't be thankful enough for it "—and to F. J. Cade :—

A letter from Stephen to-day tells me that you are in my very own Nursing Home, and in my very own room : and I must venture to write a few words, needing no sort of acknowledgment. I seem to see the chimney-pots again, and to look up at the sky with that altered aspect which it has when one is supinely contemplating it : and I could almost hear the electric bells, & listen for the marmot-like whistle that told of a doctor's coming. I wonder whether my special friends are nursing you : if they are, will you, please, tell them of my grateful remembrance ?   I do hope with all my heart that you are in such comfort as was granted to me :—not too ill or weary to enjoy the happiness of feeling kindness all round you, and Goodness all above you. . . . I shall venture to-morrow to send you a few flowers, though the garden is beginning to think of closing for repairs :—they may just remind you of one who is thinking of you.

By reason of the Bishop's illness, the Diocesan Conference was not held this year.

On Oct. 30, a meeting in support of the Western Canada Fund was held in Christ Church Hall, at which the Archbishop of York, the Bishop of Oxford, and Lord Hugh Cecil were the speakers.

On Nov. 25, after a short illness, the Bishop's younger daughter died.

On Nov. 28, he wrote to the Diocesan Magazine, of the coming General Election, and of the duty of prayer at such a time.   In December, he wrote again :—

For a long time I have been trying to think what to say in this letter for the New Year.   I have been trying so long that I must try no longer: for the Old Year is coming near its end; and there is a limit to the patience of even the kindest and most patient of editors.   So with a hopeful sort of despair I shall just say what has been in my mind all along.   It is what has come into my thoughts again and again as I look back over the year that is all but gone : it is as old as the hills, and, I think, older : but sometimes a man's eyes are opened so to see it that it looks as new as the day-break or the Spring.

It is this.—There is no learning that can be compared with learning what love and kindness are : no absolute loss or gain except the loss or gain of love and kindness : no real growth or getting on save by growing more sensitive to love and kindness, more loving and more kind.

That is all.—But I am sure that it is true.   I could prove it over and over again: from the Bible ; from poetry, and from plays, and from novels ; from people's ways, from their voices and their faces ; and from contrasted scenes in human life.— Where love and kindness come in and work, there is a change almost like that of those chemical experiments which I remember making in my youth :—save that they were not always successful. For instance, think what a contrast there is between the look, the tone of life in a London street, and the character of thought and feeling in the ward of a hospital. There is the same human material : as you go from bed to bed, you can see what the people were in their ordinary ways. But the spell of kindness has passed over them and touched their hearts : the air is charged with it : the great lesson is being learnt, and more or less rightly recited : and the great change is astir.—Some of us, perhaps, may have known the like of it in a Nursing Home.

Yes, it is the greatest lesson, the greatest gain, the greatest thing in the world : all life is just our chance of attaining it : nothing else will do instead of it, or be of any lasting use without it : neither shall silver be weighed for the price thereof. It is what makes, as we say, all the difference : it is the true test and standard of real happiness : and we shall do well to have it for the deepest meaning of our words as we wish one another a Happy New Year. We cannot guess at all what is hidden for us or for others, in the way of outward experience, of what is called prosperity or adversity, in the coming months : and we are very poor judges of what may be best, in that way, for others or for ourselves. But we cannot be wrong if we wish and pray one for another, that God may grant us, whether it be in tribulation or in welfare, in sickness or in health, in sorrow or in joy, the blessing of kindness round about us, and grace to know and prize it with humility and thankfulness, to remember it in unflagging gratitude, and to let it soften and enlighten our hearts, that they may be more sincere and constant in kindness and in love. For then we shall see the Love that is the Fount of all love, shining out through all the kindness of human hearts around us, and shining on for us if ever for a while that kindness seems to fail : it will not, I think, fail us long, if we are quietly ready to discern and welcome its return : and meanwhile we may go on just the same, if we keep thinking more and more of that Kindness and Love of God our Saviour towards man which appeared on the first Christmas Day.

So that is what I mean more than anything else, when I wish a very Happy New Year to those who read these words, and to all the Diocese which God lets me try to serve : the Diocese which, through the manifold experience of the past year, has taught me such lessons of kindness as I surely never can forget, nor, God helping me, fail to be the better for. Wonderful beyond all telling the kindness has been, in its simplicity and generosity and thoughtfulness : — shown in diverse and countless ways ;—the Christmas card a child had painted,—just a new tone in a familiar voice,—and now a great, big cheque, from friends whose names it is a joy to read, for the purchase of a motor-car.—When I was laid up in July, and my room was bright with flowers, and still more flowers came, one of my Nurses said that I should soon be a spoilt Bishop. I do hope that she was wrong : for indeed I want to be something different from that, for the sake of the Diocese which has been thus kind and good to me, and beyond telling helped me just when and where help means the very most.

1911

The motor greatly increased the happiness of this last year of his life. " The motor is mine," he writes from Cuddesdon to one of the donors, on Feb. 20, " and I've had the delight of my first run in it. I fetched it and it brought me from London this evening. As I think what a difference it promises to make, bringing a wealth of refreshment and enjoyment into my journeys, my whole heart thanks afresh the friends whose wonderful kindness has bestowed it on me, and of whom I shall often & happily think as I career about the Diocese."

On Easter Day, April 16, he preached in Cathedral to the Oxfordshire Territorial Force, and preached again in Abingdon. On Whitsun Day, June 4, he preached at Blenheim to the Yeomanry. His last confirmations at public schools were at Bradfield on May 31 and Radley on June 6. On June 10, he took part in the Investiture of the Prince of Wales with the Order of the Garter : " Such a scene," he writes, " such a glorious service, at Windsor to-day ! Beautiful almost to tears : I know I wasn't the only man with a lump in his throat." His last ordination was at Cuddesdon, on June 11. At the annual festival of the College, on June 13, he presided, according to custom, at the luncheon. The Bishop of Brechin proposed his health : and, in his reply, he said that

. . . he supposed health was one of those things which one appreciated more when, for a while, one had known the lack of it, and so health was to him a very special gladness and blessing, and he trusted that God would give him grace to use aright the health and strength He had given back to him. It had become clear to him within the last few months that he might look forward to ending his working days at Cuddesdon conscientiously ; he had tried very hard to get away, as he was quite sure the Bishop ought to live in Oxford. However, he could not let Cuddesdon. Various objections were raised— it was said by most that there was no shooting. It was quite in vain that he said for himself he had found no deficiency, and quite in vain that he offered to throw in the College—at all events, during lectures. Nothing would induce any one to take it, and he found he could not sell it for the simple reason that he could not find the right house for the Commissioners to buy instead of it. So there he was, and there he might hope to be so long as he could work, and there he meant, with a clear conscience, to enjoy to the last the happiness of being in that most beautiful place.

The Archbishop of York, in answer to a special request, has kindly given permission for the publication of the following note :—

" He had asked me to preach the sermon at the Cuddesdon Festival on June 13, 1911, and I stayed with him at Cuddesdon.   During the day we were all delighted by his freshness, almost exhilaration.   He seemed to be rejoicing in the restoration of health after his long illness : he gave the impression of a man entering on a new stage of his life with high hope and happy spirits.   At the luncheon, he spoke with all his usual charm of fancy and phrase, and with a new freedom and brightness.   He spoke very simply about his return to work, as if he enjoyed the prospect, without any trace of the weariness which had seemed before his illness to grow upon him.   He told us that he had made up his mind that Cuddesdon was still always to be his home.   There seemed to be in his speech and in his manner all day the spirit of a man who had made some inner decision which had left him free and sanguine.   Later in the day he told me that he wished very greatly to have some talk with me in the evening.   It was very late before we met in his study : but he seemed eager to use the quiet time. There was something in this eagerness which rather surprised me, especially as it was plain that he wished to speak about himself : for as you know he was very sparing in any self-disclosure.   It seemed to me that he was anxious to liberate himself of something that was, as the phrase goes, ' on his mind.'   He said he wished to speak about my sermon and the way in which it had interpreted his own thoughts about himself. My text had been 2 Tim. i. 6, 7, ' I put thee in remembrance that thou stir up the gift of God, which is in thee through the laying on of my hands.   For God gave us not a spirit of fearfulness ; but of power and love and discipline.'   I had spoken of the experiences of that blank mid-day of a man's life when the morning visions of the young man had gone, and the evening dreams of the old man had not come ; and of a 'fearfulness' which sometimes haunted the soul, taking two forms, in regard to a man's work of a certain apprehensiveness, and in regard to his inward life of that 'accidie' which he himself had sketched with such a master-hand. As to the former, I had spoken of it as a shrinking of the will before tasks once eagerly undertaken, a sinking of the heart at the challenge of ventures and calls of work once eagerly accepted. As to the latter, I had spoken of it as a faintheartedness and weariness of spirit which beset men who had accepted a high and exacting standard of inward life.

"He said that my words had somehow described what was becoming his own experience before his illness. I can only, of course, summarise an intimate conversation. The point of it was, I think, this—after his great sorrow, the death of his wife, he had determined, as the only means by which he could fortify his soul against it and prevent it clouding his whole life, to devote himself with unsparing absorption to his daily tasks of work. The result was that his work became almost, as it were, an idol which demanded an exacting and painstaking devotion. Gradually, instead of his possessing it, and retaining his own freedom, it came to possess him, and to enslave him. He came, almost unconsciously, to resent anything which might have lightened it—pushed aside, e.g., such conveniences as dictating his letters or using a motor car for his journeys. The fear of realising the blank in his home-life created by the loss of his wife's companionship led him—almost without his perceiving the tendency—to

detach himself from that home-life, from the interests
and occupations of his children, and to hold on with a
sort of grim determination to his work.   During his
illness, he had come to see what consequences had
followed from this excessive self-concentration on his
work.   He had begun to lose buoyancy of spirit ; to
let toil tell upon his nerves ; to see the problems of
his own diocese and of the Church in dark colours.
The oppression of work resulted in depression of spirit.
He became inwardly tired—in a word, dispirited.

" But his illness and the weeks of convalescence had
given him time to review himself.   He had come to
see that he had made a mistake—that he must recover
the liberty of his spirit.   He realised that the way
of escape was just to 'wait upon the Lord '—to
trust more simply in the Spirit of Power and Love
and Fortitude that had been given to him—to have
more faith in God's control of his own work, of
the diocese, of the Church.   He saw that instead of
detaching himself from home-life, he ought to have
made the most of it, and found *there*, in his sons and
daughters and their thoughts and interests, the change
and relief from work that his soul required.   He was
determined to take life more simply and trustfully—to
be less painfully fastidious in his standard of work and
to welcome rather than put aside the means by which
its burden could be lightened.   He spoke as if he felt
that life had been given back to him, to enter upon a
new stage, more resolutely hopeful and trustful, and
more ready to rely on the love of friends and children,
and the free and strong Spirit of God.

" I cannot pretend that I have in any way quoted his
words—I can only hope that I have not misinterpreted
the spirit of his talk.   When it was over, he greatly

touched me by thanking me for my sermon that day, and by asking me to give him my Blessing.

"I think you will have abundant evidence in the memories of his friends and in his own words, to show that in these last months of his life, as on that June 13 at Cuddesdon, he was like a man who had been set free, and was quietly but happily rejoicing in his freedom. And now he is free indeed."

On June 20, he was present at the Coronation Men's Meeting in Queen's Hall : and on June 22, at the Coronation, was in attendance on the Queen.

To Sir Anthony Bowlby

July 1.—This day last year we met for the first time :— and two days later, on the 3rd—well, you saved my life.—And then, day after day, it was always re-assuring & delightful to see you come into the room, or to know that you were in the house.—And as, to-night, I think over it all, I can't forego writing a word just to tell, how every day my whole heart thanks you.

You must not, please, think of answering this note ; nor yet of acknowledging in any way the two little books which I am venturing to send :—one I thought might sometimes please you on your holiday, when the last possible fish has been caught, and it's not quite bedtime : and the other I thought your daughter might some time like : for it was put together by three young ladies, between the ages of six and sixteen, the daughters of a friend of mine in Oxford. Please don't write :— and let me be, your grateful & affectionate friend.

To Mrs. Stephen Paget

July 13.—This morning's post has brought me one de- lightful letter, with the hope of a great privilege and happiness. I am quite free on Tuesday, October the 10th ; and most gladly I look forward to coming that day to marry Molly and Basil : it will be a real joy to me.

On Sunday, July 16, he was at Longworth.[1] On Saturday, July 22, he gave a great afternoon party, in Christ Church Hall, to his clergy. It was a perfect summer day ; and many hundreds of the clergy and their wives were present. He received them on the great staircase of the Hall : one who was there writes of him " standing all the afternoon, receiving the stream of guests—and such a sense of happy greeting on either side : he so happy with the recollection of all the kindness of the last year, and so proud of such a beautiful background to his party as the Hall : and the guests—I can see them now as they came streaming up—as happy to see him back in health : it was all so individual and sincere and warm-hearted." On Saturday, July 29, he was at a " King's Messengers' Festival " at South Newington, and gave a short address to the children, and pleased them by photographing some of them. His friend Lawrence Hardy went to Cuddesdon that day for the week-end : and writes of him :—

Not since those old days had I seen the Bishop so full of happiness and fun : he was just starting abroad for a holiday, he had put behind him all diocesan business and engagements, he rejoiced in the year's work after his severe illness in 1910, with all its proofs of real affection and loyalty from the diocese, and he was just like the Frank Paget of old days—(the *g* soft and the word pronounced like French, as we always used to call him). There was only a party of four in the house : Miss Church, and the Bishop, my wife, and myself. In the

---

[1] Canon Scott Holland writes of this meeeting : " He came once again to join the ' old gang ' of his familiar Oxford allies at Longworth, just before the end. He had missed the annual gathering very often : and it was a peculiar delight to us all to have him back in something like his old gaiety of spirit. He was singularly well and hopeful. He preached, in impressive simplicity, in the village church. He went off to wind up his last things before the holiday to which he was looking forward with quite a boyish glee."

garden, his son Edward, and his Chaplain, looked after a large Working‑men's Mission, which was full of interest.   We went together to early and morning church.   At lunch, the Bishop was at his best, calling up all the old memories of our Christ Church days — Archdeacon Clark's sermons, Canon Liddon, Scott Holland—his fright at having to read Dr. Pusey's last sermon in St. Mary's for him—and many such-like stories. At 2.30, we two went off to a distant church (Berrick, near Chalgrove), where he preached to the children a simple discourse but very touching; and we went to tea with the vicar : and thence, in the great heat, we walked home, about 7 miles.   He would have walked further, but spared me.   On our way we lingered talking of all the public events, especially the Parliament Bill, and the attitude of the Bishops upon it ; and revision of the Prayer-book.   He spoke of the difficulties in the Diocese, and the loyalty of all, though many differed from him.   In the evening, he and I went to the tents of the Mission in the garden, and listened to speeches on Prayer. There was an egotistic spirit in some of them, which evidently was not quite acceptable to the Bishop, who in a few words at the close brought back the subject to higher lines.   And I then said good-night, and thought he looked weary and rather sad.   Next morning I saw him for a few minutes, and was greatly struck at the change, and was very anxious.

During this last year of his life, though he was in good general health, he had more than one threatening of illness, and held his life on a very uncertain tenure. He had wished to go out to Canada for the Arch-bishops' Fund, but had been forbidden by medical advice.   On Monday, July 31, it was evident that he was in great danger : and he was taken-up in his motor, that afternoon, to London, to Welbeck House. He was attended by Sir Thomas Barlow and Sir Alfred Peace Gould : and, on Tuesday afternoon, it was found necessary to operate on him.   The con-ditions which made operation necessary were due not to anything done at the former operation, but to the inflammation which had preceded that operation. The conditions found at the second operation were such, that, even if the Bishop had recovered, it is probable that he would have lived only for a few years, perhaps for less than a year. Before the operation, he saw Miss Church, and gave her his last directions, and dictated a codicil to his will. During Tuesday night, he was very restless, with a failing pulse. On Wednesday morning, he said that he had not been in pain during the night : but he quoted the line in the Dream of Gerontius—" That sense of ruin which is worse than pain." He sent a message to Lambeth, asking that one of the Archbishop's chaplains would come and give him the Holy Communion : and the Archbishop came. After he had received the Holy Communion, he had some rest. Later in the morning, he was distressed by the heat of the day, and by the sound of the traffic : for it had not been possible for him to have the large quiet room which he had in 1910. In the afternoon, he was moved into another room : but by this time he was sinking fast. His only anxiety was lest he should not see Miss Church again before he died. His sisters were away, and came too late to see him. He saw his eldest son and Mrs. Davidson ; and he sent his blessing to his children, and to Mr. Perrin, his chaplain, who had been like a son to him : and he gave his blessing to his brother the Bishop of Stepney, and received his brother's blessing. His eldest brother, Sir John Paget, was abroad. To one who was in the room, remembering the day for her daughter's wedding, he said that he was sorry he should not be with them on that day, and he sent them his blessing. To another, who spoke

of his seeing again those whom he had loved, he said,
" So soon."   Last of all, he followed, with a steady
voice, the words of the Psalm, " The Lord is my
Shepherd."

His body was taken to Cuddesdon, and on August 5
from Cuddesdon to Oxford.   After service in the
Cathedral, it was attended to the graveside by the
Archbishops and many Bishops.   It was committed to
the grave by the Dean of Christ Church : and the
blessing was given by the Archbishop of Canterbury.
To his memory an exhibition has been founded, for
men wishing to take orders, but unable to pay for their
University course ;   preference being given to those
looking forward to work in North-West Canada.

CHAPTER IX

THESE letters were written by the Bishop to his son Bernard, in India and Burma with his Regiment, 43rd Oxfordshire Light Infantry. Some personal matters, and some of the home-news, have been left out : so have some short letters, written in great haste to catch the mail. Often he had to write in the train, or in the waiting-room of a station : and many of the letters were begun in one place and finished in another. He did not like to write letters at meetings : but there is one, a very short one, that was " written in a meeting slow enough to make it specially dull, and contentious enough to keep it from being coherent." They form a sort of diary of the last years of his life : and they must be read as a diary.

There is a break in them, between February and September 1910, when his son came home on leave.

1908

Jan. 2.—This is indeed sharp work. It's dreadful to think of your going, to think you will be so far off, to think how long you may be away, and how we shall all miss you, and how old I may be before you come back :—it makes my heart ache a bit, and I should be sorry if it didn't. But I believe it is for the welfare of your work ; and it may take you straight

267

where things are most real : and there are deeper thoughts to
check one from fear or regret :—and so I am, or will be glad.
Jan. 11, *St. Leonard's.*—I hope that the cross-country run will
come off, & that you'll lead your men to victory. If you've
had weather like ours, cross-country running must be a Spartan
exercise, in mud such as Lord Wantage has taught me to call
Crimean. I think his Life is really a wonderful book : I've
been reading it carefully, with increasing admiration. We've
had bad weather, but good walks :—yesterday to Battle, where
we couldn't see the field of Senlac or the ruins of the Abbey
that William built (with the High Altar over the spot where
Harold's body was found) because the people at the great house
(Americans now, if you please) only let you come in on Tues-
days. The last time I was there was 40 years ago :—I rode
over, almost my first venture on a horse outside a Riding-
School. *Feb.* 6.—Just twenty-four hours since we said good-
bye. You will know how constantly I have been thinking of
you, and longing that all may be going well :—so I shan't try
to tell you that. The Bishop of Southwark was dreadfully
sorry that he missed sending you his message of God-speed :—
he feels a special bond with you, I know, & cares very much.
Last night, Winnie sang to us for an hour :—I'm sure it was
partly because she felt that it had been a hard day.—I can
almost see you waving out of the window as the train went
round the curve at Waterloo. *Feb.* 12.—" The Mail goes to-
morrow : " that's a new phrase that has come into my life since
you went:—I never thought much about the mails before :
now they mean a chance not to be missed, even though it's a
short, poor letter that I send. We think of you often ;—
where you've got to, how you're faring, what you'll be looking
at & doing when this reaches you. And the " punitive ex-
pedition " becomes a centre of thought when it may con-
ceivably mean active service for you :—it will become an
absorbing centre of thought if it does. I'm glad that at the
India Office we have one of the ablest men in the Government,
one of the least likely to be thinking of popularity instead of
duty if a hard time comes. I've long respected Morley, across
wide differences of opinion : ever since I knew how he

honoured Dean Church, and ever since he got himself disliked by speaking out against an " Eight hours' day." I've just come back from Birmingham, from staying with the Bishop to bear a little part in some great Meetings which he has planned. It's wonderful to see what a hold he has got on that great place :—there's no mistaking it :—and it's just come by straightness and simplicity. I send you a tiny picture :—one I brought from Florence—just for a bookmarker—it's nothing. *Feb.* 18, *White Waltham.*—I've just come on from staying with a most delightful soldier, Major Bulkeley. He served with a Yorkshire regiment in S. Africa, and got the D.S.O. He's able, kind, humorous, & loyal, & has a most pleasant home. —We talked much of soldiering : and I wish I could remember the things he said about the strength & trust that accrue to an officer who really knows his men :—he made me feel afresh what a splendid chance it is.—He was very strong on the wisdom of having gone out to India, & especially of having gone out young. *Feb.* 27.—I write at Sonning, in between two Confirmations :—for I am in the midst of much travelling :—strangely different from yours :—for it's just running to & fro within what wd. seem to you now a tiny area. On Saturday last I was in Oxford :—I saw the Christ Church Torpid go Head of the River, after a splendid race : and I went to the meeting about the Christ Church Mission, where very pleasant, cheering things were said about " Edward Paget," and his hopping, and his good deeds generally :—delightful things for me to hear. Now I must stop : for I've got to go & see a sick man before the Confirmation.

March 3, *Winslow Hall, Bucks.*—As I write, I suppose you are at Lucknow, & well, I hope, & settling into the new conditions. I am writing in a most beautiful house, built by Sir Christopher Wren, & decorated in his time. My bedroom is oak-panelled to the ceiling, with great painted scenes on the big panels ; & the whole house is full of delightful things. But the best of it all is the host Mr. McCorquodale :—a real sportsman, first-rate in his care for his grooms and servants : —and quietly, simply keen about his Church. There are some wonderfully good people about the world, I think :—& there's

nothing so refreshing as to be with them.   We're all in a stir
about the Education Bill & the Licensing Bill.—The latter
I can hardly judge yet :—it aims right I think, but it seems a
bit peremptory & hasty.   The other, the Education Bill, seems
to me really tyrannous & iniquitous :—I hope we shall fight it
hard, & I think we may carry a good many people's consciences with us.   *March* 11.—I've just been talking to Lord
Roberts : I couldn't help telling him about you : & I must
write down at once what he said :—he asked what Regiment
you were in : and I told him you had exchanged into the 43rd
in order to get out to India, & to work : and he said : "Well,
it's a fine regiment, with a great history : " " He's quite right
to go to India " : " I'm delighted to hear it " : " I hope he'll do
well " :—" you tell him I said so."   It was all said in short,
quick sentences, rather like giving the word of command. . . .
To-day I have been up for a Wellington Governors' Meeting,
and I am writing in the train on the way back. . . . There's
been an unreasonable excitement over a private letter of the
German Emperor's to Lord Tweedmouth :—a storm in the
papers, and questions in both Houses.   The only "moral " I
can see is that if you mean a thing to be private it's very foolish
to talk of it. . . .   *March* 18.—I think your welfare has been
among the special and chief bits of happiness in the past year.
. . . Yesterday I was confirming at Lambourne, where the
great racing-stables are.   I noticed two lads specially among
the Candidates :—quiet, self-possessed, reverent, serious-looking
lads, such as it's a help to see :—and I found afterwards that
they were two of the best of the jockeys, one, I believe, already
famous, & riding for the King.—I wanted a motor to take
me on to my next Confirmation ; and five were offered :—it
was another jockey who finally sent me on.   We have dreadful
weather, with bitter cold and snow-storms :—it's been trying
work travelling from place to place ;—and I have two Confirmations most days.   *March* 25, *The Red House, Ascot.*—On
Tuesday I was at Sandhurst :—but I could not possibly get to
the R.M.C., for I was confirming at Crowthorne and at Fin-
chamstead, & going on to sleep at Winkfield : so the day was
full.—I lunched at the Rectory at Sandhurst, where there were

many enquiries about you :—and I met General Lawrence Parsons, who was, I believe, Inspector of the Artillery in India under Lord Kitchener. He talked a bit about India, and laid stress on the wisdom of never going out in the morning until you have had some food :—and he said things which it would have pleased you to hear about the Oxfordshire Light Infantry. Here I am staying with Lord Stanmore. He told me, this evening, Dr. Johnson's definition of " courteous " and " polite." " Courteous ; elegant in manners ; kind." " Polite ; elegant in manners ; glossy." *April* 2.—I was staying at Lockinge last night, and had a delightful bit of talk with Colonel Carter, who was formerly in your regiment, and whose son, I believe, is in it now. He spoke of the tone and tradition of the regiment in a way that did one's heart good :—telling me the things that were said to him by the Colonel when he joined, and how they had told on him & stuck in his mind. He made me glad afresh that it is your regiment. *April* 15, *Christ Church.*— Here I am, writing in the old home :—the place more like home to me than any other in the world. By the Dean's unfailing kindness, I have been staying here for the Oxford Confirmations : to-morrow I go to Reading for Good Friday, to take the Three Hours' Service at St. Bartholomew's :—then to London, to start for Ireland, I expect, on Easter Monday. —As I write here, I think what letters were written to you from these rooms in the old days :—I went and looked at the little grave-yard this morning. Good-bye, dearest Bernard ; for it's near midnight ; & there's much more to do this side of bed, if I can keep awake. *April* 21, *Killarney.*—We had a magnificent run, getting to Rosslare in 2½ hours : and then we went on by train to Waterford, where we stayed last night. Very delightful it was, with pleasant, kindly people, in a very comfortable but rather old-fashioned hotel. Here we are less " characteristic," but more " up-to-date ". . . . The great excitement on at the present moment is the Manchester Election :—Winston Churchill fighting to keep his seat after his entrance into the Cabinet. There are things about him that always interest me, and something that attracts me :—but I think I shall not be sorry if he's turned out. *April* 28, *Caragh*

Lake, Kerry.—Beatrice, I expect, has told you all the news of our holiday together :—a delightful holiday it has been, & to-day one of its best days, with a wonderful sight of the great cliffs that face the full Atlantic on Valentia Island.   A special pleasure in each day has been the pleasantness of the people amongst whom we travel :—there seems to be a delightful courtesy (according to Dr. Johnson's definition) and a simple dignity of self-respect in all classes, such as I have met with in no other people.

Cuddesdon, May 8.—This is not a real letter :—only just a word, lest I should be absent from the mail.   These last few days have been rather desperate—I've been writing till 1 or 2 most mornings. . . . *May 21.*—I wish you could see the beautiful embroidered stuff which you sent me in its present place and use.   It drapes the oak stand on which rests in the corner of my study that beautiful, great plàque which your uncle gave me ;—the scene from Dante, where the boat-full of little, wistful souls is crossing the waves to the Mount of Purgatory, with the stately Angel standing in the stern of the boat. . . . The scenes of that wonderful march up into the hills came before me very vividly : & I can just imagine what the first sight of the Himalayas must have been to you.   I always think that a great sea, a great sunset, and a great range of snow mountains, are the greatest sights in the world :—and I often recall what my father said once, when we were together looking at the "incomparable pomp of eve" :—"To think that beggars like us can enjoy it ". . . . Dear old Bayne is very ill :—he had a sudden heart-failure on Tuesday : and they sent him into the Acland Home, where I went to see him to-day.   He's better, I am thankful to say :—and he's just like himself, cheerful and patient and thinking about other people.   When I gave him Frida's love he laughed & said " Has Frida got any to spare ? " and before I came away he was pressing me to tell him whether there was any School in the Diocese that I wanted money for.—I don't know any one quite like him, so constant and loyal and generous.   *May 27, Lambeth Palace.*—Yesterday the Archbishop and Mrs. Davidson asked me to go abroad with them in August.   They asked me once before : and I had to say no. This time I've actually said yes :—and it is a delightful holiday to look forward to.—It's wonderfully good of them to ask me : I told the Archbishop that if he gets me out there & doesn't like me it will be an awful bore :—but they say they'll face it. It's really wonderful of them. I don't think I shall be failing any-one at home. . . . This afternoon I was crossing St. James's Park, and by good luck got an excellent sight of the French President, as he was returning, with the Prince and Princess of Wales, from the luncheon at the Guildhall.—He's a shrewd, comfortable-looking old gentleman, with no appearance of distinction about him :—just sensible and capable :—but I expect he does his own job in life very well. They're working him very hard, with all sorts of State functions on a grand scale :—and I believe he is going through it all very cheerfully and successfully.—I was told that some one asked him what he would feel like when it was all over : and he answered very sensibly, " Il ne faut pas songer à cela." . . . Bayne died very early on Monday morning. I had seen him only a few hours before ;—we prayed together, and I gave him the Blessing, & he spoke a word of thankfulness, and then said good-bye, and pressed my hand.—I can never have another friend quite like him :—& I think no one bore a truer or more reverent affec-tion towards your mother. He will be buried on Friday in the little grave-yard under the walls of the Cathedral :—& they will sing the same hymns that they sang when she was buried. *June* 11, *In the train.*—It's dreadful : I missed last week's mail : the days were busy, broken, and vagabond ;—but perhaps it's good for me : I had rather set my heart in pride on never missing a mail. . . . I write on the way back to Oxford from marrying John Egerton Warburton (who was at the House) to a daughter of Lord Newton's.—The wedding was at St. Peter's, Eaton Square :—the church was crowded :—and the centre aisle was lined by men of the Scots Guards, Warburton's regiment :—it was a beautiful sight.—But I think I'm getting rather old to run about as I used to do. Last Sunday week I was preaching at Reading & at Barkham, and staying with Mr. Wilson Noble, Leonard Noble's brother. He is a most interesting man, an amateur electrical engineer :—he has a great work-shop attached to his house :—and he has himself constructed a wireless-telegraphy machine, with which he receives messages straying about in ether. I myself heard one, or believed I did :—but you need to know what to listen for. The day before, I was lunching with the Yeomanry in their Camp at Wytham Park. It was rather amusing : I sat between the Duke of Marlborough & Winston Churchill, who is one of the officers, & of whom I took quite a fair photograph. He always interests me. . . . We are all talking and thinking a good deal about the "unrest" in India : and you, I expect, are watching, as well as talking & thinking. The people whom I have met or whose words I've read seem to believe that it was bound to come sooner or later ;—but that it might have been delayed, or come with less asperity or danger ; some say, if we had been firmer in our general policy ; some say, if we had been more conciliatory towards individuals, less dictatorial or scornful. *Waterloo Day.* — What I should desire for —— would be first that he should sit down and listen to the four Gospels, especially St. John's : that he should have them slowly, quietly, read to him : so that the picture, the Form, the Voice they bring before us might sink into his heart.—And then I should like him to watch some one like your mother, or my father, or the Bishop of Lincoln, and see the strength and purity and gentleness and brightness that Christ works in a life simply set towards Him.—Those are things that come right home to me, more than all the arguments and proofs. The arguments & proofs are needed :— they have their place & work in the whole presentation and upholding of Christianity :—and they are quite adequate for that place & work :—but it is Christ Himself, and the characters He forms and animates, that really reach the heart and win it. . . . We've just had the (Cuddesdon) Festival : I expect that other letters will have told you how delightful the Head-Master of Eton was : simple, and kind, and humorous, & brilliant : looking delightful, & behaving accordingly. Bayne has left to me all his papers & letters, to do as I like with : and this afternoon I have been looking at them. It's rather sad

work, and touching : there was a packet of your mother's
letters, and of mine : among them, one marked as the last he
had from her—just a card of invitation to dinner. One thing
after another shows what a heart he had.

July 9, *London*. . . . in the thick of the Lambeth Conference :—and very thick it is. We gathered first at Canterbury last week for a Reception, and an Opening Service in the
Cathedral : and then on Monday we began our Sessions in the
Great Library at Lambeth.—We meet in private :—250 of us
altogether, from all parts of the Anglican Communion,—India,
America, China, Japan, Australia, Africa :—two negro Bishops
from Western Equatorial Africa :—and no quarter of the globe
unrepresented. It's very tiring : for, with but a brief break
for luncheon, we sit from eleven till after five every day : and
one has to be attentive all the time. But it is also interesting
& encouraging : it shows problems in new light, from strange
points of view : and it makes one feel very deeply the range
and the power of the Anglican Communion. For the speaking is, on the whole, wonderfully good : sometimes, & not
seldom, it rises to be quite first-rate : and one feels that men
are not only saying very ably what they think, but have thought
of it very ably before they say it.—And through it all goes the
wonderful, simple, unwearied kindness of the Archbishop and
Mrs. Davidson, planning everything, entertaining the whole
250 of us at luncheon & tea every day, and never too busy to
be nice to everybody, with the unfailing tact of a kind heart.
One of those who was to have been here, Bp. Awdry of South
Tokyo, had to undergo yesterday a very severe operation. He
went into a Nursing Home for it on Tuesday, knowing that it
was critical :—but the day before he quietly came here for the
morning meeting, made his speech, & then went to Lord's
for the afternoon's cricket. Rather simple, & good, I think.

July 17.—That sight of the mountains after the rain must have
been an unveiling of real glory : I wish we had been seeing it
together. Well, a month hence I hope I may be looking at
snow mountains. Yesterday I got a talk with the Archbishop :
and after our business we laughed for pleasure to think of
Courmayeur. I can't tell how I'm longing for it : — how

I trust all happiness and restfulness may be granted to us.—
He is more & more a hero to me :—so strong, and kind, and
patient. . . . Dr. Bigg's death brings a great loss :—he has
been a true, warm-hearted friend :—and it was always a
pleasure to see him, and a delight and help to listen to him.
I think one of the very few really good things that I've done
was bearing some part in bringing about his appointment at
Christ Church. Ld. Salisbury appointed him. We shall miss
him sadly :—but I am thankful that he was spared pain, which
he dreaded, and the weariness of prolonged old age. *July* 23,
Cuddesdon.—It's an immense relief to get away into fresh,
fragrant air : as I get older I understand more the deep help of
such things, and love the country more, and London, I fear,
less. I go back on Monday for nine days more work. . . .
I've lost another friend, Louis Dyer the historian. He had
had his arm amputated for some grave trouble :—I went to see
him, & found him bright, cheerful, grateful, hopeful beyond
imagining : I never saw a man more simple & noble in a
great trial. He seemed to be going on quite well : then a
change came suddenly, & he passed away unconscious. *Aug.* 7,
Duffield.—I can imagine the sense of both loss & gain in
exchanging Ranikhut for Lucknow : the loss of some measure
of separate and independent responsibility :—the gain of getting
back to the regiment, and to friends. I write on my way back
from the Lambeth Conference. We finished our Sessions on
Wednesday :—and yesterday I came to Reading for a meeting,
& then on here for a function last night. And on the 10th,
if all be well, I'm off. We go straight through from Calais to
Martigny, in the Rhone Valley, piping hot. Dear Bernard,
I'm so looking forward to it that it seems almost too much to
think of its coming off. I know your birthday is near : I
can't remember the very day : I've got a present in my mind's
eye :—but it will be forestalled by my very best wishes. God
grant you many years of good work & happiness, with the
advancing responsibility which is what "getting-on" really
means : & with the happiness of well-earned trust : & with
strength & wisdom and patience and loyalty to bear all the
burdens. I finish in the waiting-room at Reading, so as just

to catch the mail. If all be well, my next letter will be written just under Mont Blanc,—wonderful.

Aug. 20, *Courmayeur.*—I've been having even as good a holiday as all your thought for me could devise. Monday was one of the very best days I've ever had : I started with four other men, & a guide & two porters, at 5.30 in the morning : —we climbed up to the Col du Géant, over 11,000 feet : then across the Glacier du Géant, & up a small peak called La Vierge, rising above the Glacier, & giving a most glorious view of Mt. Blanc, & the other great peaks of the same group, with the Mer de Glace sweeping round towards Chamounix. The splendour of the pure white snow, & the deep, intense blue sky, with the huge heights towering up close round us, were far beyond all words. I've had a talk here with Dr. Longstaff, the Himalayan climber & explorer. Good-bye, dearest Bernard : &, once more, God grant you many years of useful, happy, honourable life, as a good soldier, & as His servant. *Aug.* 27. . . . a glorious climb yesterday up Mt. Dolent, 12,650 feet above the sea. We started the day before, slept in a hay-hut, creeping through a gap in the roof to lie on the hay : and then set out at 2.45, in the dark, with lanterns ; and after a steep time on the Glacier & up the rocks, reached the top at 9.15. Most splendid it was : with such views as surpass all imagination & beat all telling. I went up with Canon Arnold, the Chaplain here, just we two, with two guides : & one of the guides, Henri Brocherel, had been with Dr. Longstaff in the Himalayas, when they got up above any recorded climb :—such a delightful fellow, full of interest and keenness and kindness :—I slept in his sleeping-sack, which he had had with him in the great climb. He had been at Ranikhut, & at Lucknow. The other guide had been with the Duke of the Abruzzi when he went up Mt. Ruwenzori, & with Mackinder up Mt. Kenia, in Eastern Africa, the first ascent ever made of it : so we had distinguished as well as delightful companions. I don't think I ever had a day with more glorious things to see, or more exciting climbing. *Sept.* 10, *Varallo-Sesia.*—I drove down here in a sort of omnibus, with three very gaunt horses, and very much dawdling. I should have walked : but the clouds were heavy and low, hiding the tops of all the smaller hills, and taking all the brightness out of the scene :—yet, all the same, I often wished I were walking. I've had a really splendid time this past month : with good weather, in the most glorious country :—with some of the finest walks I've ever had :—with Perrin somehow managing to send on to me hardly any letters :—and with the happiness of being with the best and kindest of people : —I can't say how good they've been to me. I do hope that I may work all the better for the wealth of refreshment and enjoyment that I have had. . . . It will be just thrilling to see those three great places, Agra and Delhi and Benares :—I think that no names in India stand out quite as those do, each with its own great, distinctive interest. . . . One special thing that I have felt in being with the Archbishop is a thing that touches all work : his unwearied, alert *interest* in everything he comes across :—the way the people make their cheese :—the way an old carpenter is making milking-pails, and what wood will do, and what won't : the laws about motor-cars, and military service, and road-mending :—everything stirred his interest ;— and, having a good knowledge of Italian, he could talk with the people about everything, to their delight and his enjoyment.

Sept. 24, *Chough's Nest, Lynton.*—This paper will bring back pleasant days and glorious sights that you and I have shared : with the happiness of coming back in the evening to the constant kindness of our hostesses, and the bright rooms, and the quick, friendly talk, we have no truer friends, I think, than they are ; and Mr. Bloxam's regard for you is quite touching. Thank you very much for the letter about your visit to the Residency :—it was most interesting & vivid :— I did not know how all the details of those great events had been kept in connexion with their scenes.—You speak of Jessie's *dream* of the Pipes :—I thought it was believed that she really heard them, far off as they were. Yesterday there came an extraordinarily good letter from Edward :—he's been working like a team of horses among the hop-pickers in Kent : — doing really good work, I'm sure : over-tasked, worried, tired, and still happy in it all. I'm very glad and thankful when I think of it. *Oct.* 2. Lynton was delightful :—I went the old walks, Hunter's Inn, Malmsmead, Watersmeet—with Sir Maurice Holzmann, who is a real, splendid walker, pounding along with a true love of it, & good for nearly twenty miles every day, if you like.—We often talked of you, & I much more often thought of you. *Oct.* 10, *Cuddesdon.*—. . . The Bishop of Reading has resigned. I had staved it off once or twice :—it would have been unwise and unkind, I think, to stave it off longer. But I shall miss him much & often :—he has been very generous and loyal : and he is a man of real ability & experience & influence. I don't know what will come next :—there is to be a Committee to consider whether the Diocese shd. be divided, or some other way taken to lighten the work :—but it's really the responsibility & anxiety that I want lightened, if it might be. *Oct.* 22.—Last Sunday I met, at a house where I was staying, Miss Wildman, who is the Superintendent, I think, of all the Nursing in Military Hospitals in India. She talked very interestingly of her work & travels :—knows Burmah well :— & made me glad that you are going to the Station with the hard name, and not to Mandalay, where I gather, malaria is apt to be very dangerous. *Oct.* 30.—This is deplorable :— Friday morning, & my letter unwritten : — and at any moment the wisdom of Quarterman may summon me, & the post go. Well, there's something in the will, though it's better to have the deed too. I've had one memorable day in the past week :—I went to the ceremony wherein Lady Wantage handed over to Reading College the Hall or Hostel she has built in memory of Lord Wantage. It is a quadrangle like that of an Oxford College, with Hall & Chapel :—it is to accommodate 76 men : & it is just a complete free gift of her own. I've never seen a thing better done all through. *Nov.* 6.—It has been a week of wandering rather.—Sunday I spent at Hanborough, near Blenheim :—a Sunday with one touching thing to mark it in memory :—one of the candidates for Confirmation, a lad of 14, dying that morning, the morning of what was to have been his Confirmation Day. I went to see his people—quiet and simple and almost broken-hearted :—with that sort of reserve which gives such great height & dignity to grief. Then on Monday I went up to Lambeth for a night ; and had a comparison of my photographs with the Archbishop's :—they declare that mine are better than his :—& only an effort of modesty makes me question it. On Wednesday I had to go to London again, & then to Reading, for a Temperance Meeting. People are in an immense state of excitement over the Licensing Bill :—I think it is a very faulty Bill :—but I am sure that change is needed, that the Public Houses ought to be greatly reduced, & that the Nation ought to have unhindered and unquestioned control over the traffic :—so I hope it will pass :—but I hope also it will be much amended. *Dec.* 3.—It is horrid to think how I have failed lately in the matter of letter-writing : but it has been rather a tremendous time, with a storm of debate & a constant strain of anxiety over the Education Bill. The Archbishop and nearly all the Bishops have been making or supporting a great effort for a peaceful settlement, though we differ a bit among ourselves as to the possible terms. The main body of the Clergy, I think, and of the more ecclesiastically minded & Conservative laymen are against the Bishops. I think it is the sort of division which is apt to come between those who have mostly to make speeches on platforms, & those who have to be responsible for a policy. *Dec.* 10. . . . the Viceroy's arrival at Lucknow. I should like to have seen you with the Colours :—I always think there is a world of symbolism and imagination and dignity about a flag :—those old Colours in the Guards' Chapel move me deeply :—and I think the Cathedral never looked so well as when we had the Colours to take care of. You will have seen the fate of the Education Bill :—that, after all the long and arduous negotiations, it has come to nothing, & has been dropped. I must own to a sense of relief, which, I expect, is rather cowardly :—for the present, we escape the tremendous storm in which we should have found ourselves if the Bill had passed : for the vast majority of the Clergy were dead against it, at all events in this part of the country. But I think that, if no settlement is reached, things will be far worse ten years hence :—it's the choice between trouble present and certain, and disaster distant and probable :—always a hard choice to make. I've found a wonderful deal of considerateness and trustfulness in many of the Clergy who have differed from me, and thought that I went too far for the sake of peace :—but they would have felt intensely the sacrifice which the Bill would have asked of them, had it become law. *Dec.* 17, *Keble College.*—It seems odd to be writing to you from Oxford rooms, and yet not from Christ Church. I am staying here with the Candidates whom I hope to ordain in the Cathedral on Sunday. They always come here for the three days before the Ordination : and I think it is a time that often means a good deal to them. Now I will rely on your discretion, and tell you a bit of private news, which you must keep strictly to yourself till it becomes public. It is almost certain that your uncle Luke will be the new Bishop of Stepney, *i.e.* a Suffragan to the Bishop of London, working specially in East London, and living there. He will be very happy there, and do first-rate work, I think :—he knows and loves East London. As I write, I expect everybody is talking about Lord Morley's statement concerning India : he was to make it in the House of Lords at 3.30 this afternoon : and there is immense interest about it.—I am glad that we have at the India Office a strong man, not likely to shirk responsibilities or to give in to clamour. The night before last I dined with the Barbers' Company in London, to celebrate the 600th anniversary of the Admission of their First Master, in 1308, when they really were Barber-Surgeons. It was a very interesting dinner, & I have never seen tables so beautiful with flowers & silver, save only at Windsor. *Cuddesdon, New Year's Eve.* . . . How can I thank you for the most beautiful and delightful of Christmas presents ? It is a splendid bit of work, and it will be among my chief treasures :—always on my standing-desk, where I may constantly see it, save when it is handed round after dinner. It gives me even all the pleasure you could wish it to give. We were a small, quiet Christmas party : but the Day was very happy. I had proffered myself to a necessitous

Parish: but at the last moment they got someone else: so I had a peaceful time at home. On Sunday I went all round the Radcliffe Infirmary, and had a talk with every patient:—it is always to me one of the happiest privileges in the year. Since then we have had a spell of tremendous cold, with heavy snow, embittering the misery of the unemployed:—it is indeed a time full of trouble. Last night, I am thankful to say, the frost broke: and we are in the unlovely slush of a welcome thaw.

1909

Jan. 7, Cuddesdon. — Burma seems much further away than India:—partly, I think, because the Indian Government, and the Secretary of State for India, and the Indian Civil Service all seem to bring India right into the field of English life. It's a constant pleasure to get the tidings of you, and to think of you and of your work:—and then to cast a look on to the immense happiness of your home-coming. I have not been away at all this winter:—it was not easy to plan:—and somehow I felt rather ashamed to be spending money on a holiday when the distress of poverty in many places is intense. The lack of employment is not, I think, working such misery in this Diocese as it is in London: still it is bad in some of the towns: & in London it has been terrible:—and there seems hardly any promise of amendment. . . . The Committee on "the Division of the Diocese, and other alternative ways of lightening the work of the Diocesan" are beginning their task: so presently, (say five years hence,) you may find me with only one County to look after, or else two Suffragan Bishops, or a motor-car, or Cuddesdon sold.—Who knows? *Jan. 14.*—Last night we had a big party here: fourteen men, undergraduates & young dons, Churchmen & Non-Conformists, who are keen about the Student Volunteer Movement, the stirring-up in the Universities of a keenness for Mission Work, came to stay here, to confer and so forth: some of them among the ablest & most promising men in Oxford, and all keen, cheerful, and unaffected. I can't imagine any such gathering in my time: and I think it means much. To-night I dined

alone, and over my dinner I had much talk with Quarterman ;
very interesting, with that shrewdness, seeing more than he
has ready words to tell. *Jan.* 21.—Last Sunday, as it were, a
year ago we had that splendid walk from Amesbury to Salisbury
& back, and went to the Cathedral, and heard the sermon on
" peace, all the days of our life."   I think that I shall always
link this Sunday with that walk.—How delightful it was :—
with the amusing incidents of our luncheon and our tea :—and
the glory of the Nave of the Cathedral :—and then the swinging
down the hill through the dark into Amesbury.   I wonder
whether we shall ever do the like again. *Jan.* 28.—Here I
am, in London and a fog,—a real, good, thick one.   It was
fairly dense, while I sat for a cheerful hour with the dentist :—
it was worse when I went to Lambeth for a meeting at 2.30 :—
and when I came out at six it was so heavy that I almost
wondered how I should find my way to Suffolk Place, where
I am staying.—It's rather weird to see the great motor-cars
lumbering out through the darkness, and all the traffic creeping
tentatively along, as blind men do. . . . You'll have read
about the strange, horrible scene at Tottenham, the two
Anarchists " running amok," & shooting everyone who interfered or seemed likely to interfere.   Yesterday I fell in with a
rustic walking near Cuddesdon : he talked about it a good
deal : & then he said " Well :—there's some as don't seem to
study neither theirselves nor yet nobody else."   I hope you
read also a very different story :—the account of Jack Binns,
the electrician on board the sinking ship, the " Republic " :—
who sat and listened for 52 hours at the " key " of the wireless
telegraphy on board, without a minute's sleep.—I think there
ought to be a V.C. for that :—but it is not a bad reward that
the wireless telegraphy served to bring help for the rescue of
the ship. *Feb.* 11.—On Tuesday I went up to town, to speak
at the College of Physicians, about a Fund for helping broken-
down doctors, & their families.   As I studied the matter, it
seemed to me very pathetic :—they have to start in life with
a great outlay on house, equipment, carriage & so forth : they
stake everything on the continuance of health & power to
work :—and they risk their health more than most men.—If

my father, for instance, had died before he was 50, we should have been almost penniless, though he had worked ceaselessly & lived most carefully.   To-day I went to assist at the Stone-laying of a new Church at Summertown :—a great ceremony, admirably arranged : but oh ! so cold.   I was up on a platform, blue with cold, with the photographers taking a series of shots :—I cd. have laughed, it was so uncomfortable :—but everyone was so kind, & so keen about the business, that I was very glad to be there.   *Feb.* 19, *London.*—Just time for just a word :—it's wretched that it should be only that :— but this week has been desperately crowded, with Convocation meetings, & some heavy work.   I'm so sorry, dear Bernard :—but I love to send my greeting even if I can do no more.—And I can't help just adding a word to say that a very delightful word about your work came round to me, never intended for me, and made me happier than I can tell you, and lit up the whole day.   *Feb.* 26.—Here we are back in mid-winter, and cold for that : and the wandering from place to place, in the series of Confirmations, has, I am bold to say, almost an air of military service about it.   The run in the open motor and the N.E. wind last night was sharp work.— But in the Confirmations themselves there are wonderful bits of happiness.—I don't think one could see anything much more touching than a beautiful, old village Church, with a simple, reverent group of old and young :—of course, it varies : but sometimes it's wonderful.   You will have heard of the anxiety here.   Quarterman went yesterday to the Middlesex Hospital.   They will keep him under observation for a few days : & then decide whether there ought to be an operation.— He has been admirable about it : sensible, self-possessed, simple, brave :—all that is best in him has come out strong.

March 5.—Quarterman has fared splendidly in hospital : all seems to have gone, thank God, quite well : & we hope he will be home soon.   *March* 11.—My letter starts in the waiting-room at Oxford : — I'm wandering about most days now :—having no Suffragan makes a good deal of difference in that regard :—and as I grow older it seems an odd sort of life : —and the winter seems more wintry.   You will have been

watching, I expect, the course of the Indian Council Bill. I
have not followed it closely, for lack of time, & I don't know
the real weight of what is said on both sides : but I rather
wish that the Lords had let Morley have his way. He is so
strong, and indifferent to public opinion, even on his own side,
that I long to see him heartily backed up :—& I believe that
it wd. help to take or keep Indian affairs quite outside party
politics : which is immensely to be desired. *March* 19.—I'm
the somebody that an ill wind blows good to. For I've missed
my train to Cropredy : and so I can write to you in the
waiting-room instead of in the train :—& I can get there in
time for the Confirmation. I wish we weren't six weeks
apart : for the last two letters have seemed to tell of rather
hard & trying work for you. . . . Life's not a level or a
smooth road ; but it's a blessing to breast the hills & trudge
over the stones with a good heart. And I think one sometimes
does one's best bits of work on the uphill bits, though one
may not know it. . . . We are in the first days of a great
alarm about the Navy. All parties are startled into unanimity,
by the report of great ship-building activity in Germany. It
seems very serious :—and a real European War wd. be such
a harm as few can now remember the like of.—And unemploy-
ment goes on :—and the air seems rather heavily charged with
anxiety. Here comes my second train. *March* 26.—I went to
Aylesbury on Tuesday, for a remarkable Confirmation,—over
80 grown-up people, of all classes,—very wonderful it was.
And I stayed the night with General Blewitt :—and that was
delightful. He knows a great deal, and he has seen much of
life and men, and seen it thoughtfully. We talked a bit about
you, & the Regiment. . . . I write on the way to Windsor,
—with five Confirmations in these two days. It's often happy
work :—but rather a strain.

April 15, *Mortehoe.*—This place will always bring back
memories of a very happy little visit here with you :—a trifle
wintry it was, and cut short, I think, by sad news : but very
happy while it lasted. I remember specially the Sunday in the
little, grey, wind-swept Church. . . . I shall think rather
anxiously of your venture in pony-training :—in England the

business about horses seems to me one of the things in which the worse man can always score off the better :—or almost always. So I hope you will go slow, whatever the pony does. *April* 22.—I remember seeing over one of the doors in the Soldiers' Institute at Aldershot the inscription " Ut migraturus habita." I've often thought of it as a good motto for one's general relation to the world : but it certainly has its special aptness for your profession. I'm very sorry they have haled you off from Maiktila so soon and suddenly : for I suppose it inevitably means expense, and I liked to think of your having the Adjutant's work and experience & responsibility. But " it's all in the swim," and there's no helping it ; and I hope this letter will find you well settled in the new quarters, and trusted with some fresh charge of work. *April* 25 (*after Mortehoe*).—I wonder what —— will do to use his leisure :—he ought to write an epoch-making book : — but late in life plunging into literature is, I expect, something like abruptly taking to sea - bathing when one's eighty. Then I met Herbert Hope, who went with me on my first reading-party in 1873 : one of the best of men, illustrating the way in which very many men are all along what they were at the end of their Oxford time :—richer in experience & sympathy, if they've used their life well :—stronger in ability, too, but keeping the same heart and mind. By the way, another, somewhat of the same sort, Emlyn Jones, of Torrington, was special in his enquiry after you :—he's doing good work, and winning great regard and trust.

May 7.—I have been in London all this week, for Convocation :—staying with the Archbishop. It's always a sort of moral sea-side to me to be with him :—he bears his great load so gallantly, with so ready a heart for kindness and sympathy, and so clear & steady a head, and so single a will. I can't be thankful enough for his friendship. *Cuddesdon, May* 28.—My best congratulations on the bison. It was a delightful story that you told of the encounter :—most exciting it must have been :—especially at the moment of the resultless click. *June* 4. —I write in the midst of the Ember Days, with ten Candidates here :—a time full of work and interest, with some strain. So

I can send only a word of greeting. It's a delightful photograph you have sent, of yourself between the horns of a bison as wide as any dilemma. There goes the gong? bell? rather cracked it is now. *June* 11.—Thank you ever so much for the beautiful, interesting, historic, mysterious thing which is up in front of me as I write :—telling within its little compass much of that wonderful East that you must know so well the look of, with still a feeling, I expect, that you have never got at the back of its head or at the bottom of its heart. *June* 21, *Berkshire Club, Reading.*—I write on my way home from a great day at Wellington :—the prize-giving, with the King & the Queen, & the Duke & Duchess of Connaught, and Prince & Princess Christian, and all sorts of people. It was a wonderful sight, and wonderfully planned : and I got some extraordinarily interesting talks : I wish I could tell you of them all, or hope to remember them for myself. But two I must tell, for they included messages to you.—Colonel Capper made immediate & special enquiry about you, and was delighted to hear of your welfare, and sent you chin-chin.—And then, I had a long and delightful talk with Lord Roberts. He bade me send you his good wishes, and also tell you that the 43rd were at Ootacamund when he was there : and that he specially remembers how, at a particular moment in some manœuvres which he was watching, the men all promptly rallied or grouped themselves round their *Captains.* I could not fully understand the excellence of this : but it had clearly struck him as the right thing rightly done : and he spoke of it as though it were a special tradition from Sir John Moore. It was a very pleasant talk : and you would have been proud to hear what he said of the Regiment.

July 20, *Missenden House, Amersham.*—A rush of work came just when I should have been writing to you.—There has been one wretched business on :—for I have had to institute proceedings against a Clergyman who persisted in doing indefensible things in Church. The case was heard yesterday :— judgement was given to-day, in my favour :—the sentence of deprivation will be pronounced a fortnight hence, unless he surrenders.—These things are a great misery :—but it would have been mere shirking if I had let him go on.   The Judge was Sir Lewis Dibdin.   I had a bit of refreshment on Saturday : for I was at a service at Chipping Norton : and after it I found Colour-Sergeant Jones waiting for me.   He is in charge of the Territorials, I believe, in that District :—he looked as smart as smart could be :—we had a delightful bit of talk. . . . I went on to a Confirmation in the Cathedral :—most beautiful it all looked : there's no place like it in the world.   From another friend of yours, Sergeant Stephens, I had also a very pleasant letter, which I think I must send you.   It seems as though you must have an extraordinarily good and pleasant lot of non-commissioned officers : and I expect you will say that's about it.   I began this letter at the house of Mr. Pembroke Stephens, an able, delightful, Irish Barrister, with whom I was staying for a function at Little Missenden :—thence I was motored over magnificently in a great "Fiat" to Twyford, where I had a stone-laying and other bits of business and pleasure, amidst the glow and happiness of good enthusiastic work. *July* 30.—We are near the end of the busiest days : and after them comes a lull, & a chance of tidying up.   To-day I go to a great gathering at Wellington ;—they are making very much of their Jubilee :—and to-morrow I lay the Foundation-stone of the new Church at Headington :—Mr. Perrin's splendid undertaking.   Last Sunday was a wonderful day : I spent it at Bromsgrove, seeing one old friend after another,—seeing the old scenes,—and then preaching in the evening.   I can't say how quickening & refreshing it was :—with such a glow of warm-heartedness through it all.   I had the old Hollyer photograph of you with me, & showed it to some of them :—& they saw the likeness of your mother in it.

Aug. 20, *Chough's Nest, Lynton.* . . . When I got here, Gilkes was staying here : and on Wednesday we all went to Simonsbath, and he & I walked most of the way home :—but not quite at that splendid pace you kept me up to.—It was a joy to get a good talk with him : for he has been my close & constant friend for 44 years,—always the same.   *Aug.* 26.—As one lives on and watches life one grows more and more sure that happiness depends vastly more on what a man is than on anything that he has or anything that happens to him : indeed I think there are some people whom nothing could make happy, and some whom nothing could make unhappy, so long as they both are what they are. And so one's best birthday wishes are made simpler :—and I wish & long for you that you may go on in all those ways which mean the most real growth and advance :—the ways of which one thinks most, and therefore, perhaps, can say least. . . . Yesterday Edward & I went that very walk of which you wrote—by the cliff to the Hunter's Inn, & back over the moor. The great cushioned backs of heather and gorse were almost as glorious as that afternoon when you and I first saw them. *Sept. 2, Cuddesdon.*—I have been getting to work at Mr. Bayne's letters and papers : —a long, strange, dusty task :—redeemed by the witness that comes out to his dutiful, painstaking ways, to his love of his mother, and to the multitude & loyalty of his friends. He deserved true friends, for such he himself was :—and he had many in his long life. *Sept. 9, Prince's Risborough.*—I write on my way to Kimble, to institute a new rector there.— Perhaps you don't think Kimble very important :—but I expect it was once on many people's lips :—for it was in the church there that Hampden refused to pay ship-money. His descendant, (direct or indirect) Lord Buckinghamshire, lives at Hampden now, not very far away :—and he has some very interesting papers of the Great Hampden's, including one in his own handwriting, showing how he really wanted to be (and perhaps in truth was) a law-abiding man. . . . The newspapers are distracted by competing discoverers of the North Pole. I find it hard to think that anybody who had really done a great thing would write of it in so bad a style as Dr. Cook's. *Sept. 16, Abingdon School.*—Here is a new crest for me to write under.—I hope to hold the Ordination on Sunday in St. Helen's, the big church here : and I came to-day, with the Chaplains and all the Candidates :—we are 27 in all : and the Head Master of Abingdon School is most kindly planning all the meals for us. . . . Everybody is talking either about the North Pole, or the Budget. There is a growing impression that the Lords will throw out the Finance Bill, and that then there will be a General Election in November :—but I can't quite believe it : I expect that quieter (and, I think, wiser) counsels will prevail, and that they will find some middle course.

Oct. 8, *Milan.* . . . Before us, if all be well, three weeks of holiday :—wholly delightful to look forward to.—Bergamo, Verona, Padua, Venice, Ferrara :—we hope for all these. I've got the most splendid appetite for a holiday, dear Bernard :— but, I just do wish, more than I can tell, that you were here to share it. . . . On the way out I have been reading the life of Beatrice d'Este,—married when she was 15 to the virtual sovereign of Milan,—about 1490 ; and thenceforward taking the lead in one of the most stirring, brilliant, eager Courts the world has ever seen. Such a wonderful story it is. *Oct.* 13, *Verona.*—I often wish that you were with us : but never more than yesterday.—For I went off,—Beatrice choosing a quieter morning,—by a steam-tram from Bergamo to Cavernago :— thence I walked through bright, fertile country to Malpaga, where one of the greatest fighting-men of Italy, a real master in counsel and war, Bartolommeo Colleone, spent his old age, and died in 1475. His Castle, now uninhabited, belongs to a certain Count Roncelli, from whom I had got an order to see it. Such a glorious, strong, interesting place : — a great space enclosed with buildings about as high as an Oxford Quad- rangle : then a very deep moat :—then the stately, fortified Castle, with its draw-bridge, its Ghibelline battlements, its noble tower, its inner quadrangle : and above all a series of wonderful frescoes, painted for Colleone, recording the proudest time of his life, when he entertained the King of Denmark, with a tournament, and a banquet, and a day's hunting.—The days were there, vivid, splendid :—and I believe he really was a fine, upright soldier,—certainly a " fust-class fightin' man." *Oct.* 21, *Baveno.*—Yesterday morning (in Venice) I went to lunch with Lady Layard. There I learnt that in the " Cosmopolitan Hospital " there was a girl whom I had confirmed : so I went off in a gondola to see her :—the Hospital is across a stretch of water, on a separate island :—thence I went by steamer to another island : & back in a little boat which I picked up there :—great fun, with glorious things to see.   *Oct.* 26, *In the Simplon Express.*—The train toils and tunnels up the Pass, where I drove with your grandfather many years ago, between Domodossola and Brieg.   It was a glorious drive :—& I remember how they unharnessed the extra horse at the top of the Pass, and let him find his own way home. . . . Here we are in the great tunnel, with an electric engine taking us through : and after the tunnel comes dinner in a Restaurant Car : and then we shut up for the night, & try to sleep till Paris.   Truly, as rather a shy lady said to me the other day, "This age we live in is a very,—a very *convenient* age."

Nov. 9, *Cuddesdon.*—It's dreadful to think what o'clock it is : —and I must be up at 6.30 for an early start and a long day. . . . I hope you had a good shoot : the start for it sounded full of interest.   I was in town last week for meetings : and I went to hear the two last speeches on the Budget, the close of the six months' discussion.—Balfour was disappointing : it was the speech of a tired man, and unconvincing.   Asquith was far better, and very able : at one point, where he flourished the flag of the Commons' supremacy over finance, it was very telling :—and you felt that a real moment in Constitutional history was in sight.   The business comes to the Lords on the 22nd : there is much talk of the Bill being thrown out, & an appeal made to the country : but last week no one, I think, really knew what would happen.—I doubt whether I shall go up for it :—it does not seem to me an issue with which Bishops have much to do.   *Nov.* 23.—I'm heartily glad that your shooting was a success :—and it must have been great fun.   I dined last Saturday with a distinguished shooter of big game :—Littledale, who nearly got to Lhassa :—his hall & dining-room are crowded with great horns & antlers, "ovis poli" and the like, & huge elk, & that like.   Last week was memorable.—On Tuesday I was at Windsor, bearing part as Chancellor in the Investiture of the King of Portugal as a Knight of the Garter.   It was a splendid, historic ceremony : the Knights in full array, sitting in Chapter : and the King & Queen at the head of the table, with their pages & attendants, and the whole thing done with great dignity.   I was just at

the side of the Queen's Chair, and had to read the Declaration
in the King's name, and one of the Admonitions. Then came
a great banquet, about 160 or 170 at table, and the great gold
plate all down the table,—a wondrous sight:—& then we all
went into the State Drawing Room, & talked.—I had very interesting talks, with Mr. Asquith, & Sir Dighton Probyn, and
Mr. Runciman, & the Duke of Norfolk, & Lord Roberts:—and
then the Queen sent for me, and was most kind and gracious:
—and looked most beautiful:—and the Duchess of Albany
also sent for me, & asked after you all with great kindness.
Then on Friday, I spoke at the huge meeting in the Albert
Hall about the Congo.—The Hall was full, save for a few
boxes, and thousands were turned away. It was most thrilling
& exciting, that vast stretch of faces, with a real intensity of
feeling and purpose. The Archbishop spoke quite admirably:
—& so did Mr. Scott Lidgett, the ablest Non-Conformist I
know. And on Thursday I preached at St. Paul's, to the
London Choirs Society:—a Choir of more than 800, and the
Cathedral full:—such a glorious, helpful service. I wish you
could have been with me all three nights. Here comes another
post. *Dec.* 3.—My very best wishes for the New Year. It is
lit up already with the hope of your coming home: may it be
in all ways, by God's Blessing, a year of welfare and happiness
for you. *Christmas Eve.* . . . I doubt whether any one knows
what is going to happen at the Election, or after it. The
Liberals are just now riding at a hard gallop, charging and
thundering away all over the country: but I think they may
have made their charge prematurely: there is a great deal of
real indifference: & perhaps some people will be frightened by
the threat of Irish Home Rule. Still, I rather expect the
Government will come back, with a reduced majority: and
then they are pledged, if they are strong enough, to curtail the
power of the Lords:—& that may be the real struggle:—more
serious and far-reaching than most people seem to see. *New
Year's Eve.* . . . I have to-day been at the funeral of Lady
Crawford—Lord Wantage's sister—a really noble, simple, kind,
clear-sighted, generous lady. The funeral was at Clifton
Hampden, a most touching scene, in perfect light and air.

On Wednesday I was bearing part in Clarke's wedding in Lichfield Cathedral. Now I am on my way to stay for three days with Lawrence Hardy : and then I go for more than a fortnight's quiet at Barmouth—joy.

1910

Jan. 6, Barmouth.—More than I can tell, I wish that you were here.   Perrin [1] and I have come here for a bit of holiday : and this afternoon we walked right over the moor under Pen-y-garn, along the old road, and there over a shoulder of the hills down on to Llwyngwril.   There was Hendre, & the gate your mother met us at that night, & the old barn, and the stream where you used to fish,—or Richard at all events. *Jan. 13.*—It has been delightful to be here with Perrin : and it has meant the refreshment of a holiday without the looming cloud of arrears of work rolling up against one's return.   For we work together at letters all the morning :—in the evening I get forward with some tasks that ought to have been done long ago : and every afternoon we get a glorious walk.   The other day I looked across to those memorable downs where you and I lost our way, on the day when "everybody was nice to us"—How pleasant those days were ! So many things came back to me as I went over the old scenes. . . . And the day after to-morrow the Election begins : and you will know the result before you get this.   Hereabouts Lloyd George is a great hero :—there's almost a fanatical enthusiasm astir for him :—and when they tried last week to hold a Unionist meeting, it was broken up.—I don't think I can remember any Election in which feeling has been so much whipped-up :— and whipped-up feeling is a bad guide when great and complex questions have to be dealt with.—It seems to me as though the rejection of the Budget by the Lords was a serious misfortune :— but whether it could have been avoided, I don't know.

[During the next few months, Bernard Paget was home on leave.   Toward the end of the time, the

---

[1] To one of his daughters, he writes at this time, "Perrin is indeed like a true son, with some of the better qualities of a father."

Bishop was ill, and underwent an operation. He
writes from Hindhead, where he had gone to recover
his strength.]

Hindhead, Sept. 12.—I am sorry I look thinner on being
enlarged :—it sounds perverse and contrary :—and I can imagine
that the effect is unfortunate. I'm getting on splendidly :—
yesterday I had, I think, my longest walk, and after it my best
night. On Saturday we motored over to Compton, where
Mrs. G. F. Watts lives, and where there is a gallery of his
pictures and sketches, with some sculpture :—quite full of
beauty and interest, and wonderful to find in the heart of the
country.—We came back through Guildford & Godalming,
and called on Mr. & Mrs. Lathbury, & had a delightful
welcome.   *Sept.* 23.—If *The Light that Failed* does not
greatly libel Aden, it must be an unattractive place. Well, it
wasn't easy to say good-bye : and the saying is apt to leave
unsaid much of what means most. It was a great happiness to
get the two or three hours at Southampton : and the scenes
stay in my memory with extraordinary vividness. The Dean
of Christ Church came here yesterday, to keep me company—
(and a delightful companion he is—) until to-morrow : then
Edward comes, to stay, I hope, to the end of my time here.—
This morning's post brought me the photograph of all my
sons : I'll spare your blushes, & not say how proud I feel of
the quartette. Such a radiant day here !—with heather & gorse
& bracken all aglow.—What a joy it will be if you & I may get
more walks together through them.—I must try to keep as
young & springy as I can for the enjoyment.

Cuddesdon, Oct. 6. . . . a wonderful happiness to be again
sitting in one's study, and taking up the threads of work.
Truly I can never come near being thankful enough for all
that has been granted me this summer and autumn. . . . By
this mail I'm sending *The Sky Pilot* :—it will seem rather
scene-painting after *John Inglesant* and *The Egoist* : but there's
reality in it, I think, and pathos & some humour. . . . I'm
sure no Bishop ever came back to find things in such wonderful order and settledness, so well dealt with, as they have been

by Perrin's wonderful care and labour. *Oct.* 14.—Yesterday Charlie Musgrave left London for Kashmir : but how far he got we don't know : for France is in a storm of strikes. . . . The railway-strike, with its arrest of all the ways of commerce and society, takes an effective means of showing the power that the workers can wield not only against employers or capitalists but against the State :—& so one understands the determined look of even a Republican government :—it sees war in the gates. *Oct.* 20.—I don't know what I should have done if Perrin had not toiled so hard to avert arrears while I was out of work :—for the fresh demands of work come tumbling on us like snow in a thaw.   But there has been much happiness in the wonderful kindness of the welcome back to work.   On Saturday, I went to see Humphrey in his rooms (in Christ Church).   He seemed very happy and comfortable : he has already found a good many friends, and Dibdin, who is on the same staircase, seems a very nice fellow, as, indeed, his father's son should be.   To-day we have had a long visit from Lord Carrington, who was most friendly :— somehow, I think the better sort of Liberal Ministers are pleasanter company than most of those with whom I more agree :—they seem to talk more in their shirt-sleeves, and to be less afraid of giving themselves away.   There is a most interesting article in to-day's *Times* on the dethroned King of Portugal . . . it seems a most pathetic story : and here he is, at twenty, turned out of his job, and unapt for any other, or, rather, handicapped with a title for life. *Oct.* 24, *G.W.R.* (*on the way back from Liverpool*).—I went to stay with the Bishop, to preach at a service held annually for doctors & surgeons & nurses :—& that was full of interest :—and as I tried to tell them to be good, I felt that no one could know better than I how good they are.   In the morning I went to the old Parish Church, where Bilbrough is, whose curates at Darlington Campbell & Perrin were, and from whose flock Wilkinson & Musgrave & Levy came :—there was a special service for the Naval Reserve :—a wonderful nice-looking set of lads.   And then I was taken to see what there is of the new Cathedral— most glorious and exciting.   I am quite sure that I have never

seen any modern building so rich in glory & beauty as the
Lady Chapel :—so splendid in dignity & in detail :—there was
a real happiness in thinking that things could be so well done.
I finish at home. Perrin motored me out : and then after
dinner I drove into Oxford again, for a meeting of the Research
Defence Society. Lord Cromer spoke well. *Westminster
Palace Hotel, Nov.* 25.—It was the saddest of telegrams that
I sent this morning :—I kept on thinking of your getting it,
longing that you may be helped and strengthened and kept
patient and trustful through all the sudden rush of sorrow,
through all the lonely wondering about it, through the long
weeks as it weighs on your heart. I'd give all I have to be
with you to-day. . . . *Cuddesdon, Dec.* 21.—We had a happy
Ordination in the Cathedral last Sunday : and Edward & I
hope to spend Christmas Day in Christ Church, staying with
the Dean :—in the afternoon I hope to go all round the
Radcliffe Infirmary.—Is it not splendid that Scott Holland is
to succeed Dr. Ince? There could not have been a better
appointment.

1911

Barmouth, Jan. 12.—Houblon and I have had a happy week
here, with a good walk every day. On Tuesday, the walk
that brings back most memories, specially of your mother, and
of you. Do you remember telling me that you thought
Edward would make a very good clergyman " because of the
way he took things " ? I've often thought it was a very true
account of the main secret of being "a very good" anything.
. . . I have ventured to send you your uncle's new book.
Truly, I'm very proud of my brothers, and of my sons.
Cuddesdon, Jan. 20. . . . the sadness of your servant's death.
It was always gladdening to think of his devotion & loyalty to
you. I should love to have earned such trust :—and in all the
sadness of his passing away there is happiness in thinking of
what you were to him, & he to you.—God grant him rest &
light. *Jan.* 27.—On Wednesday I went to Chislehampton,
for Colonel Parke's funeral. I had seen him twice during the
last stage of his long suffering :—and I had felt something of

the wonderful strength & beauty of his patience :—he was a real man, I'm sure, with true soldierliness all through him.— The service was touching, first in the tiny, homely church, where the six Dragoons in full uniform, standing round the coffin, looked so big & splendid :—& then in the little church-yard with kindred & friends & servants & villagers—people who greatly cared. *Feb.* 10.—I had a happy Sunday at Cam-bridge, with many privileges in the kindness of one's friends & in meeting a number of interesting people. I stayed with the Master of Trinity :—& I went to King's, one of the most glorious places in the world. *Lambeth, Feb.* 16.—A long day in the Convocation, then a long interview in Convocation, then a long interview, then a rush to the Middlesex Hospital to see Richard who has got a touch of jaundice & is on low diet but in high spirits, then a quiet dinner with the Miss Lawrences, then a talk with the Archbishop :—so it has come to be mid-night before I could begin my letter.—But as I think over the day I feel, as I often do, what a wonderful thing it is to have such friends as have been granted to me :—I think of one after another, and know that I never can be worthy of their kindness and trust. . . . *Privately* I may tell you that I am to be, if all be well, one of the two Bishops in attendance on the Queen at the Coronation : I'm told that Her Majesty wished it.—I am very glad & grateful : for it is a most beautiful and glorious service : and to be in attendance brings me right into the midst of it. I wish the King would command me to be in attendance at the Coronation Durbar :—then I shd. get a sight of you. But that happiness must wait for another year. *Lambeth, Feb.* 23. . . . Well, the Car has come. Yesterday it took me to Reading and back : this morning it brought us into Oxford. It is helpful and comfortable and delightful beyond all that I forecast :—it promises to make a real great difference :—and through all the enjoyment of it there goes the steady happiness of thinking of the kindness and goodness of the friends who have given it to me.—I've written to them all —between forty and fifty—one by one :—and I've had in return some letters which have deepened the gladness of the gift. . . . Yesterday I was at a great Masonic pomp over

the Stone-laying of the new Wing of the Berkshire Hospital :
—it was an odd business, but too self-conscious to be dignified.
Afterwards I went round some of the wards, which I enjoyed
much more.

Cuddesdon, March 2. . . . I wish you could see the car
rush up the hills as though they weren't there :—so swift and
quiet and strong and steady. . . . I am very often thinking
about the exchange (into the Indian Army):—I'd give a lot
to be able to talk it over with you.—I want many things for
you :—I want you to have a good career, using to the best
purpose all your powers : I want you to have, please God,
a happy life : I want you to be able to marry, if your mind &
heart are set that way : and I want you to be where you can
best help other men, of whatsoever class or colour, to make the
best of themselves. *April* 7.—Winter has turned round and
snapped at us when we thought he was going for good :—such
a black, bleak, hard N.E. wind, with bursts of snow. *April*
27.—Swanage was very pleasant : and I got some glorious
walks. But the letters waxed rather heavy : so that the
Boots one day, as he brought me my pile, said sympathetic-
ally, " Not much like a holiday." . . . *Royal Automobile Club,
Ascension Day.*—Don't think that the motor has led me into
strange and extravagant ways. I find that my membership
of our Berkshire Club, with a very modest subscription, somehow makes me an Associate of the great R.A.C., without any
further subscription :—and that thus I may come and write
my letters and have my tea in this magnificial building, far
away from the people who come up at the Athenæum and ask
me just the questions which I don't want to be asked. . . . I
have just been in the House of Lords, where the great debate
on the Parliament Bill is going on. Last night the Archbishop made a great speech which you ought to read if you
get the chance : I think it was a really thoughtful statesmanlike
utterance, such as may bring a bit of hope into what seems a
tangled and perilous plight. *Lambeth, May* 4.—I have been
staying here this week for Convocation. They have been
busy days, with some anxious and arduous work : but it makes
a great difference to have kindness and interest for the back-

ground of the days : and there is a generosity and largeness
and frankness of thought in this house which are always
refreshing :—and you watch great burdens quietly and gallantly
borne. *Cuddesdon, May* 11. . . . the Annual Meeting of the
Archdeacons and Rural Deans. We worked in the Town
Hall : but we broke the work with luncheon in Christ Church
Hall. It's a wonderful privilege to belong to that great place.
. . . Francis (the grandchild) is here, thriving and vigorous, com-
plaisantly accepting adoration, when he is not vociferous against
the whole order of things. And five other guests are here,
quite delightful :—Mr. & Mrs. Harnett, & their three children
just as nice and simple and pretty as can be. So it is a happy
houseful :—how I wish that you were here to better it all. . . .
I never read your letters in the midst of all the rest, but keep
them for a more congenial bit of the day. *May* 19. . . .
Francis still stays here : both he and the Nurse like it : so he
continues to receive the admiration of the village :—old West,
the road-mender, talked of him quite delightfully the other
day. On Tuesday I was in Westminster Abbey :—a strange
sight it is, with all the staging & galleries in course of erection,
& all the hammering going on. It looked to me as though
it would be exactly as it was in 1902. I am to have, if all
be well, the charge I had then, & to walk beside the Queen :
and I believe I am also to be one of the two Bishops who sing
the Litany :—but this is not announced. On Whitsunday I
am to be at Blenheim, to preach to the yeomanry :—it will be
like old days, with a difference,—a great difference :—but I'm
glad to be going again.

June 15.—An eventful week has passed since my last letter.
On Saturday I was at Windsor, for the Investiture of the
Prince of Wales as a Knight of the Garter. The Investiture,
in the Throne Room at the Castle, was very stately and touching :—the ceremonial like that at the Investiture of the Kings
of Norway and Portugal, but with an added touch of grace and
pathos, because the lad looked so young and modest and
simple, and one thought of the vast responsibility before him.
Then came the procession of all the Knights from the Castle,
down the hill to enter St. George's Chapel by the great west

door :—a really glorious sight, thrilling one with wonder and
delight :—the Bp. of Winchester & I walked at the end,
just in front of the King & Queen, so that we had the full
view, ever to be remembered. And then came the most
beautiful service in St. George's, such as had not been held
for 200 years :—quite full of meaning and thought and reverence.—And then a great luncheon, brilliant with gold plate,
& flowers, & uniforms, in the Castle. And Sunday had its
great joy, in Edward's ordination, a wonderful happiness.
And on Monday morning I celebrated in the College, & he
served me :—a renewal of all the happiness. Tuesday was
the College Festival, & Wednesday the Dorchester Festival :—
and both seemed to go off well and cheerily.

June 21.—I begin this week's letter in a strange environment. For I am writing in Westminster Abbey, waiting for
the last of the Rehearsals of the Coronation. Just outside the
west door is a great annexe, some sixty or seventy yards long :
crowded and busy with all sorts of people, soldiers and heralds
and bishops and pages and great ladies and dukes, with a few
princesses : it is all decorated with tapestry and armour :—it
is made to look as like an old building as possible :—and in it
all the processions are gathered and arranged. It's an odd
scene : and I can remember the time when I should have
thought it endlessly interesting. But now I find I've soon
had enough of it : and the dawdling and waste of time are
dreadful. So I've—(*Cuddesdon*, *June* 22)—Just thus far I had
got, when an interruption came : and, one way and another,
the hours got filled up :—and somehow it was very hard to
write more before this day's great service. A most wonderful,
beautiful, august, uplifting service it was, dear Bernard. I
don't think I have ever borne part in anything so great. It
seemed to me a most real Consecration of a true-hearted King
& Queen to their high calling and trust and task. All
imaginable splendour was there, in sight and sound and history
and ceremonial : no words could tell how noble & glorious &
touching it was : every scene your eye rested on, every word
& note you heard was fine and stately :—but through it went
the pure, quiet undertone of deep religion, of spiritual reality.

I was beside the Queen all the time, save when I went to the faldstools, with the Bishop of Bath & Wells, to sing the Litany :—and it was a wonderful honour, to be near so good and gracious a Lady, and waiting upon her :—and at the end she deigned to thank me. Perrin planned so well that I easily caught the 4.55, and got home in time to give mugs & medals to all the village children, and to see something of the sports in Mr. Gale's field :—very pleasant it was.

Slough, July 6.—It was a real and great distress to me that I missed last week's mail. I think the Coronation celebrations had something to do with it :—I preached at the Parish Church at Windsor on the 25th ; rushed up to London for the garden-party at Buckingham Palace on the 27th ; and again for the great service at St. Paul's on the 29th ; and so the week seemed all upset. . . . At St. Paul's, everything was magnificent :—the Cathedral thronged, up to the triforium :—and the band & choir splendid : and their Majesties sitting on a raised dais in front of the entrance to the Chancel. It was all very beautiful and reverent and stately : but I felt as if the state and the music were developed somewhat disproportionately, in comparison with the Prayers. *July 18.*—I am indeed thankful with all my heart that the fever has left you : you must use the best care you can to prevent its coming back : and I earnestly hope it won't come back. Have you a doctor whom you can thoroughly trust to give you an unbiassed, sensible, unimpulsive opinion, as a man who knows what responsibility really means ?—If you have such an one—they're not as common as blackberries,—I wish you'd ask him what kind and measure of risk there is for you in India :—whether it is reasonably prudent for you to look forward to a career mainly in India for some years : & whether much would turn on your being near the frontier, as, I imagine, the Gurkhas mostly are, rather than in the plains.—I can imagine his giving answers which, if he's a really good man, might even make it wise to re-consider the hard question about the Indian Army, or might clearly incline your choice towards the Gurkhas rather than the Cavalry, rather even than the 18th Lancers.—But of course it's no use if he's a man who wouldn't or couldn't give you a simple and trustworthy opinion. You ask about the Parliament Bill.—I think we are in a great muddle, with a good deal of risk, because on both sides the stupider and more violent people have forced on the real statesmen:—the crowd of the Unionist party forcing Ld. Lansdowne to kill the Licensing Bill & throw out the Budget :—the Labour members & the Irish and the vehement non-Conformists forcing the Cabinet to be intransigent. I think Asquith is most to be blamed, & Morley & Grey & Haldane, who ought to know better : but I do wish Ld. Lansdowne had been resolute not to bring on the crisis. As things are, we are in danger of something very like single-chamber Government, and all the risk which that means of collision later on between the Crown and the Commons, and all the risk meanwhile of unjust legislation for the sake of holding together a heterogeneous majority.—And I think the crisis need not have been provoked :—if only the tail had had the modesty to let the head decide. But I may be quite wrong : so I don't say all these things, except to you. I've been hearing about you, indirectly, from Mrs. Blewitt, whom I met at Aylesbury last Sunday, and from another friend : both of them said kind & gladdening things, & I went on my way the happier. Your keenness about the Coronation makes me ashamed that I wrote of it so poorly : but I must not try to make amends to-night : for the day has been busy, & there are other letters waiting, and it's not a memory of which one can write briefly. Indeed it is wonderful to find the unanimity of deep and thankful feeling with which all sorts of people speak of it. *July* 19. . . . just back from our Annual Diocesan Missionary Meeting. It has been held at Newbury this year : so I motored to & fro, taking with me Sir Ernest Satow, who has been staying here for it & speaking at the afternoon meeting. He is quite delightful,—a diplomatist of the very best type :—strong, able, quiet, cultivated, humorous, with great and wide experience :—I think I've never met anyone more really attractive. He spoke admirably about Missions this afternoon : dealing well with all the ordinary objections that men easily raise against them.—We had good gatherings, and a brilliant day. But I think what I cared about most was going to confirm a poor lad who is ill, and probably will not recover :—one comes away with real help from such a scene of cheerful patience and fortitude. My holiday seems delightfully near : I hope to start, if all be well, on August the 2nd, with the Archdeacon of Oxford, Miss Houblon, and Lady Constance Erskine, their cousin :—to go straight out to Brieg, in the Rhone Valley :—and thence to drive & walk up to Simplon Kulm, near the top of the Great Simplon Pass. Doesn't it sound splendid ?—more than I can tell I wish you were coming with us. *Lambeth, July* 27.— This morning I was preaching in Norwich Cathedral: the Bishop got me there for their Diocesan Missionary Festival : and I stayed with him for the night before.—It is the most glorious place : and in this wonderful sunshine it looked its very best :—and the Bishop gave me the kindest welcome :— & I had a very happy visit.—Then on the way back I halted here to see the Archbishop : and I hope to get home about midnight : so I think it's wise to write my letter while I can. I'm very unhappy about the Parliament Bill : mainly because of that rude and angry and intemperate scene in the Commons on Monday, when Hugh Cecil and F. E. Smith led a tumult and howled Asquith down. Bad temper and bad manners are enough to wreck and discredit any cause :—and there lies, I think, almost the gravest danger now. . . . Good-bye, dearest Bernard.—If all be well, I'm off for my holiday on Tuesday : —a real joy it is to look forward to it.

PART II

Written by J. M. C. Crum

CHAPTER I

Two hundred years after Marcus Aurelius died, his image had a place among the Penates of every pious family in Italy and France and Spain. He must have owed this, I think, more to the First Book of his *Meditations* than to all the others put together.

We know and love the man through those others for whom he thanks the gods—his grandfathers, teachers, friends, servants, 'almost all of them good people.'

"It is by the providence of the gods that I was subject to the emperor my father, and brought up under him, who was the properest person living to put me out of conceit with pride . . . It was the favour of the gods that I happened to meet with a brother such as mine was . . . that I had the happiness of knowing Apollonius, Rusticus, and Maximus . . . that I had the satisfaction of my mother's life and company a considerable while "—and so on.

The face of Marcus Aurelius is seen reflected in the mirror of his friendships, his admirations, his love. Describing them, he has unconsciously let us know himself.

And, so thinking, I have determined to describe the Bishop, by gathering together words of his about those whose lives and influences meant most to him—studies which he made from time to time of men whose characters most deeply influenced his. For, if you look, as he loved to do, at Holbein drawings or at Rembrandt paintings, you are likely to get near the spirit of the artist as well as the spirit of the sitters.

The further any one was allowed to enter into the thoughts of the Bishop, the more would he be felt to owe to the presence that was with him of spirits he had reverenced and loved. " Let us say our thanksgiving together," he said one day, after a Communion Service, and we read, verse about, *O sacerdotes Domini.* He spoke as if to unseen presences, and yet as if to people very near. " O ye spirits and souls of the righteous, bless ye the Lord : praise Him and magnify Him for ever."

That was not very long after Mrs. Paget's death, but there were others always living for him among the Communion of the Saints at rest. He never lost the faculty of admiring. That remained almost boyish with him to the end, and beyond his living friends were the heroes of early days, and, beyond these, History had given him an intimacy with one and another in the great multitude which no man can number. I will begin among these ; but I must not go further into the past than to where Richard Hooker stands. He may be called the first of his " mighty men." For " the first three " I expect it would be true to name Hooker, Pascal, Butler. There was Lancelot Andrewes too, but I do not think he " attained unto the first three."

There is a sermon printed in his *Spirit of Discipline* about Bishop Andrewes ; but he admits that he must speak of him " from only a fragmentary knowledge of his writings, with large indebtedness to those who have more worthily studied them."

Still it was with the greatest delight that he found the *Private Devotions* "worthily" edited by Dr. Brightman. He wished—and it is in accord with my chapter to say this—that two men especially could have welcomed the new edition : Cardinal Newman, and his father Sir James Paget, whom he remembered to have often repeated passages of *The Devotions* at family prayers.

As Hooker seemed to the Bishop to have secured for the Church of England the strength which lay in her appeal to reason, and "in his great treatise," to have "'maintained against the faithlessness of Puritan distrust and scorn, the place and dignity of human reason,' 'aided with the influence of divine grace'—showing that 'the way to be ripe in faith' is not necessarily to be 'raw in judgement,'"—so Andrewes had secured to the Church of England the strength which lay in her appeal to history.

The reader of the sermon will notice that where the Bishop claims this honour for Bishop Andrewes, other and newer names find their way into the page, and one note is a tribute to R. W. Church and another to C. Gore.

But among all teachers it was with Hooker that the Bishop most put his mind to school. Sentences from the *Ecclesiastical Polity* came to him constantly as he spoke or wrote. Perhaps the blue cover of the seventh edition of *Hooker's Works* offers a good genealogy of the Bishop's thought :—Hooker's Works edited by Mr. Keble and revised by Dean Church—Church and Paget completing the revision.

I will quote from page 6 of his Introduction to the *Study of Hooker's Fifth Book*—though I would there were a fuller-length portrait.

As a writer of English, then, and as a guide of thought,

Hooker may teach lessons which men are not ceasing yet to need. And, in himself, as illustrating the best way to live and work in a time of much controversy and confusion, he is singularly well worth studying.

Two traits stand out so brightly that they may, perhaps, be brought in here for special emphasis. They are his persevering diligence in his own proper work, and his pure unworldliness. It will presently be seen how vehement and ceaseless was the great controversy with which he had to do (a controversy, be it remembered, in which neither side would ever have been content with any recognition or liberty which was equally conceded to the other) ; and it will be seen how Hooker was placed in the very front of the struggle, to contend in the full publicity of London life, at a centre of its keenest interest, with one of the strongest and best men in the Puritan party.

But no excitement of conflict and no exultation in advantage ever drew him away from his great work and longing : the work of a student, and the longing for fuller knowledge of the truth.

He had won his way to the student's life through many difficulties—through poverty, such as made him in his undergraduate time dependent on the liberality of one patron after another ; through the vexations of academic quarrels ; through ill-health ; through the manifold hindrances of an unhappy home :—and to the labours of a student he gave himself with unceasing eagerness.

It is utterly astonishing to look at the list of the books which he uses in his work, and at the exacting thoroughness of his extant writings ; to think of the vast amount of his labour of which no trace remains ; and to remember that he was only forty-seven when he died. He adds indeed the challenge of a high example to the words in which he speaks of diligence and industry as the first duty of an educated man in days of strife ; but even more impressive than his splendid dutifulness in this regard is the simplicity with which he keeps himself unspotted alike from the conflicts and from the honours of the world. When he was called into prominence he came forward and did his best ; when the trust he bore made fighting necessary, he did not flinch from it—he held his ground, watch-

fully, skilfully, steadily, honourably ; being in the quarrel he
" bore it that the opposed might beware of him " ; bore it
without either bluster or timidity ; owning always the sincerity
and virtue of his adversary, and from him receiving as generous
a tribute of esteem.

But he loved neither fighting nor prominence ; neither
gave him any pleasure ; and therefore neither did him any
harm.   There is a clear ring of genuineness in the words
which Walton records as conveying Hooker's petition to the
Archbishop to remove him from the great place he held as
Master of ·the Temple, and to send him once more to the
quiet and obscurity of a country parsonage.   It is rare to see
a man still young (for Hooker was but thirty-eight when he
resigned the Mastership) turning away from a sphere where
he has borne a brilliant part, and betaking himself into comparative seclusion, with the simple and unselfish desire only to
do before he dies as much as he can of that which he believes
to be his proper task.   But it is perhaps even more rare for the
heat of controversy to kindle in a man the desire not to talk
but to think.   And in both ways the example of Hooker's life
may claim as much attention as the strength of his theology
and the grandeur of his style.

I name Richard Hooker for the chief of " the first
three."   If any one is modestly proud of having once
or twice read through the eight Books of the *Ecclesiastical Polity*, glancing, not too painfully, at prefaces,
notes, indices, he may be able to form some estimate
of the hours of communion with the man's mind and
spirit which would go to the re-editing of the work—
collating MSS.—tracing quotations—even correcting
proofs.   At any time, a kindred spirit would, I think,
have felt of the Bishop " this also is a friend of
Hooker."

But in some ways he was, by sympathy, nearer
akin to Pascal.   The subtlety of the French thought
and language gave him a fine pleasure in the *Lettres*

à un Provincial ; and on the *Pensées* he was hoping to
get steadily to work, when the diocese of Oxford
interfered. The hope would sometimes return to him
as of a task to which he might retire when he had
served his time as Bishop. Some of the editions had
already been collected, and the note-book was prepared. For he was fascinated by the eager intellect
which by its very eagerness had found the limits
within which intellect can move ; the keen clear
thought and speech and humour all delighted him.
But, beyond all these, he wondered and loved, when
Pascal puts by his glittering and transient successes,
and kneels, as simply as his niece Marguerite Périer
might have knelt, to adore his Redeemer.

From an unwritten book, however, it is not possible
to quote, neither can I quote the Bishop on him
whom he so often quoted, Bishop Butler ; and so
I will come to the generation preceding his own, the
generation of those who were 'old enough to be his
father.'

And among them I do not doubt that he would
have me begin with him who was his father. He
wrote some pages for the Life of Sir James Paget,
speaking especially of his religious influence. I will
give some of the words :

On "the Sundays of the old Hospital Days," as the
children grew older, "we went round some of the
wards with him, with the chance of learning patience
from his patients, and pity and gentleness and decision
from him."

He speaks of the theology that must have been
in the Sunday air, though there was much talk and
music : of Dr. Liddon's sermons at St. Paul's in the
afternoons, and of the father, in the evening, with his

book, studying with "rare strength and resoluteness of mind."

Pascal and Hooker he had studied thoroughly in early days . . . he read much of Pusey and Newman and Liddon and Lightfoot and Westcott; and everything that Church and Mozley wrote. . . . But of all authors Butler told, perhaps, most deeply on him. A few months before he died, when his bodily strength had greatly failed, and his sight was failing, I chanced to tell him I had been reading the *Analogy* again. "So have I," he said; and, speaking then with difficulty, scarcely above a whisper, he summed up with masterly justice what he thought of the book, and where it seemed to him to fall short of what is needed now for the defence and confirmation of the faith. That was more than sixty years after he had written of Pascal, "I have bought lately Pascal's *Pensées* and *Lettres à un Provincial*; and really I never remember to have read anything so nearly divine as many parts of the former are." And through all those years he had kept up, in such time as he could win for it out of the stress of practice and correspondence, the habit of theological reading. That habit told deeply on his mind. It kept his religion intellectually abreast of his science. Religion was not to him a field in which the intellect might stand at ease while the emotions went through their evolutions or conflicts : though no height stood barred to the simple and scantily taught, still he knew that the appeal—the demand—was for the whole man ; it was a field in which Pascal and Butler had needed and exerted all their powers ; and one element in his dislike of certain forms of "musical service" was that he judged them to be addressed chiefly to the senses, not the intellect. He never had any inclination to think that "the way to be ripe in faith" was "to be raw in wit and judgement." . . .

And with his habitual study of theology went, in a like tendency, two deeper habits, of which it would not be well to say much : the habit of reverence, and the habit of devotion. As the thought of what he was in these ways rises in one's mind, it brings the picture of a grace and beauty of which one longs to speak ; but even a little knowledge of what he felt about it makes one sure that it is better to be silent : and words seem coarse and blundering when they touch it. The outward tokens of his constant reverence one can recall. For all that seemed to betray irreverence in others jarred sharply on him ; a noisy, self-asserting choir, or a fussy beadle, tried his tolerance ; and if a clergyman gabbled or curtailed the prayers he would wonder whether there were no five minutes in the day that the man used worse than he might have used them in saying the service as it should be said. I never heard him tell a story or a joke that came near making fun of sacred words ; he used to say that when one was ill, and thoughts were hard to keep in order, the stupid jest would hang about the words and rob them of their power. But all his strictness and carefulness in these ways was but the partial expression of a trait that was wrought into his heart and mind—a trait that gave a quiet and natural sanctity to all his thinking about great things. Of such a trait one cannot rightly speak ; and still less do words seem just or becoming as one thinks of that yet deeper life which, more than any other power, made him what he was : through all his years of vigour and of failing strength and extreme weakness, unfailing in steadfastness and tranquillity and independence. Only those who were nearest to him could even guess at the intensity and simplicity of that inner life.

Next to this passage—these words and reticences—about his father's religious influence, may well be set a letter in which there is a suggestion of what he owed to his mother. It is from a letter written in 1888, and speaking of the difficulties of belief :—

When I think of current scepticism generally, as I come across it in society, I do not think that it *greatly* troubles me that, among those who reject Christianity, is a large number of distinguished men in art, science, politics and literature.

It may seem a paradox, but indeed I do not so mean it. It would trouble me far more if, under any great trial, my Mother's faith were to break down or prove useless, than if ten of the cleverest men I knew were to tell me that they had examined the evidence and come to the conclusion that there is nothing in Christianity : for I think that my Mother has more of the data for a right judgement in religious matters than come within the ken of any degree of cleverness, or of that ability which often suffices for distinction.   I am more cheered and confirmed by the clear faith of the loving, the patient, the unselfish, the beneficent, the humble, the thankful, the un-selfconscious, the pure in heart, than I am ever troubled by the scepticism or denials of those of whom I only *know* that they are clever,—and I think that this is logical— for religion is essentially as wide as life—and it is the former class who seem to have found out how to live ; and so they seem to have more right to be listened to (if only they could ever tell one-half they know !) than the others have secured, so long as they are only accredited as clever or distinguished.

As an introduction to what follows the quotation may be continued :—

This is very crudely and hastily put ; but I think it holds a real truth.   Of course I should be uneasy if I saw all the best and largest and richest and brightest and most sympathetic minds turning away from Christianity, for the intellect has its place in the act of faith.   But frankly I cannot say that I see anything like this.   I do not see very much, perhaps, of general society ; but, here and in my father's house, I have seen something, and I do not think that I have come into contact with any minds which so impress me with the sense of distinction, power, penetration, swiftness, fearlessness as my father's, the Dean of St. Paul's, Mr. Holland's and Mr. Gore's ; and I could easily add to this list.   It is the exact concurrence of these minds with the faith of the simplest and the best among people like my mother that makes for me the unfailing force of authority in the present day on the side of Christianity.

The first 'minds' to which he refers are 'my father's and the Dean of St. Paul's,' and so let us go on from his own father to Mrs. Paget's father, Richard William Church.   There was no judgment to which

he oftener referred later, when he himself had to judge.
"The Dean would have said" counted for much with
him.   "I wrote" (he remembers in 1906), "as I was
wont, to ask the Dean's counsel," and then quotes the
answer given in 1889.

It was the Bishop who supplied the preface to the
Dean's *Life and Letters*, and there he singles out "the
peculiar breadth of thought in deliberation and in
judgment" which marked the mind of the Dean.

"He was apt to take with him, in judging the
affairs and cases of ordinary life, a broader volume of
thought, a greater multitude of considerations, than
most men have in mind."   "He was less likely than
most men to forget in forming a judgment something
that should have been remembered."   "One constantly
felt how much his mind was carrying as it did its work."

He speaks of the dignity, the independence of his
mind ; the independence which yet had in it no note
of self-sufficiency.   For it had been won through the
sorrow and loss of 1845 when Mr. Newman seceded,
and his disciple at Oriel "after that could be no
man's disciple."

And there are other lines to be reproduced from
this portrait, "a certain quiet and simple gravity
verging towards sadness" ; a "dislike of ill-grounded
positiveness" ; an "insistence on the limitation of our
knowledge," which yet "did not stay him from saying
clearly what, so far as he could judge, he clearly
saw" ; a "sense of humour," which was in him "a
very keen and delicate sense" ; "a perfect simplicity
and lightness of manner," which guarded him from
unreality and unnaturalness in those who had to do
with him ; and then, "he could be angry. . . . One
felt that many years of quiet and hidden self-control

must lie behind the power of wielding rightly such a weapon as that anger—an anger that was just and strong and calm."

And, all the while, he seemed to live as one moving in the Presence of a Divine Holiness ; in the awe of God, not without a certain " ennobling fear."

There is a passage, too, in one of the Bishop's sermons, where he speaks of the Dean.

" No more," he has been saying, " is gained by pretending to agree than by pretending anything else," but there is the duty, always, of seeing what sympathy can be felt for those with whom one does not agree, while remaining true to one's own position—to " do full justice to an alien position."   " How hard a task that is one only realises gradually as one detects one's own failure in it, or perhaps one's own mistake in fancying that one was succeeding in it ; or, it may be, as one feels what it is to be one's self honestly and thoroughly misunderstood."

His text is—" Have salt in yourselves, and have peace one with another " ; and from the difficulty of attaining peace with alien minds without the sacrifice of any truth, he points back to the Dean.

" Few, I think, have entered more thoroughly and freely into the minds of others ; few have understood men better and done fuller justice to diverse types of thought and character, whether in the field of history or contemporary life ; yet none who knew him could think him likely to hang back or vacillate when the need came for deliberate action, for clear-cut distinction, for irrevocable venture, for costly sacrifice.

" He loved the truth and peace ; and, by God's grace he truly served both," for he guarded " that inner sternness of thought and will which counted for

so much in that great movement of Church life in
which he had lived and borne his part, that hidden
austerity which guards from softness and degeneracy
the bright hopefulness and kindness of 'the peaceable
temper.'"

Of Dr. Pusey, placed, it will be remembered, at the
highest point marked on the Bishop's schoolboy thermometer of admiration,—Dr. Pusey whose last sermon, or
rather lengthy extracts from whose last sermon, he had
read from the University pulpit—he used to speak with
reverence not unmingled with alarm ; and other leaders
of the Oxford Movement, Newman, of course, and
James Mozley, and, in a special way, Charles Marriott,
were his heroes.   But the tradition came to him
through two others, besides the Dean of St. Paul's ;
through Canon Liddon and Edward King, Bishop of
Lincoln.

Of Dr. Liddon's influence, at one time, it would
not be very easy to speak with exaggeration.

When Canon Johnston's life of Dr. Liddon was
published, the Bishop's contribution was thought to
be faint praise.   But the truth was, I fancy, that he
was explaining himself there—the public forgotten—to
his former master.   So a scholar, now grown-up, might
have appealed to one who had once been his teacher.

"I have learned from you (he is saying) ; I honour
you ; I love you : and yet, since those old Oxford days,
my life has been teaching me things which your life
allowed you to overlook.   A Bishop—and I cannot
understand how it happened, and it is a great loss that
it did happen, that you never were a Bishop—must
take into account considerations which spoil the logic
(the 'Oxford logic' Bishop Lightfoot used to call it
in Dr. Liddon) which fastens on a single train of

thought and inference, pursuing it without regard to the surrounding facts which tell upon it."

He wrote elaborately to something like this effect, and then follows one of his careful drawings of the man whom he loved, made in the name of the " friends who saw most of him, and saw him, it may be, when he was happiest."

They remember him as one who, possessing in extraordinary measure the gifts most perilous to simplicity and modesty, and so wielding those gifts that men of all sorts gathered round him in thousands and listened to him as to no other preacher, yet remained unmarred by admiration, and kept quite out of his heart all the degrading thoughts of what is called success ; remained apparently one of the least self-conscious of men, ready to enter with undivided interest into anything that was of real interest to others ; as simply grateful as a child for the simplest kindness shewn to him ; never talking about himself, nor talking as men do who, when they are silent, think much about themselves ; and making others somehow feel that it would not do to talk to him as though they thought him remarkable or great.

And then his friends remember—

How unselfishly he used his wonderful ability in ordinary conversation ; though, indeed, no conversation into which he came was really ordinary. It is hard to imagine any one talking much better than he did. The voice, the look, the manner, the perfect flexibility of tone ; the phrases that summed up everything, the reticence that suggested more than any phrase ; the gesture, or something less obtrusive than a gesture, which came in when any word would have been clumsy ; the delicate enunciation that was always precise and never prim, that lent itself alike to earnestness and fun ;—these were but the accessory graces of a mind rich with knowledge of all sorts, and swift to bring out the aptest thought, and of an imagination so vivid that every detail stood at once before it, so discerning that it saw at once the detail that meant most.

And then, behind all this, he speaks of the secret of the "strength and depth" which men felt in Dr. Liddon : they were aware in him of two influences, always present, though seldom thrust into their notice.

There was his reverence for every single human soul. "He habitually regarded men as the New Testament speaks of them."

And there was his sense of the Presence of his Lord.

There was a memorable tone that came into his words when, in preaching or in argument or in conversation he spoke of that which he condemned as slighting or disloyal to Christ. It was, quite simply, like the way in which a man fires up when any one has, even unawares, spoken rudely or contemptuously of his friend; and there are parts of his writings in which, for those at least who knew him, that same tone still sounds. It was but one sign of a real habit of thinking constantly of his Master; of a very attentive listening for His command; of an earnest, anxious desire to go straight forward in His cause, to live and die as His.

So he wrote of Dr. Liddon.

I have but few words to represent his feeling for Edward King. "Dearest and truest friend" he calls him in a letter of 1883, and "dear, dear Father" in 1885, when King became Bishop of Lincoln ; but his talk often turned towards memories of one who had in the earlier years of his ordained life an influence which told on his way of thinking and even on his way of writing and speaking. Often he would remember some illustration of the grace and charm and strength of Dr. King's manner and mind—some example of his gentle influence, his skilful love, his delicate and beautiful care in dealing with men.

" The Bishop of Lincoln's death " (he wrote) " makes a great impoverishment in my life. I had known him intimately for five and thirty years ; he had shown me wonderful kindness and trust ; and in unselfishness and gentleness and sincerity and patience he never faltered. I doubt whether any one has left more hearts feeling the poorer for his death, or more lives the better for his life—for he was just the same to all sorts and conditions of men."

During the Lambeth investigation of charges brought against Dr. King, the Bishop, who was then at Christ Church, and Mrs. Paget, with Dr. Bright, were collecting for a Defence Fund. " My wife is quite depressed at the thought of having less than fifty receipts to write and direct in the day," he wrote, when the list was being closed.

He attended a Conference held at this troublous time, and, as he was preparing to take his anxious part, Bishop Stubbs put to him across the table the first question. " Well," was the question, " and how is Richard ? " Richard was at that time five years old and the question irrelevant, but it was remembered.

It fell to the Bishop to speak, in 1901, at his first Diocesan Conference, of his great predecessor—one of whom, Dr. Moberly had said, not long before, that few men had really known him :—

That is, I think, true ; for in him, English through and through, the English quality of reserve, using almost reck-lessly at times a boundless ingenuity, kept us from seeing, save just when and as he chose, the depths of his great heart and the heights on which his spirit moved. We may wish that we had seen more of what he truly was. But men are what they are ; and by being honestly and thoroughly and fearlessly themselves they do the finest and most lasting work. And how can we tell what this Church and nation might have lost if he had forced himself away from that reserve which was as

Y

natural to him as effusiveness and exaggeration are to some men ?

When I think of his greatness, his unworldliness, his magnificent power of painstaking, of the generosity of his friendship, his "enthusiasm for intellectual equity," the splendid example of his industry, and his reverent and unselfish use of a mind majestic and robust as Bishop Butler's ; when I recall words of his that left fastened in one's heart some truth that ever since, through storm and mist, has held its place ; when I guess at the unwise plans and faulty arguments that that massive learning, that indisputable authority, kept from seeing day or doing harm, I wonder whether history, if it ever is as true and just as he tried to make it, will not place his name in the first rank of those who have had grace and power to do this Church and realm great service in our day.

He went on to speak of another who had died in the year before the Conference :—

"And then," he said, "what a loss it is that we shall never see again, in the crisis of debate, one starting from his seat and swinging forward to the space in front here, and pouring out a wealth of knowledge, pathos, humour, poetry, teaching us as only they can teach who never cease to learn. Somehow when I think that William Bright has passed beyond the veil, I cannot keep out of my mind that bit of the *Apologia* where Socrates imagines himself meeting in another world those with whom constant thought and study kept his soul in contact even here ; I find myself thinking how splendid it would be for him to talk with Athanasius and Augustine and Leo ; or to meet, perhaps, with honest souls rejoicing in the truth that they had imperfectly apprehended here—the truth he spent his life in fighting for.

"Surely we can never know another mind and heart like his ; so rich and generous, so young in interest and sympathy and enthusiasm, so keeping up the radiance and freshness of the morning when the night was close at hand ; so simply forgetful or disdainful of all else wherever the purity of truth, the Church's cause, the honour of his Lord, was even touched."

It has been said that our love towards our neighbour is, commonly, most severely tried by those who are our next-door neighbours. The above is the Bishop's portrait of him who lived on his right hand ; two years later he wrote to the Diocese, giving a portrait of him who had dwelt beside him on the other hand, Dr. Moberly :—

The common welfare, we know, is best served when each man does as much as he can of that which he can do best ; and Robert Moberly's life at Oxford answered well to that requirement. None could come to know him without learning something of the height and purity of his character, without being aware of the presence in him of a rare humility and patience and unworldliness and kindness, without seeing how great and strong a character those graces make.

But the distinctive gift he held from God, the gift which his character enabled him to use aright, was the gift of a most remarkable intellect, a power of mind, which I will even venture to call unique in the experience of recent years.

For I do not think any one in our day has shown quite such a blending of excellences commonly set in contrast, of robustness and subtlety, of tenacity and delicacy, of force and precision. For the penetration and vigour of his mind one might have claimed for him the praise which Clement the Eighth is said to have bestowed on Hooker—"nothing too hard for his understanding " : for the exactness, the indefatigable and unabashed persistence with which he enforced the fine distinctions which his keen eye saw, and his courageous judgement knew to be real, one might claim Hooker's own vindication : "the mixture of those things by speech which by nature are divided, is the mother of all error. To take away, therefore, that error which confusion breedeth, distinction is requisite. Rightly to distinguish is by conceit of mind to sever things different in nature, and to discern wherein they differ."

Before the new " next-door neighbour " had come to live in Dr. Bright's house, the Bishop had left the

Deanery. Of his own successor, once in a rather gloomy hour, he said that at least it made some amends for the thought of the failures of him who now was Bishop, to think that his great friend was so good a Dean ; and of Dr. Bright's successor, Dr. Bigg, he wrote a sketch, to be a preface to a volume of his sermons. I quote from that :—

When Dr. Bigg preached at Oxford, the power of his preaching was felt and acknowledged by many who are not apt in most matters to judge alike. Men of his own generation, severely sensitive to any deflection from the strictness of academic reserve ; undergraduates of the less literary sort, tending to think of sermons as curious exercises in a field remote from actual life ; choristers, who might not unnaturally feel that at all events University and Cathedral preaching was not addressed to them ; all these found themselves listening with a strange interest and some surprise to a preacher who did not seem to be thinking much about any of them, but somehow understood them all ; who was simply bent on his own thoughts, and yet set them all thinking. They never knew what he would say next, but when it was said it seemed the most natural thing in the world, extraordinarily well worth remembering, and likely to mean more than was at once realised. No one else preached in the same way ; but the preaching was quite untouched by anything like the taint of mannerism ; it was wholly unusual and unconventional, yet the most normal of men could not call it eccentric : the preacher never took a liberty, and never lost his own.

And so he sets himself to analyse the unusual combinations of qualities which gave Dr. Bigg his distinction :—

A mystic—" the most simple and genuine of the mystics would have hailed him as a brother, and felt that he was at home with them ; yet he never parted company with common-sense, or with ordinary ways, or with any of the prudent safeguards of sanity and sympathy. He moved among his fellows as an easy-going man, not apt to make much of differences, or to think of them as barriers to good fellowship ; yet he never struck one as content to differ, and he could be stern, even fierce, when he found himself in the thick of a controversy. His was an independent and even a lonely mind ; yet he showed a touching simplicity of pleasure when others really understood him or, with an imperfect understanding, were grateful for his teaching.   He had the true quickening gift of historical insight, and his heart would go and live in the past as thoroughly as the hearts of his great predecessors at Christ Church, Arthur Stanley and William Bright ; yet a farmer or an agricultural labourer or a man of affairs would find him curiously conversant with their concerns ; and neither in his country parish nor on the Governing Body of Christ Church could any one doubt his practical ability, his appreciation of existing circumstances.

" He took things seriously, and the pathos of life was constantly in his thoughts ; yet, besides the sense of humour which often goes with such a cast of mind, he had a healthful cheeriness, a sincere and convincing hopefulness which made him the most encouraging of counsellors."

The reader may begin to think that the Bishop indulged freely in fluent eulogy.   But it was not so. He loved to praise ; and yet his praise was spoken, especially of the Dead, with singular reserve and care. " It is better quietly to think and think again about them ; while it is best of all to try, as Pascal was bidden, for their sakes to put ourselves in the state in which they now would have us be."

He never debased the currency of praise.   If he spoke much, he thought more.

Let me give his words about two leaders whom he honoured, Archbishop Temple and Lord Salisbury.

Of the Archbishop he wrote in December 1902 :—

A man who had fought his way with such strong and pure simplicity through vast demands and difficulties, through evil report and good report, unswerving for all the world could do to make him swerve.

And then—

He went straight on ; doing the best he could ; keeping innocency and taking heed unto the thing that was right ; not expecting business to go easily, or roads to be smooth, or leisure much ; but doing all he could under the conditions he had ; and when it was done, looking to see what was to be done next.

And he quotes of him :—

One who never turned his back but marched breast forward,
  Never doubted clouds would break,
Never dreamed, though right were worsted, wrong would triumph,
  Held we fall to rise, are baffled to fight better,
          Sleep to wake.

And here is Lord Salisbury, as he spoke of him in September 1903 :—

A high example of unworldliness amidst all the world's clamour and competing ; of utter freedom from ambition ; of great strength loyally given to a great task ; of perseverance in hard work through personal sorrow and through failing health ; of a life simply, frankly, steadfastly Christian.

The foregoing appreciations are none of them connected in any special way with the Bishop's work in the Diocese. But there, too, he found many with whom he was thankful to be working.

When Archdeacon Bourke died he wrote of him as of one for whom he had felt each year a more intimate affection—of " his cheerfulness in the midst of hard work and heavy responsibility and anxiety," the cheerfulness that was not defeated by fatigue or trouble ; the hopefulness that was not discouraged by apparent failure, or by difficulties that looked insuperable ; the rare power of good judgement, strong and clear because it saw things in the true light, and so saw them distinctly and in their right proportion : " and all this light," he says, " the light of cheerfulness, of hope, of judgement, he saw, I believe, as only it can be truly seen, in God's Light. . . . The spiritual mind, the habit of communion with God, was the secret of it all."

Those were the words with which he took leave of his friend ; but since to a stranger the epitaphs of the prophets do not always carry conviction that the prophets were honoured in their own day and country, I will ask a place for the Bishop's words to Archdeacon Bourke's successor.

He invites him to the vacant office in more general terms, and then goes on :—

I must venture to add a few words of my personal feeling about it. I greatly desire that the office may be held by one with whom I can freely and trustfully take counsel, in the assurance of mutual confidence and understanding, in the certainty of unfailing loyalty and friendship ; the experience of the past years has made me sure that I should have in working with you this priceless help ; and I shall be wholly glad and thankful if I may look forward to it. . . .

Ten days later he writes :—

Your letter to-day has made me very heartily glad and grateful and thankful ; every time I think of our working together, the thought comes to me with a fresh pulse of hope ; and I feel the younger for it already. I cannot say half of what I want to say when I think of what you and Mrs. Shaw are willing to do for the sake of the Diocese, but, indeed, it touches me deeply. . . . With regard to the move, it may quite well and rightly be deferred until after August ; it is of primary importance that Wycombe (where I shall hardly dare to show my face, or pass through the station) should not be vacant for any length of time. . . . May God continue to you in the future all the blessing of the past ; and may He teach me to show you how thankful I am for your friendship and your help. —Affectionately yours, F. Oxon.

The writer of this letter wrote generous words because he thought generous thoughts. I could not show what he was if I hid all his letters to his friends ; and if I were to publish all, I think my pages would, as they went about the three counties (like Macbeth's hand), "the multitudinous see incarnadine" with blushes. Let it be allowed me then to publish only the praise of one more colleague—praise publicly made.

When the Bishop of Reading retired from the Archdeaconry of Oxford, the Bishop spoke at the Diocesan Conference :—

Many here have known him longer than I, not many can have known him better, very few, if any, can owe him more.

I have more for which to thank him as Archdeacon than you can know or I tell ; I have turned to him in all sorts of troubles, and taxed his patience shamelessly ; and he has grudged me nothing save the chance of thanking him.

If I were to try to say how much we all owed him, I should not only be quite sure of vexing him, I should also be disobeying the authority of his example — and that quite needlessly, for you know what he has been to us all.

Let us try to thank him, then, in the only way he will not blame, and cannot silence even if he would, by storing up in our hearts and carrying into the task we have to bear the loyalty, the disregard of self, the strenuous love of work which we have seen in him.

One more letter will be allowed me for the sake of the friendship that is in it, written to Dr. Pollock on the rumour that he was appointed Bishop of Norwich.

Jan. 14, 1910.

MY DEAR MASTER OF WELLINGTON—My youngest son writes to me, " Do you see that Dr. Pollock is appointed Bishop of Norwich?" I had not seen it, but I always trust the young; and so I am bold to write and tell you how glad and thankful I am. Yes, in every regard. When I think of the councils of the Bishops, there is a deep spring of hope and reassurance in looking forward to what you will bring amongst us there. And when I think of the Diocese, and the Parishes, and the Confirmation candidates, my mind turns to our talks about the boys, and to the gentleness and trust and (if I may say it) the respectfulness of your bearing towards them, and I know you will realise the opportunities of happiness in the real Pastoral work of a Bishop. And when I think of you, though I feel that you may move henceforward as one heavy-laden and sometimes weary, still, I know that you have learnt the greatness of patience, and that therefore the load and the weariness are sure to yield for you their hidden blessing. And when I think of Wellington even, I can feel that if, as I trustfully believe, the new work is God's Will for you, then quite surely He will take care of the old work. And when (as I'm afraid I always do sooner or later, and generally sooner) I think of myself, why, then, dear friend, it means more than I can tell that this new bond should bind us closer than ever together.

Forgive my venturing to write all this, and do not think that it needs any acknowledgement; and believe me to be always affectionately yours,

F. Oxon.

It was those who came nearest to the Bishop who found him most unfailing to see the good in them, to think the best of them.

I may not use, for mirrors to reflect his nature, more of those whom he loved, of those especially who worked most intimately with him in the last two or three years of his life. Yet it will be felt that this chapter has in a measure rivalled that chapter of the Roman Emperor from which it has ventured to take its origin.

CHAPTER II

I TAKE down *Hooker's Works*, Keble, Seventh Edition, Church and Paget, vol. iii., to copy out the following passage from bk. vii. chap. ii. 3.

A Bishop is a minister of God, unto whom with permanent continuance there is given not only power of administering the Word and Sacraments, which power other Presbyters have; but also a further power to ordain ecclesiastical persons, and a power of chiefty in government over Presbyters as well as Laymen, a power to be by way of jurisdiction a Pastor even to Pastors themselves.

And to a glance down the page, the words start up akin to this of "chiefty of government" and "power to be by way of jurisdiction a Pastor even to Pastors themselves," "jurisdiction," "regiment," "superiority," "superiority of power mandatory, judicial and coercive." It is therefore necessary to attempt some account of the Bishop as one who had learned from his Master, Master Richard Hooker, and others—that a Bishop is "one who hath a principal charge to guide and oversee others."

He shrank by temperament from decisions, from pronouncements. He was a cautious politician, whether in the ecclesiastical or in the civil polity. To "decide" seemed to him the real hard work that tried a man. To decide in public matters was, commonly, with him, to cast a balance between the unwisdom of venturing into motion and the unwisdom of daring to remain motionless.

" The Bishops are taunted " (he said once) " with being afraid to speak out ; and I hope often the charge is true. I should be very sorry if it were not often true of me ; for a man must be very self-confident, and careless or even contemptuous of others, if he is never afraid to speak out, however deep and difficult and complex may be the matter of which he speaks, however great the responsibility he bears."

"But " (he goes on to say) " a man may be still more afraid that he may be untrue to his task if he keep silence," and so he speaks his mind on three vexed questions.

On one question connected with Church Schools he proposed action, " for to wait when one ought not, is the height of rashness."

He had not much, in any kind of politics, of the feeling of a great life astir among multitudes of hearts, an instinct to advance, a desire for progress, waiting only for leaders to quicken it, to inspire it, to lead it on.

Some one spoke once to him in something of this sense, and his answer showed him to be thinking of society as if it were some barge or boat caught in the flood of a great river. The Great Man's office was to steer it, bending all his power to avoid, from crisis to crisis, dangers of rocks which others do not see, or see too late.

Evolution among human societies seemed to him so complex, so illusive, so *tentative* a process that he had little confidence in any one who claimed to have discovered a short and easy method for the improvement of mankind. In a world where so much experience is needed for the making of a little knowledge, he was oftener at ease among questions as to which he could remember " my father used to say . . .," and that which his father had been used to say was sometimes cautious beyond what he would himself have said.

Here are some words about medical politics from Sir James Paget's *Memoir* :—

I was always in favour of what was regarded as progress ; but my love of peace, and the habit of trying to make the best of things as they are, and my belief that legislative changes have really but little influence on the advancement of knowledge, made me a very mild reformer. I had a full share in bringing about the improvements of the last twenty years in teaching and examining and in the general management of the affairs of the College [of Surgeons] and the University [of London] ; but, whenever I look back on all this part of my work, it seems to me as if there were less good done in proportion to the time spent, than in anything in which I have been engaged.

And this has often led me to believe that in my own profession, and to suspect that in all other callings, the influence of whatever can be called politics is immensely over-rated.

If the Sentinel in *Iolanthe* is right in his opinion that—

> Every boy and every gal
> That's born into this world alive,
> Is either a little Liberal
> Or else a little Conservative,

then the Bishop was a born Conservative, one who counted the cost of a disturbance of existing relations at least as carefully as the advantage of the change proposed.

And yet, like other men (at other than Election times) he would have been ill at ease if he had been confined only to principles of Conservatism.

For with all his deference to tradition, discipline, order, he reverenced also liberty, life.

In the two aspects of his public influence which are spoken of below, in the education questions and the ecclesiastical discipline questions, he moved with great caution, and yet he moved.

In educational politics he distressed many who had found in him a leader the most conservative heart was glad to follow, by seeing a vision, which was to them only an illusion, of England opening all her schools to the denominations, in a manner that "liberal" hearts might think far off and still rejoice to see.

And in ecclesiastical politics, while his friends were some of them aghast to find him convinced by the experience of the Discipline Commission that he had never yet given its true value to law as law, he was engaged on a work whose result may be to free the Church of England from a law which three centuries have been content to leave unchanged.

So he moved, but not easily ; he decided, but with grave deliberation ; and much that is called "policy" seemed to him to live in loose thinking, and to lead to unprofitable talking.

At his first Diocesan Conference he imagined the question put to him — "And what will be your policy?" He might have pleaded inexperience, he said, as a sufficient excuse for having none :—

Yet I should not be quite frank if I merely pleaded in-experience as my excuse for not having a policy. The plain truth is that I had rather be without one if I can. I had rather trust to principles and try, God helping me, to live and work by them, seeing all I can of what is true and just, keeping it as clear and steady as I can in mind and heart, and striving with all my might to understand what it demands of me in each contingency, each group of conditions. There is the danger that a man's policy may stiffen itself towards an independent existence and set up its own claims to his deference ; that it may come to be like those melancholy diaries that people live to write, or still more seriously, like the rules that give dictates to the voice of conscience.

And so politics never came easily to him : no decision was ever to him a light affair.

" It has been a long weary business all these weeks," he writes, when the Education Bill of 1906 had reached its last stage in the House of Lords. " I am quite sure that I was never meant for politics." And to Canon Drummond a little later : " Thank you for a letter of true help and encouragement. I was very much troubled as I tried to bear my part about the Bill. I do not think I have any aptitude at all for political life ; and I felt like a fish out of water, or in very hot water. But it was all well worth while if it helped at all to hearten up the true workers in the Diocese."

I will take first the political affairs here spoken of.

I

To tell the story of the education question from 1902 to 1908 would be to wander in a wide country. I have not the necessary geography ; and I seek here only to suggest the relation of the Bishop to the Bills which, in turn, have attempted to commend themselves to the British public—Mr. Balfour's in 1902, Mr. Birrell's in 1906, Mr. M'Kenna's and Mr. Runciman's in 1908.

" Round about the Act of 1902, I have had my first experience " (he said at the Diocesan Conference in October 1903) " of having to enter, with something more than the responsibility, something less than the personal liberty of a private citizen, into the course of public affairs ; and I must own that at times I have been tempted almost to despair of seeing deep and delicate issues come out through such a tumult of conflicting and confusing forces. . . . But the despair would have been, as usual, wrong."

He had, as will be seen, a considerable journey before him still in 1903, and the tumult of conflicting and confusing forces was then at a comparatively mild stage ; but he retained his conviction that " to despair " would be, " as usual, wrong."

In May 1902 he had spoken welcoming Mr. Balfour's Bill as " an act of justice," and as " on the whole likely to help and encourage the religious education of the children."

In October the working of it is one of the " walls of difficulty " which he sees lying before us.

Already by this " long and bitter controversy " it may be that we have lost, he says, with those who strive against us, more of mutual understanding and kindness than many of us may live to regain, and that is a heavy price to pay even for justice.

He addresses himself to the vindication of the justice of receiving State-aid in Church Schools for that part of the education which the State demands for all children.

He is not shaken in his belief that the cause is just. He counsels a watchful and whole-hearted longing for peace, a readiness to sacrifice, for the sake of peace, all that we are free to sacrifice.

But what cannot be sacrificed is the " preponderant voice in the management " of Church Schools, as long as they are efficient. Those whose voluntary effort has provided and sustained them, and on whose voluntary effort they will still be largely dependent in the future, have justice in the claim to that.

He argues the rights of the case at length, and then :—

We are going to give the State a large part of the income from our endowments : the rent of our School buildings, the cost of their repairs, etc.

That is what we contribute towards the cost of the schools. . . . It is as making this contribution that we believe ourselves able honourably to receive, and justly to ask, the power to secure that purpose, the power which, with ample provisions against any misuse of it, is given us in the form of a preponderant voice in the Board of Managers. If any one were to say that for such power we ought to contribute more I could understand, though I should think him exorbitant.

If any one were to say that by no contribution, by no sacrifice, under no safeguards for individual consciences, should any body of people be able to secure the use of a public elementary school for Church teaching, I could understand him. . . . But what I cannot acquit of unfairness is the language which ignores the fact of this contribution, and which treats us as though we were merely clutching at a dole. And when people talk of public control following public money, as though that sound principle covered all the ground, they seem to me to forget that private generosity and individual sacrifices for a cause believed to be serious and sacred should among just men be either refused or recognised.

It will be remembered that on the one side, in such a Diocese as Oxford, there was a great mistrust of the Bill of 1902 among those who had, sometimes by a kind of inheritance and sometimes by the self-sacrifice of their own days, entered into an undisputed possession of the education of their parish, and that on the other side, in other parts of the country—for the feeling was but rare in the three counties—there was the resentment of those who found Church Schools supported at all by public money.   The words "Passive" and "Resistance" will recall that element in the trouble. Meanwhile other difficulties arose for any one who desired to commend the Bill to those affected by it as were the Clergy of the Oxford Diocese.

On November 13th the Bishop wrote to *The Times* concerning the amendment brought forward by Colonel Kenyon-Slaney, and adopted in the Bill.   He complained of its empowering the Managers, without any appeal beyond them, to interpret trust-deeds, to decide on what should be considered Church teaching, to deal with personal differences, and questions of misuse of power.   "The manner in which the control over religious education is now given [to the Managers] seems to me open to grave objection," he wrote.

What came to be known familiarly as "The Kenyon-Slaney Clause" was one of the alienating influences against which the Bishop had to plead.

In January 1903 he wrote to the Clergy in the Diocese, speaking of their duty towards the Act :—

"A third of a century," he said, "has passed since the last time of an importance like this to those who have in any way to do with Church Schools.   We are to work with power less independent and with opportunity less unconditioned than formerly, but we must not part with them.   There is no greater heritage than the 'power and opportunity of doing good.'   We hold them in trust for those who come after us."

From Kenyon-Slaney Clause troubles and other troubles he looks forward to the power of "the general good sense and fairness of the community" to make vexations rare and rarer—"and, anyhow," the vexations "do not seem to me to alter the plain duty of doing all we can to use and guard and hand on to our successors that privilege in regard to elementary education which the self-sacrifice and perseverance of the past have handed down to us."

In October, 1903, he alluded to the Act at the Diocesan Conference :—

I suppose none of us can remember any Bill more hotly and lengthily debated, any Act that so quickly proved hard to understand, or any change that has come into operation amidst so much controversy and hostility.

Yet he himself was full of hope :—

Already, I think, we can see the saving, the unfailing powers of equity and public spirit emerging and rising up above the agitation of prejudice and temper and misrepresentation and suspicion, and so hope grows : hope enough for us to work on by.

A year later he returns to the same subject, speaking to the same audience :—

The anxiety is penetrated with hope ; such clouds as there are may, I think, at any moment break, and let us see blue sky with the promise of a fair day. This hope of which I speak comes from what I have learnt of the working of the Act in our own three counties—of the course held, the care taken, the toil borne by those who have had given to them the hard task of administering a singularly complex and difficult Act. It would be impertinent for me to praise the loyalty and equity with which that task has been sustained ; but I do earnestly trust that nothing in our debate to-day may even seem as though we were forgetful of it. And I cannot refrain from paying, with all respect, my tribute to the public spirit which has entered into the work.

For indeed, I think that public spirit is as true a form of patriotism as can be shown in any field ; and that those who, taking fresh burdens into days already busy, or foregoing pleasures that every one would like to have, work on patiently hour after hour with nothing to look at but green cloth and blotting-paper in the joyless environment of a committee-room, are serving England as unselfishly as any men can.

And if that path of duty is not the way to glory, it is the way to other rewards, which in the long run are more worth having. If the Act had been worked everywhere as it has been among us, there would, I think, be little reason for anxiety. . . . But, unhappily, it is not so. . . .

At this Conference the complexity of the issues and the eagerness with which they were watched was illustrated by a debate on " Circular 512," in which the relations of the Board of Education to the Local Education Authorities, and of the Local Education Authorities to the Managers and Schools, were discussed by Sir Alfred Cripps and Sir William Anson.

I will only fasten on this point which emerged from it—as one on which the Bishop took hold—that " there was liberty for parents belonging to the Church of England to withdraw their children, if they pleased, from provided schools during the time of religious instruction, and to bring them to the Church or to the Church School," which seemed to him " to come nearer than any practical suggestion " he had yet heard " to the provision of religious instruction according to the wishes, belief, and convictions of parents, whether in provided or non-provided schools."

In the end of 1905, and the beginning of 1906, came the General Election, in which the Liberals were returned by an overwhelming majority—with " mandates " (it will be remembered) to do various things. The " mandate " which especially concerns us was that which resulted in Mr. Birrell's Bill.

On January 11th the Bishop wrote through *The Times* to those who would " guard the Church's teaching as a living force in English education." The maintenance of Church Schools seemed to him to be vital :—

. . . of schools, that is to say, over which those who are resolved to maintain Church teaching have an effective, though not an unshared, power of control, and to which teachers will be appointed who will give religious teaching with the reality of religious conviction.   As a Churchman, I am ready to resist strenuously any such alteration of the Act of 1902 as would have the result [of leaving the Church powerless to retain an effective part in the management of its Schools, to determine what shall be the course of religious teaching, and " to require that that teaching shall be given by those who believe it to be true "].

And I am strengthened for this resistance by the thought that the Church has always been bound to care especially for the children of the poor, and that it is their right to be taught their parents' faith that is at stake.   But it is not simply as a Churchman that I am ready thus to resist.   As one who cares about General Education, I am sure that what is most needed now is some rest from strife, some quiet time for steady work under conditions fairly understood and accepted.

The letter ends with a defence of the clerical influence that was then attacked :—

It is easy to talk about the dominance of the parson, and to make much of isolated cases in which an opportunity has been given for such talk.   But it will be a very serious thing . . . if the parson ceases to care for the School or to be able to serve it, and if from the great work of elementary education there is taken away that personal devotion and enthusiasm which in many a parish has been the most constant help for the maintenance of a true standard ; and which, however it may be slighted in the confusion of controversy, will be seen in its real value if ever it is driven from its work.

On January 31, 1906, he wrote to the Clergy and members of the Diocesan Conference in much the same strain :—

I know much of the loyalty with which [the Church Schools] have been maintained, and the sacrifices which have been made for them ; I can see something of what it may mean, especially in village life, if the heart is taken out of those who have been constant in care and toil for them.

And then, in view of the " mandate " to re-open the education question, he reviews the strength of the position of the Church Schools :—

"We have " (he says) " on our side all that the Church has done since 1870, work done under assurances and with the encouragement of the nation and in compliance with the nation's requirements. The nation has accepted this abundant service, and through that service we have, till might is right, a rightful strength on our side.

" There are three principles to keep steady and clear before our minds.

" 1. To maintain for Churchmen and for all others who desire it, the right to provide for all children whose parents wish them to receive it, as a recognised part of the elementary education, religious instruction in the faith which their parents hold.

" 2. That the Church's Creed cannot be truly represented by a combination of undenominationalism with an appendix or superstructure of distinctive doctrine.

" 3. No one shall be set to teach a faith which he does not hold."

In April, 1906, he wrote to the Diocese calling upon Churchmen to wait and see whether the Liberal Government would fulfil its difficult task " of re-conciling in calm consideration the claims of justice and the expectations that rose high in a time of excitement."

The feeling of those who are most deeply and personally concerned in the matter must tell, and we may take courage from the strong and willing expression of a widespread con-viction that " definite religious teaching " is the teaching that people want. Nothing could be more cheering and hopeful

than the abundant evidence that has told of this conviction in
one parish after another of this Diocese. I am thankful for it
with all my heart. To me it seems as though the allies I
should most desire to have are with ready keenness rallying to
the cause I have at heart, in numbers far beyond what I had
dared to hope.

This letter ends with an appeal for prayer.

Then the Bill came, and in May, 1906, he wrote to
the Incumbents and Church Wardens.

"I believe" (he writes) "that the Bill offends against the
principles of religious liberty ; violates the rights of parents ;
restricts oppressively the freedom of teachers ; deals high-
handedly with trusts ; slights and wrecks what all previous
laws have steadily encouraged ; imperils the continuance of
religious teaching in any form ; and ensures the increase of
strife.

"I believe that a strong tide of feeling is rising in the
country to reject indignantly the idea that it was for any
measure such as this that the present Government received
their power at the last Election. . . .

"In view of what [this Bill] is, I think it is our first duty
to say plainly that, as it stands, we will oppose it with all our
might ; and that, if the Government force it upon us, we shall
never acquiesce in it as a settlement of the education question."

In the following month meetings were held at
Oxford, Aylesbury, Reading, and Slough at which
these sentiments were endorsed by the Clergy and
Laity of the Diocese, Churchmen who in the three
counties had raised nearly £400,000 since the Education Bill of 1870, for the building, altering, and
improving of Schools (exclusive of repairs). I give
one extract from the speech of the Bishop at Reading
(May 16) :—

With regard to the principle that public control should
follow public money : I believe that before this Bill was

brought in, to a very great extent at least, public control did follow public money. I don't allow that hitherto denominational teaching has been paid for out of public money. I maintain that by a rough sort of an apportionment, the value of the buildings paid for that, and the public money covered the field of what is called secular instruction. Public money went over the field of what is called secular instruction, and there it was followed by public control in the presence of H.M. Inspector. I never thought of complaining of that, and I believe that Churchmen and others who care for Voluntary Schools would never have complained if the public control in that way had been made ever so stringent and exacting. Let the State see to it that the instruction is as good as can be given and received. Let the State exact as fully as it can the highest standard it can point to for this teaching. Let it come down on us as hard as it likes where we fail in this regard. It is not of that that we complain ; nor, I believe, would Churchmen have complained if simply under any state of things public money had been withheld from the field of religious education. But what we do complain of is that public control is carried into the field of religious teaching, whether public money comes there or not. There, I hold that the State is taking upon itself a function which does not rightly belong to it. It is going right away from its own principle that public control must follow public money. The Bill says expressly that no part of the expenses of denominational teaching shall fall upon the local education authority. I do not complain of that shutting out of public money from the field of denominational teaching. But when you have shut out public money, by what right do you say that this teaching shall never be in Provided Schools ? What right have you to say that denominational teaching shall only be for two days in the week in the transferred schools and shall never be given by any member of the staff ? If that is not carrying public control beyond the proposed scope of public money I am surprised. Public control is to follow public money. Yes ! But the public should have a conscience ; the public should not be quite indifferent as to the source from which their public money is drawn. A great many people who will be contributing to this money object to the predominance which it is proposed to give to undenominational teaching.

We have been told that minorities must suffer. Probably we have all recognised that that is a fact in human life : recognised it since, as children, we found ourselves in a minority in a family council deliberating as to the pleasantest employment of a holiday. Minorities must suffer ! But as I look at the Bill I think that the distribution of suffering and hardship has not been regulated by an arithmetical calculation. Those who are to suffer, it seems to me—and I trust I am not speaking unjustly—are those who want definite religious teaching. They may be in an urban area 75 per cent, which is not a minority, but they cannot get their extended facilities unless they are 80 per cent. In a country district they may be 99 per cent, which is certainly not a minority, but they cannot have denominational teaching except on two days in the week, and cannot have it given by the teacher. Surely that is not covered by the general maxim that minorities must suffer. I would ask you to look for yourselves at the advantage given to undenominational teaching—the way that it may be given in all schools, provided and transferred, at the public expense, by the trained teacher. Look at that and contrast it with the position of denominational teaching, and then see whether this is a fair and equitable use of public money which is largely drawn from those who object to this predominance of undenominational teaching. I trust that I have shown that that very sensible maxim of public control following public money has been elevated to a height to which true statesmanship would never have elevated it, above the principles of liberty, equality, and justice.

In view of the return of the House of Lords to the consideration of the Bill he wrote in September urging the Diocese to prayer ; and on October 3 at the Diocesan Conference, and at other times again, he spoke of the work of the Peers upon the Bill. " I was greatly impressed by the debate on the Bill in the House of Lords. . . . The Bill has been tried by the test of thorough and deliberate discussion ; and it has not, I think, stood the process well."

"The general tenor," he said on November 29, 1906, " of the action taken by the House of Lords is really far more in harmony with the mind of the people than the unamended Bill."

In January, 1907, he wrote to the Diocese. His fear is that this year is to see the same " very wasteful conflict " as the old year. We shall be " pleading for the recognition of principles which we cannot part with, and others cannot understand."

He rests on the thought that " the effort to reach an equitable or tolerable issue failed finally at a point where we could be quite sure of our ground. We could not surrender the liberty of the teachers in regard to Church teaching. That seemed to me the clearest subject of irreconcileable opposition ; and there, I believe, we were contending for what was plainly just."

And out of the " weary wasteful conflict " he finds two causes emerge for thankfulness, the loyalty of Churchmen, and the leading of the Archbishop of Canterbury.

A letter was sent to him in the name of nearly all the beneficed Clergy of the Diocese :—

"We recognise" (they wrote) "with sincere thankfulness the wisdom, clearness, and knowledge with which you have guided us, and also the permanent value of the strong arguments with which you have directed men's minds to the essential principles of religious equality and justice, of parents' rights and responsibilities, and of the religious liberty of teachers, which form the basis of the Church's policy on these questions. Such leadership did much to hearten your Clergy in the stress of the past, and will encourage them to face the problems of the future with hopeful patience."

It was answered by him on March 29, 1907, from Cuddesdon :—

As I contended in the Diocese and in Parliament against what I hold to be grave injustice in the Education Bill of 1906, I very often had in mind the devotion and unselfishness with which my brethren had been labouring year after year for the welfare of the children in our Schools ; and the thought of that persevering labour will be with me, I hope, unfailingly. And to that thought is added now the inspiring experience of such loyalty and sympathy and friendship as should make any man glad, and keen to work for those by whom he finds himself so generously trusted. It is little that I can do ; but in a protracted struggle every little helps ; and I count it a high privilege to bear even the least part in defending the religious education to which the Clergy, and the Teachers in our Schools, have long devoted such toil as befits a rightful and a sacred cause.

If you can in any way convey to those whose words you have conveyed to me the assurance of my true and lasting gratitude, I shall be greatly indebted to you.—I am, dear Canon Garry, very sincerely yours and theirs, F. OXON.

On February 23, 1908, Mr. M'Kenna's Bill tried its fortunes in succession to Mr. Birrell's.

One answer to it in the Diocese of Oxford might rank with Jeremiah's purchase of his cousin's field during the Babylonian invasion. It was the laying of the foundation stone of a Church School at a little village which might have been called Anathoth, but was called Holmer Green. In his speech there, in March, the Bishop counselled that when the school was finished there should be the most convenient opportunity that they could reasonably give for providing for the children of those parents who did not wish their children to have the religious education of the Church of England, such religious education as they desired for them.

Men had learned that two facts must be faced, one, that the majority of the English people did want their children religiously brought up, and the other, that English people did sincerely and really differ on matters of religion.

And in the recognition of these facts lay the hope of a satisfactory and peaceable issue.

On September 30, 1908, he spoke of the growing weariness of men at the continuance of conflict about religious education. The conviction that peace ought to be made was like a rising tide, and men had surely not learned nothing. Church people were understood to be convinced that their faith could not be represented by any undenominational teaching, as truly as Nonconformists were known to be unable to acquiesce in a system which would enforce upon their children the teaching of the Church concerning the Sacraments.

Again, the fear of tests for teachers was now qualified by an understanding that for the sake of teachers and children alike some method must be found for securing that the teaching of religion should be saved from the taint of insincerity or unreality, by being entrusted only to those who can teach it with a personal belief that it is true.

Then the Bishop turns towards a new view of the question. We have concentrated our care, he says, in the past, too exclusively upon our Voluntary Schools. The Mission of the Church is to all the children of the Church, and to all the children who but for the Church's care would be uncared for. " I am glad to believe that the sense of this wider mission has been lately growing clearer ; " and so a new aim has been suggested for effort and for prayer :—

I mean the aim of gaining the opportunity for giving in all

schools the full teaching of the Church to all children whose parents desire that they should have that teaching. It is an aim at present barred, but it is an aim which we are bound to keep in view, and for which, if it should come to seem attainable, we ought, I think, to make a great effort, and, if need be, some sacrifice, remembering our duty, long undischarged, towards those thousands of the Church's children who have no chance of attending a Church School, remembering also that those thousands are far more than they were a few years ago, and that the proportion of the Church's children in Provided Schools is constantly growing.

Two months later, on November 28, 1908, he wrote to the beneficed Clergy concerning Mr. Runciman's Bill " now before Parliament."

He repeats something of what he had said to the Conference, but writing now with the new Bill made public :—

The central principle of the proposed settlement is that the Church loses the control of Church Schools in single school parishes, and gains the opportunity of Church teaching in Provided Schools ; I was slow to accept this principle ; but I have accepted it.

The difficulties of reconciling the Clergy to such a measure will easily be understood. For while many doubted whether the price was one which could rightly be paid, no one doubted that in the Diocese of Oxford it would cost the largest surrenders and bring the smallest compensations to the Church.

The dissatisfaction felt was expressed in a letter signed by 271 incumbents and sent to the Bishop on February 9, 1909, by his dear friend Canon Drummond.

The Bill is denounced by them (1) as establishing and endowing undenominationalism as the normal religious teaching in all Public Elementary Schools ; (2) as abolishing any guarantee of fitness of training or otherwise for teachers who are to give religious instruction ; (3) as offering a "right of entry" into Council Schools too impracticable to be accepted as a compensation for the surrender of Church Schools.

The Bishop answered on March 6, 1909. By this time Mr. Runciman's Bill was dead. The amendments which he had hoped for had not been made, and others had come in their place, which had made it impossible for him to support the measure.

"In common with those who have signed the letter, I should have found myself unable to accept the terms of the late Education Bill, as that Bill stood."

Yet it did suggest the direction in which he felt hope to lie, and he offers some defence of the new principle involved in it. It was inaccurate to speak of the late Bill as establishing and endowing Undenominationalism as the normal teaching in all Public Elementary Schools.

Undenominationalism has already been for nearly forty years established and endowed as the normal (and as the only) religious teaching in all Provided Public Elementary Schools ; these schools already cover the greater part of the whole field of elementary education, and are steadily gaining more and more of that field. The Bill would actually have achieved for Church teaching the first invasion of this vast and hitherto undisputed domain of undenominationalism. . . .

And secondly, when it is said that the "right of entry into Council Schools would prove *under existing circumstances* impracticable" I answer first, that existing circumstances need not always continue to exist unchanged ; secondly, that we are plainly bound to do our utmost to secure some Church teaching for the increasing multitude of Church children in Council Schools, and that no way of bringing Church teaching into Council Schools, save by this right of entry, has yet been made clear and proved practicable ; and thirdly, that in the past very many of us have so earnestly desired this now disparaged right of entry, and found it so strenuously refused to us by those who differ from us, that it was not unnatural to set a high value on it when it seemed attainable.

I think that its true value lies somewhere between the highest and the lowest estimates of it ; and, while I fully recognise the difficulties besetting it, I believe that its effect would have depended largely upon the energy and patience with which we set ourselves to use it, and on the work of our Training Colleges.

II

A second public or political interest in which the Bishop became deeply concerned was that of Ecclesiastical Discipline.

It will have been suggested to the reader that he had set out, as a little boy at school, with boyish eagerness on the broad ocean of Church questions with a most whole-hearted determination to avoid the Erastian heresy. His heroes were those who had defied the authority of the Judicial Committee and Privy Council. The Church is spiritual. The State cannot stay it with hand or sword. Like the sentinels at Elsinore, they only

> Do it wrong, being so majestical,
> To offer it the show of violence.

And still his character made always towards order, obedience, discipline ; and he became perplexed in a Communion where the Establishment had so confused the authorities of Church and State that it was hard to find any law by which the Church should guide and control her life.

It was therefore with some distress that he found himself invited to serve on the Royal Commission appointed to consider the irregularities alleged to be prevalent in the Church of England.

In his list of engagements from June, 1904, onwards, eight days or so in the month are assigned to the work of this Commission. At first he shrank from the very name. It was entered as an engagement "in London." But the name appeared afterwards with unfailing regularity, until in June two years later, he announced that the Report was soon to be published, and that he would make it the subject of his Visitation Charge in the following autumn.

He wrote in May, 1904 :—

I rely on the prayers of the Diocese for the work of the Commission.

One of the lessons which men learn through the discipline of great anxiety is their need of prayer : they come to think of the encompassing tide of intercession as the most real help that they can seek from others. So I seek it now. [Prayer for] the Holy Spirit of Truth ; the Spirit of wisdom and understanding ; the Spirit of Counsel ; the Spirit of God's Holy Fear ; it is His unfailing help that will be needed, and that prayer must seek.

And on June 25, 1906, he wrote :—

The Report is unanimous : it is the outcome of a careful consideration of voluminous evidence ; and it rests on two years of hard work. It has a right to claim frank and serious study ; and while men are so studying it, those who have the welfare of the Church at heart will pray to Him, from Whom alone comes the grace of a right judgement in all things.

On October 5, 1904, when the Commission had been four months at work, he said at the Diocesan Conference :—

In the Visitation which I held in 1902, I spoke as though it would be a mistake to put anxiety (such as springs from the

extreme difficulty of foreseeing or imagining what is to come
of the wide, apparently intractable, divergence of some among
us in matters of ceremonial and of doctrine) in the front rank
of our cares. I spoke unadvisedly, short-sightedly. I have
come to think differently since then. . . . This care has (in
my own mind) grown too great to be held in the background,
or ordered about, or kept from becoming oppressive.

And this ominous saying was the result of two
fears which had grown upon him.

He feared that the Clergy were losing the respect
of " a considerable number of genuine and thoughtful
Churchmen who are doubting whether we are really
trustworthy, whether we are really trying to keep our
promises, whether what we have at heart is what the
Church means," and he feared the loss to the Church
as a whole " by the fact that law as law has lost its
rightful place in our thoughts."

The last words are from his Charge of 1906, from
which I will quote sentences.

Looking back over my ordained life, I can see that I have
not thought as I was bound to think of the great principle of
law : and I expect that many men on a like retrospect would
feel as I feel. Honestly, I think, the fault at the outset was
not wholly ours. We saw the processes of law always used on
one side, and sometimes against things which many thought
then, and most own now, to matter less than much that went
untouched.

We saw Courts whose authority was repudiated, condemning
hardworking clergymen to imprisonment, not without making
mistakes on points of law as to which research was then
imperfect. And we took our line with inadequate reverence
for law as law.

It seems to me, as I look back, an instance of what Bishop
Butler called " shortness of thought," and the punishment
is sure.

Further on he says :—

In 1889 I was going to a private Conference in the Jerusalem Chamber, gathered together in the hope of doing something for peace. I wrote, as I was wont, to ask Dean Church's counsel; and in his answer were these words: "Men talk defiantly because law has been so strained against the eastward position, and vestments, and the mixed chalice, that it has broken down under the strain. Law, strange to say, in England, has actually broken down under the overstrain. No one cares to observe it, because, though half a dozen men, perhaps, are made to suffer, no one feels that it has the authority which law ought to have, as the real voice of either Church or nation, and it is notoriously disregarded far and wide by both sides. The thing that everybody ought to try for is the restoration of the position of law ; law to be used for legitimate purposes, to put down real mischiefs, not to worry and disturb things which, in a Church like ours, ought to be left free."

Again he quotes : "As Bishop Creighton wrote : 'Society is founded upon law ; and the Church is bound to set an example of order and obedience to authority. Nothing can compensate for any failure in this primary duty.'" "I doubt," his own words go on, "whether many of us know how deeply men who think are judging that we have failed."

The evidences which led the Bishop to this frame of mind,—are they not written in the Blue Book ? The report arrived at was unanimous. "I shall not say anything," says the Bishop's Charge, "that I know to be at variance with the judgment of any of those with whom I served on the Commission.

The irregularities complained of fall into two divisions. Twelve practices were counted "Significant" ; significant, that is, of teaching repugnant to the doctrine of the Church of England, and these (it is recommended) should be promptly made to cease. But there were other practices which it was clear ought with equal promptitude to be made to begin.

On the one side were the twelve practices which seemed to bear away from the mind of the English Church, on the other was a wide neglect of the Church's ideal. In this Diocese, for example, there are 301 parishes in which there is ordinarily no Service at all on any week-day. That means that in nearly half of the parishes of the Diocese this purpose, this great element in the conception of the Church's life which is set forth in the Prayer Book, finds no expression, no recognition—the daily prayer of which (he says) we may see the wisdom of the Spirit-bearing Church providing thus a daily token of the reliance which we ought to place on spiritual power; a daily evidence of our belief that it is not eloquence, or organisation, or agitation, or money that really settles things; no, but the strength which prayer releases; the might, the mercy, the grace of God.

Without doubt that from which the Bishop shrank most in the work of the Commission was the necessary discussion of the conduct of the service of Holy Communion. The legal arguments concerning it seemed to him always in danger of intruding on its sanctity. They haunted him, he told me, sometimes, at the altar. I will quote one place in his Charge where he seeks to raise again the thoughts which such a dealing with them seemed to him almost to profane :—

We know how hard it is for most men, how hard, it may be, we ourselves continually find it, to keep the act of worship truly, purely spiritual; to be always lifting up our hearts to the Unseen, the Eternal, the Incomprehensible; always striving beyond the thoughts, the scenes of sense and time; always remembering that the ultimate reality of worship is in the light that no man can approach unto, and that our highest acts are but as hands stretched out, as avenues of access, towards the everlasting adoration and intercession that is on high, where Christ "ever liveth to make intercession for us": where St.

John saw "in the midst of the throne and of the four living creatures, and in the midst of the elders, a Lamb standing as though It had been slain." We know how our hearts are ever faltering away from the effort of faith, and wanting to stay at some resting-place amidst the things that are seen, amid the ways of that lower level which we think we can understand. That appeal to come up higher, to raise the venture of our hearts above all that is on earth, is made to us all ; and to answer it rightly is the soul's great task. It is a task from which men swerve in diverse ways : proffering in lieu of the uplifted venture, sometimes a moral life or activity in good works, sometimes a zeal for the cause of religion, sometimes the acceptance of a creed, sometimes the conviction that they are saved, and sometimes a worship that lingers unduly at the counterpart on earth of the supreme reality, the fount of all reality, in heaven. Out of the knowledge of our own weakness, let us learn the care we need to take lest others be weakened, lest others be allowed to halt where they should find the very spring and power for that ceaseless ascent to which God beckons all. I speak of things which I have not skill or insight to make clear. But I am sure that we have need to be trying and judging every ceremony, every form of worship, which we use for ourselves or teach to others, by this above all other tests of truth and worth, by this above all other questions : Is it indeed as "a door opened in heaven"? Is it as the soul's obedience, unhindered and unhesitating, to the Voice that says to us "Come up hither ! "?

The work on the Royal Commission was undertaken with a heavy heart, and induced in him a mood of anxiety "too great to be kept from becoming oppressive." We had failed, he held, to respect law as law, and yet it was characteristic in him that he found a consolation ready in the thought of the living and practical loyalty which he felt to be attained in the Church of England—"a very noble sort of loyalty," his Charge says, and a "loyalty which blesses both him who gives and him who takes."

The willing and intelligent allegiance of free men. That is the Gift of God to the Church of England. We can hardly think of these things without thankfulness and hope—the thankfulness and hope of those who will not forget God their Saviour, and the great things He has done for them. Such thankfulness, such hope stand foremost among the graces that make men wise and brave in times of difficulty; and we deeply need both wisdom and courage for the work, the patience, to which we are called.

The hope of a new state of law in which once more English Churchmen could be law-abiding, was advancing when the Bishop died. The letters of business, the Committees of Convocation, which resulted from the Commission, promised already some outlet from the position which seemed to him almost intolerable; but that other loyalty among the ranks of the Clergy did more to abate his anxiety, that mutual loyalty between him and his Diocese which gladdened more and more his later years as Bishop. His service on the Royal Commission may have strained it, and so may the line which he took both as to Mr. Balfour's and Mr. Runciman's Education Schemes; but the personal attachment grew each year on both sides stronger and deeper. I have written of that elsewhere, but I will make one more quotation. In November 1910 he wrote to the Diocese, " thinking again that no Bishop can ever have tried to serve a Diocese so generous in kindness as this is. But indeed in the experience of this year I have felt around me something that is even more than kindness; and I can only bow my head and thank the Giver of all Grace."

CUDDESDON.

CUDDESDON. THE DINING-ROOM.

CUDDESDON. THE STUDY.

CUDDESDON. THE BISHOP'S WRITING-TABLE.

CHAPTER III

WORK IN THREE COUNTIES

IF one might knock at the Bishop's study door again, and hear him answer, and so go in ; there he would be sitting, the arrangement, the disposal of the room seeming to have taken into itself something of his manner and mind. So Carlyle says a man's clothes declare something of what a man is, and Walter Pater thinks that a house and its gardens and its approaches become an extension of the bodily presence, and reveal the spirit of him who dwells there.

Certainly there was scarcely anything in the room but had some meaning, some personal value, to him.

The chair in which he sat and would lean back to look up, for example, was the gift of two ladies whose skill was always finding new ways of meeting wants of which he had been unconscious. Of it he had written to them adapting " the praise of the Chapter-House at York—*Ut rosa flos florum sic est domus ista domorum*— the very chair of chairs ; in which one ought to be able to answer with charity, or at least with composure, even the least welcome of letters."

On his desk before him stood an ivory figure of the Christ bound hand to hand—his father had seen it in Monmouth long ago, and rescued it from the miscellaneous surroundings of the shop where it stood for sale.

And beside it would be set a miniature that travelled with him—the clasped case always carefully opened to stand there when he returned to his writing-table.

Each picture round the room had a story. The Christ kneeling, from Bellini's "Gethsemane" in the National Gallery, for example, was copied for him by his sister-in-law. The Hollyer photograph of a chalk study by Leonardo da Vinci was a Christmas present, acknowledged—"I have been longing to write; I am heartily ashamed that my letter has been so long delayed"—on 5th March.

The books in the shelves had most of them associations with former owners, as R. W. Church; or they were author's copies, many of them; or they were editions of value, the best of them destined to go to Christ Church Library.

There was a scrap of marble on the mantelpiece brought by Dr. Liddon from the Holy Land, and thought by him to be a piece of Capernaum synagogue —the Bishop could repeat the words with which it had been given. There was, beside it, a blue hot-water-pot presented to him, on his leaving Bromsgrove, by a very poor woman, whose desire to take her own life had cost him a night out of bed; and the blue earthen-ware had taken to itself something of the price of alabaster. There were two inlaid vases of great beauty brought home by Christ Church graduates from Japan.

On a table near would be flowers—azaleas perhaps or stephanotis, and sometimes the atmosphere and temperature seemed (as in a invalid's room) to be something watched and guarded; the orderly note-paper, the two stylographs in their case, the paper-knives, one of ivory, one of silver, each in its proper place, all told of their owner's mind, his love for things

decent and in order ; and most of them had stories to
tell of friends that had planned, recommended, presented them.   There was no suggestion of the work-
shop and the shirt-sleeves, unless a clue was given by
a neat bundle of his unanswered letters, fastened with
a green-riband and a buckle, lying on the desk beside
him, and ready to disappear within it whenever he
should wish to be tidy to receive a visitor.

And yet this was his factory, and the neat bundle,
green-ribanded and buckled, was his raw material, and
he laboured here as not many men labour.   To come
back to Cuddesdon was to come and sit there and
write.   Other things were the exception.   This was
the rule.   He wrote slowly, forming each consonant
and vowel with an individual attention.   He wrote,
rather than caused another to write, the majority of his
answers.   He would have thought it discourteous to
send a postcard, inhuman to use typewriting.   He
worked at his correspondence very seriously.   Sometimes he sat over it until his mind was tired out.   If
you came suddenly upon him, at such a time, he would
look guilty and come to " attention " like a boy found
idling by an unexpected schoolmaster.   If he dictated,
he was as careful, as deliberate, as when he wrote.
Once, after a long day, I remember his looking up
with a half-smile, half-sigh, to say, " It really is most
awfully good of us to go on like this at these letters " ;
but generally the thing seemed as if it might go on for
ever and most likely would ; the mind, the voice tired,
perhaps, but the will steady, the courtesy, or affection,
or precision of the work unceasing, unfaltering.

It was his work, his means of getting into touch
with people, and he took it very seriously.

He would dictate with an earnestness which would

have surprised people who looked only for a formal answer, " Thank you with all my heart," and " for the manifold kindness of your letter."

The earnestness may, perhaps, have been damaged in transmission, as the Chaplain heard, once more, the familiar words of gratitude, and scribbled " twamh," or recognised the " manifold kindness" of the correspondent with the familiar initials " m " and " k " ; but let no one think the words came by chance. He would stop to correct. " The Rev.—— is, I believe, entirely trustworthy "—" no—would you cross that out, please—' trustworthy '—that is enough—you cannot add to a word like that." Or he would pause between the degrees of truth and faith and sincerity which he would claim at the close of a letter towards his correspondent ; or superlatives must give way to comparatives, or comparatives become mere positives.

Let me give here one example of the care with which he wrote, though he was writing to a great friend—the hostess of the " Lux Mundi " meetings at Longworth. She had asked him to make a Preface for a book, and in a first letter he had acknowledged her request some weeks before. I give the second :—

CUDDESDON, OXFORD,
29th December 1902.

DEAR MRS. ILLINGWORTH—This will be a most difficult letter to write ; and I can only, in regard to it, trust to your true kindness and generosity to make the best of my meaning and wish in writing it.

I have used the first days I have got with anything like leisure in them to read the proof sheets which you have sent me. I have now read through most of them, though it has been with many interruptions, and with the slackness of a very tired mind. And now comes my trouble ; for I find it hard to write the Preface. I ought to have foreseen that it would be thus hard ; and indeed, dear Mrs. Illingworth, I do sincerely and heartily beg your pardon. What I feel is this : that a man who writes a Preface, especially if he is charged with any sort of authority or special responsibility for others, ought himself to be able to make his own, to identify himself with, what the book says. He ought not to be urging others to lift up their minds to move on planes on which his own mind does not move. He ought not, for instance, to be calling others to use the language of a mysticism (if that is the right word) which he cannot understand for (or at least feel to be possible for definite realisation by) himself ; he ought not to incur a risk of seeming to see what he cannot affirm that he sees. He may quite sincerely and thoroughly believe that if he were other than he is, if his life had been other than it has been— less taken up with secular business, less ill-managed in the use of time—or if his temper of mind were more speculative, sympathetic, imaginative (in the good sense of the word), he would be able to make the words his own ; he may even feel that what growth he has had has brought him nearer to making them his own. But still he may feel he cannot, yet ; that he would be pointing where he has not been if he bade others use the words. And so he may have, for the sake of his own ab- solute honesty, to say, " Others must teach these things, not I."

This is my plight. It is horrid to have to write : of course, not because of the mere owning one's own limitations ; but because of the intrusiveness of implying that others, who would dislike the implication, have got on further. I can only, as I said, trust your generosity to be sure of my sincere distress in disappointing you. I just feel that we all have our own temperaments, our own gifts, our own habits of mind and work ; and that we must do the best we can with them ; heartily admiring what others have, and one's self has not ; toiling, even scrupulously, to stay within what one has, till one can gain more. I know I must often disappoint those of my friends who have what I lack ; but I think I may in the end serve them (or what they most care for) best by steadily abiding by the law of my lacking.

Once more, I am heartily sorry to have failed ; and heartily

ashamed to have been so slow in finding out my inability to
do as you wished me to do. I have but one extenuating
circumstance to plead — that the delay really comes in part
through my hearty longing to do what you asked me to do,
and my gratitude to you for having asked me. As I said, I
have not for many years written a Preface for any one's work ;
but Longworth is unlike everything else ; and so I could not
but want and try to do it. It was only when I came on the
passages in regard to which I felt as I have tried to say, that I
felt I must give it up. I do greatly hope you will know how
reluctantly I did so feel.—Believe me, dear Mrs. Illingworth,
yours most sincerely,   F. Oxon.

A third letter tells of the relief with which he
hears of the reception of the second.

CUDDESDON, OXFORD.
1st January 1903.

Dear Mrs. Illingworth—I must write just a word of
true and great gratitude for this morning's letter. It was
indeed kind of you so to understand me, and I am grateful
with all my heart.—Believe me to be, most sincerely yours,

F. Oxon.

And together with these may be printed a letter
out of which the sound of harassment has altogether
passed away. Eight years later Mrs. Illingworth had
sent him a list of the people confirmed by him that
year and the years before, at Longworth, who had
made their Communion at Easter.

SWANAGE, *19th April* 1911.

My dear Mrs. Illingworth—It was a real, refreshing
delight to get your letter this morning, and it was wonderful
kindness that sent it. Thank you indeed with all my heart ;
again and again I shall think of that Easter Day, and of
the lads trudging their two miles, and of the Angels
rejoicing all the time. Most beautiful it is, raising all
life. May God guide and guard and gladden all the work
with His continual Blessing.

I came here this evening, bringing with me the new book [Dr. Illingworth's *Divine Transcendence*]. I look forward to it as my special bit of help during the week's rest here, if all be well. Will you please give Dr. I. my very kindest remembrance ; and will you please say that when I am quite sure that I shall wholly delight in a gift I like to keep my thanks till I've read it ? But that won't be long.—Believe me to be, always very gratefully and sincerely yours,   F. Oxon.

I dare not begin sending kind remembrances ; but I shall treasure all their names, and I should like just a word said to the old farmer and his wife whom I confirmed privately.

It was the Bishop's habit of mind to maintain a high and exacting standard of carefulness in other things, as in correspondence. He was asked to speak to the children at Aston-Abbots, but he answers :—

7th February 1908.—With regard to the Children's Service I fear I must ask you to hold me excused, for the Sunday is likely to be hemmed in with work, and I should need much preparation for the Catechizing.

He lost lightness of touch and other things by it ; and he felt the loss, no doubt. One of the letters to the Diocese speaks of—

The Report of H.M. Inspector on a school in this Diocese ; in which, so far as I remember, the only fault found was this, " the Infants work rather too seriously." I hope that the Infants, with the admirable docility of early years, have shown their sense of the justice of the criticism. For myself, I mean to take it with me on my holiday.

Or again in another letter to the Diocese, after quoting Dr. Bright and Archbishop Leighton, he quotes from a book *Home is Best*, by Susan Sybilla Soulsby, this " quenching rejoinder "—" Lord bless you, child, I've no *time* to love the cat," and adds his warnings.

He was at times harassed, not careful only but care-worn ; yet it is not reasonable to assign all the blame to him, if it is remembered how great is the burden that is laid upon a modern Bishop.

When he had been Bishop seven years, he wrote in answer to a question about a clergyman in the Diocese :—

I wish I could answer it more adequately than I can. I am afraid I do not know [him] at all well ; not nearly as well as most of his neighbours. My whole impression of him is favourable ; I have never heard a word in adverse criticism. . . . But it has been one of the disappointments and failures of my work here that there are still men working in some of the little Parishes, out of the way, whom I have not really got to know and make friends with, and I often feel ashamed of it. I had looked forward to that as a special privilege of my trust, but it has been very imperfectly fulfilled.

It will, perhaps, sketch out the business of his life, if a list or two is printed of the Bishop's monthly engagements. They are not selected from among the months as being unusually full. Here is one July :—

Wantage, Stokenchurch, Oxford and Ashenden, London, London, London and Slough, London, Oxford, Aylesbury, London (three days' engagements), London and Reading, Longworth, Longworth, Oxford, Minster Lovell, Newbury, Chipping Norton, three days at Cuddesdon, Crick, Oxford, Oxford, Norwich, Wallingford and London, South Newington, Chalgrove, Nether Winchendon.

This list is chosen because it is the last month's work he did. Indeed the last place named was never visited, for he was removed to a London nursing home on the day appointed.

But I will give another—the November list, 1909 :—

Reading, Oxford, London (three times), London and

Ascot, Oxford, Mollington, Banbury, Bloxham, Aylesbury, Wooburn, Steeple Aston, Oxford, Oxford and Fenny Stratford, Oxford, Oxford and Wallingford, Oxford, the Lea, St. Paul's Cathedral, the Albert Hall (this was the Congo Meeting), Binfield, Bracknell, Wokingham, Crowthorne, Wellington, Reading, Maidenhead, Wantage.

Or let me give another list, stating it another way, in February, 1911 :—

Committees of Finance, 3 ; other committees, 6 ; sermon before the University, sermon for a Police Court Mission, dedications of a Church building and of a Mission Church, 4 Confirmations, and work in connection with "rescue and prevention," foreign missions, Canada, a hospital.

The Diocese of Oxford has 648 Parishes, and even that statement is far from carrying any just measure of the claims upon the Bishop's care. Some idea may perhaps be conveyed of the weariness to which he sank at one time by words which he wrote to the Diocese in 1902 on the news of Archbishop Temple's death. He allows the words to be printed, "tempted towards envying him." He was convinced that the work was more than could be done. Many times he spoke of a division of the Diocese. In the Diocesan Conference (September 30 and October 1, 1909) a Report was received from a Commission under the Chairmanship of Mr. A. K. Loyd, K.C., and the Conference deliberated on the methods and means of a division. Speaking at one time and another the Bishop was unvarying in his appeal. "I cannot imagine any other blessing," he said, "much greater for a man than that he should have plenty of work to do, but it is another thing altogether to have work that is left undone."

The Diocese was too large, and nothing but a

division could relieve the strain. Speaking of the help which can be given by a Bishop Suffragan he said : " The Diocesan must bear full responsibility in regard to all important questions that arise throughout the Diocese ; all the toil of thinking out hard questions and taking all responsibility must remain, in regard to the whole Diocese, with the Diocesan Bishop ; " and " to delegate work [like Confirmations] to Suffragans would be to break off a great channel of contact between the Bishop and the Diocese." It was not in those directions that the burden, the care was found—it was in attending meetings, in controversy, in decisions, in correspondence. " What saved a Bishop," he said, " was his going about among the Parishes."

To Mr. Loyd he wrote :—

I hope that the time will come when an important County containing two hundred Parishes will be regarded as a sufficient area of responsibility and care for any man ; and I believe that a Bishop who sustained a right standard of thoroughness in work would, under the present conditions of a Bishop's office, have an ample task in Oxfordshire, Berkshire, or Buckinghamshire.

One more quotation I will make from a letter to one who had contributed in support of the scheme of a Division. It is dated March 29, 1911 :—

It was a most delightful greeting that your kind letter gave me when I came home this evening ; and I am grateful with all my heart for your generous gift towards the Buckinghamshire Bishopric. I am convinced that the effort for such a division of the Diocese is a right effort, and that, if it can be carried into effect, the service which a Bishop ought to render, and must long to render, throughout a Diocese, may be fulfilled as it can hardly be when the area is so great, and the Parishes are so many as those of this Diocese. So, whenever the change is made, whether it be in my working days or not, I believe it will be for the true benefit of those whom I would fain serve far better than I can.

The car is an incalculable help, even beyond all that I forecast.

By circumstances, then, as well as to some extent by nature, the Bishop was in the way of finding his office one which overburdened him.

I do not know whether, now that they are ten years old, Mr. Kipling's *Just-so Stories* are remembered or forgotten. Perhaps the reader may be counted on as familiar with the tale of "Old Man Kangaroo" and his flight with "Yellow-Dog Dingo" in pursuit. That breathless chase became a household word at Cuddesdon, and sympathy was felt for hound and quarry.

> Kangaroo bounded away,
> His back-legs working like pistons—
> Bounded from morning till dark,
> Twenty-five feet to a bound.
> Yellow-Dog Dingo lay
> Like a yellow cloud in the distance—
> Much too busy to bark.
> My ! but they covered the ground !

He felt the homelessness of being so many nights away from Cuddesdon, so ceaselessly on the move—a week or ten days at a time. It was long before Cuddesdon became a home to the Bishop. Within a year of Mrs. Paget's death he went there, and the house long continued to be (for him) the place which was not the Deanery, the home which was not what the home at Christ Church had been.

It was not homely to him, and yet even its degree of homeliness was denied him. He thought of himself as a man of singularly little skill in adapting himself night after night to new scenes, new neighbours, bed-rooms, writing-tables.   It was not congenial to him so " to cover the ground " ; nevertheless, in the words of the nursery story spoken of above, " He had to ! "

None of his hostesses will think that there was flattery in the thanks with which he went in and came out among them.   His gratitude was true enough. Though he expressed so much, he would not diminish his expressions when he was in their carriage and out of their hearing.

Nor again will the railway servants think they failed to make him at home in railway carriages.   He was to some of them a special care and charge.   " Is not the train due to start ? " the hurrying Chaplain asked at a station which must not be named, when the Bishop was arriving only on the stroke of time.   " The train will start, Sir," was the answer, " when his Lord-ship is ready."

To travel from Paddington to Oxford, on the day when " his Lordship's " death was made known, was to feel that a very human and a very homely feeling had grown up out of the business of his railway journeys. And no Rectory or Vicarage will doubt that parishes one by one became to the Bishop homelier scenes ; still, for more than a year or two, had you taken him off his guard, you might have found him likening the life of a modern Bishop to the life of a " hunted cat."

There was a look of weariness, of melancholy, that would come into his face.   There was a tired sigh which became familiar, sometimes as an appeal for sympathy, and sometimes when he fancied himself alone—a long-drawn sigh descending, in the middle, a fifth—which would make plain to any hearer the manner of his thoughts. The work was (it is still the same) more than a man could "keep abreast of"—he often used the phrase—and there were times when he was miserable over it, or under it. Some one (who ought to have known better) said to me, "You know, if the Diocese had consisted of Cuddesdon, Wheatley and Garsington" (three villages instead of three counties) "he would have worn himself out with the care of it." If that points in the direction of a truth, then with what a joy shall it be recorded that out of the cares of a work such as three men might well be asked to divide between them, there was wrought his feeling for the Diocese, the feeling of the Diocese for him? And that is the triumph that I am recording here.

The man of whom I am trying to tell, and the circumstances in which he found himself, might have had a story which ended without any note of triumph.

"I should need much preparation for catechizing," he said of the children's service in a little village.

"There are still men whom I have not really got to know and make friends with," he says of one of 648 incumbents.

And the same care might be shown in many letters, the same wearing care and the distress it was to him to disappoint others or to do any work (as he felt) "unworthily."

"Pray for me," he said once when he was getting ready in the Vestry for some service—at Reading, I fancy it was,—"it is so dreadful to be unprepared."

And coming away from Stoke Mandeville after a service for the re-hanging of the church bells he said of his sermon, "it makes one ache all over."

And there were so many services, so many men to

2 B

get to know ; there was so much work ; even a less
scrupulous workman might have been daunted, and let
his last word be something like the long-drawn sigh
descending, in the middle, a fifth, which I have heard
in railway carriages and motor-cars, in other people's
studies and in his own.

But the melancholy grew less.   At the end it had
almost gone.   He had fought a good fight, and to live
near him was to become aware that he was fighting
well.   He needed, and he had, a real dauntlessness in
his character.   His was an almost haughty refusal to
give in to his task.

To live near him was to know that he was a brave
man.

I have been aware, sometimes, of a view of the
Bishop which looked upon him a little as some robust
and sanguine man might look upon a pale, thin, delicate
neighbour.   Men who felt themselves able to move at
ease about the world, men who take friendship (or
friendliness, at least) for granted, who like one another
without any very great surprise, and disagree from one
another without any very elaborate apology, would, to
my surprise, almost pity him as though he were some
frail and quickly-broken spirit.

To see him in that light it was necessary for the
view to be a very narrow one.   To overlook the
courage, the sporting instinct in him, it would have
been necessary to narrow the horizons of life down
almost to the limits of a prize-fighter's ring.   That his
early training left several things untaught which are
learned by most English boys, will have suggested
itself to any reader of the early pages of this book.
He himself confessed and regretted the want in
himself of a certain freedom of venture, an ease of

movement, a suppleness of character, which is the birthright of country boys who ride and shoot, and are at home among horses and hounds and guns and spaniels. He was quick to delight in the distinction of character he would find if he had to do with a man who was a fine Whip or an M.F.H., or a soldier who had seen active service. All adventure appealed to him. I have heard him describe in glowing words the courage and abandonment with which his hansom-cab had been driven. He praised such apparent reckless-nesses as being himself incapable of them. But I do not think that those whom he admired for qualities in which he seemed to himself so deficient, would have been slow to recognise that, in other fields, he too had the same distinction. He rode straight across his proper country. He could play a losing game. The fastidious scholar, the man to whom " academic " was never a word of very sinister meaning, had learned, among other things, what " chivalry " means.

More than anything else, his ten years as Bishop seem to me to have been a struggle against melancholy : but he fought a good fight, he ran a good race. He passed through doleful places. He entered upon the life with a desolate sense that life could never be again what it had been. He cared, and cared, perhaps, beyond what was right, in a certain disproportion of caring, about the disgraces in certain Parishes where he was helpless to cause the shame to cease. And the men who, by some sense of duty, were led to a contempt of his wishes or commands, in some two or three Parishes, filled his mind with foreboding for the Church.

He took things to heart as though it were a duty to feel them as deeply as possible. He would be

almost ashamed of not having passed a sleepless night,
and I have heard him quote :—

οὐ χρὴ παννύχιον εὕδειν βουληφόρον ἄνδρα.

And, outside the Diocese, general questions had power
to make him gravely anxious.   Questions ecclesiastical and questions political too.   For, indeed, a
great election victory of the party which had the
second place in his esteem, begloomed his mind like
a great public calamity.

And all the while the steady demands of his round
of work were enough to make the march heavy, uphill,
long to him ; he was struggling against melancholy.

And yet, through the ten years, and, indeed, by
help of the work they brought him, he did move on
from strength to strength, and there was no year, I
suppose, in his life in which there was quite the same
quality of disciplined gladness as in the last.

What enabled him so to win his way ?   I will try
to give an account of the forces that were on his side.
First, it would be untrue to overlook the force of his
health, his nervous power, his active, "wiry" constitution.   He had a tenacity of life which astonished
the doctors who knew him best.

He had a wonderful power of enjoying.   A holiday
was to him what holidays are to the happiest schoolboys.   To go to Switzerland, or Italy, was to begin
life again.   And even the glimpses of holiday light,
a walk in an afternoon, a concert, an hour among
pictures, found in him a fine readiness to be ten years
younger in ten minutes.

There was a spring of life in him which few would
have suspected if they had come upon him looking
worn out with work and anxiety.

Holiday freedom, and the beauty in the world of mountains, of moorland, of green English hills, delight of moving in the air and light, had a quickening power to which he was quick to respond ; but beauty in the world of character, delight in moving among men whom he loved and who loved him, had a higher power, and one more commonly within his reach.

From among letters of his friends to whom he owed most of this inspiriting I will take leave to quote.

Here are passages from his letters to one to whom he wrote very freely :—

"Thank you," he says [for some Christmas sign], "with all my heart ; and as heartily for your letter. You point me to true secrets of help. But I fear I make a very poor fight sometimes."

And, another Christmas, he wrote to him :—

In some ways Christmas does not seem to me a time that is quite easy to face ; for the thoughts of the days that are past are very vivid.

But here is another Christmas letter :—

I do not know how to thank you for a gift most welcome and beautiful, and for a letter such as has brought into this Christmas a touch of the very truest and best happiness. I know myself most unworthy of such wonderful kindness and friendship as you have given me ; but I know also how very, very much it means to me, and how hard it would be to get on without such help ; and I suppose that is why it is granted to me. I am indeed grateful and thankful for it with all my heart. May God make me less unworthy of it.

And here is a fourth Christmas letter to the same friend :—

Last night I said just a word of thanks for your letter ; but

I could not tell you half my gratitude for it.   As I said, you
have " the happy hand "—the hand that writes the words that
really help and gladden.   But indeed the happy hand is that
which the kind and true heart guides.   God grant you the
constant wealth of His Grace, that you may go on helping us
all—(you don't know how much you have helped me)—and
may He gladden you with His own Light.   Truly that Light
is " the true Light " and " no darkness can overwhelm it."—
Ever affectionately yours,   F. OXON.

" I make a shamefully poor fight against heavy-
heartedness very often," another letter to the same
friend had said, " and forget or dim the hope that is
set before us, after our time of patience, God helping
us, in this world."

But the fight has not receded, the sense of advance
is clear as you read on.

May God help me to be more steadily thankful ; and may
He sustain and bless the friendship He has granted us : so
that we may keep together as we go on our way, and if it
please Him, sometimes lighten one another's way, as you in
truth have lightened mine this Christmas.

To another friend in whom he felt the virtue he
wrote that one of his letters " came with that power
of true friendship to bid a man be trustful and hopeful
through all that is perplexing, and all that threatens
discouragement ; and, indeed, I am grateful with all
my heart."

These were chosen friends, from whom such
enheartening came very directly to him ; and from
many in other ways, through business, through his
work with them, you are aware of the same influence
renewing his strength of spirit.

The growing affection between him and old friends

and new friends in the Diocese was to him a source of life.

I will throw together letters in which this mutual helpfulness is clearly reflected. They will, I hope, give a sense of the kindness by which he found his work transfigured.

"Where love and kindness come in and work" (he wrote to the Diocese after the severe illness of 1910 from which he had recovered), "there is a change almost like that of those chemical experiments which I remember making in my youth —save that they were not always successful. For instance, what a contrast there is between the look, the tone, of life in a London street and the character of thought and feeling in the ward of a hospital. There is the same human material. As you go from bed to bed you can see what the people were in their ordinary ways, but the spell of kindness has passed over them and touched their hearts ; the air is charged with it ; the great lesson is being learnt, and more or less rightly recited ; and the great change is astir. Some of us, perhaps, may have known the like of it in a nursing home.

"Yes, it is the greatest lesson, the greatest gain, the greatest thing in the world."

It will be felt, I think, as an atmosphere in the letters which I have gathered here.

CUDDESDON, OXFORD,
25th February 1902.

MY DEAR DRUMMOND,—I cannot tell you how deeply grateful I am for the true and great kindness of the thought expressed in your letter received this morning. It is a fresh instance of a generosity which I long better to deserve. I do indeed thank you for it with all my heart.

According to the instructions which I have at present received, I am to wear at the Coronation a cope, but not a mitre. I hear, however, that it is possible that these instructions, so far as they concern me, may be altered later on ; and that I may have to wear the Garter mantle. . . .

However, since at present a cope is appointed, I asked Miss Alice Randall (as Secretary of the Diocesan Church Embroidery Society), some days ago, to be so kind as to get a design prepared for a white cope for me ; and that is how the matter now stands.

I need not say that if the cope were the gift of the Diocese it would mean to me as I wore it much that it cannot mean otherwise. And yet, my dear Drummond, I cannot help hesitating a little in regard to the generous, warm-hearted wish of which you have written to me. The thoughts that make me hesitate are these : Already I have come across needs so deep and urgent, so hard to meet, so ominous for the Church's work if they are not met, that I am almost appalled by them. The needs of Church Schools, the needs of Church building and endowment in the towns, the needs of Church restoration in the villages, and, far above all in its pathos, the poverty of the Clergy—these seem to me so grave as to give a touch of misappropriateness to the thought of spending much on a cope. I know that it would be meant simply to do honour by its beauty to the Church, and to the services and ministry of the Church; and, perhaps, if I were larger-minded I might see how this out-weighs and keeps right in the background all other thoughts in regard to it. But somehow it keeps coming back to me that if I were a Parish Priest only just able to hold on in a poor Parish, spending capital, perhaps, year after year, to keep my boys at school, and wondering how long it would last, it would, or might, make me wonder a little whether it was well for the generosity of Church people to be turned towards a glory of apparel. At another time it might be quite right ; just now, I cannot help thinking, with true gratitude, all the same, to you, that it would be better to let me go on and get the cope. I promise that it shall not do discredit to the Diocese in the eyes of those who notice such things at the Coronation, and I shall look forward to leaving it to the Diocese when I die.

I am sure that you will know that, though I ask leave thus to forgo the gift of which you had thought, my feeling about the thought of it is just the same as if I had felt free to accept

it.—Believe me, dear Drummond, very sincerely and gratefully
yours, F. Oxon.

The kindness between the Bishop and this correspondent was one of his unfailing helps ; through
agreement, for the most part, but through differences
of opinion once or twice, as the next letter will
show, written after a difficult meeting over education
questions in 1902.

I did not get home till late ; and then I found a big party
of undergraduates whom we had asked to tea ; and the post is
just going. But I will not let it go without a word of
gratitude to you—of very deep and great gratitude. I cannot
say it as I would ; but I hope you will not mind my saying
that your words and your bearing turned a day which I began
with fear into a day which I shall always remember with
thankfulness. I am grateful to you with all my heart. I
think what the day has left in my heart is the longing that, if
I am spared, I may, God helping me, work better for those
who have shown me such wonderful generosity and trust. I
know you will forgive me whatever pain I caused you. I
hope that in the outcome we may find ourselves really the
stronger in the great work of the Schools through the difficulties which look to us threatening. It has been so, I think,
more than once in the past.—Believe me, dear Drummond,
affectionately yours, F. Oxon.

The following is a letter to the Rev. W. Hewetson,
then Vicar of Thame, on the occasion of a " Quiet
Day " to be held for three Rural Deaneries.

" The service," Mr. Hewetson writes, " was, I need
not add, conducted as he wished."

CUDDESDON,
25th October 1902.

DEAR HEWETSON—Thank you heartily for the considerate
kindness of your letter. I am most thankful to hear of your

little daughter's recovery. Will you give her my kindest remembrance ?

I was going to write to you about the Celebration of the Holy Communion on Friday. I should greatly like to celebrate ; but I have, ever since I was ordained, without exception, taken the Eastward position.

If this would be at all likely to tell against your work, or to cause you trouble in any way, please let me know ; and I shall then ask you to take the service, only myself giving the Absolution and the Blessing. But if my doing as I have always done will not cause trouble at Thame, then I will celebrate.

With regard to the Mixed Chalice, we never had it at Christ Church. My own present practice is to have a little water put into the Chalice before the service begins ; and then before the Prayer for the Church Militant, to pour in wine only. If this can be so arranged I shall be glad ; but I should have no trouble at all about following the practice of the Cathedral, and using wine only, if you think it better in this case.

I am very gladly looking forward to the day. I shall drive over, if all be well, and come straight to the Church.—Always yours sincerely,   F. Oxon.

The next is but one example of his watchfulness to share the anxiety of any of the clergy when there was trouble in a parish.

LAMBETH PALACE, S.E.,
10th November 1908.

MY DEAR SHAW—You have been often in my thoughts of late, with regard to all the stir and division at Wycombe over the election to the mayoralty ; and I cannot help writing a few words to tell you how sorry I am for all the trouble you must, I expect, have felt, both in regard to the process, and in regard to its outcome. I'm afraid a good many people may have said things they had much better not have said ; and there must be some bitter feeling about ; and all such things are a hindrance to the work you love, and to some of those for whom you work.

So I am truly sorry ; I wish that there were anything that I could do.

The 37th Psalm is a help, I think, at such times.—Believe me to be, always yours most sincerely,   F. OXON.

Here may follow two letters. The first is from a lady whose son was asked by the Bishop to go to other work in the Diocese.

She wrote in illness which was painful and incurable.

Christmas Day, 1909.

Permit me to thank your Lordship for the *confidence* you place in my dear son, which I believe and hope may never prove misplaced. I taught him the Greek alphabet and to write the characters myself, before he entered school in 1886, since which time his reports and testimonials have *all* testified to the "*thoroughness*" of his work. I share the dear —— people's grief at his removal, but willingly give him up at the Master's call to a larger work. God has indeed been good to me. The dear Father now in Paradise and our children all *one in spirit*. . . . Might I ask, in confidence, that if God should call me soon your Lordship would say a word of comfort to my son ; we have been so much to each other, he being the eldest. . . . My earnest prayers will be with you and the clergy in this large Diocese. May the best blessings of this Holy Season rest upon you in your anxious charge.—Faithfully and obediently yours.

The Bishop's answer was :—

CUDDESDON,
28*th December* 1909.

DEAR MRS. ——, —In your considerateness you bade me not to answer your letter received this morning, but I cannot forgo sending a few words to tell you how deeply it touched me, and how grateful and thankful I am as I think of it. I can imagine something of the gladness which your son's good work must mean to you. It is with a clear and great hope that I think of the prospect of his work at ——, though indeed I am sorry with all my heart for those whom he will be leaving at ———. You may be sure that I shall be anxious to keep always in touch with him, and to help him in any way I can.

May God guide and guard you with His continual Blessing. —With true gratitude for the help of your prayers, I am, sincerely yours,   F. OXON.

Another reads like a twentieth-century edition of the first Christian century's manifold joy—the delight of Corinthians, Judaeans, and St. Paul—in giving and receiving (2 Corinthians ix. 12-15) :—

> CUDDESDON,
> *9th March* 1909.

DEAR NOBLE—I cannot forgo writing to tell my gratitude for the true happiness which came to me with the tidings of your generous answer to my appeal on behalf of the Candidates for Ordination ; the post looks a different thing for days after such a letter as that which brought the news of your kindness.

I greatly liked what I saw of the Candidate for whom you have made possible the realisation of his hope, and it is delightful to think of his gladness, and of the promise of his life and work ; but besides that there is the happiness of thinking that another great bit of kindness has been done, and that one's friend has done it.

I was sorry with all my heart that I just missed you that Sunday. I did not know till the Saturday night that I should be able to get over.—Believe me, dear Noble, yours always,

> F. OXON.

The following is a letter to the Vicar of Clewer St. Stephen :—

> CUDDESDON,
> *15th April* 1908.

MY DEAR NICHOLAS—It goes to my heart to hear that still you are ill, and hindered in the work of this week, and in serving those for whom, I know, you watch and pray. I can imagine a little how much the trial of being thus hindered must mean to you, and so I am bold to write just a word to tell you how sorry I am, and how greatly I trust that God may grant you help and brightness in the ever-fresh assurance of His Love and Care for you.   You will know His constant care for those whom you would fain be caring for and working for, and surely He may have some special Blessing prepared and planned for them at this time, beyond all we can ask.

Good-bye, dear Nicholas; may the Easter happiness come to you unchecked, undimmed, through all the trial.— Affectionately yours,   F. OXON.

The next is to one whose wife had been taken from him in death :—

CUDDESDON, OXFORD,
17th December 1903.

MY DEAR ——,—May God help, and uphold, and comfort you.   I cannot tell you how deeply and intensely sorry I am ; it comes back on me again and again, the thought of your heavy, heavy grief; and I long just to hold out a hand, and to try to help you to bear it.   Dear ——, I know how hard it is, and how the heart aches, till one knows not what to do.   But indeed through it all God does make known to us wonderful resources of His Mercy.   He does help us, beyond all that we can ask or think, by the kindness and gentleness that He teaches others to show us, and by the Light that changes the look of all things, and by the uplifting power of His Grace, and by showing us our task in life, and by setting us to help and think for others : so in all these ways He bears us on from day to day.   And it is just from day to day that we have to hold on ; not looking into or puzzling about the further distances of this life, but doing our best each day, with each day's task and each day's duty, trusting God to give us the strength and light which for each day we need.—Believe me, dear ——, with frequent thought of you, yours most sincerely,   F. OXON.

If the thought of your work, and of the services, is giving you anxiety, please let me help in any way I can.   For Christmas Day . . . (a suggestion follows).

The above letters need no explanation ; the one

below was written from a Parish where there had been much trouble. The Vicar, who subsequently entered the Roman Communion, was deprived, and the Bishop and the Rev. H. N. Perrin, his Chaplain, themselves took the services. Feeling in the Parish had run high. It might even be said to have been " stormy."

30th August 1909.

By God's goodness to us things have gone, in the main, quietly at ——, and there has at no point been any irreverence or interruption at any Service. I went there, with Perrin, and took all the Services on the first Sunday after the deprivation ; and—far beyond all that I, in my ὀλιγοπιστία, had thought possible—it was a Sunday of great privilege, with very much that was touching and gladdening coming out to drive one's anxiety away. Then Perrin took charge for a fortnight, including the stages of real difficulty, and then on Saturday I went and joined him there for yesterday. It was a Sunday full of encouragement, with large and reverent congregations : and I have come away with a thankful trust that there is a clear and great opportunity there for steady work, with, please God, increasing happiness.

I will finish the collection with four children's letters. First, two written to Mrs. Shaw, then at High Wycombe Vicarage.

S.E.C.R., *3rd January* 1910.

DEAR MRS. SHAW—Just a word (not to be acknowledged, please, in any way), to tell how I trust that God will grant you ever fresh assurance of His Love and Care, through the trial of Ruth's trouble. " She will be well cared for," you said in your kind letter, and indeed we can lift up our hearts to Him, and feel quite sure of that.

And from Barmouth, four days later :—

Thank you truly for this morning's kind and welcome letter. I am indeed thankful to hear that all is going well.

God grant the little patient Grace for this early trial of patience, and a happy and thorough recovery.—With true love to her, I am, yours always, F. Oxon.

The next is written to Mrs. Harnett, at Wolverton, after a visit in which tree-climbing had been part of her daughters' entertainment. The Cuddesdon trees, it seems, have peculiar advantages for this purpose. "What beautiful trees the Bishop has," a neighbour (who once was small) said of them, "and I daresay he never climbs one of them."

16th May 1911.

This is my largest paper. But if I covered it all over on both sides, I could not come near thanking you and Kathleen and Sylvia and Marigold as I want to thank you for the true happiness your letters brought me. It was just wonderful of you all to write, and your letters made the whole post seem bright. Will you give my true love to my three friends, and tell them that I wanted at once to try to write three really nice letters, but I had to write a lot of dull letters, and now it's late, and I know I can't write as I would! But, indeed, my whole heart thanks them : they brought joy into the house with their visit, and they've left some of it still hanging about the rooms and the garden, some, perhaps, up the trees, and they really must come again soon.

And then will you, please, give my affectionate remembrance to the Vicar, with my true thanks for all the kindness of the letter which he bade me not to answer ? I am indeed glad and thankful for the manifold good tidings it bore. He will know how I shall be longing to help in any way I can.— Believe me to be, always very sincerely yours,

F. Oxon.

The last letter is to Miss E. Browning, of Penn Street Vicarage, who corresponded with the Bishop with reference to so undiocesan a matter as the birthday of her cat. The letter given here acknowledges her writing after Christmas 1908.

CUDDESDON,
11th January 1909.

MY DEAR ESTHER—Thank you with all my heart for a most welcome and delightful letter. I am very glad indeed that you liked the chocolates. I do not think that you can have liked them more than I liked the honeysuckle that you gave me at Holmer Green—the summer seems to come back as I think of it.

I hope you will have a very happy New Year, and then another, quite as happy, or even happier, and then another, and another, and ever so many, all of them happy.—Ever your affectionate Bishop, F. Oxon.

If one work had to be chosen as that through which the Bishop found happiness in his office, the choice would, I do not doubt, fall upon the Confirmations. It had been so with Bishop Stubbs before him. It was so with Bishop King of Lincoln. And it was so with him.

The round of them comes each Spring. The three counties are taken in turn. In each county as many centres as possible are visited, and the round means many journeys—journeys which were heavier before the motor-car came to lighten them.

Those who have a cross-country experience of our train-service can imagine that a traffic, attentive to milk-cans rather than to men, has its disadvantages for the purposes of a Confirmation Tour. But if the Bishop was often tired as he drove out from Oxford and up Horspath Hill reading the evening post that had come in the carriage to meet him, and if he was sometimes tired when he set out next morning after working till 12 or 1 or later, answering the letters, he still found

in the Confirmations his happiest entrance into the life
of the Parishes of the Diocese.

There was for him always a pleasure in the humours
and the kindlinesses of porters and coachmen and
sextons and churchwardens, and a deeper happiness
among the candidates and their fathers and mothers.

It was Spring, and the time, first of winter aconites,
then of snowdrops, then of daffodils, in the Vicarage
gardens.   I have seen him delight to find Virgil
illustrated in the ploughing of a Berkshire field,
splendescit vomere gleba, or almost cheer the line of the
white clouds of a locomotive's steam, floating and
curling in tossed masses in the frosty air with curves
that reminded him of the Athenian horses of the
Parthenon.   And as he drove towards the villages,
bells ringing and the white flag with its red cross
flying, and the carts of candidates appeared along the
road—the Vicar perhaps sitting up beside the driver,
"bringing his sheaves with him"—or the groups of
boys and girls made their way on foot—a bunch of
white violets, or a twig of catkins in the boys' button-
holes—the homeliness and pleasantness of the scene
touched him.   And in the Vicarages themselves he
scarcely ever failed to find (or at least to leave) a
friendship.   "And a bright, pleasant Rectory it is,"
he writes of one, "such as not many lands, I think,
save ours can show ; with a cheeriness in well-doing,
and a width of interest and culture and good sense in
talk, that make one thankful and hopeful."   He did
not often fail to find some piety or shrewdness or
scholarship or loveableness "such as not many lands, I
think, save ours can show."

And the coming away from Church or Vicarage
was often a prolonged affair—the churchwardens, the

ancient sexton, the Church Lads' Brigade, the organist, the cripple in the bath-chair, all must be spoken to, whatever Bradshaw named as the time appropriate for being at the station.

His addresses to the candidates before the "laying on of hands," and to the people after it, were for the most part very much the thoughts among which his mind was moving as he read the day's services in the train, in the service-book which had been William Bright's and had his innumerable notes crowded all over its margins and between its lines.

He spoke the thoughts that were turning in his mind, and often he spoke them very simply. The country children, smooth-brushed boys on the one hand and veiled girls on the other, would gaze at him with unwavering eyes, sometimes wondering in part, perhaps, at the blue Garter-riband and the jewel, the white lawn sleeves, the scarlet hood, but feeling, surely, that one was there who cared for them, and who cared for the things of which he spoke. People would say, " he must get very tired of so many Confirmations," but the suggestion that they were monotonous was most unwelcome to his mind.

Often before or after addresses he made notes in a bound note-book. They are not easy for another to make out, but I will copy two or three of its pages, as best I can :—

PRINCES RISBOROUGH,
6th Feb. 1904.

Confirmation.

    I. The wind bloweth where it listeth, and thou hearest
        the sound thereof, but canst not tell whence it
        cometh, and whither it goeth.
      The trees bending :
      the clouds hurrying along :

the noise in the trees : down the chimney : and nothing to be seen. So is every one that is born of the Spirit :
that is the way the Spirit works.
and so many people deny it.
but those who watch and listen and want to hear, know.
So, watch, in conduct.
and listen,—the Bible.
and seek to hear,—Prayer,
and above all obey.

II. The Holy Communion : the great work of the Holy Ghost :
preparing our hearts :
hallowing the Bread and Wine :
bearing into our hearts the Presence of Christ :
helping us to live by Him.

Here is another entry. It is of what he said at the Confirmation of his second daughter and of one who was her friend and bridesmaid :—

F. & I. S. CUDDESDON, 14 *Jan.* 1904.

1 St. John v. 3 : " This is the love of God " : that love beyond and beneath all rules : " that we keep "—or rather, watchfully, consistently, thoughtfully, sustainedly, try to keep —" His Commandments."

His Commandments are not heavy, burdensome,—but rather, as showing us how to live our lives,—how to do it : so that we may not go on trying to force things, beating ourselves against barriers and limitations : but in the way of peace.

I cannot forgo making copies of three more entries :—

PADBURY, 14 *Oct.* 1903.

Dedication of Organ.
1 Cor. xii. 4 :
Gratias hodie agimus : Deum accipere, benedicere precamur : benedicere nobis et posteris.

2 C 2

Respicientes autem quotquot agnoscimus benefactores : qui rem inceperunt : qui susceperunt hortatione : qui dona dederunt, aut magna aut parva : qui laboraverunt in construendo, in parando, etiam in silvis et metallis : qui organa invenerunt (cf. Ecclus. xliv. 5), perfecerunt : organistam : sufflatorem.

(I have quoted partly for the sake of this " sufflatorem.")

Suum quisque donum dicavit : ne unum quidem superfluum : varia omnia in unum conversa.

Nonne idem in ipsa musica notandum ?—notae diversae unam efficientes harmoniam.

Vitae divinitus ordinatae parabolam accipimus : domi : inter ruricolas : in Ecclesia Dei.

Where there is grudging, envy, division : how much is hindered : how all suffer, how each suffers.

God grant us more and more of the spirit of kindness and mutual help :

that the One Spirit may guide us all in the use of the diverse gifts.

OXFORD, RADCLIFFE INFIRMARY,
18 *Oct.* 1903.

Sermon at Festival.

Hosea ii. 14 :

I. The first meaning : in regard to the Chosen People of God : who had forgotten Him : swerved from His way. She must go into exile, indeed, into the wilderness, yet only in order that there she may remember her original vocation and dignity as well as her true Lord and Love : " I will speak home to her " (Ewald).

II. The fulfilment in the experience of individual lives :

 (*a*) The wilderness of pain : sorrow : anxiety : disappointment : sickness : the enforced pause : and solitude, and stillness :
  perhaps in a life with little quiet in it.

(*b*) And how does God speak home to us? in many ways: Conscience wakes: and memory gets time: and words come back: and life is seen in its true proportion, other things dropping away.

(*c*) But one great way: the kindness, gentleness, patience, skill of those around us.

III. Was not that our Lord's own way: what His pity, His Look, Voice, Hand, must have meant:

IV. And this is committed, this Ministry, to those who work in Hospitals.

Witnesses of His Love.

———

LOUDWATER, 29*th Oct.* 1903.

Foundation Stone of New Chancel. (Very little said, by reason of rain.)

1 Cor. viii. 1:

Reading H. M. Butler's sermon on these words, and thinking over them: their lesson for to-day.

Let us get them simple—Love builds.

You will see the building rising: think of those two words: think of them in regard to your homes.

Love bonding, binding together. So, often, sorrow and trouble draw a home closer together because they call out love.

Think of them in regard to your own character.

The royal power of self-control comes with the gift of love.

Verba Psalmistae, mystice legenda:

Except the Lord, who is Love, build the house, their labour is but lost that build it.

I must take up my theme again, which is, that there did grow up between the Bishop and the Diocese a feeling which transfigured his work—some approach to that Love, the "great thing, yea, a great and thorough good," which Thomas à Kempis knew, which

" by itself makes everything that is heavy, light : and it bears evenly all that is uneven." It was growing all the while.

I remember a drive on a Sexagesima Sunday (February 15, 1903) to Witney, when he had made up his mind to refuse to go to another Diocese, with a feeling that he had chosen aright which made him light of heart. And the Diocese did respond to his choice.

At one of the Conferences he says, " Now I have, as the saying is, given myself away " (he had been speaking with unusual freedom on a difficult question), " but I do not mind that. For it only means I have thrown myself on your generosity."

Ecclesiastical Discipline and Education troubles could not chill—or at any rate could only for a while chill—his personal relation towards men whom he knew and who knew him.

And during the illness, which, a year before his death, suddenly made men anxious for his life, the love found expression which was felt for him in so many parishes. He was deeply touched, by the messages, the flowers—" When my room was bright with flowers, and still more flowers came, one of my nurses said that I should soon be a spoilt Bishop. I do hope that she was wrong ; for indeed I want to be something different from that, for the sake of the Diocese which has been thus kind and good to me, and beyond telling helped me." The thoughtfulness of people, the welcome when he returned, gave him more than the old life back.

" All along," he wrote (July 23, 1910), " I have had round me such care and comfort, such wealth of kindness, far and near, as might gladden any man. Nor has God, in spite of all my undeserving, withheld from me the light of His Countenance.

" I long that through whatsoever years He will, I may more simply and more thankfully live for Him in the service of the Diocese, to which indeed these weeks have bound my heart closer than ever before."

His son, who used to read the day's psalms to him in his illness, tells of the radiant joy with which he would welcome the old words of praise living anew with his new thankfulness.

And, among other practical kindnesses for which his illness gave his friends excuse, a motor-car was presented to him, which indeed transformed the aspects of his travelling.

Here is one of the letters he wrote in thanks for the gift :—

This evening, if all be well, the motor will be mine, and I shall be enjoying my first journey in it,—a splendid 30–34 h.p. Wolseley, a Limousine Landaulette,—as good as Vickers Maxim can turn out. As I think of all the ease and pleasure and refreshment which it promises to bring into my life, I cannot forgo writing a few words of my true gratitude to the friends of whom I shall often be thinking as I enjoy what their bounty has given me. Thank you indeed, dear Noble, for one more instance of a friendship which has gladdened me again and again.

On January 9, 1911, he wrote to Dr. Pollock, Bishop of Norwich :—

Out of the past year there rise many thoughts which I trust I shall not forget ; one is that I seem to have learnt in a new way what it means to be a Bishop, set to serve a Diocese. The kindness that came to me, in the anxiety of the summer and in the sorrow of the winter, has taught me a real love for all that wide field of sympathy and work and care ; a love like that which I had come to feel for Christ Church, and in earlier

days for my country parish. I did not know, in my dullness
and faithlessness, that one could have quite that sort of feeling
towards so big and scattered a thing as a Diocese, but, of
God's mere mercy, it has come, and it seems to light up the
thought of whatever years of work may yet remain. Of
course, I ought to have learnt it long ago, and I'm ashamed I
did not.—Always yours gratefully and affectionately,

F. Oxon.

" The sorrow of the winter," this was the death, a
month after the birth of his grandson, of his second
daughter, in whose happiness of two years' married
life he had found new happiness for himself.

One of his letters to her husband may here be
given :—

Thank you with all my heart for a letter carrying more
than any words can tell of the happiness which has been
granted to you .and to Frida. Will you give Frida my true
love, and my very best thanks for a note which has just
followed yours ? It comes, fugue-wise, like the second
enunciation of the very same theme, making one feel afresh
what a wonderful theme it is, and what glories it may work
out into, under His hand from Whom it comes.

Concerning his surviving children I will here only
say that Home, as the years went on, did give the
Bishop more of that which once seemed quite darkened
out of it, but this home-sorrow had its bearing on the
relation to the Diocese of which I set out to tell.

" The kindness and gentleness of friends," he
writes to one, " has been beyond telling, and the
Diocese seems nearer to me than ever. So indeed
God has been good to us through all the trial. Thank
God, there has been light shining through the great
sorrow."

During the year or less that remained to him of

work, Love did "much to make everything that was heavy, light."

But if it be asked why he who seemed, at times, in the undertaking of his task, to be unequal to it, was able so to advance towards a simpler, thankfuller service, the secret must ultimately be traced to where a man may hesitate to follow it ; it must be at the heart of his religion.   Here is (to look at the life from another side) the story of an elaborate and sensitive and fastidious nature—a nature gifted with qualities and powers such as make simplicity seem far away and out of reach.   Yet the story ends in simple, thankful love.   And those who were near him knew that, in the end, it must come to that.   For behind all the complexity of the character there lay a steady will to pray—an unfailing readiness to begin again, to set out afresh.

There was in him the " little child " that " leads them," the simple faith that controls the human powers and weaknesses.

I could have fancied his nature lending itself to a life of Roman, of Stoical virtue.   He could have been haughtily, austerely virtuous, keeping a conscience scrupulously clear, avoiding the breath of criticism, shrinking from the fear, even, of possible criticism ; he might have been content with Justice, Temperance, Courage, Wisdom.

He would, in a Pagan world, have fared well, I think, among the moralities in which there is no forgiving, no simple " beginning again "—fared, at least, as well as most.   There was a self-discipline which seemed to lead him by a regular progress, so that one had no sense, in his character, of shocks, of upheavals, of catastrophes as having formed it.

Impulsive, passionate natures moved in him a pitying regard such as a nurse might give to children that "will be sorry afterwards." The look of the ball-room next morning in cold daylight was present to his mind, when characters danced too wildly among the lights and flowers of to-night.

If "things are what they are, and their consequences will be what they will be," he had no "wish to be deceived."

But along with this Roman and Stoical steadiness of virtue, there was in him a great readiness to be self-dissatisfied ; a mood which welcomes "beginning again," which is glad that things in general should forgive us and be forgiven by us in turn. There was something inexorable, final, in his voice when he gave his deliberate judgment : " That was not sincere," " that was inconsiderate," " that was not right,"—and yet the culprit would have been mistaken had he thought that he had heard the " last word."

I may seem to be saying, rather cumbrously, only that he could, like other people, forgive. But I am not describing any facile process. It is not exactly "forgiving" that I am describing. It is rather a " beginning again," as though men's natures and experiences and conduct were, after all, too complex for men to judge of them. Therefore let men put the past behind them and begin again.

I think it was through the very fineness of his conscientiousness that he learned the limits of conscience. It was not so much an offended conscience as a never-satisfied conscience, which led him across the frontiers which divide the land of the Classical Virtues from the land of Christian Grace.

Trained as he was through the experience of excelling,

rather than of failure in scholarship, say, or in brilliant talk, he learned to speak of " ' success,' a word which I shudder to hear spoken " ; and I suppose the last human excellence to learn its place, the last success to be shuddered at, will always be a ' moral excellence,' a ' success in the paths of virtue.'

Yet with, perhaps, more of praise than most men win, and perhaps, more in his own nature that might have tempted him to linger where the Merits are reckoned, he found his home in Prayer, in Forgiveness, in Simplicity, in Love.   Through whatever elaborateness of thought, of self-discipline, of self-consciousness, he was making his way towards that home. Praise hurt him, you would have said sometimes. At any rate it humbled him, more and more.   Love gladdened him.   Love quickened him.   Love set him free.

From his tasks he rests—his task as Bishop of a Diocese whose demands he never felt it possible to overtake—his task as a man with a life to live, a nature to discipline, in some ways as complex and as manifold as the affairs which made up his round of duty.   And from the attempt to measure either, the office he bore and the life he lived, they will shrink farthest who lived nearest to him, or who learned most of the lesson he had to teach.

" The judgement, the estimate, *where they are*," he had said of the dead, " is formed with perfect knowledge, perfect love : and our loose guesses, our hasty impressions, our blundering words, are like voices in the noisy street outside a church."

Only, one guess we make which is not loose ; we speak of an impression which grew in those ten years ; we do not fear the charge of blundering, when we say that, to him, life's task seemed to be, in words which he used not long before he died, " to learn the Simplicity of Love " ; and when we trust that one who set himself to that task, above all other tasks, has, by Love's Grace, been taught just that, and has helped others to learn it.

THE CATHEDRAL GRAVEYARD.

LIST OF WRITINGS

1876. Two Sermons preached on All Saints' Day. By F. Paget and W. Hutchings. Pp. 32. Masters and Co., London.

1881. Concerning Spiritual Gifts : Three Addresses, together with a Sermon, etc. Pp. 64. Parker and Co., Oxford.

1882. The Redemption of Work : Addresses spoken in St. Paul's Cathedral. Pp. 46. Parker and Co., Oxford.

1884. Outlines of Church Teaching. By C. C. G., with Preface by Francis Paget. Masters and Co., London.

1886. Everlasting Punishment. Oxford House Papers, No. 11. Pp. 15.
The Grace of Courage : A Sermon. Parker and Co., Oxford.

1887. Faculties and Difficulties for Belief and Disbelief. Pp. xii, 292. Rivington's, London.
This Church and Realm : A Sermon preached at the Anniversary Festival of the English Church Union. Rivington's, London.

1888. The Works of Richard Hooker, arr. by J. Keble. Revised by R. W. Church and F. Paget. Clarendon Press, Oxford.
The Hallowing of Work : Addresses given at Eton. Pp. 62. Rivington's, London.

1889. Lux Mundi : A Series of Studies in the Religion of the Incarnation. Edited by Charles Gore. Essay on Sacraments by F. Paget. John Murray, London.
A Word to Soldiers about Christianity and Manliness. Pp. 22. Christian Knowledge Society, London.

1891. The Spirit of Discipline : Sermons . . . together with an Introductory Essay concerning Accidie. Pp. xii, 318. Longman and Co., London.

1895. Life and Letters of Dean Church. Edited by Mary Church, with Preface by F. Paget. Macmillan and Co., London.
Studies in the Christian Character : Sermons, with an Introductory Essay. Pp. xxxvi, 258. Longman and Co., London.

1899. An Introduction to the Fifth Book of Hooker's Treatise of the Laws of Ecclesiastical Polity. Pp. x, 265. Clarendon Press, Oxford.

1900. The Redemption of War : Sermons preached in the Cathedral Church of Christ. Pp. xv, 73. Longman and Co., London.

1902. A Charge delivered by the Bishop of Oxford at his Primary Visitation, 1902. Pp. 60. Longman and Co., London.
Christ the Way : Four Addresses given at Haileybury, January 11 and 13, 1902. Pp. 54. Longman and Co., London.

1904. Life and Letters of Henry Parry Liddon. By J. O. Johnston, with a concluding chapter by the Lord Bishop of Oxford. Longman and Co., London.

1905. Syllabus of Religious Instruction for Use in the Diocese of Oxford, with a Preface by the Bishop of Oxford.

1906. Plain Notes on the Church Catechism. By G. E. J. Milner, with a Preface by the Bishop of Oxford. Parker and Son, Oxford.
The Recommendations of the Royal Commission on Ecclesiastical Discipline : a Visitation Charge. Pp. 64. Longman and Co., London.

1907. Sermons at St. Paul's and Elsewhere. By H. P. Liddon, with a Preface by F. Paget. Longmans' Pocket Library of Theology.

1909. The Spirit of Christ in Common Life. By Charles Bigg, with an Introduction by the Bishop of Oxford. Longman and Co., London.
School Prayers for Use in the Diocese of Oxford. Pp. 32. James Parker and Co., Oxford.

1911. A Record of Sixty-Nine Years' Ministry. By M. R. Allnutt, with a Preface by the Lord Bishop of Oxford. Christian Knowledge Society, London, Brighton.

1912. The Sorrow of the World, with an Introductory Essay on Accidie. (Reprinted from " The Spirit of Discipline "). Pp. vi, 56. Longman and Co., London.

INDEX

399

Printed by R. & R. Clark, Limited, *Edinburgh.*